Shakespeare

For All Time

STANLEY WELLS

Shakespeare

For All Time

MACMILLAN

First published 2002 by Macmillan
an imprint of Pan Macmillan Ltd
Pan Macmillan, 20 New Wharf Road, London N1 9RR
Basingstoke and Oxford
Associated companies throughout the world
www.panmacmillan.com

ISBN 0 333 90499 0

1 3 5 7 9 8 6 4 2

A CIP catalogue record for this book is available from
the British Library.

Printed and bound in Great Britain by
The Bath Press, Bath

To my wife, Susan Hill,

who set the ball rolling

'He was not of an age, but for all time'

Ben Jonson

Contents

List of Illustrations

COLOUR PLATES

ILLUSTRATION ACKNOWLEDGEMENTS

AKG, London – 80, 86. The Art Archive – 49, 84 (Garrick Club). Ashmolean Museum, Oxford – 62. Author's Collection – 54, 98, Plate 20. Birmingham Reference Library – 109. Bodleian Library, University of Oxford – 5, 7, 22, 39, 58. Lee Brauer Photography – 34. Bridgeman Art Library – 20 (Fitzwilliam Museum, Cambridge), 21, 29 (Dulwich Picture Gallery), 24 (Private Collection), 30 (Guildhall Library, Corporation of London), 51 (Private Collection), 82 (Guildhall Art Gallery, Corporation of London), 95 (National Gallery of Scotland), 106 (Westminster Abbey, London), 114 (Herbert Art Gallery & Museum, Coventry), 115 (Central Saint Martins College of Art & Design), 127 (Private Collection), Plate 6 (Roy Miles Fine Painting), Plate 8 (Beauchamp Collection), Plate 7 (Boughton House, Northamptonshire), Plates 10 & 22 (Walker Art Gallery, Liverpool), Plate 11 (Somerset Maugham Theatre Collection), Plate 12 (Private Collection), Plates 13 & 17 (Yale Center for British Art, Paul Mellon Collection), Plate 14 (Louvre, Paris), Plate 18 (Oldham Art Gallery, Lancashire). British Library – 41; British Museum – 72, 110. Canadian Conservation Institute, Department of Canadian Heritage – 147 ('Sanders' portrait. © All rights reserved. Reproduced with permission of the Minister of Public

Works and Government Services, 2002). **Luigi Ciminaghi** – 142. **Collections** – 66 (Malcolm Crowthers). **Donald Cooper** © **Photostage** – 23, 137, 138, 141. **The College of Arms** – 13. **Colonial Williamsburg Foundation, Abby Aldrich Rockefeller Folk Art Museum, Williamsburg, VA** – Plate 16. **Country Life Picture Library** – 71 (June Buck). **Deutsches Theatermuseum** – 99, 112. **Dulwich Picture Gallery** – 28. **English Heritage** – 74 (Kenwood House, The Iveagh Bequest). **Folger Shakespeare Library** – 27, 33, 43, 57, 60, 64, 65, 70, 76, 102, 113, 126. Copyright **The Frick Collection, New York** – Plate 1. **Harvard Theatre Collection, The Houghton Library** – 44, 88, 121. © **David Hockney** – Plate 27. **Hulton Getty** – 129. **Illustrated London News Picture Library** – 89, Plate 19. **Michael Jenner** – 36. **Keats House,** London Metropolitan Archives – 90. **Kobal Collection** – 124, 125, Plate 29 (Photo: Merrick Morton). **Kunsthaus, Zurich** – 69. **Ivan Kyncl** – 42, 55. **Mander & Mitchenson Theatre Collection** – 63, 68, 83, 101, 105, 108, 111, 120, 122, 123. **The Museum of London** – 19, 32. **National Gallery of Scotland** – 77. **National Portrait Gallery, London** – 37, 59, 61, Plate 5. **John Parker Picture Library** – 31, 48. **Public Records Office, Kew** – 15, 16. **RMN** – 100 (Musée Eugène Delacroix, Paris. Photo: R. G. Ojeda), Plate 23 (Musée d'Orsay, Paris. Photo: C. Jean). **Ronald Grant Archive** – 144, 145, Plate 30 (Miramax). **The Royal Collection** © 2002, Her Majesty Queen Elizabeth II – 103. © **RSC Collection** with the permission of the Governors of the Royal Shakespeare Company – 81, 85, 96, 119, Plate 15. **SCR, London** – 134. **Shakespeare Birthplace Trust, Stratford-upon-Avon** – 3, 9 (Malcolm Davies), 12 (Malcolm Davies), 14, 50, 75, 79, 87, 91, 92, 109, 146, Plates 2, 3, 9. **Shakespeare Birthplace Trust, Shakespeare Centre Library, Stratford-upon-Avon** – 35, 38, 40, 46 (Angus McBean © RSC), 47 (Reg Wilson Collection © RSC), 52 (Tom Holte Theatre Photographic Collection), 56 (Angus McBean © RSC), 67, 93, 94, 118, 132 (Earnest Daniels), 133 (Angus McBean © RSC), 136 (Angus McBean © RSC), 139 (Tom Holte Theatre Photographic Collection), 140 (Tom Holte Theatre Photographic Collection), 143 (Gordon Goode), Plates 4 & 25. **Shakespeare Birthplace Trust, The Joe Cocks Studio Collection,** Stratford-upon-Avon – 45, 53. **Shakespeare Birthplace Trust, Records Office,** Stratford-upon-Avon – 1, 2, 4, 6, 8, 10, 11, 17, 18, 73, 116, 117. **Shakespeare's Globe, London** – 25 (Tiffany Foster), 26 & Plate 24 (John Tramper). **Stratford Festival Archives, Canada** – 135 (Terry Manzo). **Tate Gallery** – 78, Plate 21. **Victoria & Albert Museum** – 97, 104, 107, 128, 130, 131 (Theatre Museum. Photo: Houston Rogers).

Acknowledgements

My pleasure (alternating with predictable bouts of melancholy, frustration, anxiety, and self-doubt) in writing this book has been enhanced by the help and encouragement I have received from many friends and colleagues. The library staff of the Shakespeare Centre, headed by Dr Susan Brock and, for theatre records, Sylvia Morris, have been unfailingly kind and helpful, as have those of the Shakespeare Institute, James Shaw and Kate Welch. Dr Robert Bearman, Senior Archivist of the Shakespeare Birthplace Trust, has been generous with his encyclopaedic knowledge of early Stratford and Warwickshire, and I have received assistance too from members of his staff, especially Mairi MacDonald, from the Trust's Museums Department, led by Ann Donnelly, and from its photographer, Malcolm Davies. Professor Peter Holland kindly read a late draft of the script, to its advantage. Other colleagues to whom I have turned for help on a variety of topics include Dr Catherine Alexander, Professors Dennis Kennedy and Eric Rasmussen, and Patrick Spottiswoode, of Shakespeare's Globe. Georgina Morley, of Macmillan, has been wonderfully supportive and wise in advice at all stages of the enterprise, as has my agent, Vivien Green. I should not have embarked on this book without my wife's initial help and encouragement, acknowledged in the Dedication, and my daughters Jessica and Clemency have cheered me along from the sidelines. At production stage I have received great help from the copy-editor, Louise Davies, the expert picture researcher, Josine Meijer, the indexer, Sarah Ereira, and Macmillan's scholarly reader, Nick de Somogyi. And I must record a special debt of gratitude to my friend and colleague Dr Paul Edmondson, Head of Education at the Shakespeare Birthplace Trust, who has commented sagaciously on each chapter as it materialized from screen to paper, and sustained me along the way with mirth and good cheer.

STANLEY WELLS, May 2002

Preface

This book, offering an account of Shakespeare's life, writings, and afterlife, is based on a half-century's engagement with Shakespeare. Before outlining the book's overall scope and aims it may be appropriate to sketch the course of my Shakespearian activities.

My enthusiasm for Shakespeare's work was ignited by a remarkable grammar-school teacher in Hull, E. J. C. Large (the 'Mr Large' of Sir Tom Courtenay's book *Dear Tom*). He had an extraordinary capacity to bring Shakespeare to life in the classroom, reading aloud with exceptional sensitiveness, intelligence, and dramatic sense, and guiding his pupils through the text with irresistible dedication. I was first deeply stirred by Shakespeare's language through the sonnets, but theatre soon entered my life. I suppose the first Shakespeare play I saw was *Othello*, performed by Donald Wolfit and his touring company. It was largely because of the opportunities offered for seeing plays and hearing music that I chose to go to university in London, and as an undergraduate at University College between 1948 and 1951 I was fortunate to experience unforgettable performances such as Laurence Olivier's Richard III and Antony (in *Antony and Cleopatra*), Michael Redgrave's Hamlet and Macbeth, Alec Guinness's Hamlet (with a ponderous Player King from Ken Tynan), John Gielgud's Leontes in a beautiful production of *The Winter's Tale* by Peter Brook, Hugh Hunt's Chekhovian *Love's Labour's Lost*, and fine productions at the Old Vic including a *Twelfth Night* with Peggy Ashcroft. There too, at University College, I had remarkable teachers in, especially, Winifred Nowottny, earnest and intense, and Harold Jenkins, a sparklingly witty and erudite lecturer and tutor.

Later, as a schoolmaster in the country, I did what I could to emulate Mr Large as a teacher of Shakespeare. An unhappy experience that sticks in my mind is an ill-judged excursion with a group of schoolboys on a Cup Final day to a matinee of *Henry IV, Part One* in a barn-like and almost deserted theatre in Southampton in which Robert Atkins, late in his career, played Falstaff wearing a deaf-aid (not part of the characterization). Joining the Shakespeare Institute in Stratford as a graduate student in 1959 plunged me into an environment in which one lived and breathed Shakespeare; this period saw the beginnings of my long association with the Royal Shakespeare Company, first as habitual playgoer, later as director for some twenty years of the annual summer school, and latterly as vice-chairman of the governors.

Joining the staff of the Shakespeare Institute, which is part of the University of Birmingham, in 1962, I both taught Shakespeare at undergraduate and graduate level, and undertook varieties of research and publication, including the composition of a little book, *Royal Shakespeare*, on four of the theatre's productions. I worked intensively with the Institute's director, T. J. B. Spencer, from whom I learnt a lot, on the New Penguin Shakespeare edition, editing three of the plays myself. The experience thus gained led to my being invited in 1978 to head a newly formed Shakespeare department at Oxford University Press where I worked for ten years principally on the preparation of a new edition of *The Complete Works*, published in 1986 (I discuss this on pp. 384–6), and in 1988 I returned to the Shakespeare Institute as director. Retiring from that post in 1997 I have been able to continue my professional activities in the Shakespeare Centre as chairman of the Shakespeare Birthplace Trust. Throughout this time I have led the life of a professional Shakespearian, lecturing, attending and organizing conferences at home and overseas (some of them in my capacity as chairman of the International Shakespeare Association), reviewing books and performances, broadcasting, and producing editions, books, and articles.

All these activities have fed this volume, as have my interests in literature, music, and painting. Some of my travels have brought vividly home to me the fact that Shakespeare and the sense of a nation's political identity are inextricably intertwined. Invited to lecture at Grahamstown in South Africa at a time when apartheid was still in force I had scruples about the ethics of agreeing. The organizers, assuring me that the conference would be open to all, argued that it was only through the theatre and the church that protest could make itself felt. This was clearly demonstrated in Janet Suzman's politicized production of *Othello* at the Market Theatre, Johannesburg, in 1988 which offered the first black Othello in South Africa. In 1987 I was one of a group of six British Shakespeare scholars invited to Moscow for the first international conference to be held there since the inception of the Communist regime; the conference itself had political significance. We saw a performance of *Hamlet* that was clearly subversive in its intent, and learnt of other productions in which the voice of dissidence had, however covertly, made itself heard.

As the grip of Communism slowly relaxed, it became easier to travel to Eastern Europe, and in 1989 I visited Czechoslovakia at the invitation of its senior Shakespearian, Zdeněk Stríbrný, who for years had been forbidden to teach because of his liberal views. I arrived on 19 November, a date that has gone down in history as the first day of the Bloodless, or 'Velvet', Revolution by which the Communist regime was overthrown. As I was being shown round the castle I was told that there had been a spot of bother – police had beaten up students, one of whom was rumoured – falsely, as it emerged – to have died. On the following day my lecture to the Czech Academy in Prague was punctuated throughout by the rhythmical chanting of a vast procession of protesters winding their way from Wenceslaus Square to the Presidential Palace. Afterwards I stood with members of my loyal audience on a balcony to watch the seemingly endless procession stream by, the walkers waving up to the tall plate-glass windows of the National Theatre, which faces the Academy. Actors, who I was told had been prime movers with the students in the protest, waved back. Some of my planned lectures had to be cancelled because the students who might have attended them had better things to do. As the days passed, more and more processions of workers from the provinces marched through the streets. I still have the badge bearing an image of the future President Havel – a playwright whose work has been acted by the Royal Shakespeare Company – which was thrown down to me from a window as I joined the crowds thronging to see him and Alexander Dubcek, the liberal-minded former President of the Czech Communist Party, address the vast assembly that packed Wenceslaus Square – actually a long broad boulevard. Before flying home to safety – unknown to me, tanks had been massing outside Prague – I was able, too, to stand on the outskirts of the meeting of close on three quarters of a million people with which the week climaxed.

A year or two later I spoke at the inaugural conference of a Shakespeare Society in another East European country, Poland, in the war-battered city of Gdansk. Two later visits to Moscow in my capacity as literary adviser to the Animated Shakespeare series (p. 392) – a Welsh-Russian collaboration providing half-hour animated versions of a dozen plays which have done much to open up Shakespeare to young people – gave me a glimpse of the human and social problems associated with the transition from one regime to another.

The fact that, one way and another, Shakespeare can mean so much to such different kinds of people has spurred me on to write a book which will, I hope, inform and even entertain what Dr Johnson, and Virginia Woolf after him, called the 'common reader'. I have tried not to assume specialist knowledge, but I admit to a hope that I may also be able to interest those who are already well informed about Shakespeare. The first two chapters trace his life in, respectively, Stratford-upon-Avon and London. In them I offer my reading of the known facts and attempt to portray something of the social, intellectual, and theatrical context in which Shakespeare lived and worked. The third and longest chapter is the core of the book. In it I look at Shakespeare's methods of work, his evolving techniques as a poetic dramatist, the way his plays are crafted for the company to which he belonged, the range and variety of his work, the artistry with which he shaped the literary and other sources on which he drew, his use of language (including the language of silence), and his achievements as dramatist of both character and ideas. Later chapters offer an account of what has happened not only in Britain but, increasingly, worldwide as a result of Shakespeare from his time to the present: the adaptation and performance of his plays; musical, literary, dramatic and artistic offshoots; films, the critical, scholarly and editorial tradition, and so on. In writing a book that attempts at one and the same time to be biographical, critical, and historical I have had to be highly selective, and I am conscious of gaps. I hope that what surrounds them will nevertheless convey a sense of the pleasure and intellectual stimulus that Shakespeare's writings have given and continue to give, and of the degree to which they permeate the world's culture.

★

I have of course drawn extensively on standard works of reference such as the *Dictionary of National Biography* and its Supplements (27 vols., Oxford University Press, 1908–49), E. K. Chambers's *William Shakespeare: A Study of Facts and Problems* (2 vols., Oxford University Press, 1930), the Shakespearian writings of S. Schoenbaum, especially his *William Shakespeare: A Documentary Life* (Oxford University Press, 1975, revised as *A Compact Documentary Life*, 1977), Brian Vickers's six-volume collection *Shakespeare: The Critical Heritage* (Routledge, 1974–81), and *The Oxford Companion to Shakespeare*, ed. Michael Dobson and Stanley Wells (Oxford, 2001). The notes printed on pp. 405–24 do not attempt to document every statement that I make, but may, I hope, be useful to readers wishing to read more widely about the topics I discuss. Quotations from early writings are printed in modernized form unless there is a special reason to follow the original conventions. Quotations from Shakespeare are from the Oxford *Complete Works* (1986, compact edition 1988 etc.), General Editors Stanley Wells and Gary Taylor. I am grateful for the publisher's permission to draw on my essay 'Shakespeare on the English Stage' in vol. 3 of *William Shakespeare: His World, His Work, His Influence*, ed. John F. Andrews, copyright Charles Scribner's Sons (New York, 1985).

CHAPTER ONE

Shakespeare and Stratford

When we mean to build
We first survey the plot, then draw the model;
And when we see the figure of the house,
Then must we rate the cost of the erection,
Which if we find outweighs ability,
What do we then but draw anew the model
In fewer offices, or, at least, desist
To build at all?

Lord Bardolph in *Henry IV, Part Two*, 1.3.41–8

'Item I give unto my wife my second-best bed with the furniture.'

(interlined in Shakespeare's will, 25 March 1616)

WHEN THE NAME FIRST APPEARS, it is in Latin. There it stands, in the register of the parish church of Stratford-upon-Avon under the date of Wednesday, 26 April 1564: '*Gulielmus, filius Johannes Shakspere*' – William, son of John Shakespeare. Latin, because that was the language used on official documents of the time, and indeed written and spoken both formally and informally by many of the townspeople. The man who wrote the name was the officiating clergyman, probably John Bretchgirdle, MA of Christ Church, Oxford, who had been installed as vicar in 1561. He was a bachelor who spent money on scholarly books. When he died, in the following year, he left his Latin-English dictionary to the pupils of Stratford grammar school,

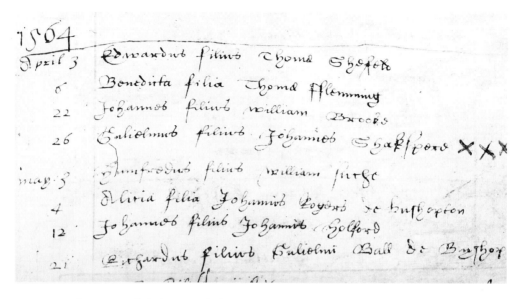

1. The entry of Shakespeare's baptism in the Stratford-upon-Avon register.
The surviving register is a copy made around 1600.

thus contributing to the later education of the infant who had mewled, and possibly puked, in his arms at the font (which survives).

Partly because many babies died soon after they were born, they were usually baptized, as the Prayer Book recommended, no later than 'the Sunday or other holy day next after the child be born'. For centuries now, Shakespeare's birthday has been celebrated on 23 April, which happens to be St George's Day, and is also the date on which he died. (A young friend of mine was reduced to tears at the thought that he died on his birthday.) The most popular alternative has been 22 April because Shakespeare's granddaughter chose that date for her marriage in 1626;[1] but the idea that she was influenced by respect for her ancestor's memory probably reflects an anachronistic enthusiasm for anniversaries.[2]

It was normal for the infant to be carried through the streets to the church by the father, attended by godparents; because baptism followed so soon after birth, mothers were usually not well enough to be present, and in any case were ineligible to attend a service until after the ceremony described in the Book of Common Prayer as 'the thanksgiving of women after childbirth, commonly called the churching of women'. But they could join in the customary, often riotous, festivities held in the house for friends and neighbours after the return from church.

This baby was lucky to survive. In July, when he was less than three months old, plague hit Stratford, carrying off a sizeable proportion of the town's inhabitants, including whole households. During the first six months of the year, twenty-two persons of a population numbering around 1,800 had been buried; the total for the rest of the year was close on 240, including four children of a single family from Henley Street, where the Shakespeares lived. As a safety measure, the August session of the town council, with John Shakespeare as a member, was held in the open air, in the garden of the Guild Chapel, with its old walnut tree and bowling green. The members, spurred no doubt by the knowledge that on that very day their town clerk was burying a son and a daughter, discussed ways of providing relief for hardship caused by the epidemic. Aldermen and burgesses contributed according to their means: John Shakespeare was assessed at one shilling – more than a whole day's wages for many workmen at the time. The grammar school closed. Some mothers fled for safety to relatives in the country.

At the time of Shakespeare's birth his father, John, was in his mid-thirties, his mother around twenty-eight. John, son of a small-scale farmer, had lived as a boy in the village of Snitterfield, some three miles north of Stratford. He probably moved into the town to learn the trade of a 'whittawer' – a tanner of white leather – and glover, which required an apprenticeship of at least seven years. Gloves featured more prominently at all levels of society then than now. They were often lined with fur, embroidered, and perfumed; when decorated with gold, silver, or jewels they could be extremely costly. On ceremonial occasions – weddings and funerals, baptisms and betrothals – they were frequently presented as gifts. When the Queen visited Cambridge in the year Shakespeare was born, the university presented her with 'four pair of Cambridge double gloves, edged and trimmed with two laces of fine gold', along with six boxes of sweets; and when actors performed at court, they were expected to wear gloves. Many portraits of Queen Elizabeth I, and of courtly ladies and gentlemen, show them either wearing or carrying them (Plate 5).

If you go to Stratford now you can see round John Shakespeare's later enlargement of the half-timbered, two-storeyed house which, along with a

goodly plot of land, 84 feet long, he had bought in 1556, perhaps in antici-
pation of his marriage.[3] The original house was of a comfortable size for a
small family. Two of the three rooms on the ground floor, the hall and the
parlour, had hearths whose fires could spread their warmth to the rest of
the building (Plate 2). There were three upper chambers, but no bathroom.
Probably there was a privy in the garden. Chamber pots and urine flasks
used at night would have been emptied in the morning on muck heaps such
as the one that John Shakespeare, before he married, was fined for keeping
too close to his and other people's houses. There may have been a kitchen
and home brewery in an outhouse; most households would have made their
own beer and ale for daily consumption. Bee-keeping, providing honey used
as a sweetener, was a common practice. Malting and brewing from locally
grown grain were – and long remained – major industries of the town; the
Shakespeare Memorial Theatre, ancestor of the Royal Shakespeare Theatre,
was founded in 1876 by the family of brewers named Flower.

2. The reconstruction of John Shakespeare's workshop in Shakespeare's Birthplace.

Like many craftsmen, John had his workshop at home, in the room across the way from the hall; it's fitted up now with tools and products of his trade – skins such as he would have tanned, gloves, purses, aprons and belts like those he made. Some of the family urine would have been put to practical use here, for softening the skins. The smells of the house would have been pungent, the less pleasant ones from the workshop mingling with those made by the baking of bread and by roasting on a spit, and, in spring and summer, with the scent of flowers and herbs from the garden. Elms and other trees grew in great profusion throughout the town.

When William was born Mary Shakespeare had already borne two baby girls, Joan and Margaret, who died in infancy. A second son, Gilbert, arrived in 1566; daughters, a new Joan – who was to be the longest-lived member of the family, dying in 1646 at the age of seventy-seven – in 1569, and an Anne in 1571; a third son, Richard, arrived in 1574. Anne, aged seven, died in 1579, when her brother William was almost fifteen. She was buried to the solemn tolling of the church bell, for which, along with a pall to be held over her coffin, her father paid eight pence. A year later the family was completed by Edmund, who like his eldest brother was to become an actor. As a child, then, Shakespeare was in a position of increasing responsibility, the eldest brother of, all told, five siblings.

Some geniuses grow in fertile ground. Mozart's father was a decent composer and a competent performer; Virginia Woolf's was a man of letters. On the other hand, among Shakespeare's contemporaries, Christopher Marlowe's father was a shoemaker, and Ben Jonson's stepfather, who brought him up, a bricklayer. Nothing that we know of Shakespeare's heredity points to a source for his talents. His mother, Mary Arden, came from a rather more prosperous farming family than his father, and seems to have been a woman of practical ability. Though she was the youngest of her father's eight daughters by his first marriage, and though he had two stepsons and two stepdaughters by his second, he appointed her one of his two executors when she was still in her late teens, and bequeathed to her 'all my land in Wilmcote called Asbies and the crop upon the ground sown and tilled as it is' along with ten marks – worth £6, six shillings and eight pence.

The family lived in a fine stone-and-timber farmhouse formerly known as Glebe Farm at Wilmcote, two or three miles from Stratford. In 2000 it

3. The upper floor of Mary Arden's House, correctly identified for the first time in 2000.

was shown that this rather than the farmhouse now known as Palmer's is the true Mary Arden's House. Like many women of the time (and many men, too) Mary made her mark rather than writing her name on a legal document, but this does not necessarily mean that she could not read, or even write. The man she married, John Shakespeare, also signed with a mark; it may seem hard to believe that one so able and successful in both business and public service was illiterate, but equally it is improbable that if he had indeed been able to write no document subscribed by him should have survived in the town's ample archives. As a sideline from his business he dealt in wool (natural enough in one who worked with animal skins) and lent money

4. *Opposite*. Holy Trinity Church, Stratford-upon-Avon (p. 8), where Shakespeare and his children were baptized, and where he, his wife and his daughter Susanna lie buried. The spire is an eighteenth-century addition.

at interest. Elected as one of the town's four constables in 1558 he rose rapidly in the corporation's hierarchy, becoming an alderman in 1565, and bailiff – the town's chief official – in 1568. In the following year he approved payments for the first recorded performances given by professional actors in the town.

Travelling players gave their initial performance before the council in the guildhall. Robert Willis, born in the same year as Shakespeare, described in his old age how, when he was a little boy, his father took him to a performance in Gloucester of 'the Mayor's play, where everyone that will goes in without money, the Mayor giving the players a reward as he thinks fit to show respect unto them'. His father 'made me stand between his legs, as he sat upon one of the benches, where we saw and heard very well'. After describing the play in well-remembered detail, he wrote some seventy years later that the sight 'took such impression in me that when I came towards man's estate it was as fresh in my memory as if I had seen it newly acted'.[4] (Curiously, his account virtually quotes from Feste's song at the end of *Twelfth Night*: 'But when I came to man's estate . . .') As the bailiff's son, the young William Shakespeare had a more privileged position; he could have accompanied his father, dressed in his scarlet robes of office and sitting in the place of honour, to see a play.

Children of respectable parents in Shakespeare's time were expected to conform to a disciplined regime. All the family would attend church on Sunday and holy days, as the law required; during his period of office as bailiff, John Shakespeare and his family would have been escorted to their seats in the front pew of the magnificent church, dedicated to the Holy Trinity, which stands by the river on the far side of the town from where they lived. Household prayers were said every morning and evening, grace before and after meals. Children were expected to show respect for their parents with a degree of formality that would provoke ribald derision in young people today.

Elizabethans had a great respect for education, which progressed rapidly during the period, but opportunities were unevenly distributed. Children like John Shakespeare and Mary Arden, brought up in rural areas, might be taught only sporadically, perhaps by local clergymen or itinerant teachers, but in towns such as Stratford-upon-Avon opportunities were greater. Between the

5. A hornbook, showing the letters of the alphabet, the vowels, the doxology, and the Lord's Prayer, such as that from which Shakespeare would have learned his letters.

ages of around five to seven, both girls and boys might attend a petty school where they would learn to recognize and pronounce their letters from a hornbook – a sheet of paper inscribed with the letters of the alphabet, a short prayer, and perhaps also combinations of vowels and consonants, covered with a layer of translucent horn and mounted on a wooden frame with a handle. A little book of dialogues printed in London when Shakespeare was nine years old shows how the horn book was put to use:

MASTER: Take the table of the cross row [alphabet] in thy left hand, and this fescue [pointer], wherewith thou shalt touch the letters one by one. Stand upright. Hold thy cap under thy arm. Hearken attentively how I shall name these letters. Mark diligently how I move my mouth. See that you may rehearse [repeat] them so, when I will have you say your lesson.[5]

And after receiving this amount of individual tuition, the boy is told, 'Go sit with thy schoolfellows, and learn that which I have taught thee.' Later he would be called back to be tested.

At his petty school, Shakespeare would have worn the gown in which young children were dressed irrespective of sex, but at the age of about seven

6. 'Big school': the upper room of the Guildhall, Stratford-upon-Avon, used in Shakespeare's time as the schoolroom. It is still part of the school.

he would have been 'breeched' – put into breeches, a sign of approaching manhood. At around this age too he would have begun to attend the King's New School, the Stratford grammar school to which his father's status in the town would have guaranteed him free admission. It was a good school, with perhaps forty boys taught at any one time by a single master, assisted by an usher, in the room above the guildhall where the council met.

With the onset of school days, life was becoming hard. Shakespeare and his schoolfellows would leave home with their satchels on their backs at around six a.m. in the summer, a bit later in the winter, and would continue their studies till the late afternoon, with few holidays. But there were occasional playing days, and Shakespeare himself gives us a glimpse of one in *The Merry Wives of Windsor*, the play in which he comes closest to portraying the life of his time. Act Four, Scene One almost seems like a little autobiographical sketch, because it's not required by the plot, and the boy who is put through his paces in Latin grammar for the benefit of his mother, Mistress Page, is named William. Seeing the teacher, Hugh Evans, out of school she realizes that ''Tis a playing day' and complains, as parents will, that her husband thinks the boy 'profits nothing in the world at his book'. Though he's off duty, the teacher feels obliged to try to prove her wrong by asking William questions. The comic point of the scene lies largely in the bawdy misunderstandings on the part of Mistress Page's uneducated friend Mistress Quickly of the Latin words that William speaks, but for us it has the additional interest of illustrating the teaching methods of the time. Asked 'What is *"lapis"'*, William correctly replies 'A stone.' Evans then asks 'What is a stone?', expecting the boy to translate the word back into Latin, but William, absent-mindedly taking the question at face value, replies, correctly but inappositely, 'A pebble', earning the rebuke 'No, it is *"lapis".'* Indelicacy intrudes as Evans asks 'What is your genitive case plural, William?' The boy answers with the genitive plural of the Latin word meaning 'this': *'Genitivo: horum, harum, horum.'* Mistress Quickly, hearing 'genitive case' as 'genital case' – and probably understanding 'case' in the slang sense of 'vagina' – and taking 'horum' to be an accusation of whoredom, exclaims in outrage 'Vengeance of Jenny's case! Fie on her! Never name her, child, if she be a whore!' When Evans rebukes her for speaking so in front of a child she indignantly turns back the accusation with *'You* do ill to teach the child such words.' Poor

William is so disconcerted that he fails his next test, but Evans finally dismisses him in a kindly manner with the words 'He is a good sprag [clever] memory.'

This scene from *The Merry Wives* includes phrases deriving directly from the book prescribed by royal proclamation as the text to be used for the teaching of Latin in grammar schools, the *Short Introduction of Grammar* written originally by William Lily, first high master of Saint Paul's School, London. Latin was the basic language of Elizabethan grammar school education. The boys had to learn to read and write in Latin, to translate passages to and from Latin, to study the grammatical and rhetorical construction of these passages, to memorize Latin writings, to write in imitation of Latin authors, to make speeches in Latin, and sometimes – as a treat – to act the Latin comedies of Plautus and Terence, which were to help mould Shakespeare's technique as a playwright and on which he draws very directly in *The Comedy of Errors*. The boys were also required to speak nothing but Latin in the classroom once they had achieved a reasonable competence in the language.

At the end of his schooldays, when he was around fifteen years old, an Elizabethan boy of average ability would have acquired as good an education in Latin language and literature as an honours graduate of the present. Documents that can be read today in the Records Office of the Shakespeare Birthplace Trust bear ample witness to the currency of Latin as a living language among Shakespeare's friends and relatives. A Stratford contemporary and friend of William Shakespeare, writer of the only surviving letter addressed to him, was Richard Quiney, who in his adult life was to devote much of his energy and considerable administrative ability to his townsfellows' welfare. Quiney was a booklover, his correspondence with fellow townsmen is conducted in a mixture of Latin and English, his wife – in a dictated letter written to him when he was in London in 1599 – advised him to read Cicero's *Epistles*,[6] and a few months earlier his son Richard, aged around eleven, wrote in Latin a touching letter asking his father to bring back from London books of blank paper for himself and his brother. The terms, affectionate but formal, in which the boy expresses gratitude that his father has 'brought him up in the studies of sacred learning' – *'educasti me in sacrae*

AN INTRODVCTION OF THE

numbre speaketh of mo then one: as Lapides, *Stones*.

Cases of Nounes.

Nounes be declined with six cases, Singularly and Pluralye the Nominatiue, the Genitiue, the Datiue, the Accusatiue, the Vocatiue, and the Ablatiue.

The Nominatiue case commeth before the Verb, and aunswereth to this question, Who or What: as Magister docet, *The Maister teacheth*.

The Genitiue case is knowen by this token Of, and aunswereth to this question, Whose or wherof: as Doctrina Magistri, *The learning of the Maister*.

The Datiue case is knowen by this token To, and aunswereth to this question, To whom, or to what: as Do librum magistro, *I giue a booke to the Maister*.

The Accusatiue case foloweth the verbe, & aunswereth to this questiõ, whome, or what: as Amo magistrum, *I loue the Maister*.

The Vocatiue case is knowen by callinge or speakinge to: as O magister, *O Maister*.

The Ablatiue case is commonly ioyned with Prepositions seruing to the Ablatiue case: as De magistro, *Of the Maister*. Coram magistro, *Before the Maister*.

Also In, with, through, for, from, by and then, after the comparatiue degree, be signes of the ablatiue case.

Articles.

ARticles are borowed of the Pronoune, and be thus declined.

Singulariter.
- Nominatiuo hic, hæc, hoc.
- Genitiuo huius.
- Datiuo huic.
- Accusatiuo hũc, hanc, hoc.
- Vocatiuo caret.
- Ablatiuo hoc, hæc, hoc.

Pluraliter.
- Nominatiuo hi, hæ, hæc.
- Genitiuo horum, harum, horum.
- Datiuo his.
- Accusatiuo hos, has, hæc.
- Vocatiuo caret.
- Ablatiuo his

Genders of Nounes.

GEnders of Nounes be seuen: the Masculine, the Feminine, the Neuter, the Commune of two, & Commune of three, the Doubtful

7. A page from Lily's *Short Introduction of Grammar* showing some of the phrases quoted in *The Merry Wives of Windsor*.

doctrinae studiis usque ad hunc diem' – illustrate a relationship between father and son characteristic of the age.[7]

It may be, of course, that young Richard Quiney's letter was composed at the behest, or at least with the disciplinary encouragement, of his schoolmaster, but many of those who learnt Latin at school continued to use it for the rest of their lives; Richard was to go on to study at Balliol College, Oxford. A younger contemporary and, it would seem, kinsman of William Shakespeare was Thomas Greene, a lawyer and aspiring poet educated at the Middle Temple who regularly writes of 'my cousin Shakespeare'. Two of Greene's children baptized in Stratford were named Anne and William, suggesting that the Shakespeares may have stood godparents to them. Of all the documents in the Records Office, perhaps the one in which we come closest to Shakespeare is a set of notes scribbled in 1614 on the day after Greene talked to the playwright and his son-in-law, John Hall, jotting down their opinions about the enclosing of land owned by Shakespeare. The very same document includes a set of Latin verses written by Greene in which he expresses anxiety consequent upon his wife's pregnancy, then in a late stage. (It came to a successful end.)[8] It is quite possible that, if letters written by Shakespeare ever turn up, they will be in Latin.

The fluency in Latin acquired by Elizabethan schoolboys, even in small towns like Stratford, meant that they could not only use the language for practical purposes, but could also both read and enjoy the great literature of the past to which they were exposed in the schoolroom. Some of them retained this capacity to the end of their days. On 1 March 1602 a London law student named John Manningham (whom we shall meet again) wrote in his notebooks that his 'cousin' (the word was often used loosely of a more or less close relative) had repeated from memory almost the whole of the first book – over six hundred lines of verse – of Virgil's *Aeneid*; two days later his entry reads 'And this day he rehearsed without book very near the whole second book of the *Aeneid*, viz. 630 verses without missing one word. A singular memory in a man of his age: 62.'[9] And pretty singular too, by our standards, that this young and not over-serious young student listened as his older relative recited in Latin at such length.

At point after point, Shakespeare's plays and poems show easy familiarity with classical texts that formed the basis of the grammar school curriculum of his time. Like Manningham's cousin, Shakespeare knew his Virgil, and also writers such as Julius Caesar and Cicero (both of whom he was to bring on stage, in *Julius Caesar*), Horace, and Livy. He was especially fond of the poetry of Ovid. He certainly knew the English verse translation by Arthur Golding, published in 1567, of Ovid's long poem *Metamorphoses*; one of Prospero's great speeches in *The Tempest*, beginning 'Ye elves of hills, brooks, standing lakes and groves', is so closely based on it as to be virtually a plagiarism. And it is equally certain that Shakespeare was closely familiar with Ovid's Latin original. Other writings by Ovid inspired him too. His long poems, *Venus and Adonis* and *The Rape of Lucrece*, are Ovidian in tone and subject matter, and the title page of the former quotes a couplet from Ovid's sensuously erotic *Amores* (which was probably not on the curriculum).

What all this helps to suggest is that, even if Shakespeare, like the school-boy of whom he writes in *As You Like It*, may have crept 'unwillingly to school', when he got there he was a keen and highly receptive pupil, inspired, perhaps, by the enthusiasm and skill of one of his teachers to a genuine love of the classics in the way that many pupils in later times have been inspired to a love of Shakespeare himself. The church, too, was a great educative force. Week by week, sometimes day by day, Shakespeare would have heard readings from the Old and the New Testaments, the homilies, and the Book of Common Prayer, along with sermons preached by the vicar and by visiting clergymen.

Arduous though the educational system was, boys who endured it found opportunities for recreation and entertainment. In his earlier years Shakespeare would have enjoyed childish pursuits such as playing with whip and top, leapfrog, hide-and-seek, and blind man's buff. As he grew older he may well have learnt to bowl, to swim in the Avon, to practise archery, to dance round the maypole, and to play football – an even rougher game, at times, then than now. The family surely kept what Shylock calls a 'harmless, necessary cat', and may have owned a pet dog like the cur Crab who behaves so badly in *The Two Gentlemen of Verona*. Fishing, hawking, and hunting were popular pursuits providing free food for pot and spit. An old local clergyman – John Frith, conceivably the man who married Shakespeare – was said to be 'unsound in religion', unable to 'preach nor read well'; but he had his uses, since 'his chiefest trade is to cure hawks that are hurt or diseased, for which purpose many do usually repair to him'.[10] Whether or not we believe the legend that as a young man Shakespeare poached deer in the grounds of the splendid Tudor mansion Charlecote House, a mile or two outside Stratford, the fact that the Shakespeare coat of arms, granted in 1596, incorporates a falcon may indicate a general interest in hunting. And at some point Shakespeare must have learned to ride a horse, essential for his later journeyings to and from London and around the country as a touring actor.

Most importantly for his later career, in Stratford he had ample opportunities to see both professional and amateur performances of plays; touring companies based in London regularly included Stratford in their itinerary during his boyhood and youth, and 'rude mechanicals' – as he was to call the artisans in *A Midsummer Night's Dream* – of the town put on entertainments, especially at Whitsuntide. In 1583, the year after Shakespeare married, the town council subsidized a performance 'by Davy Jones' (whose wife was a Hathaway) 'and his company for his pastime at Whitsuntide'. Shakespeare may have made one of that company; he may even have written the 'pastime'; he may have remembered it when he wrote *The Two Gentlemen of Verona*, in which Julia, disguised as a young man, tells how (s)he took part in such a show:

> at Pentecost,
> When all our pageants of delight were played,
> Our youth got me to play the woman's part,
> And I was trimmed in Madam Julia's gown,
> Which servèd me as fit, by all men's judgements,
> As if the garment had been made for me;
> Therefore I know she is about my height.
> And at that time I made her weep agood,
> For I did play a lamentable part.
> Madam, 'twas Ariadne, passioning
> For Theseus' perjury and unjust flight;
> Which I so lively acted with my tears
> That my poor mistress, movèd therewithal,
> Wept bitterly. (4.4.155–168)

And it is just conceivable that *The Two Gentlemen of Verona*, or an early version of it, is that very 'pageant of delight', and that Julia's words form a metatheatrical comment on the action.

As his body matured, Shakespeare must have felt both the emotional turmoil and the physical demands of what was clearly a turbulent sexuality. The evidence for this is plain to see throughout his writings. His plays, not to put too fine a point upon it, reek of sex. Some of the characters in them trade in double meanings and sexual innuendo with all the enthusiasm of adolescent lads in a changing room – though usually also with far more verbal grace and subtlety. Take, for example, a passage in his early comedy *Love's Labour's Lost* in which a group of high-spirited aristocrats are talking playfully in elegant, rhyming verse and courtly prose. Ostensibly their subject is archery, but males and females alike do all they can to exploit the sexual implications inherent in the image of an arrow penetrating a mark. 'Thou canst not hit it, hit it, hit it, my good man' sings one of the young ladies, and if she doesn't bring a sexual sense to the surface, it can scarcely be avoided in the male response 'An [if] I cannot, cannot, cannot, / An I cannot, another can.' Within a line or two the arrow becomes a prick – in a pun that Shakespeare was also to use in Sonnet 20 – stuck in the 'mark', the archer's bow hand is imagined as fondling the woman, the woman is imagined masturbating a man and causing him to ejaculate – 'Then will she get the upshoot by cleaving the pin' – yet another euphemism for penis – and, though the lady protests, with justice (though perhaps also with a giggle) 'Come, come, you talk greasily', the men round off the exchange with more dirty talk about 'pricks', 'bowls', and 'rubbing' (4.1.124–38).

This kind of chit-chat reaches its apotheosis in what is nevertheless the most romantic of Shakespeare's plays. Indeed it is characteristic of Shakespeare that he counterpoints the lyrical idealism of his young lovers in *Romeo and Juliet* with, first, the ribald bawdiness of the servants in the opening episode (often shortened in performance even now, though probably on grounds of obscurity rather than obscenity), then with the savage sexuality of Mercutio, sometimes interpreted as the outcome of frustrated, possibly subconscious desire for Romeo, and with the earthy sexual realism of Juliet's Nurse; characteristic too that, though later ages have often sentimentalized the lovers' relationship, the sexual ardour that underlies it is never disguised

8. Anne Hathaway's Cottage: the twelve-roomed farmhouse in Shottery
which belonged to the Hathaway family till 1892 when it was bought by the
Shakespeare Birthplace Trust.

and is brought fully to the surface in, for instance, Juliet's soliloquy 'Gallop apace . . .' (3.2.1–31), in which she longs for night to come so that she and Romeo can 'do their amorous rites'.

We have no direct knowledge of how Shakespeare acquired his sexual education, but it undoubtedly bore fruit earlier than was usual for young men at this time. Most of them did not marry until they were in their mid-twenties; Shakespeare was eighteen when he married Anne Hathaway, and she was three months pregnant. She was also the elder by eight years. Anne was one of the seven children of Richard Hathaway, who owned land and a house called Hewlands in Shottery, only a mile or so from Stratford. The house has long been known and shown as Anne Hathaway's Cottage, though in fact it is a substantial farmhouse. Just as Mary Arden brought her husband a legacy of ten marks, so Anne's father left her the same sum to be paid when she married.

A possible relic of William and Anne's courtship exists in one of his least distinguished sonnets, a poem which sticks out from those that surround it by its irregular form – it is written in eight-syllabled lines instead of the standard ten-syllabled – and still more by its triviality. But it is redeemed by its biographical interest, because its puns on 'hate' and 'away' add up to a declaration of love for Anne 'Hate-away', and portray the poet as an ardent, and initially unsuccessful, lover:

> Those lips that love's own hands did make
> Breathed forth the sound that said 'I hate'
> To me that languished for her sake;
> But when she saw my woeful state,
> Straight in her heart did mercy come,
> Chiding that tongue that ever sweet
> Was used in giving gentle doom,
> And taught it thus anew to greet:
> 'I hate' she altered with an end
> That followed it as gentle day
> Doth follow night who, like a fiend,
> From heaven to hell is flown away.
> > 'I hate' from hate away she threw,
> > And saved my life, saying 'not you.' (Sonnet 145)

This could easily be Shakespeare's first surviving composition, thriftily – or even sentimentally – preserved among his papers until, many years later, he was able to incorporate it into his sonnet sequence.[11]

Shakespeare's marriage licence was issued by the Bishop of Worcester, in whose diocese Stratford lay, on 27 November 1582. On the next day two Stratfordians, Fulk Sandells and John Richardson, friends of the bride's family, entered into a bond for the very large sum of £40 – twice the annual salary of Stratford's schoolmaster and its vicar – as a guarantee that there were no legal obstacles to the marriage. They would have had to testify that Shakespeare had his father's consent, necessary as he was a minor. The bishop's clerk mistakenly wrote Anne's name as 'Whateley' instead of 'Hathaway'. He made other errors; and there is no mystery about the substitution as the bond names the bride correctly as 'Anne hathwey of Stratford in the Dioces of Worcester maiden' (the last word clearly a euphemism). Nevertheless, Frank Harris, one of Shakespeare's more sensationally minded biographers, fantasized in *The Man Shakespeare* (1909) that Shakespeare had jilted an otherwise unknown Anne Whateley – 'Shakespeare's other Anne' – in favour of Anne Hathaway, and other writers have followed suit. Anthony Burgess, who also had a nice line in sensationalism, declares that 'the lovely boy that Will probably was – auburn hair, melting eyes, ready tongue, tags of Latin poetry' – had 'copulated with Anne Hathaway' with 'no talk of betrothal', a piece of 'wanton fornication, doubtless perpetrated in a ryefield in high summer', before falling in love with a putative Anne Whateley, 'sweet as May and shy as a fawn'. He was then, Burgess supposes, dragooned into a shotgun marriage with a woman he did not love.[12] This is all fiction. (The 'auburn hair' derives from an early nineteenth-century description of the colouring of Shakespeare's monument.)[13]

It used to be common, especially in books written for young people, to defend Shakespeare's reputation with the speculation that before their marriage Anne and he had been through the ritual of handfasting, a formal declaration of intent to marry, often accompanied by the exchange of rings and other gifts – gloves made by his father would have come in handy – after which sexual activity was countenanced. Certainly handfasting was common: later in life, as we shall see (p. 76), Shakespeare himself seems to have officiated at such a ceremony; and pre-marital chastity was highly valued in middle-class families. On the other hand, the urgency suggested by the terms of the marriage bond, which permitted the ceremony to take place with only one reading of the banns instead of the usual three, suggests that formalization of the union had not been long premeditated. All we can say for certain is that Shakespeare carried his baby daughter Susanna to Holy Trinity to be baptized before the whole congregation on Trinity Sunday, 26 May 1583, six months after her parents' wedding. Twins, Hamnet and Judith, followed; they were baptized on 2 February 1585. The name Hamnet is another form of Hamlet; it was common enough at the time, and the twins were very likely named after their parents' friends and neighbours, Hamnet (also known as Hamlet) and Judith Sadler; thirty years later, Shakespeare was to leave the husband money to buy a ring. It's natural to speculate whether, in writing a play with a hero bearing his son's name after Hamnet / Hamlet had died, Shakespeare was influenced by family sentiment. This was the historical name of the Danish prince, and his story was well known; still, Shakespeare chose to tell it.

Shakespeare had probably left school when he was about fifteen, some three years before Anne Hathaway conceived. He did not, like some of his Stratford contemporaries, go to a university. This may be because by this time his father's fortunes were in decline. John Shakespeare had stopped attending council meetings, and in 1586 was to be replaced as alderman because 'he doth not come to the halls when they be warned, nor hath not done of long time'. He had sold land, mortgaged a substantial part of his wife's inheritance, and was in debt. He may have needed his eldest son to help in the family business, but as a married man William could not have entered into a formal apprenticeship with his father. Perhaps he continued to live at home in the early years of his married life; his father had extended his Henley Street house in 1575, soon after the birth of his son Richard, and it was common to place a four-poster bed in parlours as well as in upper chambers – but such an arrangement would not have been conducive to literary composition.

There is no evidence that Shakespeare lived anywhere other than in Stratford before he married. But there is an intriguing theory, first propounded in 1937, that he is to be identified with one 'William Shakshafte', mentioned in 1581 in the will of a wealthy Catholic landowner, Alexander Hoghton, of Lea Hall in Lancashire.[14] Scholarly opinion on this matter has fluctuated over the years, but the theory has been strongly espoused, especially by Catholics and by members of the University of Lancaster, who in 1999 held an international conference devoted to it, linked to the proposal to found a study and performance centre at Hoghton Towers. Passions ride high, and it is not entirely easy to steer an impartial path through the arguments.

The crucial passage of Hoghton's will is his bequest to his half-brother Thomas of

> all my instruments belonging to musics, and all manner of play clothes, if he be minded to keep and do keep players; and if he will not keep and maintain players, then it is my mind and will that Sir Thomas Hesketh knight shall have the same instruments and play

clothes, and I most heartily require the said Sir Thomas to be
friendly unto Foke [i.e. Fulke] Gyllom and William Shakshafte, now
dwelling with me, and either to take them unto his service, or else
to help them to some good master.

It will strike a modern reader that Shakeshaft, however spelt, is not the same
name as 'Shakespeare'. Names were fluid in the period – Marlowe, for example, appears as 'Merlin', and Shakespeare's own name is spelt 'Shaxberd' in
documents referring to performances of plays at court in 1604–5. But it seems
relevant that in all the many references to members of Shakespeare's family
in Warwickshire records of the sixteenth century, this form has not been
found, whereas it is common in Lancashire.[15]

All the evidence on the positive side of the question is circumstantial,
and there is a lot of it. The principal known link between Stratford and
Hoghton is that an Oxford graduate, John Cottam, master of the Stratford
grammar school from September 1579 – round about the time that Shakespeare is likely to have left the school – resigned late in 1581 or early in 1582,
and returned to his family home at Tarnacre, not far from where Hoghton
lived. The area was a hotbed of illegal Catholicism, and Cottam's move
may have been motivated by the fact that his younger brother Thomas, a
Catholic priest, was arrested in 1580, arraigned with Edmund Campion in
November of that year, and executed in 1582. Supporters of the Lancashire
theory, building on a report by John Aubrey from the late seventeenth
century that Shakespeare 'had been in his younger years a schoolmaster in
the country', hypothesize that Shakespeare for some reason preceded Cottam
to Lancashire as a tutor, though Hoghton's will does not imply that Shakeshaft was a teacher, or even necessarily a musician or player. They also attach
importance to the fact that the Hoghtons and Heskeths were friendly with the
family of the Earl of Derby, to whose acting company Shakespeare may (or
may not) have belonged early in his career – but not, one has to say, before
he wooed and wed Anne Hathaway in Stratford.

A further ramification of the theory, and one of the reasons for giving space
to it here, is its implications for Shakespeare's religious beliefs. Here again we
are on shaky ground. Throughout Shakespeare's boyhood and youth his father
appears to have been a fully conforming member of the established church. In

1592, however, he was in trouble for not attending services. It was reported that this was because he feared that if he showed himself in public he would be prosecuted for being in debt, as we know he was. An alternative theory is that he was a recusant – an underground Catholic. The only support for this is a document of uncertain provenance known as the Borromeo testament, the centre of a story worth telling in its own right.

In the eighteenth century, a tall and burly Stratford wheelwright, John Jordan (1746–1809), who wrote verse and pursued antiquarian interests in his spare time, acted as a self-appointed guide and purveyor of anecdotes to visitors interested in hearing about 'that immortal man whose "muse of fire" affords entertainment to the divine, the philosopher, the metaphysician, the hero, the senator, and the poet' (as he put it). Jordan collected and embroidered upon stories already circulating, including the legends that Shakespeare poached deer at Charlecote and that, after taking part in a drinking competition in Bidford, some miles from home, he fell asleep 'beneath the umbrageous boughs of a wide-spreading crab[apple]-tree'. Next morning, according to Jordan, Shakespeare had recovered enough to boast of having drunk in many neighbouring villages:

> Piping Pebworth, dancing Marston,
> Haunted Hillborough, hungry Grafton,
> Dadgeing Exhall, papist Wixford,
> Beggarly Broom and drunken Bidford.

Jordan's endeavours came to the attention of the great scholar and editor Edmond Malone (1741–1812), who took pity on his poverty. In 1789 the vicar of Stratford, James Davenport, told Malone of the existence of a six-leaf manuscript lacking its opening now referred to as the Spiritual Last Will and Testament of John Shakespeare. The document is now known to derive from the 'Last Will of the Soul, made in health for the Christian to secure himself from the temptations of the devil at the hour of death', composed, probably in the 1570s, by the saintly Cardinal Carlo Borromeo at a time of terrible plague in Italy. The assumption is that John Shakespeare acquired a manuscript copy of this formulaic document, filled his name in the blanks (or got someone else to do it for him), and hid it (though the final paragraph asserts the writer's intention to carry it continually about him, and to have it buried with him). In 1966 an English version of the Borromeo testament, printed in tiny format in 1638, came to light, showing that the basic document mentioned by Davenport is genuine. Assured by Davenport of the authenticity of the incomplete Stratford version, Malone decided to include it in his forthcoming *History of the English Stage.* A few months later, in 1790, John Jordan sent Malone a collection of papers concerned with Shakespeare's relatives which included a manuscript copy of the will. This had now acquired an opening clearly invented by Jordan, who claimed that in 1757 a master-bricklayer, Joseph Mosely, while tiling the roof of John Shakespeare's Henley Street house, had found the will in the rafters. Malone – though he was to develop serious doubts about its authenticity – printed it as an appendix to his edition of Shakespeare from Jordan's manuscript, now in the collection of the Birmingham Reference Library.

If it's genuine, this document shows that Shakespeare's father, who had been born and brought up before the Reformation, retained – or reverted to – his Catholic faith even when it was illegal, and highly inconvenient, to do so, and that Shakespeare was brought up in a covertly Catholic household.

There is nothing inherently implausible in this. Catholics practised their faith in Warwickshire, as in many other parts of the country, sometimes secretly, sometimes openly, risking prosecution and worse. Many recusants paid a monthly fine rather than attend Church of England services. A Catholic priest, Hugh Hall, lived in disguise as a gardener in the home of Edward Arden, a wealthy landowner in North Warwickshire. Shakespeare's mother may have been related to the family; in any case, Shakespeare must have known the terrible story of Arden's son-in-law, John Somerville, who lived at Edstone, only a few miles away from Stratford. In 1583, not many months after Susanna Shakespeare was born, Somerville, 23-year-old head of an ancient Catholic family with property in both Warwickshire and Gloucestershire, and father of two young daughters, driven apparently to madness by his religious tensions, declared that he had a call to free Catholics from persecution, and was heard saying that he would go to London to shoot the Queen with his pistol. He set off, assaulting people on the way, was arrested and thrown into the Tower, admitted his intent, and under torture implicated his wife, his parents-in-law, and Hugh Hall. Somerville alone pleaded guilty, but all were sentenced to death. The women were pardoned, as was Hall, apparently because the authorities hoped to be able to get more information out of him; but Somerville and Arden were carried together in a litter to Newgate prison and shut up in separate cells. A couple of hours later, Somerville was found strangled, possibly by sympathizers wishing to protect him from the still greater horrors of public hanging, disembowelment, quartering and beheading suffered by his father-in-law on the next day. Both their heads, fixed on pikes, were set up on London Bridge as a ghastly warning to would-be traitors (Plate 4).

So, if John Shakespeare was a crypto-Catholic, he would not have been alone. But was he? His children were all baptized, and he was buried, with Anglican rites. He accepted public office, as burgess, alderman, and bailiff, which would have made it impossible for him to evade attending church services. Under his auspices as acting chamberlain in 1564, the painted images in the Guild Chapel were ordered to be defaced as part of the process of Protestantization, and in 1571, as chief alderman he attended the council meeting at which it was ordered that Romish copes and vestments remaining in the Guild Chapel should be sold off.[16] And the theory that his failure to attend church is evidence of Catholic sympathies is not supported by the documentary evidence: two certificates issued by the Commissioners for Recusancy in Warwickshire in 1592 distinguish clearly between those suspected of absence from church services for religious reasons and those suspected because there they might most easily be served with warrants for their arrest; in both lists John Shakespeare is among those of whom 'It is said that [they] come not to church for fear of process for debt.'[17]

The only positive evidence for John Shakespeare's Catholicism is the Borromeo testament, and suspicion is cast upon that by the fact that Jordan invented its opening.

The relevance of this scepticism to William Shakespeare is two-fold. First, it casts doubt upon the theory that he had a Catholic upbringing, and so may himself have had Catholic sympathies. All his life records suggest that both he and his father were conforming members of the Established Church, and the absence of dogma which is one of the most conspicuous, and highly valued, aspects of Shakespeare's writings militates against the hypothesis that he adhered strongly to a doctrinaire creed. Secondly, it leaves us free to make the natural supposition that he lived in Stratford until after he had wooed and wed Anne Hathaway and started his family.

What he did during these years, and in the period following the birth of his twins, in 1585, until he emerges on the London scene as an established playwright in 1592, we do not know. These are the so-called 'lost years'. He must have earned a living somehow. John Dowdall, a lawyer who visited Stratford in 1692, was told by one of the oldest inhabitants that Shakespeare had been apprenticed to a butcher but had 'run away from his master to London, and there was received into the playhouse as a servitor'. This implies that he lived in Stratford continuously between leaving school and going to London, with no break in Lancashire. An indirect way of investigating the matter has been to examine the plays' language in the hope that it will reveal their author's expertise in one profession or another. It's no surprise that plays written by a whittawer's son refer frequently to animal skins and their properties, to leather garments, to gloves and to the tools of the glove-maker's trade – in *The Merry Wives of Windsor*, Mistress Quickly asks if Slender wears 'a great round beard, like a glover's paring-knife' (1.4.18–19). On the other hand, Shakespeare did not have to be a glover's son to acquire this kind of information. His plays draw on so wide a range of vocabularies, sometimes quite specialized, that he could not possibly have acquired all of them through direct professional experience.

Those looking for subconscious revelations seem themselves often to have been subconsciously influenced by a desire to claim him as one of their own. The eighteenth-century scholar Edmond Malone, trained as a barrister, was sure he must have worked 'in the office of some country attorney'; the twentieth-century soldier and statesman Duff Cooper wrote a book, *Sergeant Shakespeare* (1949), trying to show that Shakespeare served 'as a soldier in the Low Countries, under the banner of the Earl of Leicester'; Lieutenant-Commander A. F. Falconer, later Professor of English at Saint Andrews, author of *Shakespeare and the Sea* (1964), considered it certain that between 1584 and 1590 Shakespeare 'came to know the sea and the navy', and that he probably reached the rank of corporal, if not lieutenant.

The diversity of conclusions that can be reached by these means shows the unreliability of the methodology, which, though it can tell us a lot about the contents and workings of Shakespeare's mind, is immensely complicated by the fact that he wrote not simply out of his head, but constantly picked up new words and ideas from a vast range of written sources, and no doubt from the conversation of people around him. This is also relevant to conjectures that he travelled abroad, in whatever capacity. Though Italy is the setting for around half of his plays, nothing in them would have required personal knowledge of the country, and he makes errors – such as Prospero's departure from 'The gates of Milan' in a barque (*The Tempest*, 1.2.130–44) – which suggest that geography was not his strong suit.

★

The Stratford record concerning William Shakespeare is completely blank for ten years after the birth of the twins except for a passing mention of him in litigation involving his father and his cousin, John Lambert, in 1587. As we shall see, he is first mentioned in print in 1592, by which time he was clearly established on the London scene. It would be nice to think that he had not left his wife to cope single-handed with Susanna, Hamnet, and Judith during their early years, but there is no evidence either way. It was inevitable that his professional career, which will be the subject of the next chapter, should centre on London. All the custom-built theatres were in London, London was the centre of the royal court, and all theatre companies aspired to be summoned to perform at court, because of both the honour and the money. Admittedly, the profession became decentred from time to time, especially when outbreaks of plague caused the authorities to ban public assemblies in the capital, as happened sometimes for months at a time – even for a year or more. In time of plague they would play exclusively in the provinces, and touring was a normal and regular activity even when there was no infection to fear. Nevertheless, London is where the action was. Moreover, Shakespeare's wife gave birth to no more children after he was twenty years old. So, it is often assumed, he left his family in Stratford, came back home only rarely, took a dark lady as his mistress, based his life in the capital, and worked there pretty well exclusively until three or four years before he died, when the springs of inspiration were drying up, and, we are told, he 'retired' to his home town. This narrative is reinforced by a statement from the unreliable John Aubrey (1626–97) that Shakespeare 'was wont to go to his native country once a year' – he doesn't say for how long.

The idea that Shakespeare was virtually a Londoner from around 1590 to 1612 rests, I suspect, largely on the mistaken notion that Stratford was a provincial backwater with few links to the capital. London is about a hundred miles from Stratford. Communications were time-consuming, but they existed, even in winter when the roads were at their worst. Shakespeare's father and Adrian Quiney, as high alderman and bailiff, journeyed to London on corporation business in January 1572, staying there for about two weeks. One of the most frequent visitors to London from Stratford was Adrian's son Richard, who worked and travelled indefatigably on behalf of his home town, as well as undertaking numerous private commissions in the capital for friends and relatives. In 1594 he rode through Gloucestershire and Oxfordshire raising money for victims of disastrous fires which had afflicted Stratford one windy day in May as a result of 'the negligence of an old woman put in trust to tend the fire of a brewhouse'.[18] One of the houses destroyed is of special interest. It belonged to Thomas Rogers, the bailiff, whose daughter Katherine – one of ten children – must have known Shakespeare's girls, and who gave birth in London in 1608 to John Harvard, founder of Harvard University. The house was splendidly rebuilt in 1595, and is now known and shown as Harvard House; its beautifully carved woodwork, which shows what excellent craftsmanship was available in Stratford, incorporates Rogers's initials with those of his wife, Alice.

Late in the following year Quiney visited London again, seeking support for victims of even more disastrous fires which had destroyed 120 homes and eighty other buildings – John Shakespeare's Henley Street house narrowly escaped, and four hundred of Stratford's inhabitants were dependent on relief. Quiney was in London at least twice in 1597, on the second visit seeking special privileges for the distressed town's manufacturing of malt at a time of severe shortage of corn and widespread poverty. He spent Christmas there, receiving letters written (one in Latin, the other in English) by Abraham Sturley on 18 and 24 January. The second of these contains a reference to Shakespeare, indicating that he was contemplating the purchase of land 'at Shottery or near about us'. And on 25 October 1598 Quiney wrote the only surviving letter addressed to Shakespeare. It's a friendly letter, though lacking the intimate revelations that we might desire. Endorsed 'To my loving good friend and countryman Mr William Shakespeare deliver

9. Harvard House.

these', it was written at the Bell Inn, in Carter Lane, close to Saint Paul's. The Bell seems to have been a regular port of call for visitors from Stratford, including William Greenway, the carrier, whose will, made in 1601, records a debt of fourteen shillings from the innkeeper. Shakespeare may well have stayed there. It was demolished in the late nineteenth century, but a plaque marks the site.

Whoever was to bear Quiney's letter to Shakespeare appears to have been expected to know where to find him. It reads:

> Loving countryman,
> I am bold of you as of a friend, craving your help with £30 upon
> Mr Bushell's and my security or Mr Mytton's with me. Mr Roswell

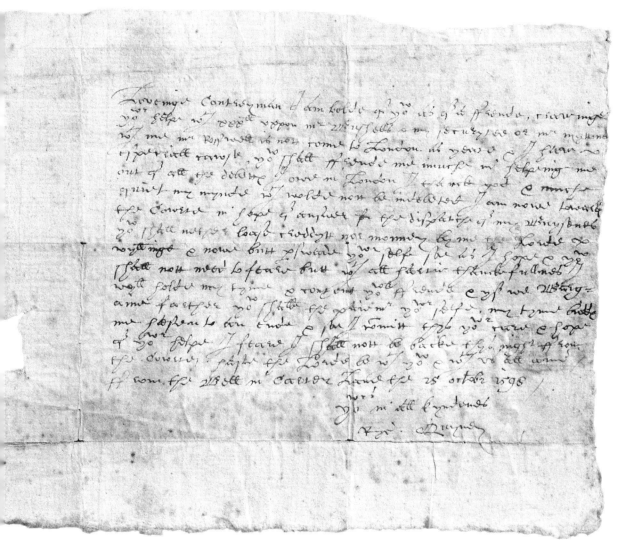

10. Letter addressed to Shakespeare from Richard Quiney, senior.

[probably Thomas Russell, a wealthy Warwickshire gentleman whom Shakespeare was to appoint overseer of his will] is not come to London as yet and I have especial cause. You shall friend me much in helping me out of all the debts I owe in London, I thank God, and much quiet my mind which would not be indebted. I am now towards the court in hope of answer for the dispatch of my business. You shall neither lose credit nor money by me, the Lord willing, and now but persuade yourself so as I hope and you shall not need to fear but with all hearty thankfulness I will hold my time and content your friend and if we bargain farther you shall be the paymaster yourself. My time bids me hasten to an end and so I commit this to your care and hope of your help. I fear I shall not be back this night from the court. Haste. The Lord be with you and with us all, Amen. From the Bell in Carter Lane, the 25 October 1598.

    Yours in all kindness,
      Ric[hard]. Quiney

The letter was preserved among Quiney's papers, so it seems not to have been delivered. We don't know whether Shakespeare lent the money. It was a large sum, and Quiney may have been asking for it on Sturley's behalf[19] rather than personally, quite possibly as a business transaction on which Shakespeare (who had recently written about usury in *The Merchant of Venice*) would receive interest. A letter to Quiney from Sturley written a few days later indicates that Quiney had expressed optimism 'that our countryman Master William Shakespeare [Mr Wm. Shak.] would procure us money', but Sturley was sceptical: 'which I will like of as I shall hear when, and where, and how', while encouraging Quiney to do all he could to bring it about. He also advised his friend to 'take heed of tobacco' – obviously regarded as a dangerous innovation – and that if he had to undertake a long journey he should 'drink some good burned [mulled] wine or aqua vitae and ale strongly mingled, without bread for a toast; and above all, keep you warm.' The carriage of the letter – probably by Greenway – from Stratford to London cost him twopence.

How long would the journey have taken Shakespeare? When Quiney rendered his accounts for his eighteen-week stay in London in 1598–9, he noted that he 'was six days going thither and coming homewards';[20] visiting London yet again in November 1601, in company with one Henry Wilson, he rode first to Oxford – a journey of some forty miles – next day to Uxbridge via High Wycombe, and on the third day to London; returning eight days later on frosty roads – their horses wore nails in their shoes to guard against slipping – they stayed overnight first at Aylesbury, then (after refreshing themselves and their horses at Banbury) rode to Walton, close to Wellesbourne (and so not far from home).[21] And it was possible to do the journey more quickly: a letter sent by Quiney from London on 3 November 1597 reached Sturley in Stratford 'late on the 5th.'[22]

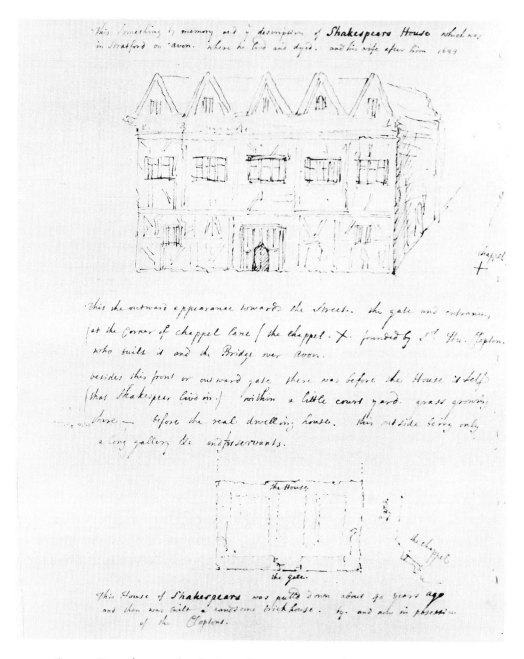

11. George Vertue's 1737 sketch, done from memory and description, of the 'front or outward gate' of New Place; the only known representation. Vertue's note records that 'the real dwelling house' stood beyond a little grassed courtyard, and that the 'outside' was 'only a long gallery &c and for servants'.

12. The five-gabled right-hand portion of the sixteenth-century Shakespeare Hotel, close to New Place.

The Quiney records show Shakespeare maintaining connections with his native town, and much other evidence shows that he did so throughout his career. On 11 August 1596 his son Hamnet was buried there. We don't know whether the boy's father was present; if the death was sudden and he was in London or on tour, news might not have reached him in time. Nor do we know what his feelings were. But we can say for certain that only a few months afterwards, in May 1597, he confirmed his commitment to Stratford by buying the town's second largest house, New Place (the largest was the College in Old Town). He paid £60 for it, and the same amount again for confirmation of his title. The century-old house lay across the road from the garden of the Guild Chapel where John Shakespeare and his fellow councillors had deliberated in the year of the playwright's birth, and close to the school the playwright had attended. It was in dilapidated condition, which meant that he had to be prepared to spend time, effort and money on improving it – a procedure which may be reflected in the speech from *Henry IV, Part Two* quoted at the head of this chapter. In January 1599 the town chamberlains, who were repairing the bridge over the Avon, paid him ten pence for a load of stone probably left over from his restoration work.

Shakespeare was still only thirty-three when he bought New Place. He had come a long way in a short time. It was a grand establishment with a frontage of over 60 feet and a depth of at least 70 feet in some parts. It had three storeys and five gables and seems to have been constructed round a courtyard and to have had ten fireplaces – not every room would have had one. It stood in ample grounds with two barns, two gardens, and two orchards; Shakespeare later bought additional land and a nearby cottage. The purchase of New Place was a statement of status and of prosperity, a declaration that its owner – who had no fixed abode in London – was first and foremost a Stratfordian. This would be more apparent than it is today if the house had survived: after being partly rebuilt in 1702, it was pulled down in 1759 by an irate owner sick of being asked for relics of the mulberry tree that Shakespeare was supposed to have planted in its garden. The site, along with the house's Great Garden, can be visited, and a glance at the five-gabled portion of the Shakespeare Hotel (p. 33), a little further up the road, may give an idea of New Place's grandeur.[23]

Bits and pieces of information in legal and other records tell us about Shakespeare's continuing Stratford presence. In 1598 he was listed as a holder of malt and corn, and in 1601 his father, who must have been over seventy years old, was buried there. By now John Shakespeare had recovered from his earlier losses and was (along with his son) officially a gentleman, having been granted a coat of arms in 1596. The seal and crest are displayed on Shakespeare's monument. John Shakespeare seems to have left no will, but his eldest son would have inherited the house now known as his birthplace, in which his mother continued to live. In the following year William greatly consolidated his possessions by the purchase, for the large sum of £320, of 107 acres of land in Old Stratford; he probably intended it as a marriage settlement for his elder daughter, Susanna. He appears not to have been around at the time the deed was signed: his brother Gilbert represented him. Later in the same year he bought a cottage with a garden amounting to a quarter of an acre in Chapel Lane, close to New Place, perhaps for a servant. In 1604 his neighbour Philip Rogers, an apothecary and dealer in tobacco,

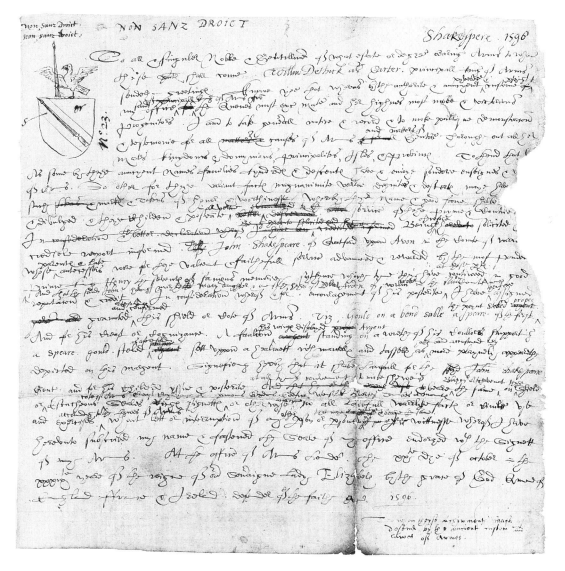

13. The coat of arms granted in 1596 to John Shakespeare and his descendants.
The motto reads 'Non Sanz Droict' – 'not without right'.

pipes, and ale bought 20 bushels of malt from members of Shakespeare's household; Shakespeare later sued him, through a solicitor, for partial non-payment. In 1605 – around the time he was writing *King Lear* – he made the most substantial of all his investments, paying £440 for an interest in the Stratford tithes. This would have resulted in an annual income of around £40.[24] Four years later, in an amply documented case, he was to sue one John Addenbrooke for a debt of £6.[25]

Shakespeare was a rich man, a householder and a landowner, possessed of a grand mansion with barns and extensive gardens, the smaller but still substantial house in which he had been born, at least one cottage with garden, a large area of land which he leased for farming, and a major investment in tithes. All this centred on Stratford, the accumulated product of years of careful husbandry of income earned from the theatre. In London, as we shall see, he had no fixed base for any length of time, and he bought no property there until the end of his life. Although he worked as an actor, which would have required him to be with his theatre company for much of the year, the meagre evidence that survives suggests that he was no star. On the other hand, he unquestionably was, for close on twenty years, his company's star playwright. He was also a major shareholder. He had tenure, which means that he would have had less need than his rivals to make his presence felt all the year round. His colleagues had every incentive to encourage him to spend time in Stratford if that would help him to write the plays on which they depended for their success. I find it hard to accept the common view that for twenty years he virtually abandoned the town where he owned a grand establishment and extensive property, where his mother and father, his wife and children, and at least some of his brothers and sisters lived.

Ever since Milton wrote of Shakespeare 'warbling his native woodnotes wild' there has prevailed an image of the playwright as one of Nature's great improvisers, an image charmingly and jokily perpetuated in the film *Shakespeare in Love*, where we see him jotting down bits of dialogue in the rafters of the theatre in the intervals of energetic love-making. This is a pleasing fiction. In real life, writing is a solitary occupation. It calls for peace and quiet. Shakespeare's plays are the product of intense imaginative and intellectual activity, deeply pondered and intricately plotted. To write them he needed space for thought. He also needed books. He was a highly literary dramatist. As he wrote he drew not only on his recollections of writings, such as the works of Ovid, that he must have read at school, but on books that he must have had open before him as he wrote. And some of them were massive folios, bigger and heavier than a modern encyclopaedia, not the sort of book he could slip into his back pocket while travelling on foot or horseback from one guildhall to another.

14. Some of the books that were most important to Shakespeare: this display shows (back row, left to right) John Gerard's *Herbal* (1597), Holinshed's *Chronicles* (1597), and Sir Thomas North's translation of Plutarch's *Lives*; (front row, left to right) Ovid's *Metamorphoses* (1603) and Montaigne's *Essays* (1603).

Can we really imagine that, having these needs, a writer who owned a splendid house in a small and relatively peaceful town in Warwickshire would not make every possible opportunity to spend time there? And is it not likely that his fellows, who relied on his literary productivity for their great financial success, encouraged him to do so? And if so, does not this modify the traditional picture of Shakespeare as a man who abandoned his family for the greater part of every year, and only resumed spending much time with them when, in the rather anachronistic term, he 'retired' to Stratford in his last years?

Shakespeare was, I suspect, our first great literary commuter. All his contemporaries who wrote for the theatre based themselves in London. Only he had the good sense to maintain a household many miles away. We know little about the contents of New Place, but my guess is that it contained a comfortable, book-lined study situated in the quietest part of the house to which Shakespeare retreated from London at every possible opportunity, and which members of the household approached at their peril when the master was at work (Plate 3).

In the later part of Shakespeare's life, his daughters made many claims on his attention. Susanna appears to have been a strong-minded woman. Legal documents from late in her life show that she had learned to write. In May 1606, then nearly twenty-six years old, she was among twenty-one Stratfordians reported to the ecclesiastical court for refusing to take Holy Communion at Easter. The Gunpowder Plot was fresh in mind, and the authorities were anxious to round up Catholic sympathizers; Susanna ignored the summons and the case was later dismissed, which probably means that, like the other defendants, she had fallen into line. More importantly, on June 1607 she married the strongly Protestant Dr John Hall, a distinguished physician, in Holy Trinity Church, and, we believe, her father made over to her the 107 acres of land that he owned in Old Stratford, while keeping a life interest in it for himself. The fine house now known as Hall's Croft was probably built for the Halls; tree-ring analysis carried out in 1999 indicates that the oldest part of the building dates from 1613.

The Halls had only one child, Elizabeth, baptized on 21 February 1608: if Susanna was not, like her mother, pregnant when she married, it was a near thing. She ran into scandal in 1613, when a disreputable rogue, John Lane, alleged not only that she had conducted an adulterous affair with a married hatter and haberdasher, Ralph Smith, but that she had contracted a venereal disease as a result. She sued Lane, who did not defend himself, for defamation of character, and won; he was excommunicated.[26]

After Susanna's father died, in 1616, she and her husband moved into New Place, where she continued to live after John Hall died, in 1635. An incident of a couple of years later raises intriguing questions about what happened to Shakespeare's books. Susanna declared in court that a bailiff and his men, having failed to collect a judgement against her late husband's estate, broke into the house 'and rashly did seize upon and take divers books, boxes, desks, moneys, bonds, bills, and other goods of great value'. Whether she got the property back we know not. She died in 1649 and is buried in Holy Trinity

next to her husband and close to her parents. The inscription on her gravestone implies that Susanna derived her intelligence from her father and her
piety from her husband, which may suggest that Shakespeare had no great
reputation for godliness:

> Witty above her sex, but that's not all,
> Wise to salvation was good Mistress Hall.
> Something of Shakespeare was in that, but this
> Wholly of him with whom she's now in bliss.

Records of Shakespeare's involvement with Stratford increase in the later
years of his life; while this may indicate that he spent more time there then,
it may also simply mean that he was more involved in the sort of activity that
got into the records. The family was dwindling. His actor brother Edmund
died in London in 1607. His mother's burial in Stratford is recorded on
9 September 1608; she must have been around seventy years old. Inheriting
her house and other property would have increased her eldest son's local
responsibilities. A document of 1611 lists him among those to be approached
for a subscription towards the mending of highways, a cause that he would
have had both professional and private reasons to support. His brother
Gilbert, of whom little is known except that he was unmarried, died in
Stratford in 1612, and his last brother, Richard, a year later. Of John and
Mary's children, only William and his sister Joan now survived.

In July 1614 yet another disastrous fire ravaged Stratford, destroying
fifty-four houses and much other property. The consequences were especially
severe for the 700 and more of the town's 2,000 or so inhabitants who drew
poor relief. Within months came proposals to enclose large areas of arable
land, including some that belonged to Shakespeare, to the north of the town,
converting it into sheep pasturage. This would have brought further hardship
along with it, reducing income and employment and increasing the price of
grain, vital to many of the town's inhabitants. A cluster of references from
later in the year onwards shows that Shakespeare was implicated, in ways that
remain obscure, in these events. Although it would be nice to think that he
was wholeheartedly a supporter of the poor, and so opposed to enclosure, the
indications are that he succeeded in sitting on the fence, safeguarding his own

interests while not offending his rich friends. One of the prime movers was William Combe, a 28-year-old landowner from whose family Shakespeare had bought some of the land in 1602. Combe's uncle John Combe had died a few months before the proposal to enclose, leaving Shakespeare £5; his fine tomb, sculpted, like Shakespeare's monument, by Gerard Johnson, may still be seen in Holy Trinity; it once bore an epitaph, alluding satirically to the rates of interest that he charged, first printed in 1618 and later said to have been composed by Shakespeare:

> Ten in the hundred here lies engraved
> A hundred to ten his soul is not saved.
> If anyone ask who lies in this tomb,
> 'O ho!' quoth the devil, ''tis my John-a-Combe.'

If Shakespeare really did write that it was a poor repayment for his legacy.

While the enclosure dispute was still raging, Shakespeare was to bequeath his sword to William's brother Thomas. The town council, fearing riots as well as serious loss of income, appealed to Shakespeare, among other landowners, not to enclose; one of their number was later to tell William Combe that 'All three fires were not so great a loss to the town as the enclosures would be.' Shakespeare stood to lose income from his tithes, and by 28 October 1614 had entered into an agreement for compensation. From November his 'cousin' Thomas Greene, Stratford's first town clerk, kept a detailed diary of events; visiting London to present a petition against enclosure, he called on Shakespeare who, with his son-in-law John Hall, had just arrived from Stratford: 'at my cousin Shakespeare coming yesterday to town I went to see him how he did.' Shakespeare, who knew all about the plans, tried to reassure Greene, saying he thought that 'there will be nothing done at all'. On 9 December Greene was part of a delegation to Combe entreating him not to go ahead, but Combe declared that when the frost broke 'the ditching would go presently forward'.

After a Council meeting on 23 December Greene wrote to Shakespeare both personally and on the council's behalf inviting support. His letter does not survive, but in a letter to another person involved Greene referred to 'the manifold miseries this borough has sustained' and to the 'above 700 poor which receive alms, whose curses and clamours will be daily poured out to God against the enterprisers of such a thing'. As the Council had feared, the dispute became acrimonious and violent. On 7 January Combe, having heard that 'some of the better sort would go to throw down the ditch', said ' "Ay, O, would they durst" in a threatening manner with very great passion and anger'. A couple of days later Greene heard that two of his townsmen 'had privately sent their spades before, and that by and by they would go throw down some of the ditch'; Greene prudently advised them to 'go in such private manner as that none might see them go lest others might perhaps follow in company and so make a riot or a mutiny'. Combe's men started to enclose the land by digging a long trench; at the very moment that an agreement was being concluded that 'there shall be no throwing down of ditches already set up . . . until after 25 March,' women and children of Bishopton and Stratford 'filled them up again'. Combe punished his tenants in the village of Welcombe, virtually depopulating it. The case dragged on until, around the time that Shakespeare died, in 1616, a letter from the chief justice told Combe that he 'should neither enclose nor lay down any arable nor plough any ancient greensward'. Even this did not deter him, but the land was not finally enclosed until well into the eighteenth century.[27]

In January 1616, Shakespeare called his lawyer to draft a will. He had stopped writing plays, and may have known that he had not long to live. Within a couple of months he had cause to change his bequests. His daughter Judith, aged thirty-one, married Richard Quiney's son Thomas, a vintner, on 10 February 1616. Wanting to tie the knot quickly, they – and the parson who performed the ceremony – took a risk: technically, marriage in Lent required a special licence, which they failed to obtain, and although the rule was often infringed, they were summoned to appear before the ecclesiastical court in Worcester. Quiney failed to turn up, and was excommunicated; Judith may have suffered the same fate. We have no reason to believe that Shakespeare disapproved of the marriage in advance, but within a few weeks, scandal highly damaging to the groom erupted. He had carried on an affair with one Margaret Wheeler, who died along with their newborn baby on 15 March. Eleven days later, only six weeks after marrying Judith, Quiney was again summoned to an ecclesiastical court, this time in the church where he had married, and was prosecuted for 'incontinence'. Confessing his

15. A page of the inventory accompanying the will of William Greenway, the Stratford carrier, listing and valuing the contents of each room in minute detail. In the hall '4 spits, a pair of cupboards, 2 pair of pot-hooks, a gridiron, 2 frying pans, 2 dripping pans, a fire shovel, a pair of tongs, a pair of links [torches], an andiron, an old pair of bellows, a sink of lead and certain wooden dishes' are collectively valued at ten shillings. As in the re-presented Birthplace, the parlour includes a bed, and painted cloths to decorate the walls.

crime and submitting himself to the court's jurisdiction, he was sentenced by the vicar who had married him to perform penance, wearing a white sheet betokening humility, before the entire congregation on three successive Sundays. Perhaps because someone – could it have been his embarrassed father-in-law? – intervened, he was lucky enough to escape with a fine of five shillings, paid to the poor of the parish, and with a less humiliating formal confession, wearing his normal clothes, before the minister of the neighbouring village of Bishopton.

The later version of Shakespeare's will was prepared on 25 March, by which time Quiney's shame must have been known – the case was to be heard on the following day. It is at once the most and the least personal document of Shakespeare's to survive: the most, because it clearly represents his fully considered, and reconsidered, views on the disposal of his estate; the least, because it is written in legal terminology, and also because it omits all mention of his books, manuscripts, and other papers which might have cast light on his life and art. It would have been normal for such possessions to be mentioned in an accompanying inventory, which is lost. The will shows Shakespeare very much as a family man and a Stratfordian: almost all the bequests outside the family are to fellow townspeople, ranging from the poor, who receive £10 (a standard sum in wills of well-off people at the time), through children such as his godson William Walker, who receives twenty shillings 'in gold' – that must have pleased the boy – to well-off friends such as Thomas Russell – overseer of the will – and Anthony and John Nash: ten years later, Anthony's son Thomas was to marry Shakespeare's granddaughter. The only Londoners receiving a mention are three of his theatre colleagues, and, as I shall suggest, there may have been a special reason for that.

The bulk of the estate, including New Place, goes to Susanna, who with her husband is the executor, and is entailed thereafter on male heirs. How different everything would have been if Hamnet had lived. Judith receives the considerable sum of £150 along with other bequests including a 'broad silver and gilt bowl': this may easily survive, a treasured possession which would be even more highly valued if its provenance were known. The rest of his plate goes to his granddaughter, Elizabeth Hall, then eight years old. The Henley Street house, along with £20 and Shakespeare's clothes, goes to

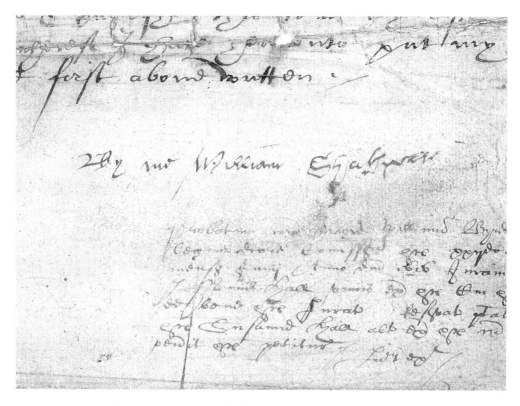

16. The signature on the last page of Shakespeare's will.

his sister Joan, whose husband, a hatter named William Hart, was soon to die; he was buried a week before Shakespeare. Perhaps by calculation, Quiney is not mentioned: but he was to give his first son, baptized on 23 November of the same year, the forename Shakespeare, probably in honour of the infant's late grandfather. The most enigmatic bequest is that of the second-best bed which is all that Shakespeare's widow receives; but she may have been automatically entitled to an interest in his estate, and certainly continued to live in New Place after his death. It is fruitless to enquire into the couple's relationship in their later years, but the idea, sometimes mooted, that their failure to produce more children after the birth of their twins shows that their marriage had collapsed is ill founded; there were large families in Stratford, like that of Thomas Rogers, but Susanna had only one child, and Judith three, like her father. A small family did not necessarily imply poor marital relations.

The signatures on the will are shaky. Shakespeare was probably already ill. The best guess – it is no more – is that he was suffering from typhoid fever.[28] He died within a month, and was buried in Holy Trinity on 25 April. This time the entry in the register is in English: 'Will Shakspere, gent': times were changing. Close on fifty years later the Stratford vicar, John Ward, was to note that 'Shakespeare, Drayton, and Ben Jonson had a merry meeting and, it seems, drank too hard, for Shakespeare died of a fever there contracted.' The poet Michael Drayton often visited Clifford Chambers, near Stratford, but there is no evidence that Jonson was ever in the neighbourhood. Tantalizingly, Ward also made a note that, in his search for information about Shakespeare, he should 'see Mrs Quiney', but he left it too late; Judith died in 1662, aged seventy-seven. Her father's last direct descendant was his granddaughter, Elizabeth, now owner of his silver-gilt bowl, who married a second husband, Sir John Bernard, but died childless in 1670.

The gravestone long believed to be Shakespeare's, up in the chancel of the church where he had been baptized, bears no name, only the epitaph beseeching the sexton not to chuck his bones in the charnel house:

> Good friend, for Jesus' sake forbear
> To dig the dust enclosed here.
> Blessed be the man that spares these stones,
> And cursed be he that moves my bones.

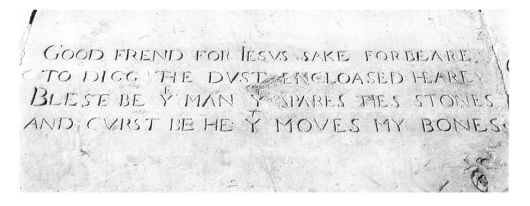

17. The epitaph on the gravestone in Holy Trinity Church traditionally regarded as Shakespeare's.

Though these lines may not sound quintessentially Shakespearian, they are written in the same metre as the Epilogue to *The Tempest* and were ascribed to Shakespeare as early as the middle of the seventeenth century.[28]

The stone, a late eighteenth- or early nineteenth-century replacement for the original, is prominently situated before the steps leading to the altar rails. Shakespeare's widow's grave, which lies to its left, bears a brass plate telling us that she was sixty-seven years old when she died in 1623 – the only evidence of her date of birth – along with a pious Latin inscription praying for her resurrection. Other members of the family lie to the right of Shakespeare. It seems rather suspicious that members of the same family, however distinguished, who died (reading from left to right) in 1623, 1616, 1647, 1635, and 1649 should be buried side by side; I sometimes toy with the thought that the stones may have been moved to provide a star line-up. And Shakespeare's stone is oddly shorter than the others – only 3 feet 7 inches long, unless part of it lies underneath the altar steps, which are a later addition. Conceivably his stone too once bore a memorial inscription, and possibly traces of it may lie hidden under the steps.

It was no doubt Shakespeare's relatives who commissioned the monument placed in the wall above his widow's gravestone. Presumably they were satisfied that it did not seriously misrepresent his appearance. Executed, like the monument to his friend John Combe, by Gerard Johnson (or Gheerart Janssen), a Dutch craftsman based in London not far from the Globe, it states that Shakespeare died on 23 April 1616 at the age of fifty-three. Like the gravestone it bears no name, but the Shakespeare arms surmount it, and the inscriptions, in both Latin and English, confirm Stratford's pride in its greatest son. The former compares him to great figures of antiquity: '*Iudicio Pylium, genio Socratem, arte Maronem, / Terra tegit, populus maeret, Olympus habet*' ('In judgement a Nestor, in genius a Socrates, in art a Virgil; the earth covers him, the people mourn him, Olympus has him'). The latter somewhat cryptically calls on the passer-by to pay tribute to his greatness as a writer:

> Stay, passenger, why goest thou by so fast?
> Read, if thou canst, whom envious death hath placed
> Within this monument: Shakespeare, with whom
> Quick nature died; whose name doth deck this tomb

Far more than cost, sith all that he hath writ
Leaves living art but page to serve his wit.

(The only sense I can make out of the last bit is that his compositions relegate the sculptor's art to the rank of a mere page – with perhaps a forced pun on the writer's 'pages' – offering service to his genius; or perhaps that all art

18. Gerard Johnson's monument to Shakespeare in
Holy Trinity Church, Stratford-upon-Avon.

subsequent to Shakespeare's is a page – servant – to his.) In fact his name does not deck the tomb, and it's not a tomb anyway; the best explanation seems to be that the inscription, and possibly the monument itself, was originally designed to be part of a free-standing tomb, abandoned perhaps on grounds of economy.

The great doors at the back of Holy Trinity open only for ceremonial occasions: weddings, funerals, civic events and, nowadays, the procession that winds each year through the streets of Shakespeare's native town to celebrate his birth. Through these doors he was carried to burial, and through them we pass to pay him homage.

As a family man and a private person, Shakespeare belongs to Stratford. But his career as a man of the theatre centred on London, and there we now follow him.

CHAPTER TWO

Shakespeare in London

'O sweet Master Shakespeare! I'll have his picture in my study at
the court.'

Gullio, in *The Return from Parnassus, Part One*, anon. (*c.*1598)

THE FIRST EXISTING REFERENCE to Shakespeare as a theatre professional,
and the earliest mention of him in print, is an insult. It is also oblique and
cryptic. Robert Greene, Cambridge-educated playwright, poet, pamphleteer,
writer of romantic tales, self-publicist, and reprobate, died in 1592 at the age
of thirty-four, reportedly after over-indulging in Rhenish wine and pickled
herring. Soon afterwards appeared a shambolically organized and hectically
written pamphlet, *Greene's Groatsworth of Wit Bought with a Million of Repen-
tance*, claiming to be composed on its author's deathbed; it was prepared
for the press, and perhaps written in part, by another minor writer, Henry
Chettle. The *Groatsworth* includes the following passage:

> there is an upstart crow, beautified with our feathers, that with his
> 'tiger's heart wrapped in a player's hide' supposes he is as well able
> to bombast out a blank verse as the best of you; and, being an
> absolute Johannes Factotum, is in his own conceit the only Shake-
> scene in a country.

'Shake-scene' clearly puns on the name Shakespeare, and 'tiger's heart
wrapped in a player's hide' paraphrases a line (1.4.138) from one of the most
memorable scenes in his play *Henry VI, Part Three*. The sneering epithet
'upstart crow' smacks of envy, and in the words 'beautified with our feathers'

Greene claims to be speaking on behalf of fellow playwrights as well as himself in resentment at the success of an actor turned playwright, whom he may also be accusing of plagiarism.

Of all allusions to Shakespeare from his own time this is, both professionally and personally, by far the least complimentary.

Soon afterwards, however, Chettle uttered a handsome apology, remarking that in his capacity as publisher's editor he could and should have 'moderated the heat' of Greene's comments, especially since Greene was dead, and declaring himself 'as sorry as if the original fault had been my fault, because myself have seen his demeanour no less civil than he excellent in the quality he professes'. And he goes on to say that 'divers of worship' – various respected persons – 'have reported his uprightness of dealing, which argues his honesty, and his facetious' – urbane, polished – 'grace in writing, that approves' – bears witness to – 'his art'.[1] This little episode shows Shakespeare emerging from the darkness of the 'lost years', established on the London scene as an upcoming actor and writer, arousing malice and envy but also admiration and respect.

How he got to London is a mystery. He may just have uprooted himself from Stratford and gone straight there to seek his fortune as a writer. It's less likely that he could have hoped to make a career as an actor if he'd had no professional experience. But we know of no non-dramatic writings (except the sonnet probably addressed to Anne Hathaway, p. 19) before he is spoken of as a playwright, and it seems more likely that he joined a travelling company as an actor, gaining experience as an all-round man of the theatre in the provinces as well as in the capital. This would help to explain why he didn't take his wife and children with him. The Queen's Men played in Stratford in 1587, five years after Shakespeare married. It was a successful company made up of some of the country's best actors. The corporation rewarded them with twenty shillings – more than they had ever paid before – and had to spend sixteen pence to repair a bench broken probably because of the press of numbers. In the same year one of the actors, William Knell, was killed in a brawl in Thame, Oxfordshire, which could easily have been on their route. It's an attractive guess – but only a guess – that Shakespeare, who may have shown promise as an amateur actor, joined them as a hired man to fill the gap. The timing is right, and he was later to rework several plays that this company owned and performed in the years before 1594. *The Famous Victories of Henry the Fifth*, *The Troublesome Reign of King John*, and *The True Tragedy of Richard the Third*, all of unknown authorship, closely anticipate his plays on English history. Most conspicuously, there are so many echoes throughout his work of the odd old tragicomedy known, to distinguish it from his own play on the same reign, as *King Leir*, that it's hard to avoid the conclusion that he gained intimate familiarity with this play by acting in it some twenty or more years before he was to transform it into his profoundest tragedy.[2]

The Queen's Men was formed primarily as a touring company, though it often played before the Queen and occasionally in public theatres in London.[3] Created in 1583 around some of the best actors of the day, it would have formed an excellent training ground for an aspiring playwright. But Shakespeare might have wished to graduate to a company with a more permanent London base. This was a crucial period in the history of the English theatre. Up to the time of Shakespeare's boyhood, plays were performed mainly by itinerant companies in makeshift premises – inns, guildhalls, great houses, bear-baiting rings. As he grew up custom-built playing places came to be constructed, but only in the capital. One called the Red Lion, of which little is known, dates from as early as 1567, but the turning point came in 1576 when James Burbage, whose son Richard was to become the greatest actor of Shakespeare's company and the inspiration for many of his finest roles, built the Theatre. Named after the amphitheatres of ancient Rome, it formed the prototype for London theatres for the next sixty and more years. Even more importantly, its construction was to provide the catalyst for an explosion in dramatic writing. Now actors had buildings that could offer ampler practical resources than had previously been available, the capital housed a population of around 200,000 persons[4] avid for entertainment, and there emerged a bevy of writers eager to exploit the new opportunities. Suddenly, drama took off. Plays became longer, more ambitious, more spectacular, more complex in construction, wider in emotional range, and better designed to show off the talents of their performers. It was the ideal moment for Shakespeare to come on the scene, and he had all the right talents to make the most of it.

Perhaps the most extraordinary feature of the new drama was its literariness. Until shortly before the building of the Theatre, all English drama had been composed in verse: the first extant play to be written entirely in prose is

The Supposes, an elegant comedy by George Gascoigne, of 1566; it had few successors for over a century. The use of prose gradually increased, especially in comedy and in comic episodes within tragedy, but playwrights had to be poets, and indeed that is what they were most frequently called. Verse is not necessarily great poetry; but many writers of plays – Greene, Marlowe, Jonson, and Chapman among them – were also distinguished poets. At no other period in the history of English literature has so high a proportion of the best writing been done for the stage. Joining the London scene, Shakespeare was able to develop his skills as a writer by acting in new plays, by rubbing shoulders with the men who were writing them, and by reading the latest books as they came from the press. He seems often to have stored books in his mind, mulling them over, perhaps subconsciously, until he was ready to make use of them. He echoes Arthur Brooke's poem *The Tragical History of Romeus and Juliet*, first published in 1562 (and reprinted in 1587, around the time Shakespeare arrived in London), in both *The Two Gentlemen of Verona* and *Henry VI, Part Three* before drawing far more closely on it for *Romeo and Juliet*. He may well have read Greene's prose romance *Pandosto* when it first appeared, in 1588: towards the end of his career he drew heavily on it for *The Winter's Tale*. Three romances first published in 1590 were to be important to him: Thomas Lodge's *Rosalynde*, which he transformed a decade later into *As You Like It*; Sir Philip Sidney's posthumous *Arcadia*, from which he borrows in *King Lear*; and Spenser's great epic poem *The Faerie Queene*,[5] echoed in several plays. And the second edition of Holinshed's *Chronicles*, of 1587, is the one that furnishes him with much of the material for his English history plays.

The greatest dramatist of Shakespeare's early years was Christopher Marlowe, Cambridge graduate, poet, translator of the classics, playwright, and government spy, born in the same year as Shakespeare but a speedier developer, who packed an amazing amount of experience as well as literary achievement into his short life. He was to die in 1593, aged twenty-nine; if Shakespeare too had died in that year, we should now regard Marlowe as the greater writer. He wrote for the Lord Admiral's Men, led by Edward Alleyn, who played at the Rose Theatre. In 1592, plays acted there included at least one instalment of Shakespeare's *Henry VI* and his *Titus Andronicus*, as well as Marlowe's sensationally popular *Jew of Malta*. One of the excitements of

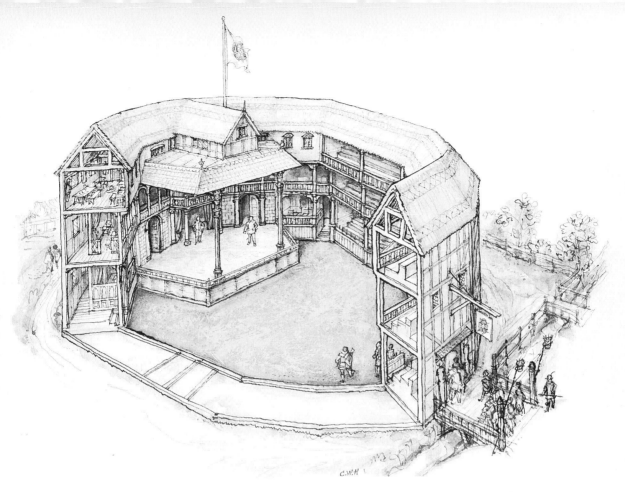

19. A drawing by C. Walter Hodges, made after the remains were discovered,
representing the Rose Theatre as enlarged in 1592 from the original structure of 1587.

seeing the remains of the Rose yield up their secrets as they were excavated
in 1989 was the realization that one was looking at the very patch of ground
where Shakespeare had stood as he learned his trade, and at the remains of
the stage on which he must have acted.

Marlowe, famous for his 'mighty line', wrote wonderfully eloquent dramatic verse in plays that Shakespeare knew and admired. *Richard II* may be
seen as a response to Marlowe's *Edward II*, *The Merchant of Venice* to *The Jew
of Malta*. More directly, in *As You Like It* Shakespeare refers to his predecessor
in the only quotation from a readily identifiable contemporary writer in all his
works: 'Dead shepherd, now I find thy saw of might: / "Who ever loved that
loved not at first sight?"' That line comes from Marlowe's sensuously beautiful and witty narrative poem *Hero and Leander*, not published while Marlowe
was alive but extended by George Chapman and published in 1598.

Hero and Leander is an early example of a literary genre which flourished in the 1590s, long poems telling stories of romantic love, inspired in style and often in subject matter by Ovid. Shakespeare may well have read it in manuscript, and when, late in 1592, the London theatres had to close because of an epidemic of plague that was to last for almost two years, he followed Marlowe's example in his own long poems, *Venus and Adonis* and *The Rape of Lucrece*, published respectively in 1593 and 1594. They maintain his links with his home town: each was printed by a Stratford man, Richard Field, two and a half years older than Shakespeare, who must have gone to the same school and whose late father's property had been evaluated by John Shakespeare in 1592.

These are virtually Shakespeare's only writings composed for print.[6] By the time he wrote them he was already an experienced dramatist who had demonstrated his versatility by producing plays of varied kinds: comedies including *The Two Gentlemen of Verona* (which I believe to be his first play), *The Taming of the Shrew*, and possibly *The Comedy of Errors* (the chronology of the early plays is particularly difficult to determine); the extraordinarily ambitious cycle of history plays on the reigns of Henry VI and Richard III; and the tragedy of *Titus Andronicus*. Plague came as a serious threat to his living; he may well have felt an urgent need for an alternative career. If so, he was remarkably successful. Nowadays the poems are among his least-known compositions, partly because fewer people read poetry than go to the theatre, but also because of changes in literary fashion. But in his own time they were phenomenally successful, frequently reprinted – more often than any of the plays – and alluded to in both printed and manuscript writings. Contemporary admirers often praise especially the sweetness of his versification, sometimes extending it to his character. So Francis Meres, in his boring but invaluable treatise *Palladis Tamia*, of 1598, writes that 'the sweet witty soul of Ovid lives in mellifluous and honey-tongued Shakespeare, witness his *Venus and Adonis*, his *Lucrece*, his sugared sonnets among his private friends, etc.'; and later, 'the Muses would speak with Shakespeare's fine-filed phrase if they would speak English'. Meres (who goes in for lists in a big way) also names Shakespeare among those who are 'the most passionate among us to bewail and bemoan the perplexities of love'. In the same year the poet Richard Barnfield praises Shakespeare's 'honey-flowing vein', declaring that his '*Venus*

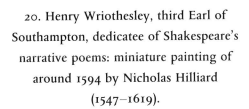

20. Henry Wriothesley, third Earl of Southampton, dedicatee of Shakespeare's narrative poems: miniature painting of around 1594 by Nicholas Hilliard (1547–1619).

and . . . *Lucrece* (sweet and chaste)' have placed his name 'in Fame's immortal book', and in 1599 John Weever writes of 'honey-tongued Shakespeare', and of the 'sugared tongues' of his characters.[7]

The poems did a lot to raise Shakespeare's literary status; in them he addresses a rather more learned and sophisticated public than in most of his plays, showing that he could compete as an imitator of the classics with university-educated men such as Marlowe and Thomas Lodge. The poems also bear witness to his rising social status. In London he was able to meet and to seek the patronage of some of the greatest men in the land. Each of the poems is dedicated to Henry Wriothesley, third Earl of Southampton, in 1593 a handsome, cultivated, and immensely accomplished nineteen-year old. In itself, this does not tell us much; the relationship between poet and patron was not necessarily close, and the terms of the earlier dedication, to *Venus and Adonis*, are relatively formal. Probably we should not read too much into the fact that as, in the poem, the young Adonis repels Venus's steamy advances, so Southampton, at the age of seventeen, had declined to marry Lady Elizabeth Vere, granddaughter of Lord Burleigh, whose ward he was, and had forfeited the enormous sum of £5,000 as a result. The earlier dedication may have been merely formal, but the warmth of the later – 'What I have done is yours, what I have to do is yours, being part in all I have, devoted yours' – suggests that Southampton had become a friend as well as a patron. Friendship with the Earl would have given Shakespeare the entrée to the family's London home, Southampton House, a centre of literary and intellectual patronage. In 1709 Nicholas Rowe, author of the first formal biography of Shakespeare, reported that Southampton gave Shakespeare a present of £1,000. The Earl was inordinately extravagant, but this is ridiculous.

By 1594 the plague had abated. Shakespeare was able to resume play writing, and the establishment of the Lord Chamberlain's Men under the patronage of Henry Carey, first Lord Hunsdon, put his career on a firm footing once and for all. He was probably a founder member: in the earliest official account to survive, of 1595, he is named along with his colleagues Will Kemp and Richard Burbage as payee for performances at court during the previous Christmas season. His position in this company is threefold. As we have seen, he was an actor – not, apparently, of any great distinction. We cannot certainly identify any of his roles: he is listed among the actor lists in two of Ben Jonson's plays as well as in his own First Folio, an epigram of around 1610 suggests he had a penchant for 'kingly parts',[8] and eighteenth-century traditions give him the Ghost in Hamlet and old Adam in *As You Like It* – not star roles (though Bernard Shaw wrote that 'the Ghost's part is one of the wonders of the play' and that this is 'the reason why Shakespear' – Shaw's idiosyncratic spelling – 'would not trust anyone else with it').[9]

Shakespeare was also a sharer, which means that he had a joint financial interest in (and responsibility for) the company's affairs. This must be the main reason for his prosperity. And he was, for well over fifteen years, their chief playwright. This made him unique. No other writer of the period had so long and stable a relationship with a single company. It gave him security, it meant that he could shape roles according to the talents of particular players, and it contributed greatly to the continuing, and growing, success of the company. Whether he had a defined contract, and whether he was paid specifically for what he wrote, we do not know. His output suggests that he was expected to provide an average of around two plays a year, and to ring the changes between tragedy and comedy. In the years between the founding of the Lord Chamberlain's Men and the building of the Globe theatre in 1599, he tended to favour comic over tragic form. This is the period of the earlier romantic comedies – *Love's Labour's Lost*, *A Midsummer Night's Dream*, *The Merchant of Venice*, and *Much Ado About Nothing*, along with the less romantic *The Merry Wives of Windsor* and the comical histories of *Henry IV, Parts One* and *Two* and *Henry V*; but it includes too the romantic tragedy of *Romeo and Juliet* and the tragical histories of *Richard II* and *King John*, and, at the end of the period, *Julius Caesar* (possibly the first play to be performed in the Globe).

The Lord Chamberlain's Men, who first performed these plays, was composed initially of around eight sharers, increasing by 1603 to a dozen, all of them actors, including, besides Shakespeare, the tragedian Richard Burbage, the comic actor and dancer Will Kemp, and John Heminges, who was to stay with the company virtually until he died, in 1630, and who served as its business manager. The sharers owned the stock of scripts, costumes, and

21. Richard Burbage (*c.* 1567–1619), Shakespeare's leading actor for most of his career, traditionally regarded as a self-portrait.

Kemps nine daies vvonder.

Performed in a daunce from
London to Norwich.

Containing the pleasure, paines and kinde entertainment
of *William Kemp* betweene *London* and that Citty
in his late Morrice.

Wherein is somewhat set downe worth note; to reprooue
the slaunders spred of him: many things merry,
nothing hurtfull.

Written by himselfe to satisfie his friends.

LONDON
Printed by *E. A.* for *Nicholas Ling*, and are to be
solde at his shop at the west doore of Saint
Paules Church. 1600.

22. Will Kemp, for several years the leading comic actor in Shakespeare's company,
dances his way from London to Norwich. He accomplished the journey of about
140 miles in nine days spread over four weeks. Kemp was accompanied by a musician,
Tom Slye, playing pipe and tabor. The Mayor of Norwich awarded him an annuity
of forty shillings, and he was also rewarded with gifts.

23. Michael Gambon, as the actor John Shank (*c.* 1580–1636), instructs a (fictional) boy player, Michael Legge (Stephen Hammerton), in Nicholas Wright's play *Cressida* (2000).

properties, and shared both expenses and profits. In addition the company employed a number of hired men on a weekly basis, three or four boy actors, each of whom seems usually to have been attached in a master-pupil relationship to one of the sharers, along with stage keepers, tiremen and women to look after the wardrobe, musicians, stage hands, and gatherers (who also could include women) to collect the cash. They also needed scribes; once a play was written a fair copy had to be made, and each actor's part transcribed along with his cues. We can see the process in action in *A Midsummer Night's Dream* when Peter Quince distributes the parts to his actors: 'Here is the scroll of every man's name which is thought fit through all Athens to play in our interlude before the Duke and Duchess on his wedding day at night.' (1.2.4–7) Bottom the weaver wants to play Thisbe as well as Pyramus, whereas Snug the joiner, who is to be Lion, needs no scroll. 'You may do it extempore, for it is nothing but roaring.' The remains of only one such script survive, for the leading role in Robert Greene's play *Orlando Furioso*. Now preserved in Dulwich College, it is made of sheets of paper cut and pasted together, and when complete must have measured around 18 feet long. That should have satisfied even Bottom.

The overall strength of the company was around twenty. All Shakespeare's plays can be performed with this number of actors, some with fewer, but this entails doubling, tripling, or even quadrupling of roles, a regular practice which playwrights needed to bear in mind as they wrote. They also had to be aware of the strengths and limitations of their performers, especially the boys, who played the women's parts as well as juvenile roles. We know little about the boys of Shakespeare's company – how old they were when they played major roles, what they looked like, how they made up – but he clearly developed great confidence in the young actors for whom he wrote roles such as Juliet, Viola, Rosalind, Cressida, and Cleopatra, which the women performers who now play them regard as the most rewarding and demanding challenges in the theatrical repertoire. A boy is presumably to be defined as a pre-pubertal male, or at least one whose voice had not yet acquired what Guiderius in *Cymbeline* calls 'the mannish crack' (4.2.237). It's easier for us to imagine boys playing girls such as Viola (in *Twelfth Night*) or Miranda (in *The Tempest*) than mature women such as Mistress Overdone (in *Measure for Measure*) or Volumnia (in *Coriolanus*), and the use of adult males for female roles in performances at the reconstructed Globe has encouraged the idea that the same thing 'must have' happened in Shakespeare's theatre (Plate 24). This is to privilege common sense over evidence. If at the old Globe, as at the new, men had played Portia and Calpurnia in *Julius Caesar* the only role left for the company's boy actors in that play would have been the page Lucius. There is no reason to believe that adult males played women's parts in the theatres of Shakespeare's time, and English theatre companies did not include women until after the restoration of the monarchy, in 1660.

There is a myth that Elizabethan actors were classed as rogues and vagabonds. This was true only of itinerant players and companies that did not enjoy the formal protection of an aristocrat, whose livery they would wear. Shakespeare's company, initially the Lord Chamberlain's Men, came under the protection of King James himself when he acceded to the English throne in 1603. Their leaders were granted 4½ yards of scarlet cloth to wear in his coronation procession the following year, in which also twelve members of the company, presumably including Shakespeare, were required to serve for most of August as Grooms of the Chamber during a state visit of the Spanish ambassador. They were each paid two shillings a day, the standard rate for Yeomen of the Guard.[10] During the next ten years – up to the time of Shakespeare's death – they played at court more often than all the other theatre companies put together: records are patchy, but we know that they gave eleven plays at court between 1 November 1604 and 31 October 1605, and that seven of them were by Shakespeare. The company's members were respectable citizens, some of whom made fortunes comparable to Shakespeare's; they were also generous to one another. John Heminges was a pillar of his local church, Saint Mary's Aldermanbury; at his death in 1630 he left to 'every of my fellows and sharers [of] his Majesty's servants . . . the sum of ten shillings apiece to make them rings for remembrance of me'; similarly the actor and musician Augustine Phillips, who died in 1605, left 'a thirty shillings piece in gold' to Shakespeare along with bequests of money to all his other colleagues, including the hired men; he was especially solicitous of his former apprentice Samuel Gilburne, to whom he bequeathed 'the sum of forty shillings and my mouse-coloured velvet hose and a white taffeta doublet, a black taffeta suit, my purple cloak, sword and dagger', and of his current apprentice James Sands, clearly a musician: he too received forty shillings, along with Phillips's bass viol, cittern, pandora and lute.[11]

Initially, the company played mainly in the Theatre and its neighbour the Curtain, both located in Shoreditch, just outside the northerly City walls. We have little direct knowledge of the structures of these playhouses, but that of the Theatre may be inferred from the fact that, in an extraordinary episode in 1599, its timbers were dismantled and reconstructed as the Globe, of which we know more.

The Theatre had been built in 1576 by James Burbage, Richard's father, on land owned by Giles Allen. In April 1597 the Burbages' lease on the land expired. By the end of the year the company moved to the nearby Curtain, and the Theatre, now unfrequented, stood empty 'in dark silence and vast solitude', as a poet put it.[12] Protracted negotiations for a renewal of the lease failed, and Allen decided to pull the building down and 'to convert the wood and timber thereof to some better use'. But the original lease had specified that, under certain conditions, Burbage could 'take down and carry away' the structure, and this his heirs[13] proceeded to do. Around Christmas 1598 they, with a dozen or so supporters and workmen, began the task of dismantling the Theatre with the intention of re-erecting it elsewhere.

It was not a trouble-free business. Allen later testified to the Queen that the Burbage faction, armed with 'swords, daggers, bills, axes and such like', being opposed by citizens seeking 'in peaceable manner to procure them to desist from that their unlawful enterprise', 'forcibly and riotously' pulled, broke, and threw down the Theatre 'in very outrageous, violent and riotous sort, to the great disturbance and terrifying not only of your subject's said servants and farmers but of divers other of your majesty's loving subjects there near inhabiting'. Over a period of several days the timbers were carted through the streets of London and across London Bridge to a site close to the Rose, where they were re-erected on new foundations to form the Globe.[14] From now on, Shakespeare's company had the great advantage of occupying its own building, and its physical characteristics, inherited in part from the Theatre, were to condition the structure of his greatest plays. This is the building for which, over the next seven or eight years, he was to write his final romantic comedies, *As You Like It* and *Twelfth Night*; his unromantic tragicomedies, *Measure for Measure*, *All's Well that Ends Well*, and the virtually unclassifiable *Troilus and Cressida*; and the culminating sequence of tragedies, *Hamlet, Othello, King Lear, Macbeth, Timon of Athens, Antony and Cleopatra*, and *Coriolanus*. The romantic tale of *Pericles*, too, though it fits more easily with the plays of his final period, was written for the Globe (see below, p. 122–4).

The precise features of this building are difficult to determine. Only one surviving drawing shows the interior of a theatre of Shakespeare's time in any detail, and until 1989, when archaeologists unearthed the foundations of the Rose, we had no physical remains. Discovery of the Rose was a momentous event for everyone interested in the theatre and drama of Shakespeare's time, and it overturned received ideas. It was smaller than we expected, the ends of the stage were tapered, not squared off, the yard was not flat but sloped towards the stage, and the structure itself was not circular but had fourteen sides. Remains of the Globe, too, survive, and enough has been uncovered to show that it had twenty sides; regrettably, full excavation of the site has not been permitted. What is left of the stage probably lies underneath Southwark Bridge, and may never be revealed.

The unique theatre drawing is the de Witt sketch of the Swan, also on the

24. Johann de Witt's drawing of the Swan Theatre, made during a visit to England
*c.*1596 and copied by Aernout van Buchel.

south bank of the Thames, and is a copy by one Dutch visitor to London of a drawing by another, which, invaluable though it is, leaves many questions unanswered. It is a composite picture, not a representation of a single occasion. Though it shows a play in performance, there is no audience except for shadowy figures in the gallery over the stage; the artist appears to have been concerned mainly to identify certain features of the structure – the protruding stage, with its supporting pillars; the minimal stage furniture; the canopy held up by stage posts; the rear wall with gates for actors to enter by; the presence behind this wall of the dressing rooms or tiring house (*mimorum aedes*); the three tiers of galleries with an entry point – *ingressus* – presumably for those members of the audience wishing to upgrade from standing in the yard, which cost one penny, to sitting in a gallery, which cost a penny more; the upper level at the back of the stage which could house spectators and could also be used by the actors for scenes set on city walls, or balconies, or at a window; the hut surmounting the whole, which would house the flying machinery; the trumpeter whose fanfares would herald a performance; and the flag bearing the theatre's emblem.

The Globe seems to have been a similar structure, and the reconstruction now operating on Bankside close to the original site offers modern playgoers the opportunity to see plays performed in conditions similar to those in which they were originally given, but some of its features remain conjectural. It is a big theatre; there is evidence that the original held over 3,000 people, twice the capacity of the Royal Shakespeare Theatre or the Olivier auditorium of the National Theatre. It was also a sophisticated theatrical instrument, ideal in its openness and its symbolism for the presentation of poetic dramas working as often as not through suggestion rather than representation. This wooden O could indeed represent the great globe itself. In it a dramatist could indicate location if he wished, verbally or with furnishings and props such as a throne, a dais, chairs and tables; but equally it could represent nowhere in particular, or more than one place at once. And the audience could see the imagined location sometimes through one character's eyes, at other times through another's, so that for example the climate of the forest in *As You Like It* and the vegetation of the island in *The Tempest* vary according to the disposition of those who find themselves there. So in *The Tempest* the amiable nonentity Adrian says to the sanguine Gonzalo 'The air breathes

25. An interior view of the reconstructed Globe Theatre on Bankside, London, showing
The Two Gentlemen of Verona in modern-dress performance in 1996.

upon us here most sweetly', to be countered with the cynical Sebastian's
'As if it had lungs, and rotten ones', and Gonzalo's 'How lush and lusty the
grass looks! How green!' receives the response from Antonio 'The ground
indeed is tawny' (2.1.49–59).

Though the establishment of theatres in London was of immense significance to Shakespeare and his fellows, plays continued to be performed
in buildings not normally used for this purpose. Importantly for both
Shakespeare's and his company's reputation, plays were often given at court
– which meant in whatever grand establishment Elizabeth or James, accompanied by her or, later, his courtiers, chose to be. Appearances at court were
prestigious, profitable, and politically significant. Noblemen and corporate
bodies might commission special performances: *The Comedy of Errors* was

26. The hall of the Middle Temple, London, showing an all-male performance of *Twelfth Night* given by the Globe company to celebrate the four-hundredth anniversary of John Manningham's record of a performance of the play there in 1602.

given at (and may even have been written for) Gray's Inn at Christmas 1594 and again at court ten years later; *Titus Andronicus* was played privately at a country house in Rutland on New Year's Day 1596; John Manningham records seeing *Twelfth Night* played in the magnificent great hall of the Middle Temple, which survives, during the Christmas season of 1601–2. A member of the Temple at this time was Thomas Greene, Shakespeare's 'cousin', who would have had a particular interest in the occasion and may even have helped to bring it about.[15] Importantly, too, companies regularly toured outside London. This influenced the way plays were written. *Twelfth Night* and *Othello* call for no resources other than those that would have been available in guildhalls or inn rooms, and other plays, such as *King Lear*, might be easily adapted. *Hamlet* needs a stage-trap for Ophelia's grave and perhaps for the appearances of the Ghost, but was played in both Oxford and Cambridge, according to the title page of the edition printed in 1603. In 1610 a don named Henry Jackson who had seen performances in Oxford remarked (in a letter written in Latin) how in tragedies the players 'moved some to tears not only by their words but even by their actions'. He singled out for special praise the boy actor's performance of Desdemona, in *Othello*, who 'by her very countenance invoked the tearful pity of those who saw her'.

We know from allusions both in manuscript and in print that Shakespeare's reputation grew rapidly during the 1590s. His name appeared on the

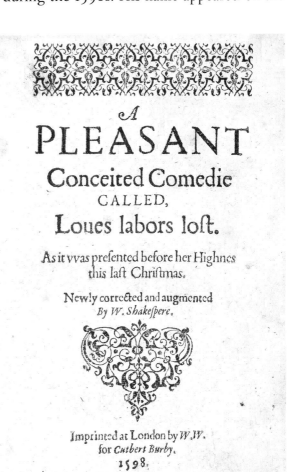

27. Title page of the second edition of *Love's Labour's Lost*, 1598, the first year in which Shakespeare's name appeared on the title page of one of his plays.

A

PLEASANT

Conceited Comedie

CALLED,

Loues labors loſt.

As it vvas preſented before her Highnes this laſt Chriſtmas.

Newly corrected and augmented
By *W. Shakeſpere.*

Imprinted at London by *W.W.*
for *Cutbert Burby.*
1598.

title page of one of his plays for the first time in 1598,[16] and in the same year Francis Meres compared him to famous comic and tragic dramatists of the ancient world: 'As Plautus and Seneca are accounted the best for comedy and tragedy among the Latins, so Shakespeare among the English is the most excellent in both kinds for the stage' – and, characteristically listing a dozen plays, he most valuably gives information that enables us to infer the latest date by which they can have been written.

Shakespeare also has a fervent admirer in the character named Gullio in the second of three lively plays of unknown authorship, known as the *Parnassus* plays, written around the turn of the century for performance by students of St John's College, Cambridge. This, however, is a double-edged compliment, because Gullio (the gull, or fool) is a conceited and affected cox-comb. He boasts to his fellow student Ingenioso how he woos his mistress in speeches larded with quotations from *Venus and Adonis* and *Romeo and Juliet*. Though Ingenioso expresses admiration to Gullio's face – 'Faith, gentleman, your reading is wonderful in our English poets!' – he comments caustically in asides addressed to the audience – 'We shall have nothing but pure Shake-speare and shreds of poetry that he hath gathered at the theatres!'

Again, 'sweet' is a favoured adjective: 'Sweet Master Shakespeare!', says Ingenioso, and at the height of his ecstasy Gullio, after quoting two lines from *Venus and Adonis*, exclaims 'O, sweet Master Shakespeare! I'll have his picture in my study at the court.' This is Shakespeare as pin-up; but it seems unlikely that a real-life Gullio would have been able to buy a likeness of his idol. In a later scene, Ingenioso recites love speeches that Gullio has persuaded him to write on his behalf in the style of Chaucer, Spenser and Shakespeare. This provides the earliest known parody of Shakespearian verse, written in the 'rhyme royal' form of *Lucrece*:

> Fair Venus, queen of beauty and of love,
> Thy red doth stain the blushing of the morn,
> Thy snowy neck shameth the milk-white dove,
> Thy presence doth this naked world adorn.
> Gazing on thee all other nymphs I scorn.
> Whene'er thou diest, slow shine that Saturday,
> Beauty and grace must sleep with thee for aye!

Preposterous though this is, it wins Gullio's rapturous acclaim: 'Let this duncified world esteem of Spenser and Chaucer, I'll worship sweet Master Shakespeare, and to honour him will lay his *Venus and Adonis* under my pillow, as we read of one – I do not well remember his name, but I am sure he was a king – slept with Homer under his bed's head.' (The name he fails to remember is Alexander the Great.)[17]

In the third of these plays (whose satirical spirit may be gauged by its description of Ben Jonson as 'the wittiest fellow of a bricklayer in England'), Shakespeare is praised again for his poems, with the reservation that he ought to tackle 'a graver subject, / Without love's languishment'. It is no doubt only a coincidence that this criticism comes shortly before Shakespeare was to turn from the predominantly comic mood of plays written in the late years of the sixteenth century to the far graver tone of those that were to follow.

In the same play Burbage and Kemp are seen auditioning recent university graduates for places in their company. Burbage suggests that as well as acting they may be able to 'pen a part', but Kemp thinks that university writers are too keen to show off their learning; they 'smell too much of that writer Ovid, and that writer *Metamorphoses*, and talk too much of "Proserpina" and "Jupiter". Why, here's our fellow Shakespeare puts them all down.' Shakespeare does not appear in person, but Burbage asks one of the aspirants to speak the opening lines of *Richard III* as an audition speech. Shakespeare's growing fame, especially as a love poet, is also witnessed around this time by the inclusion of hundreds of short extracts from his writings in the anthologies *England's Parnassus* and *Belvedere*, both published in 1600.

It's clear both from the *Parnassus* play and from an anecdote told by John Manningham (see p. 83) that Richard Burbage was especially associated in the public's mind with the role of Richard III. His reputation grew along with Shakespeare's, and each fed the other. During the 1590s Burbage vied for supremacy as a tragic actor with Edward Alleyn, of the Admiral's Men. Alleyn withdrew from the stage in 1597, and though he returned for a few years in 1600, at the urging of the Queen, before long he concentrated on his business interests. These helped to make him the most evidently wealthy and munificently philanthropic man of all those associated with the theatre in

28 & 29. Anonymous portraits of
the actor and philanthropist
Edward Alleyn and his wife Joan.

his time and perhaps in any other. From 1605 Alleyn was working on the foundation of a school and hospital to be known as the College of God's Gift at Dulwich. Dulwich College, finally set up in 1619, now houses the voluminous collection of papers relating to Alleyn's career and to that of his father-in-law, Philip Henslowe, proprietor of the Rose, which forms the greatest single source of information about the theatrical profession in Shakespeare's time. The only source of regret is that they relate to the wrong company. Contemporary portraits of Alleyn and of his first wife, Joan, show what a fine figure of a man he was – over six feet tall, exceptional for the time – and how effectively she dressed the part of a rich man's wife.

Alleyn's retirement left the field clear for his principal rival, and may have helped to precipitate the tragedies that Shakespeare wrote for Burbage in the early years of the seventeenth century. We know some of Burbage's roles from lines written after he died, in 1619:

> He's gone, and with him what a world are dead,
> Which he revived, to be revivèd so.
> No more young Hamlet, old Hieronimo,[18]
> Kind Lear, the grievèd Moor, and more beside
> That lived in him have now for ever died.

(Burbage was also commemorated in perhaps the shortest of all epitaphs: 'Exit Burbage.')[19] By and large we have to deduce his characteristics as an actor from the roles that he played, but the emphasis here on the kindness of Lear – not the most obvious quality of that irascible old man, at least in the earlier part of the play – and on Othello's grief suggests that Burbage had an outstanding ability to arouse sympathy for the characters he played. Personally, too, Burbage inspired affection: at a great banquet held a couple of months after the actor's sudden death the Earl of Pembroke, who was to be one of the dedicatees of the First Folio, could not bring himself to join in the after-dinner festivities: 'which I, being tender-hearted, could not endure to see so soon after the loss of my old acquaintance Burbage'.[20] The evening was to end with a performance of *Pericles*, in which very likely Burbage had been accustomed to play the title role.

Shakespeare's plays are remarkable for their absence of self-evident topicality. By and large, he writes about past times and distant places. Only one whole play, other than those concerned with English history, is set in England; this is *The Merry Wives of Windsor*, and even that is set off from topicality by the presence of Sir John Falstaff and by other links with plays about the reign of Henry IV. The framework to *The Taming of the Shrew*, too, has an English – indeed, a Warwickshire – setting, which for Shakespeare's audiences would have enhanced the romanticism of the Italian tale it encloses. Otherwise the plays take their audiences into Britain's distant past, or ancient Rome and Greece, or to France, Illyria, Vienna, Cyprus, or, above all, Italy. On the other hand, they do not insist on either historical or geographical precision, and can easily accommodate anachronisms, inconsistencies, and blatant topical allusions. Much late-twentieth-century criticism endeavoured to dig beneath the surface of the plays to show that, for all their appearance of remoteness, many of them engage more or less covertly with issues that affected the daily lives of their first audiences. This is often easier to suspect than to prove, but there is one conspicuous demonstration that a play was, if not written to reflect a burning issue of the day, at least found intensely relevant a few years after its composition.

When Shakespeare wrote *Richard II*, around 1595, the question of who would succeed Elizabeth as sovereign was already much in the air. The play first appeared in print in 1597, lacking the episode in which Richard finally cedes the crown to Bolingbroke. It was reprinted twice in the following year, still without the abdication episode, which is first found in the fourth edition, of 1608. This in itself is enough to suggest that the spectacle of a sovereign of England giving up his crown to a usurper was considered too politically sensitive to be presented on stage as long as the Queen was alive. Even clearer evidence that Elizabethans drew connections between this play and real life is provided by its use as an incentive to rebellion in 1601.

The Earl of Essex is the subject of one of the few unquestionable topical allusions in Shakespeare's plays, one which gives a clue to Shakespeare's stance in an urgent political issue (Plate 8). The Chorus to the fifth act of *Henry V* asks the audience to compare the triumphant reception of 'the conqu'ring Caesar' Henry on his return from France to London with that which the Earl of Essex was likely to receive when he came back from the Irish expedition on which he had embarked on 27 March 1599.

> But now behold,
> In the quick forge and working-house of thought,
> How London doth pour out her citizens.
> The Mayor and all his brethren, in best sort,
> Like to the senators of th'antique Rome
> With the plebeians swarming at their heels,
> Go forth and fetch their conqu'ring Caesar in –
> As, by a lower but high-loving likelihood,
> Were now the General of our gracious Empress –
> As, in good time he may – from Ireland coming,
> Bringing rebellion broachèd on his sword,
> How many would the peaceful city quit
> To welcome him! (5.0.22–34)

Essex was to return to London, disgraced, in September. Shakespeare's patron, the Earl of Southampton, who had accompanied Essex, preceded him in July; we are told that he and his friend the Earl of Rutland 'pass[ed] away the time in London merely in going to plays every day'.[21] During the following eighteen months Essex's discontent reached such a pitch that, abetted by Southampton, he conceived the crazy scheme of overturning the Queen and replacing her with James VI of Scotland. Matters drew towards a head in February 1601. As tension rose in London some of Essex's supporters approached Augustine Phillips and other members of the Lord Chamberlain's Men with a request that they put on a special performance of 'the play of the deposing and killing of Richard II', 'promising to get them forty shillings more than their ordinary to play it'. Sir Francis Bacon was to write that one of the ringleaders, Sir Gelly Meyrick, hoped 'to satisfy his eyes with the sight of that tragedy which he thought soon after his lord' – Essex – 'should bring from the stage to the state'. Phillips and his actor colleagues protested that the play had gone out of fashion – it was 'so old and so long out of use as that they should have small or no company at it'. This may have been disingenuous; after all the play was only a few years old. Anyhow, they gave way and put it on at the Globe on the afternoon of Saturday 7 February.

After lunching at a tavern in the City known as Gunter's, a number of the conspirators including Essex's secretary and chief adviser Henry Cuffe 'went all together to the Globe over the water where the Lord Chamberlain's men use to play and were there somewhat before the play began'. After the performance they foregathered at Essex House, and on the next day the Earl and his followers rode through the city in the vain hope of arousing enough support to overthrow the Queen and her ministers. Eleven days later, Phillips was examined as the actors' representative, and the day after that Essex and Southampton stood trial in Westminster Hall, the magnificent medieval structure completed by Richard II which is still used for state occasions. The chief prosecutor, Sir Edward Coke, invoked Richard II in his accusation that the conspirators planned to murder the Queen: 'Note but the precedents of former ages: how long lived Richard the Second after he was surprised in the same manner?' The Earls were condemned to death. After shilly-shallying from the Queen, who retained a soft spot for Essex, he was beheaded on 25 February; Southampton's sentence was commuted and he spent the rest of Elizabeth's reign in the Tower, where he had the company of a pet cat (Plate 7). So far from being blamed for their share in events, the actors were summoned to perform at court the night before Essex was executed. The title of the play is not recorded; it is unlikely to have been *Richard II*.[22]

Shakespeare's company played for the Queen for the last time on 2 February 1603; eight weeks later, on 24 March, she died. John Manningham, who was close to court circles, recorded the event in his notebook: 'This morning about three at clock Her Majesty departed this life, mildly like a lamb, easily like a ripe apple from the tree . . . I doubt not but she is amongst the royal saints in heaven in eternal joys.' Had Essex waited a while, he would have had his wish and saved his life: King James VI of Scotland was immediately proclaimed King James I of England. Manningham heard the proclamation read 'with silent joy, and no great shouting. I think the sorrow for Her Majesty's departure was so deep in many hearts they could not so suddenly show any great joy, though it could not be less than exceeding great for the succession of so worthy a king. And at night they showed it by bonfires and ringing.'[23] Within three months the new king had issued a warrant appointing 'these our servants Lawrence Fletcher, William Shakespeare, Richard Burbage, Augustine Phillips, John Heminges, Henry Condell, William Sly, Robert Armin, Richard Cowley, and the rest of their associates' to the royal

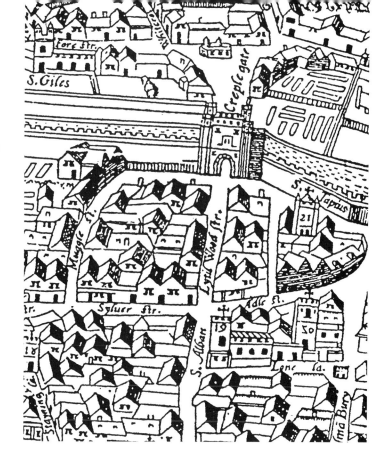

30. A detail from the map ascribed to Edward Agas (born *c.* 1540) in which the house where Shakespeare lodged with the Mountjoys can be identified at the corner of Silver and Muggle (Monkwell) Streets.

service. They were now the King's Men, acknowledged as the kingdom's pre-eminent dramatic company.

Shortly after James's accession Shakespeare was involved in a series of events which provide our only sustained glimpse into his domestic life in London, along with the most substantial and accurate report of words that he actually spoke. Regrettably, these words lack the eloquence displayed by even the least of his dramatic characters. Our information comes retrospectively, from a court case of 1612. On 7 May of that year Shakespeare was summoned to give evidence in a suit brought in the Court of Requests, London, by Stephen Belott against his father-in-law, Christopher Mountjoy. Shakespeare bore witness four days later, which suggests that he did not have to travel specially from Warwickshire; his deposition provides us with one of his few remaining signatures. Mountjoy, a Huguenot refugee who, with his wife and daughter Marie, made ladies' wigs and headdresses, lived and worked in a double house on the corner of Silver and Monkwell Streets, a respectable locality in the most northerly part of the City. The house, destroyed in the Great Fire of 1666, is identifiable on a detailed map showing the capital as it appeared in the 1550s, which seems to show the penthouse roof which would have protected goods on display in the ground-floor shop. Either Mountjoy was not the only man of his trade in this area, or he is indirectly referred to in Ben Jonson's play *Epicene*, acted in 1609, when a character says of his wife 'All her teeth were made in the Blackfriars, both her eyebrows in the Strand, and her hair in Silver Street.'[24]

Belott, Mountjoy's apprentice, had married Marie on 19 November 1604, and Shakespeare good-naturedly assisted in the marriage negotiations. According to some of the witnesses he 'persuaded' Stephen to marry Marie, and it sounds as if he may even have officiated at the ceremony of hand-fasting: a witness named Daniel Nicholas stated that the lovers 'were made sure by Master Shakespeare by giving their consent, and agreed to marry, and did marry'.[25] At first the couple continued to live with Marie's parents, but relations deteriorated, especially after her mother died in 1606, and there were quarrels over money matters. Eventually Belott went to law over a claim that Mountjoy had broken promises to pay a marriage portion of £60 and to leave Marie £200 in his will. All the witnesses were asked an identical set of questions somewhat loaded on Belott's behalf – for example, 'what parcels of goods or household stuff' Mountjoy had promised, and whether what he actually gave included 'one old feather bed, one old feather bolster, a flock bolster, a thin green rug . . . a dozen of napkins of coarse diaper, two short tablecloths, six short towels and one long one . . . two pairs of little scissors', and so on. Joan Johnson, a basket-maker's wife of Ealing who had worked as a servant to Mountjoy, testified that her employer had asked 'one Mr Shakespeare that lay in the house' to act as go-between in the marriage nego-tiations. In his deposition, 'William Shakespeare of Stratford-upon-Avon', described as 'of the age of forty-eight years or thereabouts', declared that he had known Belott and Mountjoy 'for the space of ten years or thereabouts', which suggests that he may have 'lain' in the house – whether continuously or sporadically – for at least two years before the marriage. He had known Belott when he was working for Mountjoy, regarding him as 'a very good and industrious servant'. Mountjoy had shown the young man 'great good will and affection' and had 'made a motion' to him of marriage with his daughter. Mrs Mountjoy 'did solicit and entreat' Shakespeare to 'move and persuade' Belott 'to effect the said marriage' and Shakespeare had complied.

On money matters Shakespeare is studiously non-committal. Though Mountjoy had promised to give Belott 'a portion', Shakespeare could not remember exactly how much nor when it was to be paid, nor did he know that Mountjoy had promised to leave the couple £200. He knew nothing about the 'implements and necessaries of household stuff' that Mountjoy had handed over. But he affirmed that Belott had been living in the house and that they had 'had amongst themselves many conferences' – conversations – 'about their marriage which afterwards was consummated and solemnized'. (Whether in that order is not clear.) In the end the case was referred to the elders of the French church in London. They found in favour of Belott but awarded him only 20 nobles – £6, thirteen shillings and four pence, roughly the value of the goods he had taken out of the house – which Mountjoy, who was leading a dissolute life, had not paid a year later.

From this case it is apparent that Shakespeare was a trusted friend of the Mountjoy family.[26] Where else in London did he lodge? We have far less evidence of his presence in the capital than in Stratford. In 1597 – the year he bought New Place – he is listed in records for the parish of St Helen's, Bishopsgate – reasonably convenient of access to the Theatre and the Curtain – among those who are 'dead, departed', or 'gone out of the said ward'. The occasion of this negative piece of evidence was a tax assessment. Government required payment of a tax on possessions of one shilling in the pound. In October of the previous year his goods had been assessed at the value of £5, and by November of the following year he had moved away. So he owed, and does not appear to have paid, five shillings. The highest assessment in the ward was £300. Methods of assessment may have been rough and ready, but the low valuation of his possessions in Bishopsgate does not suggest that he had put down any roots. While living there he would have been most likely to worship at St Helen's Church. This still stands, much restored, having survived two IRA attacks during the 1990s. Its exterior is unprepossessing, but inside it is light and airy with many fine monuments which give an impression of the sort of people that Shakespeare may have known and from whom he could have picked up useful information. One memorial, for instance, bearing a representation of a galleon, commemorates Alderman Richard Staper, who died in 1608, as 'the greatest merchant in his time, the chiefest actor in discovery of the trades of Turkey and East India, a man

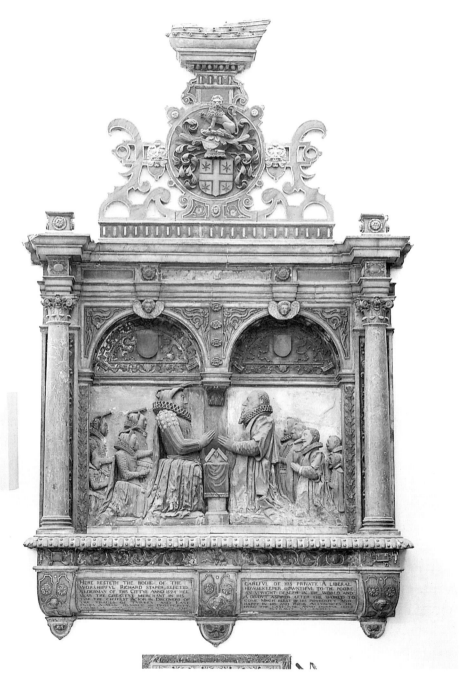

31. The monument to Richard Staper in St Helen's Church, Bishopsgate, showing him
with his wife and family, is surmounted by a representation of a galleon.

humble in prosperity'. He seems to have been a bit of a Puritan, judging by the fact that he left orders that at his burial 'I will have no drinking made before the going to the Church as is now used'. Shakespeare might surely have had fascinating conversations with Staper about his travels.

Another monument in the same church commemorates the life and achievements of Martin Bond, citizen and haberdasher. His father, William, had hired out to Francis Drake the ship, later known as *The Golden Hind*, in which Drake was to circumnavigate the globe, and Martin himself was a signatory to the second Charter of Virginia. His monument is surmounted by a fine bas-relief showing him in his tent guarded by sentries and with a groom holding his horse. The inscription tells us that Bond 'was captain in the year 1588 at the camp at Tilbury' – where of course Elizabeth delivered her famous speech declaring 'I have the body but of a weak and feeble woman; but I have the heart and stomach of a king.' In later life, says the inscription, he 'remained captain of the trained bands of this city until his death. He was a Merchant Adventurer and free of the company of haber-dashers. He lived to the age of 85 and died in May 1643.' This means that he was only six years older than Shakespeare, with whom he may well have swapped many an anecdote.

On 1 October 1598 Shakespeare was again listed among tax defaulters in Bishopsgate, this time for the sum of thirteen shillings and four pence, but still on goods valued at £5. This implies that in the meantime he had moved away from Bishopsgate, and then gone back again, though not necessarily to the same lodgings. Then in a document of a year or so later his debt is listed as the business of the Sheriff of Surrey and Sussex and was referred to the Bishop of Winchester. The only area in which the bishop had juris-diction was the liberty of the Clink in Southwark, close to the newly erected Globe. Shakespeare appears to have been on the move again, but it is, as Schoenbaum remarks, 'a curious fact that his name has not been traced in any of the annual lists of residents of the Clink parish (St Saviour's) compiled by the officers who made the rounds to collect tokens purchased by church-goers for Easter Communion, which was compulsory'.[27] Again Shakespeare is more remarkable for his absence than for his presence.

This is the sum of our knowledge of Shakespeare as a resident of London: a temporary incumbent of several different premises, where he seems to have kept few belongings, over a period of some eight years, during which he was making major purchases of property and land in his home town, where his family lived. Where he lodged after leaving the Mountjoy household we don't know, but he may well have returned to Southwark. On 31 December 1607, at the time of the Great Frost so vividly imagined by Virginia Woolf in her novel *Orlando* (1928), when the Thames froze so hard that ale was sold from tents erected on the ice, the great bell of what is now Southwark Cathedral tolled for the funeral of a man described in the burial register as 'Edmund Shakespeare, a player'. The Cathedral's fee book gives slightly more detail: 'Edmund Shakespeare, a player, buried in the church, with a forenoon knell of the great bell, 20 shillings.' This is almost certainly William's youngest brother, baptized in Stratford in 1580. A few months before the burial the register of St Giles without Cripplegate – not far from Silver Street, where

32. Frost fair on the Thames; a model from the Museum of London, based on contemporary evidence.

the Mountjoys lived – records the burial of an infant, 'Edward Shakespeare, son of Edward Shakespeare player, base born.' The father's name is presumably a slip for Edmund, or possibly an alternative form. Nothing more is known of Edmund. Presumably he had followed his brother to London to seek a living as an actor. He may not have had much success; his name is not recorded as a member of the King's Men or of any other company, but it seems likely that William paid his not inconsiderable funeral expenses. Edmund had no memorial in his time, but his burial is recorded on a stone in the floor of Southwark Cathedral, which also boasts a more elaborate memorial to his brother.

In 1613, when Shakespeare's career as a playwright was practically over, he bought his only substantial London property, a gatehouse in Blackfriars which had previously been a Catholic hideaway. According to a document of 1596 it had been 'in time past suspected and searched for papists but no good done for want of good knowledge of the back doors and bye-ways and of the dark corners'. It cost Shakespeare £140 – more than New Place – but he rented it to a John Robinson, and seems never to have lived in it himself; he probably regarded it as an investment. It appears to have been demolished in the late eighteenth century to make way for a new bridge.[28]

The Mountjoy household interconnects with Shakespeare's life at several points. A witness in the lawsuit was George Wilkins, described as a victualler, or innkeeper. When the Belotts first set themselves up independently, probably after a row with Mountjoy the year after they were married, they lodged with Wilkins, who deposed that he would not have given more than £5 for the goods they brought with them. A colourful character, he often appeared in court in his own right; his inn was a riotous establishment which doubled as a brothel.[29] Only three months before giving evidence in the Mountjoy case he had 'outrageously beaten one Judith Walton and stamped upon her so that she was carried home in a chair'. But Wilkins was also a playwright who had worked closely with Shakespeare. He wrote an accomplished and successful play, *The Miseries of Enforced Marriage*, acted by the King's Men by 1607, when it was published; he probably collaborated with Shakespeare on *Pericles*, performed at the Globe around the end of 1607; and he wrote the book of that play, a derivative novel called *The Painful Adventures of Pericles Prince of Tyre*, published in 1608.

Another link between Shakespeare and the Mountjoy household is the even more picturesque figure of Simon Forman (1552–1611), who left by far the fullest eyewitness accounts of performances of any of Shakespeare's plays. Forman was an astrologer, magician, and physician whose voluminous notebooks – still not adequately investigated – offer astonishingly intimate glimpses into his own life and that of many of his contemporaries.[30] Confidentially consulted by thousands of men and (especially) women of all walks of life, including theatre people, about their health, things they had lost, anxieties about what might happen to friends and relatives, and for insight into the future, he noted their medical symptoms and their horoscopes, recorded the advice that he gave them, chronicled innumerable sexual encounters, many of them with his patients, and even recounted his dreams – including one in which the Queen propositioned him. Mrs Mountjoy consulted him first in 1597, when she was thirty, in the hope that he could tell her how to recover jewels and money lost from her purse. Ten days later she returned, with symptoms that Forman diagnosed as signs of pregnancy; he predicted a miscarriage. There are hints too that she was conducting an illicit affair with a Mr Wood, who lived close by and whose wife asked whether she would be well advised to join her as a shopkeeper.

A reader of Forman's papers would inevitably form the impression that London in Shakespeare's time (as at any other) was a hotbed of illicit sexual activity such as Shakespeare himself portrays, transposed to a foreign setting, in the brothel scenes of *Measure for Measure* and *Pericles* and, more gently but closer to home, the Eastcheap scenes of Parts One and Two of *Henry IV*. This may well be true. In some people's minds prostitution and the theatre were closely linked. According to Philip Stubbes – admittedly a Puritan opponent of theatre – sexual pleasure was an invariable sequel to play-going: 'these goodly pageants being ended, every mate sorts to his mate, everyone brings another homeward of their way very friendly, and in their secret conclaves covertly they play the sodomites or worse.'[31] Philip Henslowe and Edward Alleyn ran brothels as well as playhouses, watermen ferried across the Thames clients of the prostitutes as well as the theatres of Southwark.

At a less professional level, one of Forman's patients, Emilia Lanier, was mistress of Lord Hunsdon, patron of Shakespeare's company, and mother of Hunsdon's illegitimate son. She was also, in a paradox characteristic of the period, a religious poet of some talent, author of *Salve Deus Rex Judaeorum*, of 1611 (the poems are written in English). The historian A. L. Rowse proclaimed his belief that she was Shakespeare's as well as Hunsdon's mistress, the dark lady of the Sonnets.[32] That hypothesis has not been substantiated, but there are reasons to suppose that Shakespeare had extra-marital affairs. Indeed, he seems to have taken pride in this if we believe Sonnet 31, where he speaks of 'the trophies of my lovers gone'. In March 1601, John Manningham, whose cousin had such a good memory for Latin verse, picked up a story circulating in London society which suggests that Shakespeare had a reputation as both a lecher and a wit.

> Upon a time when [Richard] Burbage played Richard III there was a citizen grew so far in liking with him that before she went from the play she appointed him to come that night unto her by the name of Richard III. Shakespeare, overhearing their conclusion, went before, was entertained, and at his game ere Burbage came. Then message being brought that Richard III was at the door, Shakespeare caused return to be made that William the Conqueror was before Richard III.

Manningham adds, as if to help him to tell the tale effectively, 'Shakespeare's name William'. The anecdote must have been well known, because Manningham's is not the only version to have survived; it is told also, in more elaborate but less authentic detail, in a book published in 1759, Thomas Wilkes's *General View of the Stage*. Wilkes must have got it from a different source, since Manningham's notebooks were not known in his time.[33] It sounds, perhaps, too neat to be true, but the fact that it could be told at all indicates that it had at least a surface plausibility. And it's interesting that a year or two later Shakespeare was to write two plays – *All's Well That Ends Well* and *Measure for Measure* – in both of which one man substitutes for another in a woman's bed. (Admittedly this was a common narrative device.)

Apart from this, information about Shakespeare's sex life after the early years of his marriage is hard to come by, and mainly deductive. Eric Partridge, whose book *Shakespeare's Bawdy* was the first systematic study of Shakespeare's sexual language, deduced that Shakespeare was 'an exceedingly knowledgeable amorist, a versatile connoisseur, and a highly artistic, an ingeniously skilful, practitioner of love-making, who could have taught Ovid rather more than that facile doctrinaire could have taught him; he evidently knew of, and probably he practised, an artifice accessible to few – one that I cannot becomingly mention here, though I felt it obligatory to touch on it, very briefly, in the Glossary'.[34] There is something unpleasant about that remark; it is as if Partridge were implying, and covertly boasting, that he too was a sophisticated man of the world; and the reference to an esoteric artifice – whatever it may be – is coy.[35]

Far more direct information about Shakespeare's intimate life can be derived from his Sonnets – provided, that is, that we take them to be autobiographical. 154 in number, they first appeared in print in 1609, but may have been composed over a long period of time; Meres writes in 1598 of Shakespeare's 'sugared sonnets to his private friends', and we have seen (p. 19) that Shakespeare probably wrote one of them while he was still a teenager. They were published with a dedication, signed not by Shakespeare but with the initials of the publisher, Thomas Thorpe, to 'Mr W. H.', described as their 'onlie begetter', whatever that may mean. The identity of Mr W. H. has given rise to endless speculation. Possibly it is a deliberately cryptic reference to Henry Wriothesley, Earl of Southampton, who has in any case been the favourite candidate for the 'beauteous and lovely youth' (54) to whom many of the poems appear to be addressed.

The Sonnets are a miscellaneous bunch of poems, varying greatly in poetic style and quality. They gain a spurious air of coherence by the manner in which they were assembled before publication along with the fact that all but three[36] are composed in the fourteen-line stanza, with a concluding couplet, that has come to be known as the Shakespearian sonnet form. While some of them seem intensely personal in utterance, others are more formal and public in tone. Most of them are poems of friendship or of love, but one of the finest – 146, beginning 'Poor soul, the centre of my sinful earth' – is a spiritual meditation with a closing couplet that would seem at home among John Donne's Holy Sonnets; addressing his soul, the poet writes:

> So shalt thou feed on death, that feeds on men,
> And death once dead, there's no more dying then.

TO. THE .ONLIE. BEGETTER. OF.
THESE . INSVING . SONNETS.
M^r. W. H.   ALL .HAPPINESSE.
AND .THAT. ETERNITIE.
PROMISED.

BY.

OVR. EVER-LIVING. POET.

WISHETH.

THE . WELL-WISHING.
ADVENTVRER . IN.
SETTING.
FORTH.

T. T.

33. The dedication, signed with the initials of the publisher, Thomas Thorpe,
to *Shakespeare's Sonnets* as originally printed in 1609. Few if any published sentences
have given rise to so much speculation and controversy.

No clear narrative emerges from the collection, but we learn, usually obliquely, that the poet has a younger friend whom he loves dearly but who arouses his jealousy by being friendly with another poet, and that the youth is seduced by the author's mistress, unflatteringly described in 137 as 'the bay where all men ride'.

By my reckoning thirty of the poems, all among the first 126, are indisputably addressed to, or primarily concern, a man; thirteen are clearly about a woman – the 'dark lady' – and these are all in the later part of the collection, from 127 onwards. One, 144 – 'Two loves I have, of comfort and despair' – shows the poet torn between a man and a woman. All the remainder (excluding 146) could have either a male or a female as their topic, though up to 126 context is likely to suggest a male. Some of the poems which, judging by their place within the collection, are written to a man are regularly anthologized as gender-free love poems: 'Shall I compare thee to a summer's day?', addressed by many a swain to his beloved, may seem more likely from its place in the sequence to be addressed to the fair (which may mean simply 'attractive' or 'beautiful') friend; so even may 'Let me not to the marriage of true minds' (116), frequently read at heterosexual marriages. It is unclear whether there is more than one friend, and the only name that emerges is Shakespeare's own, Will. We learn that because the poet indulges in elaborate wordplay on it:

> Whoever hath her wish, thou hast thy Will,
> And Will to boot, and Will in overplus.
> More than enough am I that vex thee still,
> To thy sweet will making addition thus.
> Wilt thou, whose will is large and spacious,
> Not once vouchsafe to hide my will in thine?
> Shall will in others seem right gracious,
> And in my will no fair acceptance shine?
> The sea, all water, yet receives rain still,
> And in abundance addeth to his store;
> So thou, being rich in Will, add to thy Will
> One will of mine to make thy large Will more.

Let no unkind no fair beseechers kill;
Think all but one, and me in that one Will. (135)

That is a complicated poem, its wordplay bitter rather than comic, simultaneously erotic and intellectual. In it, the word 'Will' accumulates successively
and simultaneously a range of significances including the personal name –
which may be both that of the poet and of a rival for the woman's favours
– 'will' as desire, and 'will' as both vagina and penis – or 'willy'.

Most of the first seventeen poems urge a young man to marry and beget
offspring; they are often conjectured to have been written on commission
from a parent. These are among the more formal poems, but even so, some
are warm in tone: the young man (assuming there is only one) is addressed
as 'love' and 'dear my love' (13), and the poet is 'all in war with time for
love' of him (15). Many of the final group, from 127 onwards, known collectively though perhaps unhelpfully as the dark lady sonnets, read like
intensely private utterances. Though some of them are ostensibly addressed
to a woman, dark in colouring and in soul, it is hard to believe that the
poet would have wished her to read them. Hard too to believe that he
would have wished his wife and daughters to do so, if they are really personal
poems rather than quasi-dramatic fictions, speeches from an unwritten play,
as it were.

The question of whether the Sonnets are autobiographical revelations
of Shakespeare's inner self, or whether they are primarily literary exercises
(even though they must still derive ultimately from personal emotional
experience) has vexed readers for at least two centuries. 'With these poems
Shakespeare unlocked his heart', wrote Wordsworth. 'If so, the less Shakespeare he', responded Browning.[37] Shakespeare was a dramatist who could
speak for people far different from himself, as we see from the vast range of
characters in his plays. If he could write to order the anguished speeches
of, say, Angelo, in *Measure for Measure*, or of Hamlet or Othello in their
most passionate moments, he could also have written poems on the basis of
imagined rather than actual experience.

As a scholar, I have to admit this. But if I were required to jump over
the fence rather than sit on it, I should have to come out with the view that
many of the Sonnets, including – indeed, especially – those that seem most

revelatory of sexual infatuation and self-disgust, are private poems, personal and almost confessional in nature, like the erotic drawings of Henry Fuseli, J. M. W. Turner, or Duncan Grant. I think this partly because, considered as a fictional sequence designed to chart the stages of a series of relationships, the Sonnets are a failure. No clear narrative emerges.

If we accept the Sonnets as revelations of Shakespeare's private life, we must take those concerned with the dark woman as reflections of an adulterous affair which gave the poet as much shame as pleasure. Despising himself for indulging his lust, he takes consolation only in the thought that he is not alone in folly:

> Th'expense of spirit in a waste of shame
> Is lust in action; and till action, lust
> Is perjured, murd'rous, bloody, full of blame,
> Savage, extreme, rude, cruel, not to trust,
> Enjoyed no sooner but despisèd straight,
> Past reason hunted, and no sooner had
> Past reason hated as a swallowed bait
> On purpose laid to make the taker mad;
> Mad in pursuit and in possession so,
> Had, having, and in quest to have, extreme;
> A bliss in proof and proved, a very woe;
> Before, a joy proposed; behind, a dream.
>   All this the world well knows, yet none knows well
>   To shun the heaven that leads men to this hell. (129)

The relationship with the young man, though it has its ups and downs, is far happier. Whether it is sexual is a matter of endless debate. Eric Partridge, who deduced that Shakespeare was a 'knowledgeable amorist', deduced too that he was exclusively heterosexual. This view has been strongly challenged in recent years. In his plays Shakespeare presents many intense friendships between men (and a smaller number between women). Commentators on both plays and Sonnets have invoked Renaissance notions of male friendship as a way of explaining that during the period men commonly used the language of love in addressing one another without this implying that they were lovers. The most explicitly sexual male-to-male relationship in the plays is that between Achilles and Patroclus in *Troilus and Cressida*, which derives from classical sources. Thersites reductively calls Patroclus Achilles's 'masculine whore' (5.1.17); Patroclus himself more sympathetically speaks of Achilles's 'great love' to him (3.3.214). Among other friendships that have often, in post-Freudian times, been interpreted as sexual are those between Antonio and Bassanio in *The Merchant of Venice* and Antonio and Sebastian in *Twelfth Night*; the second Antonio not only says 'come what may, I do adore thee so / That danger shall seem sport, and I will go' (2.1.42–3), he also speaks of his 'desire, / More sharp than filèd steel' (3.3.3–4). That is strong language. The first time the Sonnets were reprinted, in 1640, pronouns in a few of them were altered from male to female as if in deference to the requirements of decorum (p. 177).

Those who believe that Shakespeare himself was sexually attracted to men, and may have had one or more male lovers, derive their evidence principally from the Sonnets. They have to contend with what appears to be an explicit denial of a sexual element in the relationship between the poet and his friend in Sonnet 20:

> . . . for a woman wert thou first created,
> Till nature as she wrought thee fell a-doting,
> And by addition me of thee defeated
> By adding one thing to my purpose nothing.
> > But since she pricked thee out for woman's pleasure,
> > Mine be thy love and thy love's use their treasure.

The ostensible meaning of these lines is that the poet has no use for the other man's sexual parts – his 'thing' (a common euphemism for the penis, played on for example by Viola disguised as a boy in *Twelfth Night* – 'A little thing would make me tell them how much I lack of a man', 3.4.293–4), even though he finds the rest of him as attractive as he would find a woman. But, it can be argued, this Sonnet is placed early in the sequence – relationships alter with the passage of time – and whatever the poet says about the young man's prick, the earlier part of the poem shows that he thinks of its owner as of a woman whom he might desire:

> A woman's face with nature's own hand painted
> Hast thou, the master-mistress of my passion;
> A woman's gentle heart, but not acquainted
> With shifting change as is false women's fashion . . .

One of the complicating factors in the autobiographical interpretation of the Sonnets is the fact that those concerned with a young man present a highly idealized picture of the relationship which contrasts violently with the disillusioned view of the woman. The most popular, lyrically beautiful sonnets all occur in the first part of the collection. Is the contrast, we may ask, part of the artistic design? Is Shakespeare deliberately overturning the conventions of love poetry, playing with them rather than portraying things as they are? Or is the idealism, perhaps, indicative of a subconscious sexual response which the poet himself does not recognize? Many of the poems indicate a highly charged emotional relationship in which a psychologist might identify a homoerotic element that might or might not be acknowledged by either or both of the men. The most explicitly sexual poems are those concerned with the woman, especially the defiantly lewd Sonnet 151:

> My soul doth tell my body that he may
> Triumph in love; flesh stays no farther reason,
> But rising at thy name doth point out thee
> As his triumphant prize. Proud of this pride,
> He is contented thy poor drudge to be,
> To stand in thy affairs, fall by thy side.
>   No want of conscience hold it that I call
>   Her 'love' for whose dear love I rise and fall.

But sonnets addressed to the 'sweet boy' (108), if not blatantly sexual, use the language of love: 'Lord of my love' (26), 'my friend and I are one' (42), 'thou mine, I thine', 'eternal love' (108), 'my lovely boy' (126). And many of those in the earlier part of the sequence that are indeterminately addressed are drenched in the language of longing and desire, of sadness in absence and joy at thoughts of the friend's 'sweet love' (29), speaking of sleepless nights during which the poet's thoughts make 'a zealous pilgrimage' to the beloved

(27, 61), of mutual possession and shared identity (31, 36, 39), of the poet as 'slave' to his friend's 'desire' (57), of fears of loss (64), of dependency (75, 'So are you to my thoughts as food to life'). It would be a naïve young man who, addressed in these terms, did not regard himself as the object of desire. If Shakespeare himself did not, in the fullest sense of the word, love a man, he certainly understood the feelings of those who do.

★

As we have seen, Richard Burbage may have been Shakespeare's sexual rival; he was certainly his professional collaborator. During the early years of King James's reign their company continued at the Globe, but a change came in 1608 when Burbage formed a syndicate of seven men, including Shakespeare, to take over an additional playing space in an old Dominican monastery in the Blackfriars area of London which had previously served for performances by boys' companies. Blackfriars was an exclusive area whose residents had successfully objected to James Burbage's proposal to take over the auditorium when his lease on the Theatre ran out in 1597. The Blackfriars theatre was very different from the Globe – a rectangular, roofed space, particularly useful for winter performances, with a much smaller capacity. The stage occupied one end of the room and the audience sat – not stood – in rows before it, in galleries round the sides, and even in seats on the stage itself. Admission prices were higher – a basic sixpence instead of one penny.

The change in playing conditions affected the dramaturgy of plays written for the newly available space. As it was enclosed, artificial lighting was needed, and because candles have to be renewed, intervals in performances were introduced; Shakespeare's late plays are more clearly divided into five acts than his earlier. Musicians played between the acts as well as before performances. Softer music was preferred – woodwind rather than brass – and spectacular effects, such as flights from above and magic devices like the disappearing table in *The Tempest*, were more easily presented.

Use of the Blackfriars in addition to the Globe coincides with the last major shift in Shakespeare's dramatic style. This is the period of the romances – *The Winter's Tale* and *Cymbeline*, *The Tempest* and the collaborative *All is True* (*Henry VIII*), *The Two Noble Kinsmen* and the lost *Cardenio*. These plays make more use of spectacle, music, and dance than most of their predecessors, but

34. The interior of the Shenandoah Shakespeare's reconstruction of the Blackfriars
playhouse in Staunton, Virginia, 2001.

before attributing the change to the acquisition of the Blackfriars we should
remember that *Pericles*, performed before this happened, shares many of the
same characteristics. The Blackfriars was primarily a winter house; the company continued to perform at the Globe, for the court, and on tour. It would
have been impractical of their dramatists to write plays that could not adapt
to a variety of playing conditions.

Simon Forman's most valuable contribution to knowledge of Shakespeare
comes with accounts of visits to the Globe in his notebook *The Book of Plays
and Notes thereof per Formans for Common Policy* – the meaning of 'per Formans'
is obscure, but he seems to mean 'for conducting myself in the ordinary affairs
of life'. In other words, his play-going is directed to practical ends. His notes
on performances of *Macbeth, Cymbeline*, and *The Winter's Tale*, inadequate

though in some respects they are, are by far the fullest contemporary accounts of performance of plays by Shakespeare.[38] Mostly he summarizes the plots, but in *Macbeth*, which he saw on 20 April 1611, he was deeply impressed by the emotional impact of the episode following Duncan's murder and of the banquet scene, in which Macbeth 'fell into a great passion of fear and fury' on seeing Banquo's ghost. As a medical man, he took a particular interest in the sleepwalking: 'Observe also how Macbeth's queen did rise in the night in her sleep, and walked and talked and confessed all. And the doctor noted her words.' From the antics of Autolycus in *The Winter's Tale*, which he saw on 15 May, he drew the moral 'Beware of trusting feigned beggars or fawning fellows'. Perhaps it says something about the attitude of audiences to performers that he always uses the names of characters, not of the actors playing them.

Forman was to meet his end later that year in circumstances as bizarre as any in his extraordinary life. One Sunday, his wife teasingly asked him whether he or she would die first. He replied that he would die before the following Thursday night. Day followed day and 'he was well'. On the Thursday evening 'He went down to the waterside and took a pair of oars to go to some buildings he was in hand with in Puddle Dock. Being in the middle of the Thames he presently fell down, only saying "An impost, an impost!" ['an abscess, an abscess!'] and so died.' A storm broke out.[39]

On the afternoon of Tuesday, 29 June 1613, the King's Men suffered a terrible blow. They were giving one of the earliest performances of Shakespeare and Fletcher's play about Henry VIII to a full house when a burning scrap of rag or paper from a cannon that had been fired as a sound effect wafted up into the thatch and ignited it. Within less than an hour the theatre had burnt to the ground. Miraculously, the diplomat Sir Henry Wotton wrote in a letter to his nephew Sir Edmund Bacon, 'nothing did perish but wood and straw and a few forsaken cloaks; only one man had his breeches set on fire, that would perhaps have broiled him if he had not by the benefit of a provident wit put it out with bottle ale.' Another account tells us that the only casualty was a man 'who was scalded by the fire by adventuring in to save a child which otherwise had been burnt'. The occasion was newsworthy; reports of the fire mean that this is the most circumstantially recorded early performance of any of Shakespeare's plays. They also show clearly that the play, re-named *Henry VIII* when it was printed in 1623, was performed under the title of *All is True*. These words form the refrain of a ballad which an enterprising versifier wrote and circulated within twenty-four hours of the conflagration. Three of its stanzas run:

> Out run the knights, out run the lords,
> And there was great ado;
> Some lost their hats, and some their swords,
> Then out run Burbage too;
> The reprobates, though drunk on Monday,
> Prayed for the fool and Henry Condye [Condell];
> *O sorrow, pitiful sorrow,*
> *And yet all this is true.*

> The periwigs and drumheads fry
> Like to a burning firkin;
> A woeful burning did betide
> To many a good buff jerkin.
> Then with swoll'n eyes, like drunken Fleming's,
> Distressèd stood old stuttering Heminges.
> *O sorrow, pitiful sorrow,*
> *And yet all this is true.*

> No shower his rain did there down force
> In all that sunshine weather
> To save that great renownèd house,
> Nor thou, O alehouse, neither.
> Had it begun below, sans doubt,
> Their wives for fear had pissed it out.
> *O sorrow, pitiful sorrow,*
> *And yet all this is true.*

Wise after the event, the ballad-maker advised the actors to use any money they might otherwise have spent on whores in saving up to buy tiles, not thatch, in rebuilding the theatre. The second Globe, built on the foundations of the first and in use within a year, was indeed tiled, whether or not as a result of continency on the part of the actors.

With sad appropriateness, the burning of the Globe virtually coincides with the end of Shakespeare's career as a writer. Three months before the fire he had collaborated with his old friend Richard Burbage, an accomplished painter as well as actor, in one of the least of his compositions, now lost. Jointly they had devised an impresa – a painted paper or paste-board shield with emblems or mottoes – for Southampton's play-going friend the Earl of Rutland to wield as he rode in the tournament on King James's Accession Day, 24 March. A week later the Earl's steward recorded a payment of forty-four shillings in gold 'to Mr Shakespeare . . . about my lord's impresa' along with the same sum to Burbage 'for painting and making it'.

Shakespeare's last certain visit to London was in November 1614, after he had stopped writing for the theatre, when Thomas Greene spoke to him and his son-in-law, John Hall, about the Welcombe enclosures (pp. 40–1). He may have been there again the following year for litigation involving his gatehouse. It's sometimes regarded as odd that his death in 1616 was marked by no printed tributes from his London friends. But poems often circulated extensively in manuscript, and a memorial sonnet written soon after he died survives in at least twenty-seven handwritten copies transcribed into commonplace books under a variety of titles.[40] Composed by William Basse, a minor poet, it first appeared in print, for no obvious reason, in a collection of poems by John Donne of 1633. Basse proposes a high honour: burial in Westminster Abbey. To make this possible some of the present incumbents will have to shove up a bit:

> Renownèd Spenser, lie a thought more nigh
> To learnèd Chaucer; and rare Beaumont, lie
> A little nearer Spenser, to make room
> For Shakespeare in your threefold, fourfold tomb.

When all four are in the same bed, the poet says, they may lie undisturbed until Doomsday since 'hardly will a fifth / Betwixt this day and that by Fate be slain.' (In fact the fourth was to be Shakespeare's friend and rival Ben Jonson.) Chaucer and Spenser are the poets with whom Shakespeare had been

Mr. WILLIAM
SHAKESPEARES
COMEDIES,
HISTORIES, &
TRAGEDIES.

Publiſhed according to the True Originall Copies.

L O N D O N
Printed by Iſaac Iaggard, and Ed. Blount. 1623.

35. The title page of the First Folio edition of Shakespeare's plays with the engraving of the author by Martin Droeshout.

grouped in the *Parnassus* play; the dramatist Beaumont may seem a surprising bedfellow, but his memory was green as Basse wrote: Beaumont died on 6 March 1616, only a few weeks before Shakespeare, and was buried in the Abbey three days later. Basse goes on to suggest that if room can't be made in the Abbey, then the 'rare tragedian Shakespeare' may sleep alone 'Under this carvèd marble of thine own'. It is as if Basse were submitting his lines for possible publication on a Stratford tombstone.

Shakespeare's family's tribute is the monumental bust placed on the wall of Holy Trinity Church, Stratford. It provides one of the only two likenesses of the man with a strong claim to authenticity. His colleagues' tribute is the First Folio edition of his plays, published in 1623. The title-page illustration, a copper engraving by Martin Droeshout, is the other plausible likeness. It was probably done from a miniature or drawing, and is approved by Ben Jonson in the lines printed on the facing page. As part of its preliminary matter the Folio prints commendatory poems, some of which may well have been written soon after Shakespeare died. Some of these poems afford links with Stratford. One was written by Leonard Digges, stepson of Thomas Russell, overseer of Shakespeare's will. Digges's clumsy lines refer to Shakespeare's 'Stratford monument' as if it were already in place. Ben Jonson too, in his far more substantial and accomplished eulogy 'To the Memory of My Beloved the Author, Mr William Shakespeare, and What He Hath Left Us', apostrophizes Shakespeare as 'Sweet swan of Avon!' Jonson had read Basse's poem, and takes issue with it:

> My Shakespeare, rise! *I* will not lodge thee by
> Chaucer, or Spenser, or bid Beaumont lie
> A little further to make thee a room.
> Thou art a monument without a tomb.

We don't know when the Folio was first planned, but my guess is that Shakespeare discussed it with his colleagues during his last years. The men who took prime responsibility for the book were John Heminges and Henry Condell. They did so, they declare, 'without ambition either of self-profit or fame, only to keep the memory of so worthy a friend and fellow alive as was our Shakespeare'. It was a brave gesture. They were actors with no experience of editorial work, and they carried out their complex task, or at least oversaw its execution by others, with great diligence. Their names appear at the end of the Dedication to the Earls of Pembroke and Montgomery, in which they write of the brother Earls as Shakespeare's admirers and patrons. And Heminges and Condell also sign the preface addressed 'To the great variety of Readers'. In both documents they deplore the fact that Shakespeare has not 'lived to have set forth and overseen his own writings'. It seems significant that the Folio was put together by the only colleagues named in Shakespeare's will except for Richard Burbage, who had died in 1619. Is it

not possible, even likely, that they had earned their bequests by a promise to oversee the compilation of a volume which would preserve in print eighteen plays that had not previously been published, and to provide improved texts of those that had already appeared in print?

Heminges and Condell have their own memorial. The church where they worshipped, Saint Mary's, Aldermanbury, was destroyed by the Great Fire of London in 1666. Restored by Christopher Wren, it suffered again in the Second World War. The remains were removed to Westminster College in Fulton, Missouri and reconstructed as a memorial to Winston Churchill. Now the site is empty, but a pleasant garden nearby has as its centrepiece a privately donated statue erected in 1896. On each side of the plinth plaques commemorate the achievement of Heminges and Condell in assembling the Folio. Higher up is a model of the Folio itself, and the whole is surmounted by a bust of Shakespeare. The plays are Shakespeare's greatest legacy to the world, and the First Folio is by far his most important memorial because without it many of the plays, including some of the finest, might well have suffered the same fate as the lost *Cardenio*. In Sonnet 65 Shakespeare had lamented that neither 'brass, nor stone, nor earth, nor boundless sea, / But sad mortality o'ersways their power.' Leonard Digges, in his commendatory lines, picked up on this when he wrote that the Folio, 'When brass and marble fade, shall make thee look / Fresh to all ages.' The marble of Shakespeare's monument endures virtually unchanged in Stratford; the plays of the Folio are a more fluid memorial, metamorphosing constantly like living organisms as they interact with successive generations of readers, spectators, and interpreters.

36. *Opposite*. Probably the only monument ever dedicated to a book: the memorial in Love Lane, in the City of London, commemorating Heminges and Condell and their achievement in preparing the First Folio.

CHAPTER THREE

Shakespeare the Writer

Give me that man

Who . . .

Can call the banished auditor home and tie

His ear with golden chains to his melody;

Can draw with adamantine pen even creatures

Forged out of th'hammer on tiptoe to reach up

And from rare silence clap their brawny hands

T'applaud what their charmed soul scarce understands.

Thomas Dekker (*c.*1572–1632), Prologue to
If this be not a Good Play, the Devil is in it (1611)

. . . let but Falstaff come,

Hal, Poins, the rest, you scarce shall have a room,

All is so pestered. Let but Beatrice

And Benedick be seen, lo, in a trice

The Cockpit galleries, boxes, all are full

To hear Malvolio, that cross-gartered gull.

Brief, there is nothing in his wit-fraught book

Whose sound we would not hear, on whose worth look;

Like old-coined gold, whose lines in every page

Shall pass true current to succeeding age.

Leonard Digges, in Shakespeare's *Poems* (1640)

37. Joseph Severn's painting of John Keats reading in his house in Hampstead. His engraving of Shakespeare (p. 266) presides over him.

JOHN KEATS, who adored Shakespeare, wrote in a letter of March 1819 that it would be a great delight 'to know in what position Shakespeare sat when he began writing "To be or not to be"'.[1] This is not possible, but we can deduce quite a lot about how Shakespeare went about his business of writing plays, and the attempt to do so may help us to understand why they are as they are.

We may start with the physical act of writing. Shakespeare must usually have written with a quill pen formed from a feather taken from a goose's wing, which required frequent remaking and a separate supply of ink. The portability of the fountain or ballpoint pen was not available to him; he may occasionally have used a pencil made of graphite, discovered in England in the year of his birth. This means that he would have been more bound to a table or desk than modern writers, who have greater freedom of movement.

The texte hand.

All men are by nature equal, made all by one workman of like myre, ι howsoeuer we deceaue our selues, as dere vnto God is the porest begger, as the moste pompous Prince liuing in the worlde. Plato

Aa Bb Cc Dd E Ff Sg Hh Ii.
Kk Ll M m Nn O Po p Qq Rr Ss.
Tt Uu w Xx Yy Zz ꝛ.

B

38. A woodcut engraving showing the formation of letters in the secretary hand, the one most practised by Shakespeare, from *A Booke Containing Divers Sortes of Hands* (1571), by a French writing master, Jean de Beauchesne, assisted for the English edition by John Baildon.

39. An early owner of the 1602 edition of Jean de Beauchesne and John Baildon's book containing this illustration of good and bad ways of holding a quill pen has practised writing on the book itself. It may remind us of Sam Goldwyn's comment on Shakespeare's works: 'Fantastic! And it was all written with a feather!'

HOVV YOV OVGHT TO
hold your Penne.

Good

Naught

Good

Naught

He would have written on one side only of sheets of paper, which was expensive; this may have been a deterrent to extensive revision while composing. According to Heminges and Condell in their epistle to readers of the First Folio, 'His mind and hand went together, and what he thought he uttered with that easiness that we have scarce received from him a blot in his papers.' Perhaps they had said the same to Ben Jonson who wrote 'I remember the players have often mentioned it as an honour to Shakespeare that in his writing, whatsoever he penned, he never blotted out line. My answer hath been "Would he had blotted a thousand".' And defending himself against the accusation that this was 'a malevolent speech', Jonson went on to pay tribute to Shakespeare in words that seem all the more genuine for not being effusive. 'I loved the man, and do honour his memory – on this side idolatry – as much as any.' Jonson went on to say, 'He was indeed honest, and of an open and free nature; had an excellent fantasy, brave notions, and gentle expressions' –

40. Ben Jonson: an engraving, *c.*1622–6, by Robert Vaughan; the Latin inscription, meaning 'a true likeness of the most learned of poets, Ben Jonson', emphasizes his pride in his scholarship.

which is to say, an excellent imagination, fine ideas, and noble powers of expression – 'wherein he flowed with that facility' – that is, poured it all out with such ease – 'that sometime it was necessary he should be stopped.' The gist of Jonson's criticism is that Shakespeare lacked discipline: 'His wit was in his own power; would the rule of it had been so too.' Still, 'he redeemed his vices with his virtues. There was ever more in him to be praised than to be pardoned.'[2]

In these passages from notebooks eventually published under the title of *Timber* Jonson vacillates between praise and censure, giving with one hand what he takes away with the other. In his tribute printed in the Folio, however, he is readier to admit that, in practising his art, Shakespeare did in fact 'blot' lines: the man 'Who casts to write a living line must sweat / (Such as thine are) and strike the second heat / Upon the muses' anvil.' And as we shall see, there is evidence from the texts themselves that this was so, at least in some plays.

Whereas with, for example, Keats we can study manuscripts to see how the finished work of art took shape in successive drafts, no incontestably genuine manuscript of any of Shakespeare's works is known to survive. The only certain specimens of his handwriting are half a dozen signatures. There is, however, a dramatic manuscript to which he almost certainly contributed. This is the play of *Sir Thomas More*, a heavily revised document preserved in the British Library with no indication of who wrote it. Evidence from handwriting and style suggests that it was first written, probably in the early 1590s, by two dramatists, Anthony Munday and Henry Chettle, working in collaboration, and that Munday then wrote it out as a fair copy. The Master of the Revels, who was responsible for licensing and censoring plays, wrote marginal notes criticizing it on political grounds and requiring revisions which were made by Chettle and by several other writers. Even so the play was never put into final shape, and was neither acted nor printed in its own time. It has occasionally been performed, notably in Nottingham in 1964, when Ian McKellen played More, but although individual episodes are effective it does not form a coherent whole.

Since late in the nineteenth century many scholars have believed that one of the revisers was Shakespeare. The principal passage in what is known as Hand D impressively portrays events leading up to the riots of Londoners against foreign immigrants on 'Ill May Day', 1517. More, sent by the authorities as a peacemaker, subdues the rioters in powerful and humane speeches of controlled rhetoric: to the demand that foreigners – 'strangers' – be expelled he responds:

> Grant them removed, and grant that this your noise
> Hath chid down all the majesty of England.
> Imagine that you see the wretched strangers,
> Their babies at their backs, with their poor luggage
> Plodding to th' ports and coasts for transportation,
> And that you sit as kings in your desires,
> Authority quite silenced by your brawl
> And you in ruff of your opinions clothed:
> What had you got? I'll tell you. You had taught
> How insolence and strong hand should prevail,
> How order should be quelled – and by this pattern
> Not one of you should live an agèd man,
> For other ruffians as their fancies wrought
> With selfsame hand, self reasons, and self right
> Would shark on you, and men like ravenous fishes
> Would feed on one another.

This scene's plea for tolerance in the face of racial bigotry and jingoistic exclusiveness can speak powerfully to modern listeners. In style, it is comparable to passages in Shakespeare's English history plays and to the opening scene of *Coriolanus*. It uses images characteristic of Shakespeare: for instance, the idea of men feeding on each other like fishes is to crop up again in the first published edition of *King Lear*, when the Duke of Albany prophesies that 'Humanity must perforce prey on itself, / Like monsters of the deep.' (*The History of King Lear*, 17.48–9) The handwriting is at least compatible with that of Shakespeare's known signatures. It's not unreasonable, then, to look at the scene for evidence of his methods of composition.

The writer uses what is known as the secretary hand characteristic of the period but difficult for modern readers to decipher without special training – and even then there are problems. As the illustration shows, the layout of the manuscript differs from that used for a printed text. Initial words in lines of verse are not capitalized, as they normally are in all early printed texts of Shakespeare's plays except (for no very obvious reason) the first (1600) edition of *The Merchant of Venice*. Each speech is followed by a rule, and names of the speakers are written in the left margin. The only stage directions are for characters to enter (no one leaves the stage in this passage). Punctuation is almost non-existent, as if Shakespeare's ideas were indeed flowing with such facility that he had no time to bother about such details. Similarly, names of speakers and words within the text are often abbreviated. Spelling, as was customary in the period, is fluid, closer to the phonetic than modern practice but not consistently so. Our word 'sheriff' appears as 'Shreiff', 'shreef', 'shreeve', 'Shreiue' and 'Shreue' – all monosyllables – within five lines. However fast the author may have been composing, he incorporated second thoughts as he wrote. 'Blotting' of three consecutive lines, with interlined substitutions, can be seen in the page reproduced; lesser changes are apparent throughout. The passage quoted above appears, in so far as modern typography can represent it, as follows:

> graunt them remoued and graunt that this yor ~y~ noyce
> hath Chidd downe all the matie of Ingland
> ymagin that yo^u see the wretched straingers
>   w^t
> their babyes at their backe, ~and~ their poor lugage
> plodding tooth porte and coste for transportacion
> and that yo^u sytt as kinge in your desyres
> aucthoryty quyte sylenct by yor braule
> and yo^u in ruff of yor ~yo~ opynions clothd
> what had yo^u gott · , · Ile tell yo^u, yo^u had taught
> how insolenc and strong hand shoold prevayle
> how orderd shoold be quelld, and by this patterne
> not on of yo^u shoold lyve an aged man
> for other ruffians as their fancies wrought
> wth sealf same hand sealf reasons and sealf right
> woold shark on yo^u and men lyke ravenous fishes
> woold feed on on another.

41. A page from the manuscript of *Sir Thomas More*: probably the only manuscript of Shakespeare's to survive other than his signatures.

At the end of the first of these lines it looks as if Shakespeare – we will assume it is he – started to write a word beginning with 'y' but changed his mind. In the fourth line he cancelled 'and', substituting 'with'. In the eighth line he seems to have been about to repeat 'your' and then deleted the 'yo'. The passage is full of spellings that are irregular by our standards but would have been acceptable in their time – 'babyes', 'coste' (for coast), 'sytt', 'shoold', 'woold', and so on; but in the eleventh line 'orderd' appears to be a slip of the pen for 'order', or 'ordere'. At one or two points in the original, the writer (who seems not to have been fully familiar with the rest of the play) left the speaker's name open.

All other information about Shakespeare's working methods comes from printed texts. These are deficient in many respects. Shakespeare himself prepared none of them for publication except the narrative poems. He was above all a man of the theatre, writing scripts for performance, not for reading. Only about half of his plays appeared in print during his lifetime, in the flimsy little paperback form of the quarto, and there is no sign that he had anything to do with their publication. Unlike, for example, Ben Jonson, he wrote no dedications for them, no lists of characters or epistles to the reader. Nor did he do anything to help the reader to envisage the action in the manner of, for example, Bernard Shaw, whose stage directions sometimes amount to little essays on the characters. And when Heminges and Condell put the rest of the plays into print, in the Folio, they too printed what are essentially theatre texts.

These printed texts bear out the impression created by the *More* manuscript about Shakespeare's working methods. They are not infallible guides to what stood in the manuscript lying behind them because the process of putting a play into print generally involved a certain amount of tidying up. In writing a play, Shakespeare did not necessarily start at the beginning and go straight through to the end. He may have drafted passages several times before incorporating them into the complete script, uncharitably known as 'foul papers', which represented his own final draft (in so far as any theatrical script is final), and this may have been transcribed, by himself or a professional scribe, for the theatre or for printing, producing a fair copy. There is reason to believe that Heminges and Condell, in preparing the Folio, employed Ralph Crane, a scribe who worked for the King's Men, to make copies of certain texts, and that he imposed some of his personal habits of presentation on them. In the printing house, too, compositors undertook a degree of regularization. But standards varied, and in some texts incompetence on the part of workmen was compounded by their having to work from an ill-presented manuscript.

Perhaps the worst printed of all the early texts of Shakespeare is the first edition of *King Lear*, of 1608, in which verse is often printed as prose, prose sometimes as verse, and there are many grotesque errors sometimes producing total nonsense. In a speech of Edgar's, for instance, the compositor, apparently totally mystified by his manuscript, set the words 'swithald footed thrice the old, a nellthu night more and her nine fold'. After a number of copies had been printed, someone in the printing house must have peered again at the papers before him, making a half-hearted effort to improve this by altering it to 'swithald footed thrice the old, he met the night mare and her nine fold'. Modern editors print the passage as 'Swithin (or 'Swithold') footed thrice the wold, / He met the night mare and her ninefold' (and even that takes a lot of explaining). But when the first edition was reprinted in 1619, with no input from the author (who was dead), the printers did a respectable job of sorting out many of the more obvious problems. (Even so, they were obviously working from a copy in which Edgar's words had not been corrected, as they printed 'anelthu night Moore'.)

For all the printers' efforts, the texts of some plays preserve features which clearly – and sometimes interestingly – reflect oddities of the manuscript. In the 1599 edition of *Romeo and Juliet*, for example, at the end of the balcony scene (2.1) Romeo says:

> The grey-eyed morn smiles on the frowning night,
> Chequ'ring the eastern clouds with streaks of light,
> And darkness fleckted like a drunkard reels
> From forth day's pathway, made by Titan's wheels.

Immediately after that, the Friar enters saying:

The grey-eyed morn smiles on the frowning night,
Checking the eastern clouds with streaks of light,
And fleckled darkness like a drunkard reels
From forth day's path and Titan's burning wheels.[3]

It looks as if Shakespeare, having written the first version of these lines for Romeo, immediately decided both that they would come better from the Friar, on his first entrance, and that he could polish them up a bit, so wrote down a new version while failing to show clearly that he intended the first to be deleted. As a result, both got into print.

An even clearer example of the same sort of thing, and one that gives a still more illuminating glimpse into Shakespeare's workshop, comes at a climactic point of *Love's Labour's Lost* where in both the first printed text, of 1598, and its reprint in the 1623 Folio, Biron's great speech on love appears in two separate versions one after the other. What Shakespeare first wrote includes the following:

From women's eyes this doctrine I derive:
They are the grounds, the books, the academes,
From whence doth spring the true Promethean fire.
Why, universal plodding poisons up
The nimble spirits in our arteries,
As motion and long-during action tires
The sinewy vigour of the traveller.
Now, for not looking on a woman's face
You have in that forsworn the use of eyes,
And study too, the causer of your vow.
For where is any author in the world
Teaches such beauty as a woman's eye?
Learning is but an adjunct to ourself,
And where we are our learning likewise is.
Then when ourselves we see in ladies' eyes,
With ourselves,
Do we not likewise see our learning there?

42. 'Let us once lose our oaths to find ourselves' (4.3.337): Ralph Fiennes as Biron with Bernard Wright as Longueville, Simon Russell Beale as the King, and Paterson Joseph as Dumaine in Terry Hands's Royal Shakespeare Company production of *Love's Labour's Lost*, 1990.

This passage begins well but loses impetus, petering out at the end as if Shakespeare were aware that he had got himself into a tangle. So he retraced his steps, seeing the opportunity for lots of improvements on the way, and produced a wonderfully exhilarating paean in praise of love:

O, we have made a vow to study, lords,
And in that vow we have forsworn our books;
For when would you, my liege, or you, or you,
In leaden contemplation have found out
Such fiery numbers as the prompting eyes
Of beauty's tutors have enriched you with?
Other slow arts entirely keep the brain,
And therefore, finding barren practisers,
Scarce show a harvest of their heavy toil.
But love, first learnèd in a lady's eyes,
Lives not alone immurèd in the brain,
But with the motion of all elements
Courses as swift as thought in every power,
And gives to every power a double power,
Above their function and their offices.
It adds a precious seeing to the eye –
A lover's eyes will gaze an eagle blind.
A lover's ear will hear the lowest sound
When the suspicious head of theft is stopped.
Love's feeling is more soft and sensible
Than are the tender horns of cockled snails.
Love's tongue proves dainty Bacchus gross in taste.
For valour, is not love a Hercules,
Still climbing trees in the Hesperides?
Subtle as Sphinx, as sweet and musical
As bright Apollo's lute strung with his hair;
And when love speaks, the voice of all the gods
Make heaven drowsy with the harmony.
Never durst poet touch a pen to write
Until his ink were tempered with love's sighs.
O, then his lines would ravish savage ears,
And plant in tyrants mild humility.
From women's eyes this doctrine I derive.
They sparkle still the right Promethean fire.
They are the books, the arts, the academes,

That show, contain, and nourish all the world,
Else none at all in aught proves excellent.
Then fools you were these women to forswear,
Or keeping what is sworn, you will prove fools.
For wisdom's sake – a word that all men love –
Or for love's sake – a word that loves all men –
Or for men's sake – the authors of these women –
Or women's sake – by whom we men are men –
Let us once lose our oaths to find ourselves,
Or else we lose ourselves to keep our oaths.
It is religion to be thus forsworn,
For charity itself fulfils the law,
And who can sever love from charity? (4.3.294–341)

The existence of these two passages one after the other both disproves and
supports contemporary statements about Shakespeare's methods of composition. It disproves the idea that he 'never blotted line'; here he has blotted, if
not a thousand, at least seventeen in one go. But it supports the view that his
verse 'flowed' with great 'facility' once he was on track: the later version picks
up a few phrases from the earlier but develops them into a sustained verse
paragraph of incomparable energy and eloquence.

★

As Shakespeare wrote he must have been more conscious than most playwrights of the actors on whom he depended. The closeness of his association
for much of his career with a single, and exceptionally stable, company of
actors meant that he could tailor roles to the talents of individual performers.
Again, occasional anomalies (ironed out by modern editors) in printed texts
show him doing so. In the first edition of *Much Ado About Nothing*, for
example, certain speeches belonging to the comic constable Dogberry and his
sidekick Verges are ascribed not to the characters but to the actors (Will)
Kemp and (Richard) Cowley. The impression of confidence in his interpreters
that this creates is reinforced by other features of early texts such as the fact
that at times, in the haste of composition, Shakespeare – as in the *More* manuscript – did not trouble to sort out the distribution of roles among certain

Watch 1 And that Counte Claudio did meane vppon his wordes, to difgrace Hero before the whole affemblie, and not marrie her.

Kemp O villaine! thou wilt be condemnd into euerlafting redemption for this.

Sexton VVhat elfe?   *Watch* This is all.

Sexton And this is more mafters then you can deny, prince Iohn is this morning fecretlie ftolne awaie : Hero was in this manner accufde, in this verie manner refufde , and vppon the griefe of this fodainlie died : Maifter Conftable, let thefe men be bound , and brought to Leonatoes, I will goe before and fhew him their examination.

Conftable Come, let them be opiniond.

Couley Let them be in the hands of Coxcombe.

Kemp Gods my life, wheres the Sexton? let him write down the Princes officer Coxcombe: come, bind them, thou naughty varlet.

Couley Away, you are an affe, you are an affe.

Kemp Dooft thou not fufpect my place ? dooft thou not fufpect my yeeres? O that he were here to write me downe an affe! but maifters , remember that I am an affe, though it bee not written downe, yet forget not that I am n affe : No thou villaine, thou art full of pietie as fhal be prou de vpon thee by good witnes, I am a wife fellow, and which is more, an officer, and which is more, a houfholder, and which is more, as pretty a peece of flefh as anie is in Meffina , and one that knowes the Law, goe to, and a rich fellow enough, go to, and a fellow that hath had loffes, and on that hath two gownes, and euery thing hanfome about him : bring him away: O that I had bin writ dowhe an affe!   *exit.*

Enter Leonato and his brother.

Brother If you go on thus, you will kill your felfe,
And tis not wifedome thus to fecond griefe,
Againft your felfe.

Leonato I pray thee ceafe thy counfaile,
Which falles into mine eares as profitleffe,
As water in a fyue: giue not me counfaile,

Nor

groups of speakers such as the citizens in *Coriolanus*, leaving this task to the point at which the script was put into production.

Even clearer evidence that Shakespeare wrote as a member of the company who would translate his scripts into staged action is provided by the frequent absence of information which is crucial to the play's effect. Primarily he is concerned with writing words to be spoken, not with directing how they should be spoken or what action should accompany them. He usually gives instructions for who is to come on stage, though even these are not entirely reliable. For example in the first printing of *Much Ado* (which appears to have been made from a draft that had undergone little if any tidying up, and which therefore brings us exceptionally close to the process of composition), Innogen, mother of Hero, is instructed to enter both at the opening of the play and later, but says nothing and takes no part in the action; almost certainly Shakespeare had second thoughts about writing a part for her, perhaps because he realized that he would need his full complement of boy actors for the roles of Beatrice, Hero, Margaret, Ursula, and Benedick's boy. Editors and directors almost invariably expunge her.

Exits are less reliably provided, presumably on the grounds that an actor could be trusted to know when he had to leave. This makes room for creative assumption; for example, there is no point at which Macbeth's Porter is directed to leave the stage in the Folio text, nor do the words give any clue as to whether he should go off as soon as he has finished speaking or stay on stage as an ironic presence during the discovery that Duncan has been murdered. Far less frequently does Shakespeare give any indication (except – and it is an important exception, as his speeches are full of implicit stage directions – what may be gleaned from the speeches themselves) of the character to whom words should be addressed, what gestures or actions might accompany them, the tone in which they should be delivered, whether they should be spoken aside or directed to persons on stage, or of action which may be

43. *Opposite.* A page from the first edition of *Much Ado About Nothing*, printed directly from Shakespeare's working papers; this shows him using actors' names (*Couley and Kemp*) for the characters (Verges and Dogberry) they are to portray, generic instead of personal names ('*Sexton*' for '*Verges*', '*Constable*' for Dogberry, '*Brother*' for '*Antonio*'), and non-specific labels ('*Watch* 1, *Watch*').

crucial to the play's effect. Both instrumental and vocal music of many kinds is important to his plays, for songs, dances, battle scenes, visions, and so on. Some at least of the actors could sing and play, and expert professional musicians were available – drummers, trumpeters, oboists, flautists, lutenists, players of horns and recorders; but no incidental music and few if any original settings for songs survive.[4] (This lack has had the merit of stimulating hundreds of excellent songs for later performances.) Cues and lyrics are not always given; we do not know, for example, what words Lucius sang to Brutus in the tent scene (*Julius Caesar*, 4.2.317), and there is no lyric for the fairies' song of blessing at the end of *A Midsummer Night's Dream* (5.2.30). Significantly, music cues are less common in texts printed from Shakespeare's original manuscripts than in those influenced by the theatre, as if the provision of music had to be decided on in rehearsal. All this means that many points in the plays are open to variations of interpretation on the most practical level.

A few examples will help to indicate the extent to which Shakespeare left decisions either to be communicated by himself or to be made in collaboration with his actors in rehearsal. A crucial matter is the age of his characters. Just occasionally the dialogue provides precise – or fairly precise – clues. In *Romeo and Juliet* the information that Juliet is 'not yet fourteen' at the start of the action is repeatedly hammered home, as if Shakespeare attached special importance to her youth. In *King Lear*, Kent roundly declares 'I have years on my back forty-eight', and Lear, more vaguely, says he is 'fourscore and upward'. Some characters appear to age at an unnatural rate during the course of the action. Hamlet, a student (whatever that may imply) at the start of the play is, if we believe the gravedigger (5.1.140–58), thirty years old not all that much later; and Macbeth, initially a vigorous warrior, talks of himself as an old man in the last act (5.3.24–6). And his wife's age is indeterminate; she used to be played as a middle-aged battleaxe, but in recent years, partly under the influence of explorations of the play's sexual subtext, she has been getting younger and younger – and sexier and sexier. In *Much Ado About Nothing*, Beatrice and Benedick are clearly older than Hero and Claudio, who are obviously young, but the age gap could be anything from two or three to twenty or more years. Modern directors have exploited the latitude left them by the text, this time by often playing them as middle-aged, creating a more autumnal mood than productions that use younger actors.

44 & 45. The nineteenth-century American actress Charlotte Cushman (pp. 291–2) presents a very different image of Lady Macbeth from Sinéad Cusack (above), seen here in the production directed by Adrian Noble for the Royal Shakespeare Company in 1986.

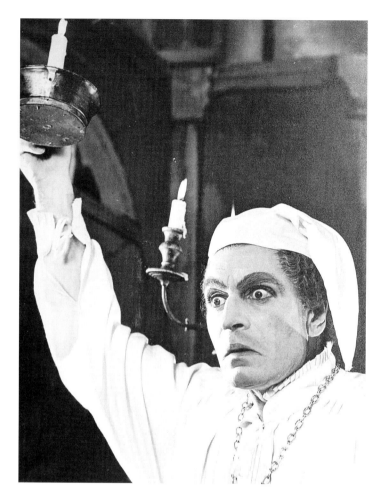

46. 'My masters,
are you mad?' (2.3.83):
Laurence Olivier as
Malvolio in John
Gielgud's production
of *Twelfth Night*,
Shakespeare
Memorial Theatre,
Stratford-upon-Avon,
1955.

Rather similarly, Shakespeare's stage directions fail to give essential information even at crucial stages of the action. The effect is rather as if a novel
by Dickens or Jane Austen had survived with its dialogue intact but its
narration only fragmentarily preserved. We may think of the scene of revelry
(2.3) in *Twelfth Night*, where a climactically comic action is represented in the
text by no more than the bare direction '*They sing the catch*'. The director and
actors between them must build up the mirth to a high pitch which is then
harshly and ludicrously punctured by the entry of the pompous Malvolio – a
moment which is usually manipulated to raise a big laugh simply on the basis
of Malvolio's grotesquely comic appearance, since he has been rudely aroused
from bed, an effect of which the text gives no hint in another rudimentary

direction, '*Enter Malvolio*'. Stage directions do little to convey the excitement of battle scenes and of fights such as the duel between Laertes and Hamlet, and Macduff's killing of Macbeth, and at many points the dialogue is open to so wide a range of interpretation as to affect our overall view of the play itself. How for example should Shylock, in *The Merchant of Venice*, make his final exit? The last words he speaks are 'I pray you give me leave to go from hence. / I am not well. Send the deed after me, / And I will sign it.' The Duke says 'Get thee gone, but do it', and Graziano adds:

> In christ'ning shalt thou have two godfathers.
> Had I been judge thou shouldst have had ten more,
> To bring thee to the gallows, not the font. (4.1.395–7)

And Shylock goes. Many actors, such as Henry Irving and Laurence Olivier, have felt the need to give him a 'big' exit, expressive of accumulated emotion sufficient to create a tragic effect. Others, such as Patrick Stewart in a John Barton production, have portrayed not tragic depths but a cringing self-abasement.

The dialogue itself, too, is often open to variant interpretation in the absence of any indication from Shakespeare as to how he wished it to be performed – if, indeed, he had any clear idea about such matters before his actors set to work. King Lear's apostrophe to the storm – 'Blow, wind, and crack your cheeks!' – is usually a loud howl of anguish; Donald Sinden spoke the words in a stage whisper, arguing that they are 'an invocation that a storm *should* happen, rather than a comment on one that is already happening.' There has been much argument about whether Macbeth, in the lines originally printed as 'this my Hand will rather / The multitudinous Seas incarnadine, / Making the Greene one, Red', should say 'Making the green, one red' or 'Making the green one, red'. Shakespeare's dialogue often permits, even demands, pauses that may be more eloquent than words. In *Measure for Measure*, at the moment when Isabella has to decide whether to ask the Duke to pardon Angelo, who has wronged her, Peter Brook, in his 1950 Stratford production, had Barbara Jefford hold as long a pause as she thought the audience could bear before kneeling and allowing the claims of mercy to override those of justice. And the ending of the same play, where the Duke proposes

47. 'For your lovely sake /
Give me your hand, and say
you will be mine' (*Measure for
Measure*, 5.1.490–1). Isabella
(Estelle Kohler) is bewildered
to receive an inopportune
proposal of marriage from
the Duke (Sebastian Shaw)
in John Barton's Royal
Shakespeare Company
production (1970).

marriage to Isabella and she makes no verbal response, has never been the same since John Barton, overturning the previously invariable assumption that no girl could possibly turn down a duke, caused his actress not to accept the Duke's offer.

★

How long it took Shakespeare to write a play we cannot be sure. No doubt some took longer than others, and the matter is complicated by uncertainties about exactly what he wrote and when he wrote it. Greene's insult of 1592 suggests that Shakespeare had already established a reputation by then; probably he had been writing since before 1590, and he certainly went on doing so until around 1614. The only major interruption to his career as a playwright seems to have been that caused by plague in 1593 to 1594, when he wrote the narrative poems. As the table shows, the traditional canon of his work consists of thirty-eight plays. Not all of them are his own unaided work – collaboration was a fact of life in the theatre of his time. Perhaps this is why, in the Epilogue to *Henry V* – possibly first spoken by Shakespeare himself – he discreetly indicates single authorship:

> Thus far, with rough and all-unable pen,
> Our bending author hath pursued the story . . .[5]

Scholars have often conjectured on the basis of style and quality that Shakespeare worked with other writers early in his career, especially in *Titus Andronicus* and *Henry VI, Part One*, and this is not impossible. In recent years

---

A CONJECTURAL CHRONOLOGY OF SHAKESPEARE'S WORKS

A few of Shakespeare's plays can be pretty precisely dated. The allusion to the Earl of Essex in the chorus to Act 5 of *Henry V*, for instance, could only have been written in 1599 (p. 72) But for many of the plays we have only vague information, such as dates of publication which may have occurred long after composition, dates of performances which may not have been the first, or inclusion in Francis Meres's list (p. 54) which tells us only that the plays listed there must have been written by 1598, when his book was published. The chronology of the early plays is particularly difficult to establish. The following table is based on the 'Canon and Chronology' section in *William Shakespeare: A Textual Companion*, by Stanley Wells and Gary Taylor, with John Jowett and William Montgomery (1987), where more detailed information and discussion may be found.

1590–1	*The Two Gentlemen of Verona*		*1599–1600*	*As You Like It*
	The Taming of the Shrew		*1600–1*	*Hamlet*
1591	*The First Part of the Contention (Henry VI, Part Two)*			*Twelfth Night*
	Richard, Duke of York (Henry VI, Part Three)		*1602*	*Troilus and Cressida*
1592	*Henry VI, Part One*		*1593–1603*	*The Sonnets*
	Titus Andronicus		*1603*	*Measure for Measure*
1592–3	*Richard III*		*1603–4*	*A Lover's Complaint*
	Venus and Adonis			*Sir Thomas More*
1593–4	*The Rape of Lucrece*			*Othello*
1594	*The Comedy of Errors*		*1604–5*	*All's Well That Ends Well*
1594–5	*Love's Labour's Lost*		*1605*	*Timon of Athens*
1595	*Richard II*		*1605–6*	*King Lear*
	Romeo and Juliet		*1606*	*Macbeth*
	A Midsummer Night's Dream			*Antony and Cleopatra*
1596	*King John*		*1607*	*Pericles*
1596–7	*The Merchant of Venice*		*1608*	*Coriolanus*
	Henry IV, Part One		*1609*	*The Winter's Tale*
1597–8	*The Merry Wives of Windsor*		*1610*	*Cymbeline*
	Henry IV, Part Two		*1611*	*The Tempest*
1598	*Much Ado About Nothing*		*1613*	*Henry VIII (All is True)*
1598–9	*Henry V*		*1613–14*	*The Two Noble Kinsmen*
1599	*Julius Caesar*			

the belief that he wrote parts, even perhaps all, of the play of *Edward III*, which was printed anonymously in 1596, has been growing, supported by elaborate if not infallible stylistic tests, and after hovering for decades on the fringes of the canon the play has been accepted into their editions by some editors.[6]

After 1594, when Shakespeare's career with the Lord Chamberlain's Men was fully under way, he seems to have preferred to work alone until towards the end of his career. Two possibly collaborative and late plays, *Pericles* and *Timon of Athens*, survive only in problematic texts – more problematic, of course, in their original state than in the tidied-up versions quite properly presented by editors. *Pericles* – a very popular play in its own time – was published as Shakespeare's in 1609, probably a couple of years after it was first acted.[7] There are fine passages in the first part of the play, but it is a cliché of criticism that 'the authentic Shakespearian voice' is not heard until the beginning of the third act,[8] with the hero's Lear-like apostrophe to the storm:

> The god of this great vast rebuke these surges
> Which wash both heav'n and hell; and thou that hast
> Upon the winds command, bind them in brass,
> Having called them from the deep. (11.1–4)

Much in the rest of the play, especially the climactic episode of reunion between Pericles and his daughter Marina, which in dramatic tension outshines even that between Lear and Cordelia, is glorious. But the first two acts are so odd in style, with so many apparent errors, that they have usually been supposed to derive from a mangled manuscript originally written by or in collaboration with another writer, perhaps the nefarious George Wilkins (see p. 81), who certainly wrote the book of the play, published in 1608, before the play itself appeared in print. His book's title is *The Painful Adventures of Pericles Prince of Tyre, Being the True History of the Play of Pericles, as it was lately presented by the worthy and ancient poet John Gower.*

48. *Opposite.* 'From ashes ancient Gower is come' (*Pericles*, 1.2): the memorial to John Gower in Southwark Cathedral.

For all the text's manifest faults, *Pericles* was reprinted three times in the next ten years; in 1629 Jonson enviously referred to it as a 'mouldy tale';[9] but Heminges and Condell omitted it from the Folio. Nevertheless it has regularly been accepted as part of the canon since the middle of the seventeenth century.

The other seriously problematic play, *Timon of Athens* – a tragedy of very uncertain date which survives only in the incomplete draft printed in the Folio – was probably written jointly by Shakespeare and Thomas Middleton (1580–1627), who may have had a hand in *Measure for Measure*, and who went on to become one of the most successful dramatists of his time. Middleton also seems to have worked on *Macbeth*, though as reviser rather than collaborator. The scenes involving Hecate, Queen of the Witches, are written in a style very different from the rest of the play and indeed from anything else in the Shakespeare canon; they include the first lines of two songs also found in Middleton's play *The Witch*, and there is good reason to believe that the text of *Macbeth* as it has come down to us was revised by Middleton some years after Shakespeare originally wrote it, perhaps after he died.

Whereas evidence for collaboration with Middleton is inferential, we have clear documentary evidence that Shakespeare also collaborated with another young colleague, John Fletcher (1579–1625), who also was to go on to great things both with Francis Beaumont and under his own steam. *The Two Noble Kinsmen* first appeared in print in 1634, after both its authors had died, ascribed to 'the memorable worthies of their time Mr John Fletcher and Mr William Shakespeare, Gent'. It was not included in the Folio, presumably because Heminges and Condell knew that it was not Shakespeare's unaided work, and only in recent years has it begun to appear in collected editions of Shakespeare. Its first recorded revival in the theatre (apart from a seventeenth-century adaptation, *The Rivals*, by William Davenant) was in London at the Old Vic in 1928; it was not performed by the Stratford company until it was chosen to open the Swan Theatre, in 1986. Since the middle of the nineteenth century, too, scholars have believed because of its style that the play first acted as *All is True* was also written in collaboration with Fletcher and that it was included, and retitled *Henry VIII*, in the Folio to make a neat ending to the history cycle.

It is natural to wonder if there was any special reason why Shakespeare was most certainly active as a collaborator in his late years. To write in this way is not necessarily easier, so the idea that he was becoming tired, or ill, does not provide a convincing explanation. Conceivably his colleagues, worried that he was in danger of losing touch with the public, persuaded him that he should listen to the ideas of younger writers more in tune with the times. The verbal style of late plays such as *Cymbeline* and, to a lesser extent, *The Tempest* is often highly involuted, turning inward upon itself rather than outwardly to address the audience. Sometimes verbal obscurity can serve a clear dramatic purpose, as in the agonized self-searching of Leontes, in *The Winter's Tale*, when, ostensibly addressing his son Mamillius, he tortures himself with speculation about the source of his wife's supposed infidelity:

> Sweet villain,
> Most dear'st, my collop! Can thy dam – may't be? –
> Affection, thy intention stabs the centre.
> Thou dost make possible things not so held,
> Communicat'st with dreams – how can this be? –
> With what's unreal thou coactive art,
> And fellow'st nothing. Then 'tis very credent
> Thou mayst co-join with something, and thou dost –
> And that beyond commission; and I find it –
> And that to the infection of my brains
> And hard'ning of my brows. (1.2.138–48)

These lines, with their self-address, their abstractions, their difficult diction and their contorted syntax, are virtually impossible to paraphrase – no wonder Leontes's friend Polixenes asks 'What means Sicilia?' – but even in their obscurity are wonderfully expressive of his bemused mental condition. But in other late plays the poet seems almost to be writing for himself, as if unconcerned that an unfortunate actor is going to have to try to make an audience understand at first hearing what he is on about. In *The Two Noble Kinsmen* more than in *All is True* (or *Henry VIII*) this stylistic habit makes it relatively easy to discern which passages come from Shakespeare's pen. As Charles Lamb put it, 'Shakspeare mingles every thing, he runs line into line, embarrasses sentences and metaphors; before one idea has burst its shell, another is hatched and clamorous for disclosure.'[10] A conspicuous example is the speech in the first scene in which one of three queens, widows of kings killed in the siege of Thebes, addresses Hippolyta:

> Honoured Hippolyta,
> Most dreaded Amazon, that hast slain
> The scythe-tusked boar, that with thy arm, as strong
> As it is white, wast near to make the male
> To thy sex captive, but that this, thy lord —
> Born to uphold creation in that honour
> First nature styled it in — shrunk thee into
> The bound thou wast o'erflowing, at once subduing
> Thy force and thy affection; soldieress,
> That equally canst poise sternness with pity,
> Whom now I know hath much more power on him
> Than ever he had on thee, who ow'st his strength,
> And his love too, who is a servant for
> The tenor of thy speech; dear glass of ladies,
> Bid him that we, whom flaming war doth scorch,
> Under the shadow of his sword may cool us.
> Require him he advance it o'er our heads.
> Speak't in a woman's key, like such a woman
> As any of us three. Weep ere you fail.
> Lend us a knee:
> But touch the ground for us no longer time
> Than a dove's motion when the head's plucked off.
> Tell him, if he i'th' blood-sized field lay swoll'n,
> Showing his teeth, grinning at the moon,
> What you would do. (*The Two Noble Kinsmen*, 1.1.77–101)

That is a virtuoso piece of verse composition. Only a writer of long experience in handling the blank verse line could have achieved its complex rhetoric, with its sixteen-line first sentence, tortuous in construction, piling subordinate clauses one on top of another, some in apposition, some subordinate to others; with its qualifying and parenthetical clauses, its figurative language, its mixture of concrete and abstract expressions, its coined compounds ('scythe-tusked' and, later, 'blood-sized'), its invented word ('soldieress'), its inversions and ellipses and elisions, its run-on verse lines and feminine endings, and the grotesque imagery of the concluding lines. Making no concessions to either speaker or hearer, it amounts almost to a parody of Shakespeare's late style, and the bizarre image chosen to convey the brevity of the time that Hippolyta should kneel – 'no longer time / Than a dove's motion when the head's plucked off' – has a surreal, almost mad quality. Brilliant though the writing is, it is scarcely theatrical; in the 1986 Swan production, nine lines of the speech were omitted. The scenes of the play generally attributed to Fletcher are easier in style, less subtle in expression but, in my experience, more theatrically effective. So it is not impossible that Shakespeare finally withdrew from theatrical composition, and may even have been encouraged by his colleagues to do so, because he had lost the taste for overt theatricality. In other words, he got the sack.

If we are assessing Shakespeare's complete output we need also to mention two lost plays. In his list of 1598, Francis Meres mentioned a comedy called *Love's Labour's Won*. This was usually assumed to be an alternative title for an existing play, most plausibly *The Taming of the Shrew*, until the discovery in 1953 of a fragment of a bookseller's list of items sold in August 1603 that had been used in the binding of a book published in 1637 or 1638.[11] This also names *Love's Labour's Won*, from which it would appear that this is the title of a play that had appeared in print under that name. There is nothing inherently implausible about this. Hundreds of works by contemporaries of Shakespeare are known by their titles alone, either because they never reached print or because printed copies were read out of existence. Play texts were flimsy; they would normally be sold unbound in editions of a few hundred copies, and rarely reached libraries. Several editions of Shakespeare plays only narrowly escaped oblivion; the more popular they were, the more likely they were to be read to pieces. We have only a single sheet of the first printing of *Henry IV, Part One*, only one copy of the first edition of *Venus and Adonis*, and only two, both imperfect, of the first, short quarto (1603) of *Hamlet*. The earliest, 1594 edition of *Titus Andronicus* was not discovered until 1904, when a copy – still the only one known to exist – turned up in Sweden.[12] What is more surprising is that if, as we must suppose, an independent Shakespeare play called *Love's Labour's Won* really did exist, it was not included in the Folio. Perhaps one day a copy will emerge.

We know more about the other lost play, but it seems never to have reached print. This is *Cardenio*. The name is that of a character in Part One of Cervantes's *Don Quixote*, published in an English translation in 1612. A play of this name (give or take the usual fluidity of spelling) was presented by the King's Men at court on 20 May 1613 and on 9 July before the ambassador of the Duke of Savoy, and in 1653 a play called '*The History of Cardenio*, by Mr Fletcher and Shakespeare' was registered for publication. It was apparently not printed, but there must have been at least one manuscript. In 1728 Lewis Theobald, whose edition of Shakespeare's complete works was to appear five years later, published a play based on the story of Cardenio called *Double Falsehood, or The Distrest Lovers*, claiming to have revised and adapted it from one 'originally written by W. Shakespeare'. A respectable tragicomedy, it had already been acted at Drury Lane and was to receive a number of later performances. There is no good reason to doubt that Theobald really did have before him as he wrote a genuine manuscript of a play written by Shakespeare and Fletcher in collaboration, and it is exciting to speculate that such a manuscript may lurk undiscovered on a library shelf or in a chest of old papers. But in 1770 a newspaper reported that 'the original manuscript' on which Theobald based his play was 'treasured up in the Museum of Covent Garden playhouse'. The theatre and its library burned to the ground in 1808.

The likelihood then that Shakespeare wrote or collaborated in up to forty plays over a career lasting some twenty to twenty-five years gives him an average output of around two plays a year, slowing down somewhat in his later years. This is considerable but not phenomenal. Comparison with contemporary dramatists is not easy because many of them also worked in collaboration, and some were more prolific as non-dramatic writers. Marlowe, with seven plays in seven years (along with the odd bit of spying, translating, and verse writing) lags a little behind Shakespeare, who also was busy with other functions, as actor and administrator. Ben Jonson wrote fewer and less varied plays over a longer career which saw the composition also of much lyric verse and many court masques. Some twenty years after Shakespeare died Richard Brome, author of *The Antipodes* and other plays, had a contract – the earliest that we know about – by which he appears to have been expected to compose three plays each year; he did not succeed.[13] Thomas Heywood boasted of having had 'either a hand or at least a main finger' in some 220 plays, a career average of around five a year, though only around twenty-four survive, and posterity has taken no great interest in them.

If Shakespeare was not phenomenally prolific, his steadiness of production and consistency of achievement are remarkable by any standards. So is his success over the full generic range of tragedy, comedy and history, emphasized in the full title of the Folio (*Mr William Shakespeare's Comedies, Histories, and Tragedies*); this versatility would have been immensely valuable to his colleagues, who needed a varied repertoire in the hope of keeping public interest at a high pitch. Shakespeare was never a slave to genre. Even the lightest of his comedies include serious elements, and his tragedies were to shock neoclassical critics by their failure to remain serious from beginning to end. *Othello* has a bawdy clown appearing in a couple of scenes (though often ignored in performance and criticism); *Macbeth* has its sinisterly comic Porter (too often trivialized in modern productions); in *Antony and Cleopatra* it is a clown who brings Cleopatra the asp that will kill her. And the comic gravediggers in *Hamlet* are essential to the play's central preoccupation with death and its effects, both physical and spiritual, upon human beings.

Shakespeare's versatility can be seen even within the traditional generic categories. His comedies range from plays as light in tone as *The Comedy of Errors* and *The Taming of the Shrew* through the more wholeheartedly romantic *Twelfth Night* and *As You Like It* to plays of ethical debate such as *Measure for Measure* and *All's Well That Ends Well* and to the high symbolism and disdain of generic purity exhibited in *The Winter's Tale*, *Cymbeline*, and *The Tempest*. Some of his English history plays are in tragic, others in comic form: the supremely comic Falstaff originates in a play of English history. The tragedy of *Romeo and Juliet*, for part of its length, has the tone of a romantic comedy. Throughout *Hamlet* Shakespeare maintains a comic perspective on the action through Polonius, the gravediggers, Osric and, not least, through the wit and irony of Hamlet himself. *King Lear*, for all its emotional intensity, is shot through with rough humour and sardonic wit and even, in the reunion of Lear and Cordelia, seems briefly as if it might be about to end like a romance.

Shakespeare's success over so wide an emotional and intellectual range marks him out not only from most, if not all, of his contemporaries, but also from virtually any English writer of any period. Is there anyone – dramatist, playwright, poet, novelist – who bears comparison with him in this respect?[14] No doubt his versatility came in part as a response to external pressures exerted by his colleagues, but it is also a measure of his ambition. We see this early in his career when he seems deliberately to be demonstrating his capacity to write in a wide range of modes, showing off his classicism in plays as different as *The Comedy of Errors* and *Titus Andronicus*, and his ability to construct epic drama of unprecedented scope in the three plays based on the reign of Henry VI followed by, and culminating in, *Richard III*. Similarly, when he writes his long poems, he casts one of them, *Venus and Adonis*, in comic, the other, *The Rape of Lucrece*, in tragic mode. Admittedly, he favours some dramatic kinds over others at different periods of his career. His English history plays (except for the collaborative *All is True* or *Henry VIII*) all come before the acquisition of the Globe, in 1599. Comic form predominates, even in English history plays, from around 1595 to beyond the composition of *Hamlet* around 1600; there is a shift to tragedy and tragicomedy from *Julius Caesar* (probably 1599) through to *Antony and Cleopatra* and *Coriolanus* (around 1608) – though the contrast between the poetic extravagance of the former and the austere reserve of the latter is enough to indicate how wide a poetic and emotional range tragedy in his hands could encompass. And finally come those late plays, or romances, or tragicomedies, or whatever we choose to call them, from *Pericles* to *The Tempest* and beyond, whose very generic indeterminacy sums up the comprehensiveness of his vision.

★

Bernard Shaw once tartly praised Shakespeare's 'gift of telling a story (provided someone else told it to him first)'.[15] This is only partly unfair. The invention of narrative was not Shakespeare's greatest strength, nor should we value him as highly as we do if it had been. He used stories for the exploration of human behaviour, for the creation of theatrically effective situations, for their emotional and comic potential, and for the intellectual stimulus that they could provoke. He borrowed the basic narrative material of almost all his plays from books, whether fictional, theatrical, legendary, mythical, historical, or factual. The collected reprint of his narrative and dramatic sources compiled by Geoffrey Bullough runs to eight thick volumes.[16] Many of them come from history, both classical and English. Two of his greatest – and fattest – source books are Sir Thomas North's *Lives of the Noble Grecians and Romans* of 1579, translated from a French version of the Greek historian Plutarch's work, and the *Chronicles of England, Scotland, and Ireland* by Raphael Holinshed, published in 1577 and then greatly enlarged ten years later, which incorporates much material from earlier chronicles. And Shakespeare does nothing to disguise his plays' derivativeness: indeed he sometimes draws attention to it, as when he brings a copy of Ovid on stage in the Ovid-inspired *Titus Andronicus* – 'My mother gave it me', says Young Lucius (4.1.43) – or in *The Winter's Tale*, where repeated references to an 'old tale' would have reminded audiences that the story derives from his old enemy Robert Greene's romance *Pandosto*.

As I have said, Shakespeare had a preference for the past and for the geographically remote. This is surely because it freed his imagination from the claims of actuality, allowing him to operate in worlds of myth and symbol. Yet he is far from being an abstract dramatist. Behind his characters lie the personifications of late medieval morality plays such as *Everyman*, depicting the battle between good and evil influences for a man's soul; but to compare such a play with *Richard III*, or *Othello*, or *Macbeth*, is to see how far Shakespeare has left his models behind. Constantly in his plays we observe a tension between the general and the particular, the abstract and the concrete, moralizing reflectiveness and localizing particularity. And although he frequently draws on pre-existing stories, the plotting of his plays – the layout and structuring of the narrative, the disposition of the scenes, the variations of perspective through which the events are seen – is his own. This is true even when he is working with a pre-existing play, as in *The Comedy of Errors*, which, though it includes episodes and characters of his own devising, is closely indebted to *Menaechmi* by the Roman dramatist Plautus, a comedy which Shakespeare may have read at school.

It is his shortest play, and unique in that it makes no explicit use of music (though directors usually employ incidental music to link scenes, and indeed have often compensated for the text's brevity by padding it out with songs – Trevor Nunn's RSC version of 1976 won the Society of West End Theatre Managers' award as the best musical of the year). Performed during student

revels at Gray's Inn in 1594, it may have been written for that occasion.
It used to be regarded as Shakespeare's earliest play, but the mastery of its
construction makes this unlikely. Though Shakespeare takes over basic comic
situations resulting from the presence within Ephesus of adult twin brothers
who have been parted from birth, one seeking the other, he greatly com-
plicates the action by making their servants twins too, thus increasing the
possibilities, even inevitabilities, of comic confusion. Whereas in Plautus
there is no one whom the visiting brother, Antipholus of Syracuse, is likely
to take for anyone else, in Shakespeare he too can be wrong, about the
servants, both of them confusingly and improbably named Dromio. Every
character in Shakespeare's play knows, and may encounter, either a twin
master or servant or both, and so is liable to error, except for the Abbess, who
appears only in the last scene; the fact that she is not susceptible to error suits
her function of resolving the complexities of the action. Characteristically,
doubling the twins enhances the play's witty intellectuality. The plotting
of *The Comedy of Errors* is an intellectual feat of some magnitude, akin to the
composition of a fugue. But it is also characteristic of Shakespeare to broaden
the play's emotional range by adding the wholly serious framework, derived
from another classical story which he was to use again close to the end of his
career in *Pericles*, of Egeon, father of the twin masters condemned to die
unless he can find someone to pay his debts by the end of the single day in
which the action, copying neoclassical precedent, takes place. Egeon (like
Antonio in *Twelfth Night*) is a still centre to the play, and his distress when,
as he believes, the son he has brought up from birth rejects him, provides the
catalyst for a climax in which, for the first time in Shakespeare's output,
laughter and pathos intermingle in a manner that has come to be thought of
as peculiarly Shakespearian (Plate 25).

It was less easy for Shakespeare to alter narrative material when he
was drawing on well-known historical events. Brutus could not but murder
Julius Caesar, and Bolingbroke's usurpation of Richard II's throne was
predetermined; there was no way in which Mark Antony could not have an
affair with Cleopatra, and the audience would have lynched Shakespeare's
actors if Henry V had failed to win the Battle of Agincourt. But Shakespeare could and did adjust less centrally significant facts to suit his artistic
design. A structural foundation of *Henry IV, Part One* is the parallel between

two young men who give the impression of being the same age, the King's reprobate son Prince Hal and Hotspur, the honour-hungry offspring of the King's opponent the Earl of Northumberland. In fact Hotspur was the older man by twenty-three years. Frequently Shakespeare telescopes events to enhance their dramatic impact. *Julius Caesar* owes a lot in both incident and language to North's Plutarch, but the magnificent sweep of action from the Lupercal games of the opening scene through the assassination of Caesar to the death of Cinna the poet, murdered because he has the same name as one of the conspirators, draws upon not just one but three of Plutarch's lives, those of Caesar, Brutus, and Antony, in a masterly compression of the historical time scheme and reorganization of events in the interests of dramatic effect.

As he gained experience, too, Shakespeare became increasingly willing not simply to reorganize historical material but to add to it. Though his three earliest English history plays, on the reign of Henry VI, are extraordinary in their deployment of a mass of disparate material, by comparison with later plays they stick relatively closely to the chronicles on which they are based. Then suddenly, in *Richard III*, Shakespeare draws all the threads together in a more consciously patterned rhetorical and theatrical structure of action which exhibits the same kind of intellectual control as is evident in *The Comedy of Errors*, different though the plays are in most other respects. Richard dominates both action and counter-action to an extent that makes it easy to think of this play as an ironic tragedy rather than a chronicle history, and the closing scene, with the parallelisms of Richard's and Richmond's dreams and the alternating blessings and curses of the ghosts of characters from all the earlier plays in the sequence, provides a coping stone to the four plays which justifies the twentieth-century practice of considering and performing them as a tetralogy. The same degree of patterning is evident in another English history play which is tragic in structure, the subsequent *Richard II*, one of Shakespeare's only four plays to be written exclusively in verse (the others, all early, are *King John* and the first and third of the plays about Henry VI).

Already in these plays Shakespeare adds and invents material to amplify and extend his historical sources, but not until *Henry IV, Part One* does he thread through the historical action a fully developed sequence of fictional scenes. He does so with triumphant success. Written at the same period as some of his finest comedies, the Henry IV plays, culminating in *Henry V*, move history into the theatrical and imaginative realms of comedy, ending as they do with both victory and marriage for the young prince whose exploits link all three plays. Above all, they do so in the character of Sir John Falstaff, who, though he has his origins in the historical Sir John Oldcastle, later Lord Cobham (and indeed bore the name of Oldcastle until the play was censored before publication as the result of objections from the current holder of the title), so far transcends his forebear that he has come to be regarded as Shakespeare's greatest comic creation.

The word 'creation' is of course a metaphor. Like all Shakespeare's characters, Falstaff is ultimately neither more nor less than the result of the impact on readers or spectators of the words that Shakespeare penned, different in every reader's mind and in every actor's performance, but like just a few other of those characters – Hamlet, Shylock, Romeo – he has come to be thought of as if he had an independent existence. 'Not only witty in [him]self, but the cause that wit is in other men',[17] Falstaff is, as we shall see in later chapters, a prolifically seminal figure who has engendered a multitude of literary, dramatic, musical, cinematic, and other offspring. He has acquired a life of his own, but this should not lead us to underestimate the integrity of his complex function in the history plays. In Part One, which is the more obviously schematic, he figures as the deflator of Hotspur's neurotic obsession with honour and as a surrogate father to the Prince; in Part Two, older and more melancholy, he both focuses the play's poetic preoccupation with the depredations of time and serves as a measure of the sacrifices in humanity demanded by the duties of kingship. The journey from the opening of the Prince's first soliloquy, 'I know you all', as he reflects on his tavern associates in Part One, to his 'I know you not, old man', as, newly enthroned, he rejects Falstaff at the end of Part Two is poignant and troubling.

At times Shakespeare's additions to his inherited narratives are clearly intended as reflections on the action, linking specific events to broader systems of ideas. In the poem *Venus and Adonis* Adonis's stallion lusts after a mare and gallops off to the woods with her, frustrating Adonis's attempts to escape from Venus's importunities; the contrast between the animal's uninhibited sexuality and Adonis's bashfulness forms a kind of comic subplot. In plays,

49. John Collier's 1904 painting of Herbert Beerbohm Tree as Falstaff in
The Merry Wives of Windsor, with Madge Kendal as Mistress Ford and Ellen Terry (left)
as Mistress Page, shows a traditional visualization of the character first seen
in the illustration to *The Wits* (p. 184).

such episodes – 'mirror scenes' as they are sometimes called – are often
only tenuously related to the plot, and for that reason could be omitted in
performance, but nevertheless provide invaluable clues to the significances
that Shakespeare perceived in his narrative. The scene of the gardeners
(3.4) in *Richard II* is an example. These men's profession is metaphorical, their
characterization rudimentary, their manner of speech little differentiated from
that of their social superiors. England has repeatedly been compared to a
garden, now the comparison is actualized in a blatantly emblematic episode

as the head gardener portrays his domain as a microcosm of the country with himself as king:

> . . . Bolingbroke
> Hath seized the wasteful King. O, what pity is it
> That he had not so trimmed and dressed his land
> As we this garden! We at time of year
> Do wound the bark, the skin of our fruit trees,
> Lest, being over-proud in sap and blood,
> With too much riches it confound itself.
> Had he done so to great and growing men,
> They might have lived to bear, and he to taste,
> Their fruits of duty. Superfluous branches
> We lop away, that bearing boughs may live.
> Had he done so, himself had borne the crown,
> Which waste of idle hours hath quite thrown down. (3.4.55–67)

This scene, objectifying a verbal metaphor into character and action, provides a virtual paradigm of poetic drama as, in the critic G. Wilson Knight's phrase, an 'expanded metaphor',[18] and similar instances can be found in many other plays, though some of them display their technique less explicitly. I think of the no less emblematic representation of the follies and horrors of civil war in the episode (2.5) in *Richard, Duke of York* (or *Henry VI, Part Three*), in which we see successively a soldier who has unknowingly killed his father and a father who has unknowingly killed his son; of the murder of Cinna the poet, in *Julius Caesar* (3.3), clearly invented as an illustration of the horrible consequences of mob rule; or in *King Lear* the conversation (4.5) between mad Lear and blind Gloucester which releases Lear's misanthropy and misogyny, or that in *Macbeth* (2.4) between Ross and an Old Man (it is characteristic of this type of scene for characters not to have personal names) in which the unnaturalness of Macbeth's murder of Duncan is reflected in nature:

> OLD MAN: 'Tis unnatural,
> Even like the deed that's done. On Tuesday last
> A falcon, tow'ring in her pride of place,
> Was by a mousing owl hawked at and killed.

ROSS: And Duncan's horses – a thing most strange and certain –
Beauteous and swift, the minions of their race,
Turned wild in nature, broke their stalls, flung out,
Contending 'gainst obedience, as they would
Make war with mankind. (2.4.10–18)

There are numerous other means by which Shakespeare broadens the scope of his inherited stories. Sometimes he adds invented characters, or ones based on only a hint in the original, who are more important as commentators or foils than as participants in the plot. In *Romeo and Juliet* the Nurse's earthy and unselfconscious sexuality sets off Juliet's initial innocence just as Mercutio's sophisticatedly bawdy and cynical wit sets off Romeo's romanticism. And as Mercutio inadvertently and tragically lets Romeo down with the rash act that, resulting in his death, turns the direction of the play from romantic comedy to tragedy, so too the Nurse fails Juliet by her inability to understand the depth of her love for Romeo. In *Macbeth*, Banquo – killed off by both Macbeth and the playwright when he is no longer needed – serves as a kind of norm against which Macbeth's descent into evil is measured, rather as Horatio, who 'is not passion's slave' (3.2.70), acts as a calm sounding board to Hamlet's emotional turbulence.

Shakespeare frequently adds clowns and fools to the base story as comic commentators on serious or romantic action as well as to add to a play's entertainment value. The word 'clown' had not acquired its modern sense of a circus entertainer, but was used rather of a comic rustic, a buffoon or uneducated countryman who might nevertheless embody unsophisticated virtue and common sense. *The Two Gentlemen of Verona* takes bits of its plot from a romantic tale, *Diana*, by the Portuguese writer Jorge de Montemajor,[19] but Shakespeare weaves into the story of young love and betrayed friendship episodes involving comic servants of his romantic heroes, Speed and Lance (not to speak of Lance's dog, Crab), who in both words and deeds comment satirically on their masters' follies. These are the forerunners of a sequence of characters whose exploits, sometimes developed into a full-blown subplot, diversify primarily romantic plots in the comedies – one thinks of Lancelot Gobbo in *The Merchant of Venice*, Dogberry and the watch in *Much Ado About Nothing*, Sir Toby Belch, Sir Andrew Aguecheek, and Maria in *Twelfth Night*.

50. *We Three Loggerheads*: an early painting of Tom Derry and Archie Armstrong, court fools to King James I, with coxcombs and bauble.

As usual with Shakespeare, there are practical as well as artistic reasons for these features of his plays. The use of different groups of characters within a single play caters for the needs of a variety of actors, reduces the demands of individual actors by spreading the load, makes space for changes of costume, increases the emotional range of the play, and adds to its entertainment value.

A close relative of the clown is the fool, a character type that Shakespeare often adds to his sources and that he developed with great subtlety and orig- inality. It has its origins in life: both 'natural' and 'wise' fools were maintained in great houses, the former providing involuntary entertainment through their mental incapacity, the latter more sophisticated professional entertainers whose appearance of folly was part of their act. In Shakespeare's time they wore distinctive costume, a 'motley' – multicoloured – coat and a coxcomb, and carried a bauble – a stick with a fool's head, sometimes with a bladder on the end. This makes them difficult to translate into updated productions, but directors have found modern counterparts in circus clowns, music hall entertainers, and cheeky pageboys. Shakespeare's fools are mostly wise; they hover on the edges of the play's action, enabled by their classlessness to move easily between high and low characters, glancing obliquely in anecdote, jest, and song at the follies of their social betters: 'He uses his folly like a stalking-horse, and under the presentation of that he shoots his wit,' says the Duke in *As You Like It* of Touchstone, whose name, meaning a piece of stone used to test the quality of gold or silver alloys, hints at his function.

Entertainers within the play, the fools entertain the audience too, both directly in songs and comic set pieces such as Touchstone's disquisition on the lie (5.4.67–101), and indirectly in a complex interplay of significances perceived by the audience but not necessarily apparent to the characters for whom they are intended. Paradoxes associated with wisdom, or wit, and folly, the possibility that a 'wise' man such as Malvolio in *Twelfth Night* may be more truly foolish than the fool Feste or even the drunken Sir Toby Belch, and that fools may exhibit their own kind of wisdom, recur endlessly in Shakespeare's plays. Paradoxically wiser than those around them, fools live on a threshold of communication which can induce a strong sense of melancholy. Touchstone is Shakespeare's most robust fool, with something of the clown about him; more subtle and more characteristic is Feste, who entertains the lovesick Orsino with the intense melancholy of a song which, as Orsino says, 'dallies with the innocence of love, / Like the old age':

> Come away, come away death,
>   And in sad cypress let me be laid.
> Fie away, fie away breath,
>   I am slain by a fair cruel maid.
> My shroud of white, stuck all with yew,
>   O prepare it.
> My part of death no one so true
>   Did share it.
>
> Not a flower, not a flower sweet
>   On my black coffin let there be strewn.

> Not a friend, not a friend greet
>> My poor corpse, where my bones shall be thrown.
> A thousand thousand sighs to save,
> Lay me O where
> Sad true lover never find my grave,
>> To weep there. (*Twelfth Night*, 2.4.50–65)

Actors have suggested that the song's extremity of lovesickness obliquely mocks Orsino's, but if there is an element of send-up here, it is virtually submerged in sympathy. And no one could be more sympathetic than the apotheosis of Shakespeare's use of the character type, the Fool of *King Lear*, whose very namelessness assists the sense of a disembodied intelligence existing purely for the sake of his master (like Ariel in *The Tempest*). Lear's Fool accompanies him into the storm with selfless loyalty – 'But I will tarry, the fool will stay, / And let the wise man fly' – and goes to bed in the noontide of his life when Lear's folly burns away in madness.

As Shakespeare sought narratives which he could turn into drama he must have had an eye open for episodes that he could develop into extended stretches of theatrically effective action. Some such scenes are relatively simple in structure – the overhearing scene (4.3) in *Love's Labour's Lost*, in which each of the lords reveals that he has broken his vow by succumbing to love, succeeds by the brilliant neatness of its design, the balcony scene (2.1) in *Romeo and Juliet* is for most of its length a duet, and Lady Macbeth's sleep-walking (5.1) is little more than an interrupted soliloquy. But it is easy to underestimate the amount of imagination, intellectual skill, and sheer practical stagecraft that went into the fashioning of such ambitious and extended scenes as the trial of Shylock (4.1) in *The Merchant of Venice*, the forum scene (3.2) in *Julius Caesar*, the play scene (3.2) in *Hamlet*, the opening scene of *King Lear*, the multi-perspective overhearing scene (5.1) in *Troilus and Cressida*, the banquet scene (3.4) in *Macbeth*, and the amazingly complex denouement (5.6) of *Cymbeline*, in which revelation succeeds revelation with dizzying virtuosity. The playwright had not only to imagine himself into the minds of the characters in these situations, and to write their speeches, he had also to shape and plot the scenes with concern for dramatic pace and rhythm, for the practical resources of his stage, and in such a way that his actors had time to make their entrances, and to change costume when necessary, and that they never needed to be in two places at once.

Before Shakespeare sat down to write he had to do a lot of preparatory work. More for some plays than for others. A few give the impression of being composed on the wing. There are signs in the first printing of *Much Ado About Nothing*, brilliant though it is, that Shakespeare made it up as he went along – for instance, at one point the text as first printed reads '*Enter the Prince, Hero, Leonato, John and Borachio, and Conrad*' even though only Don Pedro (who was called Don Peter at the start of the play) takes part in the following dialogue with Benedick, who is already on stage. There is a legend that *The Merry Wives of Windsor* was written hastily to please Queen Elizabeth by showing Falstaff in love. Literary critics have complained that the Falstaff of this play is a pale shadow of his other self, and the play notably includes a far higher proportion of prose over verse than any other. But the plotting is dextrous and the dialogue lively; audiences rarely complain.

Most of Shakespeare's plays, however, bear witness to a massive amount of what Dante Gabriel Rossetti called 'fundamental brainwork'.[20] *Romeo and Juliet*, though greatly valued for its lyricism, is architectonic in layout and design, its action punctuated by the three appearances of the Prince, always as an authority figure – first as he stills the brawl between the followers of Montague and Capulet, next at the climax of the second violent episode, culminating in the death of Mercutio, and finally as he enters to preside over the investigation into the lovers' deaths and to apportion responsibility for them. The play's characters are carefully conceived to complement and contrast with one another, the preparations for the Capulets' ball at which Romeo first sees Juliet are ironically echoed by those for her marriage to Paris, and each of the play's three love duets – one in the evening, at the ball, the second at night, in the garden, and the third at dawn as the lovers, now married, prepare to part – is interrupted by calls from the Nurse. Before Shakespeare started to write the dialogue of this play he must have worked out a ground plan as thoroughly as if he had been designing an intricate building (a process which, incidentally, he describes in some detail at *Henry IV, Part Two*, 1.3.41–62, in the lines quoted as the epigraph to Chapter One and written at around the time he was buying, and probably renovating, New Place).

And some plays, as I have suggested, grew in his mind over a long period of time. An extreme example is *King Lear*, particularly understandable in that it has often been regarded as his most profound and deeply pondered study of human identity. Discussing Shakespeare's early career (p. 51) I mentioned his indebtedness to a tragicomedy of anonymous authorship known as *King Leir* dating from before 1594 in which he may have acted as a young man. Lear's banishment of Cordelia without a dowry is foreshadowed in so early a play as *The Two Gentlemen of Verona* when the Duke, complaining about his daughter Silvia's refusal to marry the man he intends for her, complains:

> She is peevish, sullen, froward,
> Proud, disobedient, stubborn, lacking duty,
> Neither regarding that she is my child,
> Nor fearing me as if I were her father.
> And may I say to thee, this pride of hers
> Upon advice hath drawn my love from her,
> And where I thought the remnant of mine age
> Should have been cherished by her child-like duty,
> I now am full resolved to take a wife,
> And turn her out to who will take her in.
> Then let her beauty be her wedding dower,
> For me and my possessions she esteems not. (3.1.68–79)

Verbal resemblances to *King Leir* in plays as different from one another as *Richard III*, *Richard II*, *Henry V*, *As You Like It*, and *Hamlet* suggest that Shakespeare frequently mulled over his memories of the old play (which did not reach print until 1605, by which time Shakespeare may already have written his own *Lear*). Though there is no question that *King Leir* provided many ideas for *King Lear*, Shakespeare totally outstrips it in every way, transforming the layout, adding the parallel plot of the Earl of Gloucester and his sons Edgar and Edmund, inventing the Fool, fundamentally changing the play's ethos from Christian to pagan, altering the conclusion – none of the many versions of the story before his ends tragically – writing dialogue which creates an immensely subtle network of interconnected images and motifs, and using the tale as a carrier of a vast range of stimuli to thought about, especially, man's relation to society and to the universe.

Shakespeare is often praised for his ability to portray individual character. Certainly he was immensely interested in, and observant of, quirks of human behaviour, and some of his plays fascinatingly explore the psychology of exceptional people. Hamlet as well as Falstaff has exerted unending appeal as a character who appears to have an existence outside his play, and even minor characters – Barnardine in *Measure for Measure*, Silence in *Henry IV, Part Two*, Doctor Pinch in *The Comedy of Errors* – may spring to life as the result of things they say or do. Whereas some of Shakespeare's major characters may be thought of as specimens of ordinary humanity writ large – the kings of the English history plays, Othello, Claudius and Gertrude in *Hamlet* – others inhabit, at least in part, a world of allegory and parable – Timon of Athens, Iago, even Macbeth, and the heroines of the late romances, with their generalizing names – Perdita, the lost one; Miranda, to be wondered at; Marina, child of the sea. Perhaps most quirkily individual of all are the central figures of the late tragedies *Antony and Cleopatra* and *Coriolanus*, reflecting a similar preoccupation in Plutarch. Always, however, character is subsumed in a larger design, and frequently enough, as I have indicated, characters are more important as symbols or functions than as individuals. Some roles, such as the soldier who has killed his father, or Time in *The Winter's Tale*, are patently symbolical; others, such as murderers, messengers, and servants, are primarily functional, and though Shakespeare may give individualizing touches to them and to, for instance, authority figures like the Dukes in *The Comedy of Errors*, *Romeo and Juliet*, and *The Merchant of Venice*, they exist as part of the play's overall design rather than in their own right.

As I have mentioned in relation to Falstaff, character is the result both of extrapolation by the reader and of theatrical projection. Anyone who has taken part in amateur play-readings, or watched poor productions, will know how the mere words alone cannot be relied upon to give a sense of human individuality in the various roles. In the classroom, any teacher who succeeds in persuading schoolchildren that Falstaff is funny must be a genius. The audience's apprehension of character in its totality depends upon the realization in performance of a subtext, the bringing together by the actor of innumerable hints in the text – and sometimes a decision to ignore others so as not to overcrowd the canvas – in the attempt to create the impression of an integrated, if at times relevantly inconsistent, personality.

Ideas were no less important to Shakespeare than characters. His education had taught him to appreciate the value of dialectic. Renaissance students were encouraged in the Ciceronian technique of arguing both sides of the question ('*disputatio in utramque partem*') as a means to truth, a technique that underpins many of Shakespeare's plays, creating a potential ambiguity of response which leaves them endlessly open to variety of interpretation. In *The Merchant of Venice*, the Jews as well as the Christians may command sympathy. In *Coriolanus*, the patricians are as open to criticism as the plebeians. In *The Tempest*, Prospero does not occupy all the moral high ground in the dispute with Caliban (Plate 23). Shakespeare's most virtuous characters have touches of human fallibility, and most of his villains have a moment at which, with the sudden, brief opening up of a new perspective, we see them as 'desperately mortal', like the drunken murderer Barnardine in *Measure for Measure*; even the cowardly Paroles in *All's Well That Ends Well* is allowed his claim 'There's place and means for every man alive.' (4.3.341)

Some of Shakespeare's plays bring to the surface commonplace debating themes of the period: between justice and mercy in *The Merchant of Venice* and *Measure for Measure*; between nature and nurture (or natural and acquired ability), in *All's Well That Ends Well*, *The Winter's Tale*, and *The Tempest*; between the respective merits of court and country, prominent in the meditations of Shakespeare's English kings on the burdens of royalty and in pastoral plays, especially *As You Like It*, but extending even as far as *King Lear* in the contrast between court and heath. *Timon of Athens* is virtually a parable about the true nature of wealth. In *The Winter's Tale*, the unusually abstract debate (4.4.79–103) between the innocent Perdita and her lover's father, the disguised Polixenes, about the relationship between art and nature focuses and brings to the surface ideas that underlie the entire play and that find dramatic expression in the amazing final scene in which art *becomes* nature as the apparent statue of Hermione melts into life. In the same play, the preoccupation with the beneficial and destructive effects of time that Shakespeare demonstrates at all stages of his career is objectified in the actual presence of Time as Chorus. *Measure for Measure* excitingly stages moral debates between Isabella and Angelo, and two crucial scenes in *Troilus and Cressida*, perhaps the most overtly philosophical of the plays (and the most linguistically taxing), show us first the Greek leaders debating why after seven years of siege they have still not defeated Troy, and then the Trojans debating the worth of Helen and expanding from this into a general discussion of the subjectivity of value. It is potentially reductive to pursue one set of ideas in a Shakespeare play at the expense of others, but this should not cause us to ignore their omnipresence.

I have emphasized Shakespeare's general reliance on pre-existing narratives, but there are just a few plays in which he owes so little that so far as the plot goes they may be regarded as products of his unassisted imagination, and so particularly revealing of the way his mind worked when left to its own devices.[21] They are all comedies – Dr Johnson was to say that this was the form that came most congenially to him: 'in his comic scenes, he seems to produce without labour, what no labour can improve . . . His tragedy seems to be skill, his comedy to be instinct.'[22] The three principally invented plays are *Love's Labour's Lost*, *A Midsummer Night's Dream*, and *The Tempest*. In spite of the absence of strong narrative sources, all these plays are fantastic and literary in inspiration. *Love's Labour's Lost* may have been suggested by events in recent French history, *A Midsummer Night's Dream* is slightly indebted to Chaucer's Knight's Tale (which Shakespeare and Fletcher were to use more fully in *The Two Noble Kinsmen*) and to Golding's Ovid for *Pyramus and Thisbe*, and *The Tempest* draws on travellers' accounts of voyages to the New World for the opening storm. All three plays are full of classical references, and *The Tempest*, as I have noted, virtually quotes from Ovid in Prospero's great speech (5.1.33–57) beginning 'Ye elves of hills, brooks, standing lakes and groves', as well as from the French essayist Montaigne. All are exceptionally neat in design: *The Tempest*, along with the early *Comedy of Errors*, is Shakespeare's only play to observe the neoclassical unities of time, place, and action. *Love's Labour's Lost* and *The Tempest* particularly base themselves on patterns of ideas, with characters exemplifying them – in *Love's Labour's Lost*, for instance, Holofernes and Sir Nathaniel bear witness to the sterility that would result if the lords' foolish plan of abjuring women for learning were to succeed, while the uninhibited Costard and Jaquenetta stand for the opposite extreme. *A Midsummer Night's Dream* is centrally preoccupied with imagination, and all three plays relate closely to Shakespeare's own art; *Love's Labour's Lost* is profoundly concerned with the uses and abuses of language, Prospero in *The Tempest* (who in function resembles Oberon in *A Midsummer Night's Dream*, the one served by Robin Goodfellow (or Puck), the other by Ariel), is the artist at the centre of his play, the dreamer of dreams and conjuror-up of visions, and has with reason been compared to Shakespeare himself.[23]

Each play includes within itself one or more dramatic entertainment – the masque of Muscovites and the pageant of the Nine Worthies in *Love's Labour's Lost*, *The Lamentable Tragedy of Pyramus and Thisbe* in *A Midsummer Night's Dream*, and the masque in *The Tempest*. The two later plays make explicit use of supernatural figures – the fairy court in *A Midsummer Night's Dream*, Prospero, Ariel, and the goddesses of the masque in *The Tempest*. And each includes at the other extreme earthy, this-worldly roles – Costard, Bottom, Caliban. Each play, too, has a vein of didacticism, *Love's Labour's Lost* and *A Midsummer Night's Dream* in their emphasis on the need for courtesy in human affairs, *The Tempest* in its celebration, in both the courtship of Ferdinand and Miranda and the masque offered on their betrothal, of the values of chastity and temperance.

One could go on, but it is surely clear that all three plays draw from the same well of inspiration. In them Shakespeare affirms the importance of the imagination in human life, the fact that a world of dreams can grow, as Hippolyta says in *A Midsummer Night's Dream*, 'to something of great constancy' (5.1.26). But he shows too his awareness of the fragility of the works of man, the vulnerability of Prospero's great vision to the evil of a Caliban:

> The cloud-capped towers, the gorgeous palaces,
> The solemn temples, the great globe itself,
> Yea, all which it inherit, shall dissolve;
> And, like this insubstantial pageant faded,
> Leave not a rack behind. (4.1.152–6)

★

In writing about Shakespeare's plays, so far I have said only a little about his language. He was writing at a time of great linguistic ferment. Many English books and even plays were still being written in Latin. Elizabeth and James attended performances of Latin plays in the universities; Francis Bacon is only the best known of many authors to write extensively in Latin, largely because this was the best way to achieve an international readership.[24] Sir Thomas Bodley, founder of the Bodleian Library in Oxford, deliberately excluded plays from his collections; in 1605 only thirty-six of close on 6,000 books held by the library were in English.[25] Though writers for the popular theatre naturally wrote in English, many plays, including Shakespeare's, incorporate Latin tags and allusions to Latin literature. The English language was struggling to achieve a vocabulary and expressive power comparable to that offered by Latin.[26] This process involved much coining of new words, often on the basis of, especially, Latin and French, and encouraged the use of old words in new forms, senses, and combinations. Shakespeare was an indefatigable innovator. The list-maker Francis Meres justly praised him, among others, as a poet by whom 'the English tongue is mightily enriched, and gorgeously invested in rare ornaments and resplendent habiliments'. It has been calculated that Shakespeare's works use an exceptionally large vocabulary of anywhere between 20,000 and 30,000 words (precision is impossible both because of the difficulty of defining exactly what we mean by a word – do compounds and negative forms count, for instance? – and because of textual variants).[27] Many of these words were new to the language – or at least to print.[28] Some words apparently coined by Shakespeare, such as accommodation, addiction, comply, discontent, frugal, and reinforcement, are still in common use; many others are no longer current.[29]

Pervasive influences on Shakespeare's vocabulary are the Bible and the Book of Common Prayer, and the proverbial language of his time (itself much influenced by the Bible).[30] These would have come to him by word of mouth as well as through reading, but the wide extent of his vocabulary is largely a consequence of the highly derivative, literary aspects of his work. Inevitably the language of his major sources – Holinshed, Plutarch, and so on – seeps through into his plays; he did not disdain at times to borrow their wording to an extent that nowadays would result in accusations of plagiarism. At his least inspired he did so almost mechanically. One of the more tedious scenes in Shakespeare is that in *Henry V* (1.2) in which the Archbishop of Canterbury instructs the young king in his rights to the French throne. We can almost see Shakespeare yawning as he dutifully turns Holinshed into the blankest of blank verse. Here is Holinshed:

> Hugh Capet also, who usurped the crown upon Charles Duke of
> Lorraine, the sole heir male of the line and stock of Charles the

Great, to make his title seem true and appear good, though indeed it was stark naught, conveyed himself as heir to the lady Lingard, daughter to King Charlemagne, son to Louis the Emperor, that was son to Charles the Great.

Now Shakespeare, with borrowed words underlined:

> <u>Hugh Capet also – who usurped the crown</u>
> Of <u>Charles</u> the <u>Duke of Lorraine, sole heir male</u>
> <u>Of the true line and stock of Charles the Great</u> –
> <u>To</u> fine <u>his title</u> with some shows of truth,
> <u>Though</u> in pure truth it was corrupt and <u>naught</u>,
> <u>Conveyed himself as heir to th' Lady Lingard</u>,
> <u>Daughter to Charlemain</u>, who was the <u>son</u>
> <u>To Louis the Emperor</u>, and Louis the <u>son</u>
> Of <u>Charles the Great</u>. (1.2.69–77)

Very little effort has gone into that. A similar process of mechanical adaptation is at work in another of Shakespeare's less widely admired episodes, the earlier part of the 'English' scene (4.3) in *Macbeth*.

At other times, however, Shakespeare's verbal borrowing, though scarcely less extensive, is far more creative. In *Antony and Cleopatra*, where he has a more inspiring source in North's adaptation of Plutarch, his imagination takes fire and he transforms fine prose into great dramatic verse. Plutarch describes how, when Cleopatra first set out to meet Antony, she took to her barge,

the poop whereof was of gold, the sails of purple, and the oars of silver, which kept stroke in rowing after the sound of the music of flutes, oboes, citterns, viols and such other instruments as they played upon in the barge. And now for the person of herself: she was laid under a pavilion of cloth of gold of tissue, apparelled and attired like the goddess Venus commonly drawn in picture; and hard by her, on either hand of her, pretty fair boys apparelled as painters do set forth god Cupid, with little fans in their hands, with the which they fanned wind upon her. Her ladies and gentlewomen also, the

51. A vision of Cleopatra by Lawrence Alma-Tadema (1836–1912).

fairest of them were apparelled like the nymphs Nereides, which are the mermaids of the waters, and like the graces, some steering the helm, others tending the tackle and ropes of the barge, out of the which there came a wonderful passing sweet savour of perfumes that perfumed the wharf's side, pestered with innumerable multitudes of people.

Shakespeare alters the placing of the episode so that it comes after we have experienced Cleopatra in many moods, turns Plutarch's lyrical description into an erotic vision, and adds to its piquancy by putting it into the mouth of the detached observer Enobarbus who has seemed least likely to be seduced by Cleopatra's wiles. It is extraordinary how much of North's phraseology remains in lines that nevertheless achieve complete poetic independence:

> The <u>poop</u> was beaten <u>gold</u>;
> <u>Purple the sails</u>, and so perfumèd that
> The winds were love-sick with them. <u>The oars</u> were <u>silver</u>,
> Which to the tune of <u>flutes</u> <u>kept stroke</u>, and made
> The water which they beat to follow faster,
> As amorous of their strokes. <u>For her</u> own <u>person</u>,
> It beggared all description. She did lie
> In her <u>pavilion – cloth of gold, of tissue –</u>
> O'er-<u>picturing</u> that <u>Venus</u> where we see
> The fancy outwork nature. On each side her
> Stood <u>pretty</u> dimpled boys, like smiling <u>Cupids</u>,
> With divers-coloured <u>fans</u> whose <u>wind</u> did seem
> To glow the delicate cheeks which they did cool,
> And what they undid did . . .
> Her <u>gentlewomen, like the Nereides</u>,
> So many <u>mermaids</u>, tended her i'th' eyes,
> And made their bends adornings. At the <u>helm</u>
> A seeming <u>mermaid</u> steers. The silken <u>tackle</u>
> Swell with the touches of those flower-soft hands
> That yarely frame the office. From the barge
> A strange invisible <u>perfume</u> hits the sense
> Of the adjacent <u>wharfs</u>. The city cast
> Her <u>people</u> out upon her . . . (2.2.199–221)

Needless to say, Shakespeare read many books other than those that supplied him with stories, and of course he heard, and learned, roles in plays other than his own. He may well, like many of his contemporaries, have kept a commonplace book in which he jotted down memorable sayings and observations that might come in useful for future use: 'My tables, / My tables – meet it is I set it down / That one may smile and smile and be a villain', as Hamlet does (1.5.107–9). Shakespeare read like a magpie, constantly pecking at new words, often dropping them after they had served his purpose once or twice. Around the time he wrote *King Lear*, for example, he read Samuel Harsnet's *Declaration of Popish Impostures* and John Florio's translation of Montaigne's *Essays*, both published in 1603, apparently picking up from them many unusual words – 'compeer', 'handy-dandy' from Florio, 'auricular' 'corky', bo-peep', 'conspirant' from Harsnet – which appear in this play alone.

Language was immensely important to Shakespeare, and he is properly revered as our greatest poet, but I hope to have made clear that I do not subscribe to the commonly expressed view that the greatness of his plays lies entirely in 'the words'. He was not simply a poet who wrote in dramatic form. He was a poetic dramatist because, at his best, he conceived of story, plot, action, character, and language as a whole, one deeply interrelated with the other. Full appreciation of his work demands a multi-levelled response. Nevertheless, as later chapters of this book will show, his work can make an impact in adaptation, translation, and even in the wordless forms of the silent film and ballet. And the language of the plays needs to be apprehended as poetry and prose meant not to be read but to be heard in a theatre, not merely to be spoken but to be carried on the voice and projected by the body of a well-suited actor, occasionally in the presence only of the audience but mostly as one of a group of other men and (nowadays) women listening or not listening, reacting or not reacting, in ways that add to the verbal meaning of what is being said. Taken by itself, the tirade that Adriana, in *The Comedy of Errors* (2.2.113–49), fires off against the man she wrongly believes to be her husband is an entirely serious expression of wifely jealousy; seen to be addressed to the innocent and uncomprehending man who has never met her before, it becomes a complex piece of high comedy.

This means that reading plays calls for a kind of imaginative activity quite different from that required by the reading of lyric or epic poetry, or novels and discursive prose. Shakespeare's prose and verse need to be judged by the standards of drama, not literature. The dramatic situation may call at times for bombast, hyperbole, understatement, banality, repetitiveness, linguistic obscurity and stylistic disjunction which would be unacceptable in writing meant simply to be read. This is not to say that every stylistic infelicity can be explained and excused on the grounds that it serves the needs of the theatre. Throughout his career Shakespeare was capable of prolixity, unnecessary obscurity, awkwardness of expression, pedestrian versifying and verbal inelegance. Even in his greatest plays we sometimes sense him struggling with plot at the expense of language, or allowing his pen to run away with him in speeches of greater length than the situation warrants.

Having admitted that Shakespeare was fallible, we must immediately acknowledge that there is no stage of his career at which he does not display that mastery of the English language which, for all his merits as a dramatic plotter, a thinker, a portrayer of human character, is responsible for his pre-eminence as the greatest of poets as well as the greatest of dramatists. Even in his earliest plays he emerges fully formed as a poet and prose writer of exceptional accomplishment. There must have been earlier writings still, if only schoolboy exercises, that have not survived. It is in his early plays and the narrative poems that his rhetorical education most clearly shows itself. It was a training in formal devices, figures of speech with formidable names mostly derived from Latin or Greek, some of them still in common use – hyperbole, irony, parable, metaphor, simile – others known only to specialists – anaphora (repetition of a word at the beginning of a sequence of clauses or phrases), epistrophe (the same word ending a sequence of clauses), antimetabole (repetition of words in inverted order), epanalepsis (repetition of the same word at the beginning and end of a line), and so on.[31] These terms were drilled into Elizabethan schoolboys as a basis for their composition of prose – primarily in Latin, but inevitably with a knock-on effect on English – as well as verse.

The effect of this training on poetic composition could be stilted, and may seem excessively formal to modern tastes. The structure of much of Shakespeare's early verse lies skeletally close to the surface, drawing attention in reading to the artistry of the writer rather than conveying the impression of natural, spontaneous utterance. Nevertheless this is the mode in which the plays succeeded on the stages of their time, and actors capable of translating it into performance can still create in their audiences a sense of the passions behind the rhetoric, the person within the style.

We have evidence that this was so in Shakespeare's time in two of the very few examples of contemporary response to a play in performance. Insulting

52. 'I give thee this to dry thy cheeks withal' (*Richard, Duke of York*, 1.4.84):
Peggy Ashcroft as Margaret taunts Donald Sinden as York with a napkin soaked
in the blood of his slaughtered youngest son, Rutland.

Shakespeare in his *Groatsworth of Wit* Robert Greene alluded to a line,
'O tiger's heart wrapped in a woman's hide!', from the play known originally
as *Richard, Duke of York*, but later more familiar as *Henry VI, Part Three*.
The line occurs in the middle of a 38-line speech of sophisticated rhetoric
from the Duke of York in response to a 42-line diatribe from his captor
Queen Margaret, taunting him with the death of his sons. On the page these

long speeches may seem static and unexciting, but no one who saw the Peter
Hall / John Barton production of 1963 will forget the controlled ferocity with
which Peggy Ashcroft's Margaret verbally attacked Donald Sinden's tethered
York as she unleashed her fury at him, or his counter-attack:

> YORK: O tiger's heart wrapped in a woman's hide!
>   How couldst thou drain the life-blood of the child
>   To bid the father wipe his eyes withal,
>   And yet be seen to bear a woman's face?
>   Women are soft, mild, pitiful, and flexible –
>   Thou stern, obdurate, flinty, rough, remorseless.
>   Bidd'st thou me rage? Why, now thou hast thy wish.
>   Wouldst have me weep? Why, now thou hast thy will.
>   For raging wind blows up incessant showers,
>   And when the rage allays the rain begins.
>   These tears are my sweet Rutland's obsequies,
>   And every drop cries vengeance for his death
>   'Gainst thee, fell Clifford, and thee, false Frenchwoman.
>   (1.4.138–150)

The power of these speeches in Elizabethan performance helps to explain
why Greene could expect his readers to identify his near-quotation.

The other rhetorical passage commemorated in contemporary record is
in *Henry VI, Part One* (probably written after *Part Two* and *Part Three*). The
stalwart English warrior Lord Talbot, Earl of Shrewsbury, grieves over the
body of his son John, valiantly slain in battle:

> SERVANT: O my dear lord, lo where your son is borne.
> TALBOT: Thou antic death, which laugh'st us here to scorn,
>   Anon from thy insulting tyranny,
>   Coupled in bonds of perpetuity,
>   Two Talbots wingèd through the lither [yielding] sky
>   In thy despite shall scape mortality.
>   (*To John*) O thou whose wounds become hard-favoured death,
>   Speak to thy father ere thou yield thy breath.

Brave death by speaking, whether he will or no;
Imagine him a Frenchman and thy foe. –
Poor boy, he smiles, methinks, as who should say
‘Had death been French, then death had died today’.
Come, come, and lay him in his father’s arms.
        Soldiers lay John in Talbot’s arms
My spirit can no longer bear these harms.
Soldiers, adieu. I have what I would have,
Now my old arms are young John Talbot’s grave.
    (4.7.17–32)

And he dies. Again, these formal, polished words, this time in rhyme, are totally implausible as the dying utterance of a grieving man of war. Yet Thomas Nashe, poet, playwright and pamphleteer, bears witness to its profoundly moving effect in performances given probably at the Rose Theatre in 1592:

> How would it have joyed brave Talbot, the terror of the French, to think that after he had lien two hundred years in his tomb he should triumph again on the stage, and have his bones new-embalmed with the tears of ten thousand spectators at least (at several [i.e. various] times) who in the tragedian that represents his person imagine they behold him fresh bleeding![32]

This is also one of a number of passages suggesting an uninhibited degree of emotionalism in the reactions of Elizabethan theatre-goers.

The discovery of the theatrical power of Shakespeare’s rhetoric (and also of that of some of his contemporaries, especially Marlowe in *Tamburlaine* and *Edward II*) when delivered with proper understanding of the balance between identification and distancing that it calls for is an achievement of the modern theatre, responsible for the rehabilitation of, especially, the early histories and *Titus Andronicus*. It resembles the rehabilitation of baroque opera as the result of the study of early musical performance styles. Just as there was a time not all that long ago when operas by Handel that are now part of the staple repertoire were considered unperformable, so *Titus Andronicus*, before the landmark Stratford productions of Peter Brook (1955) and Deborah Warner (1987), was

53. 'Ah, now thou turn'st away
thy face for shame.' (2.4.28):
Lavinia (Sonia Ritter) and
Marcus Andronicus (Donald
Sumpter) in Deborah
Warner's Royal Shakespeare
Company production of
Titus Andronicus, 1987.

generally regarded as an excrescence on the canon. But *Titus's* technique still meets with misunderstanding. A common sticking point is the 47–line speech of Marcus Andronicus on seeing his niece Lavinia with *'her hands cut off and her tongue cut out, and ravished'*. The poetic accomplishment of Marcus's lines is not in doubt. They are elegantly written in an Ovidian style and with direct references to the classical legend on which the episode is based.

> Alas, a crimson river of warm blood,
> Like to a bubbling fountain stirred with wind,
> Doth rise and fall between thy rosèd lips,
> Coming and going with thy honey breath.

But sure some Tereus hath deflowered thee
And, lest thou shouldst detect him, cut thy tongue.
Ah, now thou turn'st away thy face for shame,
And notwithstanding all this loss of blood,
As from a conduit with three issuing spouts,
Yet do thy cheeks look red as Titan's face
Blushing to be encountered with a cloud.
Shall I speak for thee? Shall I say 'tis so?
O that I knew thy heart, and knew the beast,
That I might rail at him to ease my mind! (2.4.22–35)

With its similes and metaphors, its alliterations and conventional epithets, its classical allusions and (necessarily) rhetorical questions, this is consciously artificial writing, more obviously of its time than, for instance, Hamlet's soliloquies (though they too have their share of rhetorical devices). But Frank Kermode is unfair in stating that Marcus 'is making poetry about the extraordinary appearance of Lavinia, and making it exactly as he would if he were in a non-dramatic poem'.[33] The verse is constantly conscious of the silent presence of the raped and mutilated woman, addressing her directly, giving cues for her reactions, and allowing for poignant pauses as she gestures or moves in response to what Marcus says. Naturalistically, the problem is that Lavinia is in urgent need of practical help, and it is absurd that Marcus should waste time in talking before doing something about her plight. Julie Taymor, in her bold and imaginative film, shortens the speech and takes advantage of the freedoms of the medium by causing Marcus to approach Lavinia from afar, only slowly realizing what has happened to her (after all, he has not read the stage direction). Peter Brook, in a production which showed that Titus (played by Laurence Olivier at the peak of his form) is a great tragic role, omitted it altogether. But this is poetic, not naturalistic drama. Deborah Warner showed her awareness of this in a production which plumbed the play's rhetoric for its deep sources, bringing them to the surface so that even the most artificial verbal structures became expressive of emotion. Marcus's speech, spoken in hushed tones and with the traumatized figure of Lavinia quivering before us, became a deeply moving attempt, enacted outside time, to master the facts, and thus to survive the shock, of a previously unimagined horror. In its own time, *Titus Andronicus* was one of Shakespeare's most popular plays; we have no right to assume that it was acted with less understanding then than in this revelatory production.

Shakespeare's rhetorical training underpins not only the high drama of the early histories and of *Titus Andronicus* but also the lyrical verse found mostly in the comedies, and even the comic prose. It is seen at its most obvious in set pieces such as Henry VI's highly patterned meditation (*Richard, Duke of York*, 2.5.1–54) on how much happier he would be as a peasant than as a king, a classic expression of the pastoral ideal which anticipates similar expressions of discontent from both Henry IV and Henry V and which also looks forward to the more detailed examination of pastoralism in *As You Like It*. The literariness of the early plays, however dramatically effective they may be, is evident from the many links between the poems of 1593–4 and plays written around the same time. In *The Comedy of Errors*, for instance, Dromio of Syracuse, describing the kitchen wench, 'spherical, like a globe', who has laid claim to him offers to 'find out countries in her', and proceeds to do so in a brilliant set piece of prose comedy (3.2.116–44). The device is essentially the same as that in *Venus and Adonis* in which Venus, trying to seduce Adonis, describes her body as a park in which he shall be a deer:

> Feed where thou wilt, on mountain or in dale;
> Graze on my lips, and if those hills be dry,
> Stray lower, where the pleasant fountains lie. (232–4)

Rhyme schemes and metrical patterns associated with lyrical, especially amatory verse are particularly common among the early plays, which also are much concerned with love. During the early 1590s the sonnet form enjoyed a great vogue; probably most of Shakespeare's sonnets were written then, and the verse form of the sonnet, either complete, or with additional lines, or abbreviated to its last six lines (which is also the stanza form of *Venus and Adonis*) crops up frequently in, for instance, *Love's Labour's Lost*, in which the lords compose sonnets to their ladies, and in *Romeo and Juliet*, which has a sonnet as its prologue and as a Chorus to its second act; in which the words of the lovers on their first meeting are cast in the form of a sonnet; and in which the Prince's concluding speech is in the six-line stanza form.

A Midsummer Night's Dream is a virtual anthology of lyric forms. As Shakespeare's career progressed his use of rhyme dwindled, in keeping with the submersion of other formal devices beneath the surface of his verse.

Among rhetorical figures studied in schools were various forms of wordplay, and Shakespeare's works of all periods are shot through with puns and quibbles, double entendres and comic misunderstandings, often of extreme ingenuity, and sometimes dependent on esoteric significances and lost allusions which make them incomprehensible to the modern theatre-goer and even at times to the scholar. Dr Johnson considered this a vice and said so at length, culminating in the judgement that 'A quibble was to him the fatal Cleopatra for which he lost the world, and was content to lose it',[34] thus turning Shakespeare into a latterday Mark Antony. Wordplay in the early comedies is especially liable to bore the modern reader, and to force actors into paroxysms of gestural ingenuity in the effort to make theatrical sense of the bawdy double meanings in passages such as:

> SPEED: Why then, how stands the matter with them?
> LANCE: Marry, thus: when it stands well with him it stands well with her.
> SPEED: What an ass art thou! I understand thee not.
> LANCE: What a block art thou, that thou canst not! My staff understands me
> SPEED: What thou sayst?
> LANCE: Ay, and what I do too.
> (*The Two Gentlemen of Verona*, 2.5.19–26)

Max Beerbohm deftly parodied that kind of writing in a lament for the absence of Shakespearian comic relief in Shaw's play about prize-fighting, *The Admirable Bashville*:

> SECOND POLICEMAN: Canst tell me of this prize-fight? Is't within law?
> FIRST POLICEMAN: Aye! To't. For what does a man prize highest? A fight. But no man fights what he prizes, else is he no man, being not manly, nor yet unmannerly. Argal, if he fight the prize, then

is not the prize his, save in misprision, and 'tis no prize-fight
within the meaning of the act.

SECOND POLICEMAN: Marry, I like thy wit, etc., etc.[35]

Modern playgoers, however, have been educated into an easier acceptance of
wordplay than neoclassical and nineteenth-century readers, partly as a result
of its serious use in post-Freudian literature, above all by James Joyce, and by
critical studies that have illuminated the contribution it can make to the plays'
verbal texture. The serious pun was to become one of Shakespeare's most
successful devices, a means by which he could create multiple layers of meaning and suggest in his characters a complexity of response which adds to their
appearance of psychological reality. 'I'll gild the faces of the grooms withal,'
says Lady Macbeth, 'For it must seem their guilt.' (2.2.54–5) And Othello,
quenching the taper that he holds in his hand, condemns Desdemona with
'Put out the light, and then put out the light.' (5.2.7)

Throughout Shakespeare's career the blank verse line – 'But soft, what
light from yonder window breaks'[36] is a typical example – remained his
staple medium for dramatic verse, often varied with a wide range of metrical
devices, shorter and longer lines, and rhyme in couplets and other combinations. As his experience grew, his treatment of the medium increased
in flexibility, approximating, when it suited his dramatic purpose, more
and more closely to the rhythms of ordinary speech and then, towards
the end of his career, reaching a degree of rhythmical and linguistic complexity – as in the passage from *The Two Noble Kinsmen* quoted on p. 126
– that is no less stylized and artificial in its way than the overt rhetoricism
of the early style. An obvious comparison to a musician would be with the
changes in Beethoven's handling of sonata form and of melodic line from
beginning to end of his career. This is not necessarily to say that in any
absolute sense Shakespeare (or Beethoven) improved. Though Biron's long
speech quoted on pp. 112–13 is more regular in rhythm than, say, Hamlet's
soliloquies, I resist the idea that it is for that reason 'inferior', just as I also
resist the categorization of Shakespeare's later comedies as 'mature comedies',
as if there were anything immature about so assured and finished a masterpiece as *A Midsummer Night's Dream.*

Still it would be hard to deny that the development in Shakespeare's handling of blank verse resulted in an increase in his technical armoury, enabling greater subtlety of expression, density of poetic texture, and depth of psychological suggestiveness. As his mastery increased, his technique became less and less apparent, as if intuition were taking over from intellectual effort. There is something of a breakthrough in *Romeo and Juliet*, whose stylistic range in both prose and verse is greater than that of any play previously written by Shakespeare or anyone else. Particularly forward-looking in terms of Shakespeare's style is the representation in the Nurse's speeches of an undisciplined mind flitting inconsequentially from one topic to another –

> But, as I said,
> On Lammas Eve at night shall she be fourteen,
> That shall she, marry, I remember it well.
> 'Tis since the earthquake now eleven years,
> And she was weaned – I never shall forget it –
> Of all the days of the year upon that day,
> For I had then laid wormwood to my dug,
> Sitting in the sun under the dovehouse wall. (1.3.22–9)

Though these lines play with variations on the basic rhythm of blank verse, they readily accommodate colloquial phrases, repetitions, and digressions in a manner that creates the impression of naturally idiosyncratic speech. This is both brilliantly successful in itself and anticipative of a technique that reaches a high point in Hamlet's soliloquies:

> That it should come to this –
> But two months dead – nay not so much, not two –
> So excellent a king, that was to this
> Hyperion to a satyr, so loving to my mother
> That he might not beteem the winds of heaven
> Visit her face too roughly! Heaven and earth,
> Must I remember? Why, she would hang on him
> As if increase of appetite had grown
> By what it fed on, and yet within a month –
> Let me not think on't; frailty, thy name is woman –

> A little month, or ere those shoes were old
> With which she followed my poor father's body,
> Like Niobe, all tears, why she, even she –
> O God, a beast that wants discourse of reason
> Would have mourned longer! – married with mine uncle,
> My father's brother, but no more like my father
> Than I to Hercules . . . (1.2.137–53)

This torrent of words which, with its tortured syntax, self-interruptions and corrections, exclamations and rhetorical questions, creates the impression of a passionate disorder within the speaker's mind is nevertheless the result of consummate ordering of words on the part of the playwright. For all its impression of spontaneous utterance it bears traces of the earlier rhetorical style in its classical allusions, antitheses, alliterations, similes, metaphors, and shifts from the particular to the general. And its dramatic impact is created partly by the violent contrast in style between Hamlet's self-revelatory immediacy as he opens up his mind to the audience and the self-concealing falsity of Claudius's oily diplomacy to the court in the speeches that go before it:

> Though yet of Hamlet our dear brother's death
> The memory be green, and that it us befitted
> To bear our hearts in grief and our whole kingdom
> To be contracted in one brow of woe,
> Yet so far hath discretion fought with nature
> That we with wisest sorrow think on him
> Together with remembrance of ourselves. (1.2.1–7)

(It has not taken Claudius long to learn to use the royal plural.) The contrast between his and Hamlet's speeches serves as a reminder that Shakespeare's development of style was, as it were, cumulative rather than progressive; he didn't stop being able to write in one manner because he learned to do so in another. And the increased fluency of his verse has a counterpart in his handling of prose, traditionally regarded as the less exalted medium and associated with low-life characters and comedy. Even in his earliest plays Shakespeare writes set pieces whose artistry is no less real for being projected

54. 'Now the dog all this while sheds not a tear nor speaks a word' (*The Two Gentlemen of Verona*, 2.3.30–31): a watercolour drawing of Lance and his dog, Crab, by Richard Westall (1765–1836).

in the diction and rhythms of everyday speech. Clowns such as Lance in *The Two Gentlemen of Verona*, Grumio in *The Taming of the Shrew*, and Costard in *Love's Labour's Lost* make immediate contact with their audiences in speeches such as Lance's complaint about his dog Crab – perhaps the best non-speaking role in the canon:

> LANCE (*to the audience*): Nay, 'twill be this hour ere I have done weeping. All the kind of the Lances have this very fault. I have received my proportion, like the prodigious son, and am going with Sir Proteus to the Imperial's court. I think Crab, my dog, be the sourest-natured dog that lives. My mother weeping, my father wailing, my sister crying, our maid howling, our cat wringing her hands, and all our house in a great perplexity, yet did not this cruel-hearted cur shed one tear. He is a stone, a very pebble-stone, and has no more pity in him than a dog. A Jew would have

wept to have seen our parting. Why, my grandam, having no eyes, look you, wept herself blind at my parting. Nay, I'll show you the manner of it. This shoe is my father. No, this left shoe is my father. No, no, this left shoe is my mother. Nay, that cannot be so, neither. Yes, it is so, it is so, it hath the worser sole. This shoe with the hole in it is my mother, and this my father. A vengeance on't, there 'tis. Now, sir, this staff is my sister, for, look you, she is as white as a lily and as small as a wand. This hat is Nan our maid. I am the dog. No, the dog is himself, and I am the dog. O, the dog is me, and I am myself. Ay, so, so. Now come I to my father. 'Father, your blessing.' Now should not the shoe speak a word for weeping. Now should I kiss my father. Well, he weeps on. Now come I to my mother. O that she could speak now, like a moved woman. Well, I kiss her. Why, there 'tis. Here's my mother's breath up and down. Now come I to my sister. Mark the moan she makes. – Now the dog all this while sheds not a tear nor speaks a word. But see how I lay the dust with my tears. (*The Two Gentlemen of Verona*, 2.3.1–32)

As Shakespeare's career progressed he experimented freely with the medium. In *Much Ado About Nothing*, the emotional honesty of Beatrice and Benedick, who mainly speak prose, contrasts favourably with the hollow verse of Claudio and Hero, and in *As You Like It* the most truly poetical love scenes and speeches are in prose: 'O coz, coz, coz, my pretty little coz, that thou didst know how many fathom deep I am in love. But it cannot be sounded. My affection hath an unknown bottom, like the Bay of Portugal', says Rosalind (4.1.195–8). Some of Shakespeare's most vividly characterized roles – Shylock, Malvolio, Mistress Quickly, Iago, above all Falstaff – are written largely or entirely in prose. In tragedy, one of the reasons that Hamlet seems so protean a figure, so responsive to experience and eloquent in expression, is the ease with which he shifts from one register to another. And in *King Lear* it is often not easy to tell where prose ends and verse begins.

Though Shakespeare never ceased to be a poetic dramatist, in certain plays written towards the end of his career he seems to cultivate a linguistic austerity that avoids sensuousness and charm while cultivating intensity and

55. 'How fares your majesty?' (5.2.718): Mercadé (Griffith Jones), the messenger of death, presides over the last scene of *Love's Labour's Lost* in Terry Hands's Royal Shakespeare Company production, 1990.

functionality. I think especially of *King Lear* and *Coriolanus*, plays from which it would be hard to draw extracts suitable for anthologies of poetic beauties. But there is no straight line in his stylistic progress. None of his plays is poetically richer than *Antony and Cleopatra*, written between *Lear* and *Coriolanus*, and what were to be his final solo-authored works, *The Winter's Tale*, *Cymbeline* and *The Tempest*, are extraordinary for the profoundly imaginative quality of their language. Yet throughout his career he knew the value of simplicity. Though *Love's Labour's Lost* is a virtuoso display of linguistic exuberance the most important communication is made not through words but in between them, as it were, when the messenger Mercadé, entering at first unnoticed on a scene of uproarious mirth, brings the Princess news of her father's death:

MERCADÉ:	The King your father –
PRINCESS:	Dead, for my life.
MERCADÉ:	Even so. My tale is told. (5.2.712–13)

There are few more theatrically potent moments in the canon. It is paralleled by many other points at which words of great simplicity, having in themselves no obvious rhetorical or poetic power, make a devastating impact because of their placing. In *The Merchant of Venice*, Shylock's 'I am not well' as, acknowledging defeat, he begs to be allowed to leave the court room;[37] Prince Harry's 'I do; I will' as reality rises to the surface of the fiction he has been enacting in the Eastcheap tavern and he recognizes that he will indeed have to banish Falstaff;[38] in *Antony and Cleopatra*, Cleopatra's 'Husband, I come' as she prepares to meet Mark Antony 'where souls do couch on flowers';[39] in *Pericles* 'A terrible childbed hast thou had, my dear'[40] as Pericles prepares for the burial at sea of his supposedly dead wife just after she has given birth to their daughter; in *The Winter's Tale* Leontes's 'O, she's warm!'[41] as art gives way to life and *his* supposedly dead wife is restored to him; and in *The Tempest*, Prospero's ''Tis new to thee' in response to Miranda's 'O brave new world / That has such people in't':[42] these are among many moments when Shakespeare abandons rhetoric in the confidence that simple statement is all the situation requires. The most powerful sustained example of the method comes in *King Lear*. Lear's reunion with Cordelia (4.6) is heralded by a mighty image:

> Thou art a soul in bliss, but I am bound
> Upon a wheel of fire, that mine own tears
> Do scald like molten lead.

But after that the episode is sustained by a succession of entirely plain, largely monosyllabic phrases: 'You must not kneel' . . . 'I think this lady to be my child, Cordelia. / And so I am, I am' . . . 'No cause, no cause'. . . 'I am old and foolish'.

There are even points at which, rather than write meaningful words, Shakespeare instructs the actor to express wordless emotion. On the printed page, the elementary signifier 'O', occurring at a climactic moment, can have a seriously anti-climactic effect. But Shakespeare asks his actors to convey many varied emotions through it – and sometimes leaves it up to the actor to decide exactly what should be conveyed. It can have brilliant comic force:

putting Octavius Caesar's case to Cleopatra, Thidias, with a painfully con-
trived attempt to give her a let-out, explains:

> He knows that you embraced not Antony
> As you did love, but as you fearèd him.
> (*Antony and Cleopatra*, 3.13.55–7)

56. 'You are a spirit, I know' (5.1.42): the reunion of Lear (John Gielgud) and Cordelia
(Peggy Ashcroft) in the production by John Gielgud and Anthony Quayle,
Shakespeare Memorial Theatre, Stratford-upon-Avon, 1950.

'O', says Cleopatra, but her apparently impassive reply can convey a world of meaning. At some points the dialogue indicates pretty clearly what Shakespeare was aiming at. After Desdemona's death has been discovered, Othello falls on the bed with the inarticulate cry 'O, O, O!' to which Emilia responds 'Nay, lie thee down and roar';[43] and in Lady Macbeth's sleep-walking her 'O, O, O!' is glossed by the doctor's comment 'What a sigh is there! The heart is sorely charged.'[44] On a number of occasions Shakespeare uses 'O' as a climactic if inarticulate expression of suffering, as in Othello's 'O Desdemon! Dead Desdemon! Dead! O! O!',[45] and at the moment of death in Hamlet's 'O, O, O, O!' which follows 'The rest is silence' in the Folio text, and Lear's 'O, O, O, O!' which is almost the last sound he makes in the quarto text. And Shakespeare knows that silence itself is one of the actor's most potent tools. *'Holds her by the hand, silent'* is the direction in the Folio text at the emotional climax of *Coriolanus* as the hero struggles with the decision whether to yield to his mother's pleas on behalf of Rome knowing that, in doing so, he will bring about his own death.[46]

To say that Shakespeare's language is inherently dramatic is not to deny that its power and beauty can withstand quotation out of context just as his plots can be retold in narrative or even wordless form without losing all their force. Over the centuries, many anthologies of 'beauties of Shakespeare' have appeared; I have committed one myself.[47] Individual speeches – 'I know a bank . . .',[i] 'The quality of mercy . . .',[ii] 'All the world's a stage',[iii] 'She never told her love . . .',[iv] 'Our revels now are ended . . .'[v] – are learned and quoted as if they were poems in their own right, often with more concern for sound than content. Shakespeare's language has a quality, difficult to define, of memorability that has caused many phrases to enter the common language so that they are no longer thought of as quotations: 'more sinned against than sinning',[vi] 'more in sorrow than in anger',[vii] 'green-eyed jealousy',[viii] 'at one fell swoop',[ix] 'the wish is father to the thought'.[x] The richness and density of

---

i. *A Midsummer Night's Dream*, 2.1.249 ii. *The Merchant of Venice*, 4.1.181 iii. *As You Like It*, 2.7.139 iv. *Twelfth Night*, 2.4.110 v. *The Tempest*, 4.1.148 vi. *King Lear*, 3.2.60 vii. *Hamlet*, 1.2.229–30 viii. *The Merchant of Venice*, 3.2.110 ix. *Macbeth*, 4.3.220 x. *Henry IV, Part Two*, 4.3.221 ('thy wish was father, Harry, to that thought')

Shakespeare's dialogue mean that his plays have much to offer to the reader, and, as we shall see when we look at their reception during the Romantic period, there have been times in the history of even the English theatre when performance texts were so badly mutilated that sensitive readers lost faith in the plays' theatrical viability and declared them actable only in the theatre of the mind.

Shakespeare did not work in a professional vacuum. The changes in his dramatic style and technique over the course of his career are not simply a matter of personal, interior development. He responded to shifts in theatrical and poetic fashion and to the innovations of successive fellow dramatists such as Marlowe, Jonson, Chapman, Middleton, and Fletcher. In doing so he acknowledged a responsibility to entertain, in the broadest sense of that word, but he was not afraid of challenging his audiences. Whatever Hamlet's opinions of the groundlings, playgoers who made popular successes of some of the most intellectually, linguistically, and emotionally demanding – and indeed some of the longest – play scripts ever written do not deserve the condescension and contempt often meted out to them. Shakespeare fulfilled his obligations to his audiences in ways that preserved his artistic integrity and furthered his artistic ambition. It is easy to trace both derivative and recurring elements in his plays, but not to accuse him of abandoning the search for new modes of expression or of falling back on formulaic templates for play composition.

This is a reason why it is possible to think of individual plays as units of a larger whole. What people mean when they use the word 'Shakespeare' varies. It may be simply the man from Stratford in any capacity. It may be a subject studied in schools – 'Have you read much Shakespeare?' – 'No, *it* wasn't on the syllabus'. It may also refer to an impression of the constantly evolving mind and imagination from which all the works emanated, as when Coleridge speaks of 'myriad-minded Shakespeare.'[48] T. S. Eliot overstated the case when he wrote that 'the full meaning of any one of his plays is not in itself alone, but in that play in the order in which it was written, in its relation to all of Shakespeare's other plays, earlier and later: we must know all of Shakespeare's work in order to know any of it'.[49] Still, if all the Shakespeare plays had come down to us anonymously, or with the names of different, otherwise unknown dramatists attached to each of them – *Hamlet*, by Samuel Smiley, *Othello*, by James Nero, *Macbeth*, by Ian McNab, and so on – something would have been lost. I find it interesting that the same mind, at different stages of its evolution, was responsible for both *The Comedy of Errors* and *King Lear* – two very disparate plays both portraying a man who suffers loss of a sense of identity amounting to madness as a consequence of rejection by those he loves best; that (to quote Keats) one man could take 'as much delight in conceiving an Iago as an Imogen';[50] that the writer of the idealizing sonnets to the young man could write with such anguish and self-disgust of his relationship with the dark lady; that the self-delighting poet of *Love's Labour's Lost* and *Venus and Adonis* became the author of the philo-sophically contorted *Troilus and Cressida*; and that the man who could portray such depths of suffering and despair in *Titus Andronicus*, *Othello*, and *King Lear* could offer the consolations apparent in *Hamlet*, *Antony and Cleopatra*, and *The Winter's Tale*. To think about both the links between Shakespeare's plays and the diversity of his achievement may help to explain why an additional meaning of the word 'Shakespeare' is, to quote the words of the *Oxford English Dictionary*, 'A person (occas. a thing) comparable to Shakespeare, esp. as being pre-eminent in a particular sphere.'

Far more than I have found space for in this chapter could be said (and has been said by many other writers) about how Shakespeare wrote his plays and what he accomplished in them. What I have written is intended as a prelude to an account of his extraordinary reputation and influence, and by way of introduction to that I should like to try, however sketchily, to define some of the characteristics of his work that are responsible for its endurance.

Writing of Shakespeare's methods of composition I noted that his texts as they have come down to us leave much unsaid. Stage business, age and appearance of characters, inflections of language, even allocation of speeches are often open to interpretation. This is complicated by uncertainties result-ing from absence of authoritative manuscripts along with deficiencies in the process of transmission – the fact, for instance, that *Hamlet* survives in three substantially different editions, of 1603, 1604, and 1623, and that no one can be sure of their exact relationship. I should not put these factors high on a list of reasons for Shakespeare's enduring popularity, as similar things could be said of other, less highly admired writers; but they help to explain why his plays can go on revealing new interpretative possibilities.

Far more important in this respect, and more special to Shakespeare, is his technique of presenting characters and their actions from their own point of view, arguing as it were on both sides of the question, so that differing balances of sympathies will be suggested in each production (or critical reading) of *The Merchant of Venice* between Jews and Christians, or of *Coriolanus* between patricians and plebeians.

As an artist, Shakespeare invites an aesthetic response. The shapeliness and subtlety of design in units ranging from the phrase, through verse and prose paragraphs, scenes and longer stretches of action to the play's totality have over the centuries been sources of pleasure, as have the wit, lyricism, and epigrammatic concision of much of his writing. And his plays make room for songs and dances, displays of swordsmanship, theatrical shows and spectacle. These qualities are part and parcel of Shakespeare's profession as an entertainer. He and his actors had to 'strive to please' their audiences 'every day', as Feste sings at the end of *Twelfth Night*. One way in which they did so was by displaying the artistry of both the writer and the performer. And the exceptional opportunities and challenges that Shakespeare provides for actors help to explain his enduring appeal even to those who can earn far more money in film or television than in the classical theatre. This appeal is bound up with Shakespeare's reputation as a creator of character. Many roles in his plays, predominantly comic like Bottom, Falstaff, Beatrice and Benedick, Malvolio, and Rosalind, tragic like Richard II and Richard III, Hamlet, Othello, and Lear, and tragicomic like Angelo and Isabella in *Measure for Measure*, Pericles, Leontes, and Prospero have become touchstones of the actor's art; actors want to play them, and audiences want to see their favourites in these roles.

Related to this are the exceptional fullness and density of texture of Shakespeare's plays. Some – *Hamlet, Coriolanus, Cymbeline, Richard III*, for example – are exceptionally long by the standards of their own and indeed any other time. Though the Chorus to *Romeo and Juliet* speaks of 'the two-hours' traffic of our stage', it is hard to believe that most of the plays, even when performed without interruption, did not last longer than this. And it is not just a matter of length. Shakespeare packs an extraordinary amount and range of material into his structures, so that, for example, the tragedies are simultaneously studies of individual states of mind and of issues of government and statecraft, and the comedies hold in balance both romantic and anti-romantic attitudes to love and friendship. And much of his writing is linguistically complex and dense, holding us up to examine simultaneously more than one layer of the verbal texture rather than propelling us forward on a single stream of consciousness. This means that no reading or performance can encompass the full range of any one play. It would be a remarkable reader who could respond in a single reading, even on a subconscious level, to the full range of Shakespeare's allusiveness, his linguistic cross-references, his punning and wordplay and his rhetorical subtleties. Selection is inevitable. Many books on Shakespeare show that anything approaching a full exegesis of a single text will of necessity be many times longer than the text itself. And any actor who tried to unpack every detail of a major role would be in danger of over-loading his performance. This richness of detail means that Shakespeare's most complex plays contain within themselves infinite numbers of possible other plays, depending on how the kaleidoscope is shaken.

I have remarked upon Shakespeare's preference for mythic and legendary tales set in distant places and past times. As we have seen with *Richard II*, his plays may have had topical applications, he may even at times have used history to cloak a concern with contemporary politics, but he is not ostensi-bly and primarily a topical dramatist, and this has helped to create a sense that he is, as Jonson wrote, 'not of an age but for all time'. His plays, though firmly grounded in particularity, are about things that matter to most people in most places at most times, they give classic dramatic and poetic expres-sion to great commonplaces of human existence – love and friendship, hatred and malice, family relationships, parting and reunion, success and failure, loneliness and community, joy and grief, aggression and fear, good and bad government of both the self and the commonwealth. This helps to explain why they are capable of both temporal and cultural translation.

So do their structural strengths, even independent of their particularized language. It is possible to strip some, at least, of the plays right down to their basic story lines, enjoying, for example, *Macbeth* as a murder story or *Romeo and Juliet* as a tale of personal love and family feuding without losing all sense of meaning, as we can see from the enduring and international (if not wholly deserved) success of Mary and Charles Lamb's *Tales from Shakespeare*, in which the plays were first introduced to China and Japan, or even in silent films and wordless ballet versions. Nor are they resistant to linguistic translation. It is an insult to the content of Shakespeare's dramatic writing to claim that it must lose everything in translation. Certainly some of its stylistic qualities, especially those relying on rhythm, rhyme, and wordplay, are likely to suffer. But skilful translators may succeed in replacing them with other qualities which, deriving from the original and attempting to recreate its linguistic theatricality, are nevertheless consonant with the language into which the translation is being made. In any case English-speaking listeners require translation too, even if only that which occurs at the moment of impact as we adjust to the obsolete and archaic qualities of the language of Shakespeare's time. Listeners and readers who depend on a modern translation have the advantage in that the translation will attempt to render intelligible difficulties which native speakers have to endure. It is even possible, heretical though it may be to say so, that translation will improve on the original.

An additional reason for Shakespeare's enduring appeal, and one that marks him out from many other dramatists (while linking him with some of the greatest, such as the Greek tragedians and in his own time, especially, John Webster) is his concern with man not only in society but also in relation to the universe. To this extent, whatever his personal beliefs, he is in the most important sense of the word a religious writer: not a proponent of any particular religion, but a writer who is aware, and makes his spectators aware, of the mystery of things, of mankind's impulse to seek, however unavailingly, for an understanding of how we came to be on earth as well as how we should conduct ourselves now that we are here. This is why he often writes of the explicitly supernatural – in *Hamlet, A Midsummer Night's Dream, Macbeth,* or *The Tempest* – and why even plays that are not directly concerned with other-worldly matters nevertheless invoke a sense of a world elsewhere, as in the contrasting meditations on death by the Duke – 'Be absolute for death. Either death or life / Shall thereby be the sweeter . . .' – and then Claudio – 'Ay, but to die, and go we know not where; / To lie in cold obstruction, and to rot . . .' – in *Measure for Measure* (3.1), or in *Twelfth Night*, Viola's 'And what should I do in Illyria? / My brother, he is in Elysium' (1.2.2–3). And this is why too, *King Lear*, its action determinedly abstracted from the consolations of Christianity, has, with its relentless battering at the gates of the unknown, its profound examination of what differentiates man from the beasts, come to be regarded as Shakespeare's greatest play.

CHAPTER FOUR

The Growth of the Legend: 1623–1744

Shakespeare, whom you and every playhouse bill
Style the divine, the matchless, what you will,
For gain, not glory, winged his roving flight,
And grew immortal in his own despite.

Alexander Pope, 'The First Epistle of the
Second Book of Horace, Imitated' (1737)

FOR MANY YEARS AFTER the publication of the First Folio in 1623 there was little to suggest that Shakespeare would come to be regarded as the greatest dramatist of his generation, let alone of all time. Though Ben Jonson's output was smaller and more limited, his comedies were frequently revived, as were the plays of Francis Beaumont and John Fletcher. New plays, some of them by new dramatists, clamoured for attention, but the King's Men continued to perform Shakespeare. Records are patchy, but we know of revivals of seventeen different plays by Shakespeare, some of them several times, during the quarter century or so after he died. It is in the nature of things that most of the performances we know about were given at court – that is, wherever the royal family was – where *The Winter's Tale* seems to have been a particular favourite. Mouldy though Jonson thought *Pericles*, it was acted at Whitehall after a great feast for the French Ambassador in 1619 and at the Globe in 1631, presumably in a better text than has survived.

Mostly we can only guess why particular plays were chosen, but, rather as Essex's supporters had seen political relevance in *Richard II* during the reign of Queen Elizabeth, so *Henry VIII* assumed topicality at a time of national crisis in the reign of Charles I. The intensely unpopular George Villiers, Duke of Buckingham, overweening favourite successively of James I and of his son Charles, commissioned a performance of the play at the Globe on 29 July 1628, no doubt seeking for parallels between his own situation and that of the Buckingham (no relative) in the play. According to a contemporary letter writer 'he stayed till the Duke of Buckingham was beheaded, and then departed', but would have done better to wait: 'he should rather have seen the fall of Cardinal Wolsey, who was a more lively type of himself, having governed this kingdom eighteen years, as he hath done fourteen'.[1] Within a month the Duke was dead not, as he had feared, as the result of action on behalf of the state but at the hands of a disaffected army officer, John Felton, who, though hailed as a national hero for the deed, was hanged at Tyburn.

Other history plays continued to be acted, though the largely fictional Falstaff was already so dominant a character that reference is made to performances at court of the first and second parts of *Falstaff* rather than of *Henry IV*. Perhaps Falstaff's presence in the cast was the main reason for the revival of *The Merry Wives of Windsor* in 1638. *Richard II*, even though it had been regarded as 'old' and 'long out of use' in 1599 (p. 73), was revived at the Globe in 1631, and *Richard III* at court for the birthday of Queen Henrietta Maria, who loved plays and often performed in court masques, 'it being the first play the Queen saw since her Majesty's delivery of the Duke of York', on 17 November 1633. A few days later the King and Queen enjoyed *The Taming of the Shrew*, and not long after that both *Cymbeline* and *The Winter's Tale*, all performed by the King's Men. Tragedies, too, continued in the repertory, *Othello*, *Hamlet* and *Julius Caesar* all being given before the King and Queen in the winter of 1636–7. Only the King's Men had the right to play Shakespeare, but in 1627 his friend John Heminges, who continued as their business man, paid the Master of the Revels £5 to 'forbid the playing of Shakespeare's plays' by a company performing at the Red Bull.

The plays and especially the poems continued, too, to reappear in print. The 1623 Folio itself was a success: a second edition, with John Milton's first, and anonymously, published poem 'An Epitaph on the Admirable Dramatic Poet, W. Shakespeare' followed in 1632, nine years after the first, whereas it was twenty-four years before the 1616 Folio of Jonson's *Works* was followed by a greatly enlarged second edition. The Shakespeare Folio was to appear again in 1663 with a second issue the following year adding *Pericles* and six other plays not now believed to be by Shakespeare, and then again in 1685. Other plays were independently reprinted from time to time, few of them after 1639. Understandably, *Venus and Adonis* and *The Rape of Lucrece* outstripped the plays in number of printed editions; after all they were intended to be read, though paradoxically they had been omitted from the Folio (perhaps because their original publishers would not let them go); but they went out of fashion after the middle of the century. *Venus and Adonis* went through at least fifteen reprints until 1635, but only one more, in 1675, till the end of the century; *The Rape of Lucrece* lagged behind, with eight editions up to 1632, then one more in 1655; the latter has the special interest of including as its frontispiece the first illustration of any of Shakespeare's works done for an edition, and the first with any pretensions as a work of art: an engraving by William Faithorne (see overleaf) showing Lucrece about to stab herself, to the surprise of her husband, surmounted by an oval miniature of Shakespeare based on the Droeshout engraving.

Perhaps most surprisingly to us, the publication in 1609 of the Sonnets seems to have been a failure. They were not reprinted until 1640 when all but eight of them reappeared in an underhand way in a curious volume published by John Benson misleadingly entitled *Poems Written by Wil. Shakespeare Gent.* This disguises the Sonnets by altering their order, sometimes running several together as if they were a single poem, giving them banal titles such as 'An Invitation to Marriage' (for an amalgam of sonnets from the opening sequence), 'Love's Relief', 'Two Faithful Friends', 'The Picture of True Love', 'Self-flattery of her Beauty', and altering pronouns in three of the sonnets (Nos. 101, 104, and 108, where 'sweet boy' becomes 'sweet love') so that they appear to refer to a female instead of a male. It seems clear that Benson was making at least a token effort to slew the poems in the direction of conventional, boy-to-girl love lyrics. The volume does not include the narrative poems, and adds many verses by writers including Thomas Heywood, Jonson, and Beaumont without identifying them, along with an appendix of 'excellent poems . . . by other gentlemen'.

Benson also printed a Preface implying that all the poems in the volume are by Shakespeare and that they had not previously been published. He claims that they are 'serene, clear, and elegantly plain, such gentle strains as shall recreate and not perplex your brain, no intricate or cloudy stuff to

57. William Faithorne's engraving for the title page of the 1655 edition of
The Rape of Lucrece.

puzzle intellect, but perfect eloquence'. Readers who have puzzled over the more cryptic of the Sonnets may wonder whether these words can really have been written about the poems they know and possibly love. They would be justified in their scepticism; not until 1950 was it shown (and it is still little known) that Benson did not in fact write these sentences as a response to the poems in his volume but that he plagiarized the bulk of his Preface from a poem by Thomas May that has nothing to do with Shakespeare or with the poems that Benson prints.[2]

May was one of the followers and disciples of Ben Jonson, poets and playwrights who styled themselves the Sons, or Tribe, of Ben. The closest equivalent for Shakespeare was William Davenant (1606–68), who may have been Shakespeare's godson, possibly even his natural son. Davenant is in numerous ways the central figure in the development of Shakespeare's reputation during the seventeenth century, and his influence extended well beyond that. Before he was born his mother Jane (or Jennet), like Mrs Mountjoy before her, consulted Simon Forman about her gynaecological troubles – within four years, between 1593 and 1597, she had given birth to five children who were either stillborn or died in infancy. Her husband was a wine-broker, a cultivated, serious-minded man who became Mayor of Oxford and was later described as 'an admirer and lover of plays and play-makers, especially Shakespeare'.[3] This is a taste he could have fostered while living in London; early in the new century he and his wife moved to Oxford, where they kept a large tavern with more than twenty rooms in the centre of the city. Their son William was born there in 1606. Our knowledge of Shakespeare's relationship with the family depends largely but not entirely on the gossipy John Aubrey in his late-seventeenth-century *Brief Lives*. Though Aubrey passes on much unreliable hearsay, he was personally acquainted with two of William Davenant's brothers and his sister and had studied at Oxford; much of what he wrote was implicitly endorsed by the Oxford antiquarian Anthony Wood, so it cannot be dismissed out of hand. Aubrey reported that Shakespeare 'was wont to go into Warwickshire once a year, and did commonly in his journey lie' at the Davenants' tavern. If so, this must have been as a family guest, since taverns (unlike inns) were not lodging houses. Mrs Davenant 'was a very beautiful woman, and of a very good wit, and of conversation extremely agreeable'. William Davenant's

58. William Davenant
crowned with bays as
Poet Laureate: William
Faithorne's engraving
(1662), after a portrait
by John Greenhill, does
nothing to disguise his
syphilitic nose.

brother Robert, a parson, had told Aubrey that Shakespeare had 'given him a hundred kisses' (presumably as a baby).

There was a traditional Oxford belief, which Davenant's most scholarly biographer sees no reason to dismiss, that William Shakespeare stood godfather to William Davenant.[4] A possible objection is that though Shakespeare bequeathed twenty shillings in gold to his seven-year-old godson William Walker, he left not a penny to the ten-year old Davenant. But this might be explained if Davenant was, as he liked to claim, Shakespeare's natural but unacknowledged son; Aubrey says that he 'would sometimes, when he was pleasant over a glass of wine, say that it seemed to him that he writ with the very spirit that Shakespeare [did], and seemed contented enough to be thought his son'. This legend fostered a theory, popular in the early years of the twentieth century, that Jane Davenant was the dark lady of Shakespeare's Sonnets.

59. The Chandos portrait of Shakespeare.

Whatever the truth of Davenant's parentage, there is no question that he fervently admired Shakespeare. A graceful ode 'In Remembrance of Master William Shakespeare' appeared in his collection of poems entitled *Madagascar, with other poems* in 1638, the year in which he became Poet Laureate; it warns any poets who may wish 'To welcome Nature in the early spring' – the time of Shakespeare's death – to avoid the Avon since there the flowers and trees will be in mourning, and the river has wept itself away so that instead of 'a river your mocked eye / Will find a shallow brook'. Davenant also appears to have owned the only portrait allegedly of Shakespeare likely to have been painted in his lifetime. This is the frequently reproduced and imitated Chandos portrait – the one with the earring – so called because it was once owned by the Duke of Chandos; in 1856 it became the first picture presented to the National Portrait Gallery, where it still hangs.[5]

One of Davenant's closest friends was the poet Sir John Suckling, best known as author of the lyric 'Why so pale and wan, fond lover?' and as inventor of the game of cribbage. He too was a passionate admirer of Shakespeare, and echoes his works in a number of his writings. Suckling had himself painted, probably in 1638, the year in which he died, by Anthony Van Dyck, holding a copy of either the First or the Second Folio open at *Hamlet* (Plate 1). The choice of subject matter appears to have been intended not simply as an expression of hero worship but as a kind of artistic manifesto. Literary theorists were increasingly insistent that artists should follow rules of composition derived from the classics – an attitude that was to form a topic of heated argument for well over a century. Suckling is known to have dissociated himself from it, most explicitly on the occasion of a debate at Eton College, in the rooms of one of its fellows, John Hales, who had declared that he would demonstrate Shakespeare's superiority to all 'the ancient poets'. His challengers, according to one of several variant accounts, had 'a great many books' sent down from London, and the matter was thoroughly debated by a distinguished and learned assembly. In conclusion judges chosen from among them 'unanimously gave the preference to Shakespeare'.[6]

Van Dyck's painting bears the Latin motto '*nec et quaesiveris extra*' – 'do not seek outside your self' – a quotation from the Latin poet Persius resembling Sir Philip Sidney's 'Look in thy heart and write'. This appears to be intended as an assertion of an artist's right to exercise personal judgement, to prefer a native writer over the classics, and thus also of Shakespeare's own right to be judged by standards other than those derived from ancient writers.[7] And the fact that the book is open at *Hamlet*, which portrays the most inward-looking of Shakespeare's heroes, reinforces this interpretation.

Davenant's most significant contribution to the story of Shakespeare lies in his work as a man of the theatre. A prolific writer of plays mainly for the indoor, covered Blackfriars playhouse, he was also much involved in the production of spectacular court masques employing elaborate scenery and stage machines. All this activity suffered severe disruption in 1642 when Parliament, ostensibly to 'appease and avert the wrath of God', forbade the performance of stage plays. During the Civil War many of the actors, like Davenant, fought on the King's side. In 1643 Queen Henrietta Maria, on her way after her return from France at the head of a loyalist army to re-join the

King at Oxford, was met in Stratford by his nephew Prince Rupert and held court at New Place, where she stayed for two nights as guest of Susanna Hall, whose father's plays she had often enjoyed. The Globe was pulled down in 1644 to make room for housing, as was the Blackfriars playhouse, which had fallen into a sad state of disrepair, in 1655.

In spite of the Government's efforts theatrical activity was not completely suppressed. At least three of Shakespeare's plays were adapted and abbreviated as 'drolls', brief entertainments performed at fairs, in taverns, and even in surviving theatres, many of which were printed as collections in 1662 and 1673 by Francis Kirkman with a frontispiece which, though it should not be taken as evidence of the way in which plays were staged, gives the first representations of Falstaff and Mistress Quickly ('Hostess'). *The Gravemakers* is based only on the graveyard scene from *Hamlet*; the popularity of Falstaff accounted for *The Bouncing Knight*, which draws on five scenes from *Henry IV, Part One*. The title page of the original, anonymous publication in 1661 of *The Merry Conceited Humours of Bottom the Weaver* announces that it is offered for amateur as well as for professional performance to add to 'the general mirth that is likely very suddenly to happen about the King's coronation'. It claims that the piece has 'often been acted by some of His Majesty's comedians, and lately privately presented by several apprentices for their harmless recreation with great applause'. Gerard Langbaine (1656–92), perhaps the first serious Shakespeare scholar, says that it 'used to be acted at Bartholomew Fair and other markets in the country, by strollers'.[8] This is the earliest of many versions of *A Midsummer Night's Dream* to centre on the play within the play, though it includes other passages; of especial interest is the suggestion among 'The Names of the Actors' that the performers of Oberon and Titania may double Theseus and Hippolyta, and that those who enact Pyramus, Thisbe, and Wall 'likewise may present three fairies'. This anticipates Peter Brook's ground-breaking 1970 RSC production (pp. 374–5) both in the doubling and in having the fairies played by adult males – as may have happened in Shakespeare's time.

In the later part of the period between the overthrow of the monarchy and the restoration to the throne of King Charles II, Davenant, who had been knighted for his war service, managed to evade the prohibition on plays by staging quasi-operatic entertainments drawing on the conventions of the

Changling

The Queene

Simpleton

S.r I Falstafe

French Dancing Ma.

Hostes

Clause

60. The frontispiece to *The Wits* (1662), a collection of drolls published by Francis Kirkman, possibly depicting an improvised stage, shows Falstaff and the Hostess (Mistress Quickly).

indoor theatres in which he had worked before the war. His work with scenic staging bore fruit with the resumption of theatrical activity on the restoration in May 1660 of King Charles II, which saw a seismic shift in the conditions under which plays were presented. For a few months some of the old practices were resumed, but in August Davenant, along with the courtier and playwright Thomas Killigrew, received a royal patent authorizing each of them to form a company of actors and to build a playhouse, creating a virtual monopoly of theatrical activity in the capital. Their companies played initially in converted indoor tennis courts, but in 1663 Killigrew moved to a former riding school off Drury Lane. Davenant, in rivalry, commissioned Christopher Wren to plan a new theatre, and though Davenant himself died in 1668 (as laureate, he was buried in Westminster Abbey) his company transferred to this new Duke's House (Dorset Garden Theatre) in 1671. In the following year Killigrew's theatre burned down and he too commissioned Wren to design a new building which became the ancestor of all the succeeding Drury Lanes.

The new theatre buildings were different from the public playhouses of Shakespeare's time in crucial ways. They were enclosed, and smaller than their forebears. Their stages projected less prominently into the auditorium, and the forestage was marked off from the rear by an embellished proscenium arch such as Inigo Jones had employed for court masques. Entries could be made through doors at each side of the proscenium; a curtain could conceal the arch from the audience; scenery could be painted on wings and on pairs of flats. Staging was highly conventionalized; in general actors spoke from the forestage. The settings, which were more like illustrations than representational scenery, and which often did duty for many different plays, changed in front of the audience; it was unusual for the curtain to fall between acts. A green carpet signified that the play was a tragedy (this custom was observed until well into the nineteenth century). Lighting was provided by chandeliers (such as can be seen in the frontispiece to *The Wits*) hanging above the performers in outdoor as well as indoor scenes. Spectators often crowded on to the stage. Above all, from very early on in the new era women's parts were played by women. The age of the professional actress had arrived.

Like the staging methods, the Restoration audience was closer to that of the earlier private theatres and court performances than to that of the public playhouses. Royal influence was strong. Whereas earlier the theatre had gone to the court, now the court attended the theatre, and imposed its tastes upon it. Higher admission prices resulted in more exclusive and fashion-conscious audiences. Demand for plays was great, and in the absence of an adequate supply of new ones, many written before the Restoration were revived. But tastes had changed, with the result that some older plays rapidly dropped out of the repertoire, while others were heavily adapted to make them more suitable both for the new theatre conditions and for the tastes of spectators.

All this had a crucial effect on the staging of Shakespeare. The right to perform his plays was divided between Davenant's and Killigrew's companies. Davenant was awarded *The Tempest, Measure for Measure, Much Ado About Nothing, Romeo and Juliet, Twelfth Night, Henry VIII, King Lear, Macbeth, Hamlet,* and *Pericles,* all of which he declared he would 'reform and make fit for the company of actors appointed under his direction and command'. This phrasing acknowledges that the plays had come to seem old-fashioned. Spectators with neoclassical leanings found Shakespeare barbarously free in his plotting. Those who went to the theatre hoping for music, dancing, and spectacular stage effects were liable to find him dull. And to both theatre-goers and readers his language seemed dated. John Dryden was to write in 1679 that 'it must be allowed to the present age that the tongue in general is so much refined since Shakespeare's time that many of his words and more of his phrases are scarce intelligible, and of those which we understand, some are ungrammatical, others coarse, and his whole style is so pestered with figurative expressions that it is as affected as it is obscure'.[9]

Plays of the past were commodities that must submit to adaptation or perish. There was no sense that staging methods should adapt themselves to the demands of texts written in a different era: indeed, it was to be close on two centuries before such an historical sense was to develop. Even *Hamlet* seemed out of date to the diarist John Evelyn, who wrote in 1661, 'The old play began to disgust this refined age.'[10] But Evelyn was not much of a theatre-goer, and this is the only reference to Shakespeare in his voluminous diaries. In the same year Samuel Pepys noted seeing the same play performed in a manner that he realized was new: it was, he wrote, 'done with scenes very well, but above all Betterton did the Prince's part beyond imagination'. Pepys saw *Hamlet* again twice that year, and again in 1668 he was 'mightily pleased with it, but above all with Betterton, the best part, I believe, that ever man acted'.

Unlike Evelyn, for Pepys 'going to a play or the like' was among 'the greatest real comforts' that he could expect in the world; he vowed frequently, occasionally with success, to abstain from the pleasure. Between 1660 and 1669 he records some 350 visits to the theatre, including forty-one performances of twelve plays by Shakespeare, some of them in adapted form.[11] He admired *Hamlet* greatly. He saw *Macbeth* nine times and *The Tempest* eight, but clearly Shakespeare was not dominant in the repertoire. Nor was Shakespeare's name necessarily much of an attraction in itself – Pepys mentions it only once in his records of theatre visits, and Davenant's published versions of *The Two Noble Kinsmen* (as *The Rivals*, based mainly on passages now attributed to Fletcher) and *Macbeth* do not mention their original author.

Pepys was ambivalent in his reactions to Shakespeare. He had bad experiences in 1662: seeing *Romeo and Juliet* for the first time, he thought it 'the play of itself the worst that ever I heard in my life'; later that year he went to *A Midsummer Night's Dream* 'which I have never seen before, nor shall ever again, for it is the most insipid ridiculous play that ever I saw in my life'. But the occasion was at least partially redeemed by 'some good dancing and some handsome women, which was all my pleasure'. He was best pleased by the Davenant and Dryden adaptations. Three visits to Davenant's *Macbeth* within four months elicited the judgement that it was 'a most excellent play in all respects, but especially in divertissement, though it be a deep tragedy', and 'though I have seen it often, yet is it one of the best plays for a stage, and variety of dancing and music, that ever I saw'. *The Tempest* pleased on repeated occasions because 'it is so full of variety, and particularly this day I took pleasure to learn the tune of the seaman's dance, which I have much desire to be perfect in, and have made myself so'. 'Variety of dancing and music' was to be a feature of the staging of Shakespeare's plays for many decades to come. In 1726, for instance, *Macbeth* as given at Drury Lane had 'not only all songs, dances, and other decorations proper to the play' – i.e. to Davenant's play – but 'several additional entertainments, viz. after the first act, the Musette by Y. Rainton and Miss Robinson, after the second, the eighth of Corelli's concertos, after the third a wooden shoe dance by

Mr Sandham's children, after the fourth a Dutch skipper by Mr Sandham, after the fifth "La Peirette" by Mr Rogers the Peirror [Pierrot?] and Mrs Brent'.[12] Well into the nineteenth century such additions to the main fare of the evening were customarily given.

Davenant, notwithstanding his veneration for his putative father and all his works, was more radical in his treatment of texts than Killigrew, though his 1661 *Hamlet* for Betterton was relatively unaltered apart from stylistic changes and the omission of around 850 lines – a considerable number, but no more than in most modern stage performances of this exceptionally long text, and far fewer than in most film versions. Davenant's next adaptation however showed how far it was possible to go. *The Law Against Lovers* (1662) combines the main plot of *Measure for Measure* with the Benedick and Beatrice episodes of *Much Ado About Nothing*, omits the 'low' comic episodes, and makes many other alterations and additions. Essentially this is a new play opportunistically cobbled together out of bits of old ones. Pepys thought it 'a good play and well performed, especially the little girl's (whom I never saw act before) dancing and singing', but an anonymous satirist complained that Davenant

> Was a far better cook than a poet,
> And only he the art of it had
> Of two good plays to make one bad.

The Law Against Lovers was not revived after the year of its first performance, but two other adaptations by Davenant were not merely successful in their own time but exerted their influence for many decades, even centuries, to come.

Davenant's *Macbeth*, of 1663–4, reshapes the play according to the tenets of neoclassical criticism, refining, and in the process diluting, its language ('The devil damn thee black, thou cream-faced loon!' becomes 'Now friend, what means thy change of countenance?') and giving the tragedy a more explicit moral purpose with an emphasis on the folly of ambition. Malcolm calls for Macbeth's corpse to

> Hang upon
> A pinnacle in Dunsinane, to show

> To future ages what to those is due
> Who others' right by lawless power pursue.

On a more practical level, Davenant fattens the actresses' parts (arranging a meeting between Lady Macbeth and Lady Macduff, for example) and adds to the spectacle, especially by elaborating the witch scenes with song, dance, and flying machines. In doing so he took several steps further the process by which Middleton, it would seem, had himself elaborated Shakespeare's play by adding the Hecate scenes which, though modern editors print them, are virtually never performed. Indeed it seems likely that Davenant worked not from Shakespeare's play as printed in the Folio but from a manuscript used by Shakespeare's company, since he gives the full text of Hecate's songs which are represented only by their first lines in the Folio. His changes brought the play closer to the condition of opera, as John Downes, prompter to the Duke's company, recognized when he wrote of its 'being dressed in all its finery, as new clothes, new scenes, machines – as flyings for the Witches', and said (with an eye to the business side of things) that 'with all the singing and dancing in it . . . it being all excellently performed, being in the nature of an opera it recompensed double the expense'.[13] Davenant's version totally supplanted Shakespeare's play on the stage until David Garrick's performance in 1744, and it was more than a century after that before standard acting texts abandoned all of Davenant's changes. The singing witches were especially popular.

Davenant enlisted the help of his younger colleague John Dryden (1631–1700), already a successful poet and playwright who was to succeed him as Poet Laureate, for his adaptation of *The Tempest* (subtitled *The Enchanted Island*) that was successfully performed in 1667. Though this is already one of Shakespeare's most regularly constructed plays, Davenant and Dryden add to its symmetry by providing a sister, Dorinda, for Miranda and a brother, Hippolito, for Ferdinand. Dryden, in a Preface written after Davenant's death, praised this as a masterstroke: 'as he was a man of quick and piercing imagination . . . he designed the counterpart to Shakespeare's plot, namely, that of a man who had never seen a woman, that by this means these two characters of innocence and love might the more illustrate and commend each other.' In a curious reversal of earlier practice, Hippolito was played by a woman because, the Prologue explains:

> We . . . by our dearth of youths are forced t'employ
> One of our women to present a boy –
> And that's a transformation you will say
> Exceeding all the magic in the play.

Restoration actresses had no great reputation for chastity, as the Prologue implies:

> Whate'er she was before the play began,
> All you shall see of her is perfect man;
> Or if your fancy will be farther led
> To find her woman, it must be abed.[14]

The tone of the young people's scenes treads a knife edge between innocent charm and smutty lubricity. It would be hard to maintain an appearance of chaste naïvety in passages such as that in which Miranda brings an all-too phallic sword to the wounded Hippolito: 'I am come to ease you', she says, unwrapping the sword. He replies: 'Alas, I feel the cold air come to me. My wound shoots worse than ever.' Miranda 'wipes and anoints the sword', asking 'Does it still grieve you?' Hippolito responds 'Now methinks there's something laid just upon it.'

> MIRANDA: Do you feel no ease?
> HIPPOLITO: Yes, yes, upon the sudden all the pain
> 　　　Is leaving me, sweet heaven, how I am eased!

The Dryden/Davenant *Tempest* was itself adapted in 1674 in a spectacularly operatic version by Thomas Shadwell with music by John Bannister, Pelham Humfrey, and Matthew Locke; Henry Purcell composed a new score for performance in 1690. These adaptations kept Shakespeare's play off the stage until the late eighteenth century; Hippolito and Dorinda remained in the cast list until 1838. (The operatic version was revived at the Old Vic in 1959 for the tercentenary of Purcell's birth.)[15]

Other Shakespeare plays too could be seen in the early years of the Restoration. Killigrew presented John Lacy's *Sauny the Scot*, mostly a prose paraphrase of *The Taming of the Shrew*, with its setting removed from Verona to London, in 1667; 'Sauny' is Petruccio's servant Grumio rewritten as a starring role for Lacy. Davenant's company gave *Twelfth Night* (from 1661); James Howard adapted *Romeo and Juliet* into a tragicomedy, now lost, 'preserving Romeo and Juliet alive, so that when the tragedy was revived again, 'twas played alternately, tragical one day and tragicomical another for several days together', wrote Downes, according to whom *Lear* was played 'as written'. But it is Davenant's *Macbeth*, his acting version of *Hamlet*, and his and Dryden's *Tempest* that were to be of continuing importance in the history of Shakespeare on the stage.

Dryden was the most genuinely creative of the adapters, the one most capable of treating Shakespeare as Shakespeare himself had treated his sources, making of them works of art with their own independent validity. So his *All for Love, or the World Well Lost* (1678), though it is influenced by *Antony and Cleopatra*, is a fine heroic tragedy in its own right. His *Troilus and Cressida, or Truth Found Too Late* draws more heavily on the Shakespeare play (from which he 'undertook to remove that heap of rubbish under which many excellent thoughts lay wholly buried'). Dryden's version was successfully acted between 1679 and 1734; if his strictures on Shakespeare seem absurdly condescending and uncomprehending it is worth remembering that as late as 1920 the theatre historian G. C. D. Odell could write that Dryden's 'play as a play is better, I believe, than Shakespeare's, which is hardly a play at all'.[16] Indeed, we have no record of any performance of Shakespeare's *Troilus and Cressida* from its own time until the twentieth century; its present high reputation represents the success of efforts to apply the historical imagination to studies of theatre and drama.

As earlier, Shakespeare's plays were found relevant to the contemporary political situation: an adaptation of *Richard II* (1681) by Nahum Tate (son of the curiously named Faithful Teate) was suppressed after its second performance because it was thought to reflect unfavourably upon the monarchy, and two avowedly anti-Catholic plays (1681 and 1682) by John Crowne deriving from *Henry VI* were also suppressed. Whereas Tate's *Ingratitude of a Commonwealth* (1682) based on *Coriolanus* failed, his version of *King Lear*, played at Dorset Garden with Betterton as Lear in 1681, survived to become one of the most successful, and in its way notorious, plays of the English stage.

Like Dryden with *Troilus and Cressida*, Tate congratulated himself on his perspicacity in recognizing merits in the original play beneath all its self-evident faults. He found it 'a heap of jewels unstrung and unpolished, yet so dazzling in their disorder that I soon perceived I had seized a treasure'. Above all, he had 'the good fortune to light on one expedient to rectify what was wanting in the regulation and probability of the tale, which was, to run through the whole a love betwixt Edgar and Cordelia, that never changed word with each other in the original'. Tate's method required him to make 'the tale conclude in a success to the innocent distressed persons.' So, in the final scene, Lear presents Edgar with Cordelia:

> Take her crowned,
> Th'imperial grace fresh blooming on her brow.

Gloucester confers his blessing, Kent adds 'Old Kent throws in his hearty wishes too', and Lear suggests to Gloucester,

> Thou, Kent, and I, retired to some cool cell,
> Will gently pass our short reserves of time
> In calm reflection on our fortunes past.

The play ends with a resoundingly moral couplet as Edgar lauds his bride:

> Thy bright example shall convince the world
> – Whatever storms of fortune are decreed –
> That truth and virtue shall at last succeed.

Tate's other changes include the total omission of the Fool and a hotting up of Edmund's sexual intrigue with the wicked sisters.

It is easy to scoff at Tate's *Lear* for its reductiveness, its simplistic neatness of structure, its evasion of tragedy, and its moralistic triteness. His version pales into triviality when compared to its source. Yet Tate's version has been one of the most frequently performed plays in the history of English drama. It continued to be acted (though with an increasing number of reversions to Shakespeare's dialogue) until 1838 when W. C. Macready restored the Fool in what was still a much shortened text. Tate would be easier to forgive had he not been so appallingly successful.

It would be possible to discuss many more adaptations of Shakespeare's plays made during this period. An anonymous version of *A Midsummer Night's Dream* of 1692, *The Fairy Queen*, is of interest mainly because it formed a framework for an unrelated series of spectacular scenes with marvellous music by Henry Purcell, often performed on their own as *The Fairy Queen*; Purcell set no words of Shakespeare's play.[17] Rather similarly, Charles Gildon's *Measure for Measure, or Beauty the Best Advocate* (1700) offers a simplified version of Shakespeare's play in which, as a birthday present, Angelo is presented with Purcell's opera *Dido and Aeneas* arranged as a four-part masque. The epilogue, spoken by Shakespeare's Ghost, suggests an undercurrent of guilt about the ethics of adaptation:

> Enough, your cruelty alive, I knew –
> And must I dead be persecuted too?
> My ghost can bear no more, but comes to rage.
> My plays by scribblers mangled have I seen.
> . . . . .
> O, if Macbeth or Hamlet ever pleased,
> Or Desdemona e'er your passions raised,
> If Brutus or the bleeding Caesar e'er
> Inspired your pity or provoked your fear,
> Let me no more endure such mighty wrongs
> By scribblers' folly or by actors' wrongs.

Charles Johnson's *Love in a Forest* (1723), which combines parts of *As You Like It* with the perennially popular Pyramus and Thisbe scenes from *A Midsummer Night's Dream*, is of interest mainly as a rare attempt to put the romantic comedies, largely neglected since the closing of the theatres, back into circulation. But the adaptation that was to be more influential even than Tate's *Lear* is Colley Cibber's of *Richard III*, first acted in 1699.

This is shorter than the original and has fewer characters; the role of Richard, in which Cibber, an excellent actor in foppish roles, fancied himself, is fattened, while even such major characters as Queen Margaret, Clarence,

61. Thomas Betterton,
by an artist of the
school of Godfrey
Kneller (1646–1723).

Edward IV, and Hastings disappear. Not unintelligently, Cibber opens with episodes showing the death of Henry VI, so providing background information lacking in the original play. This practice has been followed even in productions not primarily based on Cibber, including F. R. Benson's short silent film of 1911, filmed on the stage of the Stratford Memorial Theatre.[18] About one third of Cibber's play is in his own words; these include passages that have passed into the language and are sometimes thought to be by Shakespeare: 'Off with his head; so much for Buckingham', and 'Richard's himself again'. The rest is cobbled together with contributions from most of Shakespeare's other history plays. Though in most respects immeasurably inferior to its model, Cibber's play has great melodramatic potential and provided a virtuoso vehicle of stunning effectiveness for generations of tragic actors. It supplanted Shakespeare's play until the late nineteenth century,

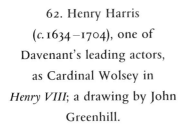

62. Henry Harris (*c.*1634–1704), one of Davenant's leading actors, as Cardinal Wolsey in *Henry VIII*; a drawing by John Greenhill.

influencing in structure and even in language Laurence Olivier's film of 1955, and perhaps still affects the play's theatrical image.

If the story so far has been rather of the way plays were adapted than performed, this is largely because accounts of performance are scarce and patchy. Few of the new breed of actresses shone in Shakespeare, partly because of the neglect of the comedies that provide their best opportunities. Unquestionably the leading male actor from the early years of the Restoration till he died in 1710 was Thomas Betterton (?1635–1710), who excelled as Othello, Brutus, Henry VIII, Hotspur (in his younger days), Falstaff, and, supremely, Hamlet, which he continued to play into his seventies. He was instructed in the role by Davenant who, according to a legend passed on by Downes, had learned about it from a 'Mr Taylor of the Blackfriars Company', who himself was 'instructed by the author Mr Shakespeare'.

63. James Quin as Coriolanus.

Taylor didn't join the King's Men till after Shakespeare died, so the story is probably not true, but it suggests that value attached to links with the pre-Commonwealth theatre. In *Henry VIII* Betterton played the King to the Wolsey of Henry Harris, subject of the first known portrait of an actor in a Shakespeare role.

Betterton's acting style seems to have been characterized by restraint, con- siderable powers of impersonation, great vocal control, and an extraordinary capacity to command the rapt attention of an audience. Cibber described how he 'made the Ghost equally terrible to the spectator as to himself',[19] and an anonymous critic records how 'when Hamlet utters this line, upon the Ghost's leaving the stage, ". . . *See – where he goes – ev'n now – out at the portal*" the whole audience hath remained in a dead silence for near a minute, and then – as if recovering all at once from their astonishment – have joined as one man in a thunder of universal applause'.[20] Both Betterton's speaking and his movements would seem inordinately stylized to us, but he was able to convince contemporary theatre-goers of the reality of the passions that he portrayed. His principal leading ladies were his wife Mary Saunderson (*c.*1637–1712), Elizabeth Barry (1658–1713), and Anne Brace-girdle (*c.*1663–1748), but sadly little evidence survives of their performances in Shakespearian roles.

Of all actors the one who seems to have reached the farthest extreme of stylization without altogether forfeiting the respect of audiences is James Quin (1693–1766), who made a great hit as Falstaff in 1720 and remained a leading performer until he retired in 1751. The engraving of him as Coriolanus in James Thomson's play (only distantly related to Shakespeare's) which illustrates the plume, full wig, tutu, and truncheon that were among the conventional appurtenances of the tragic hero cannot but seem ludicrous now. He spent the closing years of his career in rivalry with the young David Garrick, of whose acting style he declared, 'If the young fellow is right, I and the rest of the players have been all wrong.' Quin's declamatory artificiality induced one of the violent reactions that recur periodically in the history of acting, and the prime agent of reaction was Charles Macklin (1699–1797), famous above all for his Shylock, a role that he first played in 1741. Before then it had generally been given to low comedians in a version by George Granville, Lord Lansdowne. Macklin's text was closer to the original, leaving Shylock's role almost complete. 'This is the Jew / That Shakespeare drew' proclaimed a couplet attributed, probably falsely, to Alexander Pope. Macklin retained the hooked nose and red hair traditionally associated with the role, adding a red beard and hat based on his extensive reading about Jews and Venice. He played the character with a passion and ferocity that, it is reported, were to render George II sleepless (after, not during the performance). During the first performance, according to an account attributed to Macklin himself, at his portrayal of 'the contrasted passions of joy for the Merchant's losses and grief for the elopement of Jessica . . . The whole house was in an uproar of applause – and I was obliged to pause between the speeches, to give it vent, so as to be heard.'[21] (This passage gives the impression of a volatility of audience response, with applause frequently interrupting the performance, which recurs again and again in accounts of acting from Shakespeare's own time at least to the end of the nineteenth century.)

The publication of texts of the plays as acted during the interregnum and in Restoration theatres foreshadowed a long-standing practice, which was particularly prevalent during the Victorian era and has still not completely died out, of offering to the public acting editions which could serve as souvenirs of particular productions. These were relatively ephemeral. Single-text editions of the original plays dwindled in number during the later part of the seventeenth century, and transmission of the 'authentic' text depended mainly on successive reprints of the Folio. Though these incorporated intelligent attempts to correct error and to improve presentation, they also introduced corruption and did not represent a systematic attempt to edit the texts in any modern sense of the word. A new era arrived when the publisher Jacob Tonson who, followed by his great-nephew of the same name, was to exert major influence over Shakespeare's publishing fortunes for half a century, decided that the Folio had had its day.

Tonson made a fortune out of Milton's *Paradise Lost* and worked closely, though not always amicably, with Dryden, who described him satirically in lines written under his portrait:

> With leering looks, bull-faced, and freckled fair;
> With two left legs, and Judas-coloured hair,
> And frowzy pores, that taint the ambient air.

(Pope also called him 'left-legged Jacob', so there must have been something odd about his gait.) Around 1708 Tonson commissioned Nicholas Rowe to prepare a new edition of Shakespeare's plays in the smaller format in which he had already issued plays by Aphra Behn and Milton's poems. Like the Folio, this edition, published in six volumes in 1709, is essentially one for the gentleman's library, not for the theatre practitioner or the casual purchaser.[22]

Rowe, born in 1674, was a prolific poet and playwright whose most successful play, *Jane Shore* (1714), was professedly written 'in imitation of Shakespeare's style'. In editing Shakespeare's complete plays Rowe inaugurated a practice which has prevailed with very few exceptions to the present day, of revising the text of the most recently published edition, which for him was the Fourth Folio, of 1685. His revision is often perfunctory in the extreme. He did nothing to rethink the Folio's contents, retaining the apocryphal plays added in 1685 and still omitting the poems (which however appeared separately also in 1709, with the sonnets reprinted from Benson's edition). He restored passages of *Hamlet* from a late printing of the edition published in 1604, and made a number of sensible corrections throughout the volume, but his main purpose, and the one that, for better or for worse, has had the longest-lasting influence on our apprehension of Shakespeare, was to bring the presentation of the plays up to date. He alters spelling and punctuation to conform with the practice of his day. He continues the process begun in the Folio of dividing the plays into acts and, less systematically, scenes, like plays of his own time. He provides each of them with lists of the characters, arranged in order of social status and naming men before women, usually followed with a statement of the general location of the action – 'Scene partly at Venice, and partly at Belmont, the Seat of Portia upon the Continent' for *The Merchant of Venice* – and for some of the plays, especially those that were in the repertoire of the theatres of his time, he provides indications of the location of individual scenes. In this he often has in mind stock scenery that would have been used in the theatre for places such as 'a palace', 'the street', 'a prison', 'a wood', 'a heath'. Occasionally indeed he precisely calls for the staging methods of the day: 'Scene draws' – i. e. the painted shutters are drawn apart – 'and discovers Juliet on a bed' and, in *Macbeth*, 'A dark Cave, in the middle a great Cauldron burning' and, for the Witches, 'They rise from the Stage, and fly away'. Although these editorial practices often convey an impression of the plays very different from that which they would originally have created, they have been followed by generations of editors; the provision of scene locators for plays that would originally have been performed on an unlocalized stage is only slowly being abandoned, and although in planning the Oxford edition of *The Complete Works* I was strongly tempted not to mark act and scene divisions, I finally and reluctantly decided against a step that would have created difficult problems in referring to the plays, while inviting the designer to minimize their prominence.

Rowe's edition was advertised as 'adorned with cuts' – engravings. Except for the *Lucrece* mentioned above, this was the first time that an edition of Shakespeare had been illustrated with anything other than the Droeshout engraving. The anonymous illustrations to the plays, like the presentation of the text, also bring them partly up to date. As in contemporary stagings, many of the characters are dressed in modern clothes – full-bottomed wigs and three-cornered hats for gentlemen, hoods and shawls for ladies. And a number of the illustrations reflect contemporary stage practice, either real or imagined. Many of them, such as those to *Henry V* and *A Midsummer Night's Dream*, have landscape or interior backgrounds such as would have been painted on flats; and in that to *Richard III* the ghost of Richmond is seen emerging from the floor as out of a stage trap.

Rowe's edition is significant too for its provision of the first formal biography of Shakespeare. During the seventeenth century sporadic attempts had been made to collect and record information about Shakespeare's life. Some of them, such as John Aubrey's, long remained in manuscript, but Rowe seems not to have known them. He had help from Betterton, to whose performance of Hamlet he pays eloquent tribute, and whose 'veneration for the memory of Shakespeare . . . engaged him to make a journey into Warwickshire on purpose to gather up what remains he could of a name for which he had so great a value'. It's Rowe who reports that, in spite of all his efforts, he could discover nothing of Shakespeare as an actor except that 'the top of his performance was the Ghost in his own *Hamlet*'. Rowe also offers criticism of his author, appreciative of his powers of characterization – 'Falstaff is allowed by everybody to be a masterpiece' – and not without originality in his assessment of *The Merchant of Venice*: 'though we have seen that play received and acted as a comedy' – this would have been in Granville's adaptation – 'and the part of the Jew performed by an excellent comedian, yet I cannot but think it was designed tragically by the author. There appears in it such a deadly spirit of revenge, such a savage fierceness and fellness, and such a bloody designation of cruelty and mischief, as cannot agree either with the style or characters of comedy.' This shrewdly anticipates Macklin's reinterpretation of the role. Rowe's biographical essay, factually inaccurate and inadequate though it is,

64. 'We split! We split!' (1.1.58). The frontispiece to *The Tempest* in Rowe's edition. Prospero with his staff is to be seen on the island at the far left, and Ariel hovers over the mast.

was reprinted with variations in many subsequent editions and was to remain the standard account of the life for close on a century.

Nicholas Rowe edited the plays from the point of view of a man of the theatre. Shakespeare's next editor, the great poet Alexander Pope (1688–1744), whose edition, also published by Tonson, and also in six volumes, appeared from 1723 to 1725, took the diametrically opposed approach of a man of letters; indeed, Pope displayed contempt for Shakespeare's actors, whom he blamed for supposed additions and omissions, redistribution of speeches, and interpolation of spectacle.[23] Admirably, he was more systematic than Rowe in consulting early quartos and emending the text from them, and in modernizing spelling and punctuation; less admirably, he imposed his own literary taste on Shakespeare and on his readers in emendations deriving from his own imagination – 'all our yesterdays have lighted fools / The way to study [for 'dusty'] death' (*Macbeth*, 5.5.21–2) – in attempts to make Shakespeare's grammar and the metre of his verse conform to his own standards, and notoriously in expressing criticism of his author through officious presentation of his text. 'Some suspect passages which are excessively bad . . . are degraded to the bottom of the page.' Pope especially disliked comic wordplay, so much of *The Comedy of Errors* – already the shortest play – is ditched, as is the Porter's speech in *Macbeth*. He is harsh on the clown scenes in *The Two Gentlemen of Verona*, which he suspects may have been interpolated by 'the actors'; they are 'composed of the most trifling conceits to be accounted for only by the gross taste of the age he lived in'. He wishes he 'had authority to leave them out', but failing that has at least been able to 'set a mark of reprobation' – three daggers – 'upon them throughout this edition'. And in fact he did omit many passages, totally without authority. On the other hand 'some of the most shining passages are distinguished by commas in the margin'; speeches such as Prospero's 'Our revels now are ended' and 'Ye elves of hills . . .' receive marks of commendation, and really good scenes, such as the banquet scene (3.4) in *Macbeth*, have a star placed beside them, as in a child's exercise book. Rather similarly, the edition includes analytical indexes (not compiled by Pope himself) to, for example, 'thoughts and sentiments' and a 'table of the most considerable' speeches offering readers guidance to the tastiest and most uplifting bits – a kind of do-it-yourself Shakespeare anthology.

Unsurprisingly, Pope's waspishness stung critics into retaliatory action, stimulating the first complete scholarly monograph to be written on Shakespeare. This is Lewis Theobald's *Shakespeare Restored*, of 1726, subtitled 'An attempt designed not only to correct Mr Pope's most erroneous edition of this poet, but likewise to restore the true reading of Shakespeare in all the editions of his works hitherto published'. Theobald's most famous attempt to restore a true reading comes in Mistress Quickly's account of Falstaff's death (*Henry V*, 2.3.9–25); the Folio has 'after I saw him fumble with the Sheets, and play with Flowers, and smile vpon his fingers end, I knew there was but one way: for his Nose was as sharpe as a Pen, and a Table of greene fields'. Arguing strongly against Pope's ingenious but fictional explanation that the final clause represents an intrusive direction for a table to be carried in by a property man (otherwise unknown to fame) named Greenfield, Theobald, assisted by his knowledge of the handwriting of Shakespeare's time, came up with the suggestion that what Quickly should actually say is 'a babbled of green fields'. This brilliant reading has stood the test of time and is accepted by almost all scholars.[24]

Theobald's book became the centre of a squabble conducted in part at a high literary level. His play *Double Falsehood*, claiming, as we have seen, to be based on the lost *Cardenio*, was acted in the year after his attack on Pope appeared. In the second, 1728 edition of Pope's Shakespeare 'a thing called the *Double Falsehood*' was named among 'those wretched plays' falsely attributed to Shakespeare; nevertheless, Pope incorporated many of Theobald's best emendations. In the same year appeared *The Dunciad*, Pope's long satirical poem which has 'piddling Theobald' as its chief dunce. Theobald did not take the insult lying down. His book had demonstrated that he was far better qualified as an editor of Shakespeare than Pope, and Tonson was persuaded to commission him to prepare yet another edition, which appeared in 1733. Theobald's editorial work was more thorough than that of either Rowe or Pope, he provided many explanatory notes based on his exceptionally wide reading in the literature of Shakespeare's time, and his edition, long undervalued, is now recognized as one of the most important of all contributions to the editorial tradition.

By contrast, its expensively produced and highly priced successor of 1744, prepared by Thomas Hanmer, a Tory politician who retired from the post of Speaker of the House of Commons in 1721 to devote himself to literature and his garden, is one of the worst, distinguished only by its elegant bindings and handsome typography – it is the first Shakespeare edition to be published by Oxford University Press – and its fine engravings by Hubert Gravelot, mostly of charming, Watteau-esque drawings by Francis Hayman. Hanmer based his edition closely on Pope's while consigning to the foot of the page even more passages that he disliked than his predecessor. He emends by intuition, in *Othello* altering the description of Cassio as 'a fellow almost damned in a fair wife' to '. . . damn'd in a fair phyz [i.e. physiognomy, face]' on the grounds that 'Cassio's beauty is often hinted at, which it is natural enough for other rough soldiers to treat with scorn'. In *The Winter's Tale* he alters the setting of the pastoral scenes from Bohemia (which notoriously has no coast) to Bythinia, considering Bohemia 'a blunder and an absurdity of which Shakespeare in justice ought not to be thought capable' (this change was to be adopted by the no less literal-minded Victorian actor-manager Charles Kean in his 1856 production).

All editors adopt a critical attitude to the texts they present, though few of them go as far as Pope and Hanmer in practical application of their opinions. Theatrical adaptation is a more extreme form of practical criticism, the author reshaping the play according to principles of playwriting, however unconsciously formulated, different from those that lie behind the original. As we have seen, some of the Restoration adaptations are accompanied by prefaces and other documents expressing views of the Shakespeare play, generally as a way of justifying attempts to improve it. More formal literary criticism was slow to develop and, when appreciative, tended strongly to praise Shakespeare as a writer who owed more to nature than to art. In 'L'Allegro' (*c.*1632) Milton writes of him as 'fancy's child' who warbles 'his native woodnotes wild', and around 1661 Thomas Fuller, in his *Worthies of England* (published posthumously in 1662) wrote that 'his learning was very little' and that 'nature itself' was all his art. Mistaken though this view is, it produced from Fuller a memorable contrast between Shakespeare and Jonson,

> which two I behold like a Spanish great galleon and an English man-of-war: Master Jonson, like the former, was built far higher in learning: solid but slow in his performances. Shakespeare, with the English man-of-war, lesser in bulk but lighter in sailing, could turn

65. 'No more, no more' (*As You Like It*, 1.2.205). Orlando throws Charles the wrestler and wins Rosalind's heart in Francis Hayman's drawing engraved for Hanmer's edition.

with all tides, tack about, and take advantage of all winds by the quickness of his wit and invention.[25]

At around the same time Margaret Cavendish, Duchess of Newcastle (herself a dramatist) was anticipating a long line of character criticism when, in a rambling but shrewd letter published in 1664 which constitutes 'the first critical prose essay on Shakespeare',[26] she wrote that 'Shakespeare did not want wit to express to the life all sorts of persons . . . one would think he had been transformed into every one of those persons he hath described.'[27] She even compliments him with the notion that 'one would think that he had been metamorphosed from a man to a woman, for who could describe Cleopatra better than he hath done, and many other females of his own creating . . .' Excellence of characterization is a theme too of the Preface to Pope's edition, with its fulsome if exaggerated claim that 'every single character in Shakespeare is as much an individual as those in life itself . . . had all the speeches been printed without the very names of the speakers I believe one might have applied them with certainty to every speaker.' Try putting that into practice with characters such as Ross, Angus, and Menteith in *Macbeth*, whose names sound like those of railway stations along a minor branch line in Scotland, and who have no more individuality.

Slowly Shakespeare's reputation was overtaking that of all his rivals. Though Dryden was often both explicitly and implicitly censorious, in his *Essay of Dramatic Poesy* (1668) he praises Shakespeare as 'the man who of all modern, and perhaps ancient, poets had the largest and most comprehensive soul'. The first historian of the English theatre, Gerard Langbaine, who claimed to own copies of 980 English plays and masques along with drolls and interludes, declares in his pioneering *Account of the English Dramatic Poets* (1692) 'I esteem his plays beyond any that have ever been published in this language', and makes the first serious attempt to identify the literary sources of Shakespeare's works.

There were dissentients from the chorus of praise, most pungently Thomas Rymer, who had written a tragedy in rhymed verse, *Edgar, or the English Monarch*, conforming to the dramatic laws of antiquity. The fact that it remained unacted may have fuelled his sustained and ferocious attacks in his treatise *A Short View of Tragedy* (1693) on *Julius Caesar* and, especially,

Othello, which he describes as 'none other than a bloody farce, without salt or savour'. Looking for morals in the play, he says that it offers 'a caution to all maidens of quality how, without their parents' consent, they run away with blackamoors' and 'a warning to all good wives that they look well to their linen'. Appalling to us in its social attitudes – 'with us a Moor might marry some little drab or small-coal wench' – and uncomprehending in its literalism, Rymer's criticism forms a salutary lesson in the danger of applying inappropriate criteria to a work of art. As even Dryden wisely wrote, 'we know, in spite of Mr Rymer, that genius alone is a greater virtue (if I may so call it) than all other qualifications put together . . . I reverence Mr Rymer's learning, but I detest his ill nature and arrogance.'[28] But the conflict between admiration for Shakespeare's 'natural' genius and anxiety about his violation of principles of composition derived from the ancients was to continue for many decades, largely unsustained by understanding that his works are informed by an artistry that is different from, but no less valid and rigorous, than theirs.

In the early decades of the eighteenth century Shakespeare is frequently discussed, usually appreciatively, in essays appearing in the *Tatler*, the *Spectator*, and in the columns of the burgeoning newspaper industry. Artists had begun to illustrate his works, mostly so far in editions though in 1727 William Hogarth (1697–1764) started work on his painting *Falstaff Examining his Recruits*, probably the first independent illustration of a Shakespeare play by a major artist, a subject which gives scope for Hogarth's talents for satirical characterization. Like many later paintings it assumes artistic licence to conflate separate moments of the same play (here *Henry IV, Part Two*): Falstaff's interrogation of Shallow's men in the earlier part of Act Three, Scene Two, merges with the later moment when Bardolph slips him a bribe 'to free Mouldy and Bullcalf' (Plate 12). And in 1728 Hogarth made an engraving of *Henry VIII and Anne Boleyn* probably based on the lavish Drury Lane production of the previous year in which the procession for Anne's coronation closely imitated that for George II, crowned only a couple of weeks before. This episode was so popular that it was soon given independently as an afterpiece to unrelated plays.

Before long, too, serious efforts were made to formalize Shakespeare's pre-eminence among British cultural icons. In 1735 a bust was included in the

66. The Scheemakers
statue in Westminster
Abbey.

Temple of British Worthies at Stowe, and soon afterwards attempts were in
hand to give him that place in the national pantheon, Westminster Abbey,
that he had been unable to fill on his death. No shoving up was necessary:
1741 saw the erection of a handsome statue designed by William Kent,
sculpted by Peter Scheemakers and paid for by public subscription. Originally it showed Shakespeare pointing to a blank scroll, but this caused such

ridicule that the dean had the gap supplied by a passage misquoted from *The Tempest* which draws on the association already made between Shakespeare and Prospero:

> The Cloud cupt Tow'rs,
> The Gorgeous Palaces,
> The Solemn Temples,
> The Great Globe itself
> Yea all which it inherit
> Shall Dissolve;
> And like the baseless Fabrick of a Vision
> Leave not a wreck behind.

In 1736 the *Daily Journal* had printed an anonymous piece announcing 'a noble attempt to revive the stage by a club of women of the first quality and fashion'. This was the Shakespeare Ladies' Club, headed by the Countess of Shaftesbury, whose members supported the Abbey project and who campaigned successfully for an increase in the number of performances of Shakespeare's plays, especially the comedies, which had been largely neglected. Perhaps their greatest achievement lay in stimulating the 1740 production at Drury Lane of *As You Like It*, with the delightful and still popular songs of Thomas Arne, which provided Hannah Pritchard with her first great triumph in the role of Rosalind, so paving the way for her historic partnership with Garrick; she also played Viola in *Twelfth Night* in the following year. In the following theatre season, one in every four performances was of a Shakespeare play. This was an auspicious year too as that in which David Garrick, who was to dominate the Shakespearian scene for many years to come, made his first appearance in London.

★

What of Shakespeare overseas? In his own time, remarkably, *Hamlet* and *Richard II* had been acted aboard an East India ship, the *Dragon*, when it had been long becalmed off the coast of Sierra Leone. The ship's captain, William Keeling, recorded in his diary for 5 September 1607 'we gave the tragedy of *Hamlet*', and for 30 September that Captain William Hawkins, commander of his sister ship the *Hector*, 'dined with me, when my company acted *King Richard the Second*'. Then, six months later, 'I invited Captain Hawkins to a fish dinner, and had *Hamlet* acted aboard me; which I permit to keep my people from idleness and unlawful games, or sleep.' The deck of a ship closely resembled the stage of the Globe:

> A wooden stage is indistinguishable from a wooden deck, a trap door resembles a ship's hatch, a tiring house façade is remarkably similar to a forecastle, a theatre's 'cellarage' is structurally parallel to below-decks.[41]

Both plays performed had reached print, and we can only assume that Keeling had had the foresight to include one or more copies in his ship's stores.

Companies of English actors who toured Germany and neighbouring countries in and after Shakespeare's lifetime included in their repertoires garbled versions of some of his plays, initially in English but later in German translation. One of these, *Der Bestrafte Brudermord* – known in English as *Fratricide Punished* – survives in a text of 1710 and has occasionally been performed in modern times as a curiosity; only about one fifth the length of the original, it reaches a climax of absurdity when Hamlet, threatened on both sides by two assassins, asks permission to pray, after which he will give the signal for them to fire; he does so but falls flat on his face at that very moment, with the result that they shoot each other.[30]

The first direct translation into German comes only at the very end of this period, 1741, when Baron von Borck, Prussian Ambassador to England – impelled, he claimed, by nothing more creditable than idleness – turned *Julius Caesar*, prose and all, into alexandrines.[31] No doubt because of its classical subject matter and relative chasteness of style, the same play had special appeal for Voltaire who, exiled to England between 1726 and 1729, read and saw some of Shakespeare's tragedies, was influenced by them in plays that he wrote himself, and translated speeches from *Hamlet*; his version of 'To be or not to be' is said to be the first translation of Shakespeare into French. It occurs in the *Philosophical Letters*, printed in English translation in 1733 then in French in the following year, in which he tells his countrymen of Shakespeare's 'natural and sublime genius' which nevertheless lacked 'the smallest spark of taste' and was 'devoid of the remotest idea of the rules'. As a good neoclassicist he had very ambivalent feelings even about *Hamlet* which is, he was to write later,

> a coarse and barbarous piece, which would not be tolerated by the lowest rabble of France and Italy. In it Hamlet becomes mad in the second act, his mistress becomes mad in the third; the prince kills the father of his mistress under pretence of killing a rat, and the heroine throws herself into the river. A grave is dug upon the stage; the grave-diggers indulge in quibbles worthy of themselves, while holding in their hands the skulls of the dead. Prince Hamlet replies to their abominable vulgarities by stuff not less disgusting. During this time one of the actors makes the conquest of Poland. Hamlet, his mother, and his step-father drink together upon the stage. They sing at the table, they quarrel, they beat one another, they kill one another. One would suppose this work to be the fruit of the imagination of a drunken savage. Nevertheless, the play contains some sublime strokes worthy of the greatest geniuses. It seems as if nature had been pleased to bring together in the head of Shakespeare whatever there is most forcible and grand, along with whatever is of lowest and most detestable that coarseness without wit can exhibit.[32]

By the early 1740s, then, Shakespeare's pre-eminence in Britain was assured. His plays were performed in increasing numbers; many of them were still given in heavily adapted form, but the voice of protest was heard, efforts were slowly being made to restore original texts, and the repertoire was expanding, largely as the result of the efforts of the Ladies' Club. Publication proceeded apace, and understanding of textual matters was increasing by fits and starts. A modest amount of music had been composed for and inspired by the plays. Critical studies were pretty rudimentary, there was little understanding of the theatrical conditions of Shakespeare's time, and studies of his life and of his language were primitive. Overseas, Shakespeare had not yet made much headway. That would soon change.

CHAPTER FIVE

The Age of Garrick – Shakespeare Celebrated: 1741–1789

Our Shakespeare compared is to no man,
Nor Frenchman nor Grecian nor Roman,
Their swans are all geese to the Avon's sweet swan,
And the man of all men was a Warwickshire man,
    Warwickshire man,
    Avon's swan,
And the man of all men was a Warwickshire man.

David Garrick, from *Shakespeare's Garland* (1769),
songs for the Stratford Jubilee

DAVID GARRICK DOMINATES the story of Shakespeare from the time of his debut as Richard III in 1741 until he died in 1779. He was one of the greatest and most versatile actors in the history of the British theatre, and he excelled in an unusually wide range of Shakespearian roles. He was a successful playwright who applied his talents to the adaptation, and to some extent the restoration, of Shakespeare's plays. He was an exceptionally capable manager who instituted major reforms in theatre administration and in the production of plays. His interest in the history of the drama led him to compile an important collection of early printed texts. His veneration for Shakespeare was largely responsible for putting Stratford-upon-Avon on the map as the centre of Shakespearian pilgrimage and stimulated other creative artists – writers, painters, sculptors, and composers – to contribute to the

A Copy of the PLAY BILL *that announced the first appearance of* Mr. GARRICK.

October 19th, 1741.

GOODMAN'S FIELDS.

At the late Theatre in Goodman's Fields, this Day will be performed,

A Concert of Vocal and Instrumental Music,
DIVIDED INTO TWO PARTS.

TICKETS AT THREE, TWO, AND ONE SHILLING.

Places for the Boxes to be taken at the Fleece Tavern, near the Theatre.

N. B. Between the Two Parts of the Concert will be presented an Historical Play, called the

LIFE AND DEATH OF

King Richard the Third.

CONTAINING THE DISTRESSES OF K. HENRY VI.

The artful acquisition of the Crown by King Richard.

The Murder of Young King Edward V. and his Brother in the Tower,

THE LANDING OF THE EARL OF RICHMOND,

And the Death of King Richard in the memorable Battle of Bosworth Field, being the last that was fought between the Houses of York and Lancaster; with many other true Historical Passages.

The Part of King Richard by A GENTLEMAN,
(Who never appeared on any Stage),

King Henry, by Mr. GIFFARD,   Richmond, Mr. MARSHALL,

Prince Edward, by Miss HIPPISLEY,   Duke of York, Miss NAYLOR,

Duke of Buckingham, Mr. PATERSON,   Duke of Norfolk, Mr. BLAKES,   Lord Stanley, Mr. PAGETT,

Oxford, Mr. VAUGHAN,   Tressel, Mr. W. GIFFARD,   Catesby, Mr. MARR,   Ratcliff, Mr. CROFTS,

Blunt, Mr. NAYLOR,   Tyrrel, Mr. PUTTENHAM,   Lord Mayor, Mr. DUNSTALL.

The Queen, Mrs. STEEL,   Duchess of York, Mrs. YATES,

And the Part of Lady Anne, by Mrs. GIFFARD.

WITH

Entertainments of Dancing,
By Mons. FROMET,   Madame DAVALT,   and the Two Masters and Miss GRANIER.

To which will be added a Ballad Opera, of One Act, called

The Virgin Unmask'd.

The Part of Lucy, by Miss HIPPISLEY.

Both of which will be performed Gratis, by Persons for their Diversion.

The Concert will begin exactly at Six o'Clock.

67. The playbill for Garrick's sensational first appearance as Richard III, ostensibly part of a programme of 'vocal and instrumental music'.

celebration and reinterpretation of the man who was central to his professional life.

Received ideas about Shakespearian acting had already taken a severe knock from Macklin's reinterpretation of Shylock (pp. 197–8) when Garrick, aged twenty-four, created a sensation by his performance as Richard III in Cibber's adaptation at the small theatre in Goodman's Fields in the East End of London. As this was not one of the two patent theatres, Drury Lane and Covent Garden, which since 1737 had enjoyed exclusive rights to present plays, the management observed the fiction, as the playbill shows, that the theatre was no longer a theatre and that the play, along with the customary after-piece, a ballad opera called *The Virgin Unmasked*, was no more than a free gift to those paying to attend 'a concert of vocal and instrumental music'. The playbill's claim that Garrick had 'never appeared on any stage' was not true; indeed, he had already performed at this same theatre, anonymously, as Harlequin in a pantomime. His success as Richard was instantaneous, and he was rapidly engaged to play at Drury Lane, which he managed jointly from 1747 to 1776. A reviewer praised his debut performance in terms that indicate what he was reacting against:

> He is not less happy in his mien and gait, in which he is neither strutting nor mincing, neither stiff nor slouching. When three or four are on the stage with him, he is attentive to whatever is spoke, and never drops his characters when he has finished a speech by either looking contemptuously on an inferior performer, unnecessary spitting, or suffering his eyes to wander through the whole circle of spectators . . .[1]

One wonders exactly how much spitting was acceptable.

Four years later William Hogarth, in one of the finest and most frequently reproduced of all theatrical paintings, portrayed Garrick at a climactic moment of the role as Richard wakes from his ghost-ridden dream:

> Give me a horse! Bind up my wounds!
> Have mercy, Heaven! Ha, soft! – 'Twas but a dream –
> But then so terrible it shakes my soul.[2]

Garrick's backward stretching pose with outstretched hand is not unsuggestive of conventional ways of representing horror; but then, no acting is ever totally naturalistic (Plate 10).

The art of theatre criticism, both formal and informal, was beginning to develop in Garrick's time, and did so all the more rapidly because of the admiration he inspired; also, he loved to be painted; there are probably more paintings and engravings of him in his roles than of any other actor. As a result we have more detailed descriptions and representations of his acting than of any of his predecessors (and many of his successors). Like Betterton, he was especially famous as Hamlet, which he played repeatedly from 1742 until he retired at the age of fifty-nine in 1776. The German philosopher and scientist Georg Christoph Lichtenberg sent back home wonderfully detailed and eloquent accounts of his performance while visiting England in 1775. Garrick's 'start' on seeing the Ghost – aided, astonishingly, by the use of a mechanical wig which could be manipulated to cause his shock of hair to rise on the words 'Look, my lord, it comes'[3] – was a well-known 'point' in his performance; Lichtenberg tells how,

> as Hamlet moves towards the back of the stage slightly to the left and turns his back on the audience, Horatio starts, and saying: 'Look, my lord, it comes', points to the right, where the ghost has already appeared and stands motionless, before anyone is aware of him. At these words Garrick turns sharply and at the same moment staggers back two or three paces with his knees giving way under him; his hat falls to the ground and both his arms, especially the left, are stretched out nearly to their full length, with the hands as high as his head, the right arm more bent and the hand lower, and the fingers apart; his mouth is open: thus he stands rooted to the spot, with legs apart, but no loss of dignity, supported by his friends, who are better acquainted with the apparition and fear lest he should collapse . . . At last he speaks, not at the beginning, but at the end of a breath, with a trembling voice: 'Angels and ministers of grace defend us!', words which supply anything this scene may lack and make it one of the greatest and most terrible which will ever be played on any stage.[4]

Henry Fielding paid an oblique tribute to Garrick's Hamlet in his novel *Tom Jones* (1749) with Mr Partridge's reaction 'He the best player! Why, I could act as well myself, I am sure, if I had seen a ghost, I should have looked in the very same manner, and had done just as he did – the King for my money; he speaks all his words distinctly, half as loud again as the others – anybody may see he's an actor.'

Garrick's attitude to Shakespeare's texts was ambivalent. Though he often used the standard adaptations, his veneration for Shakespeare – combined with his acute sense of theatricality – frequently prompted him to restore passages of the original dialogue. For *King Lear*, which he played with great success from as early as 1742, when he was only twenty-five, he mostly used Tate's adaptation, though in 1756 he announced it 'with restorations from Shakespeare'. While keeping an abbreviated version of Tate's love story as well as the happy ending, he restored many of Shakespeare's lines. One of his Cordelias was the beautiful Susannah Cibber, who was painted in the role (sans Garrick, surprisingly) with great theatrical flair by Pieter van Bleeck in 1755; using a canvas over nine feet square, he depicts her with her maid Arante as she is about to be saved by Poor Tom from two ruffians employed by Edmund (Plate 14). Garrick's last performance as Lear evoked an extraordinary tribute from the journalist and man-about-town Sir Henry Bate Dudley (1745–1824), also known as 'The Fighting Parson':

> The curse at the close of the first act, – his phrenetic appeal to heaven at the end of the second on Regan's ingratitude, were two such enthusiastic scenes of human exertion, that they caused a kind of momentary petrefaction through the house, which he soon dissolved as universally into tears. – Even the unfeeling Regan and Goneril, forgetful of their characteristic cruelty, played through the whole of their parts with aching bosoms and streaming eyes. – In a word, we never saw before so exquisite a theatrical performance, or one so loudly and universally applauded.[5]

For all his restorations, Garrick's instincts as a practical man of the theatre seeking maximum effectiveness on the stages of his time led him both to add passages of his own composition to the earlier adaptations and to make wholly new versions. His divided mind is demonstrated by the Prologue to his rewriting of *The Winter's Tale* as *Florizel and Perdita* (1756) in which he declares his 'plan, / To lose no drop of that immortal man' even though the play that follows sluices away most of the first three acts. In 1744, before he became manager of Drury Lane, he announced that he would put on *Macbeth*, which since 1700 had been played some 200 times in the Davenant version, 'as written by Shakespeare'. This is said to have provoked Quin to ask 'What does he mean? Don't *I* play it as Shakespeare wrote it?' Nevertheless Garrick cut some 270 lines and added explanatory passages. He substituted a servant for Macbeth's Porter, omitted the murder of Lady Macduff and her son, and used some of Davenant's elaborations in the witch scenes. Garrick had a special talent for expiring on stage, excelling 'in the expression of convulsive throes and dying agonies'. Shakespeare had failed to provide Macbeth with a dying speech. Davenant had gone some way to supplying the deficiency by giving him the moralistic last words 'Farewell, vain World, and what's most vain in it – Ambition.' Garrick filled the gap more amply but no less edifyingly:

> 'Tis done! the scene of life will quickly close.
> Ambition's vain, delusive dreams are fled,
> And now I wake to darkness, guilt and horror.
> I cannot bear it! Let me shake it off –
> 'Twa' not be; my soul is clogged with blood.
> I cannot rise! I dare not ask for mercy.
> It is too late, hell drags me down. I sink,
> I sink – Oh! my soul is lost forever!
> Oh! (*Dies*)

In spite of the echoes of Marlowe's Faustus, this is claptrap. But Garrick transformed it with his acting, provoking the critic Francis Gentleman to ask 'Who has heard his speech, after receiving his death wound, uttered with the utmost agony of body and mind, but trembles at the idea of future punishment, and almost pities the expiring wretch, though stained with crimes of the deepest dye?' Macbeth was one of Garrick's finest roles until 1768, when he gave it up following the death of Hannah Pritchard, who matched him as Lady Macbeth. Zoffany's literalistic painting of them in the scene after the murder of Duncan is an interesting record, not least of Garrick's comparatively short stature; Fuseli's version, though he is said to have sketched it during a performance, is a far more creative representation of the passions behind it (see overleaf).

Some of Garrick's adaptations, like Davenant's, were to affect the staging of Shakespeare's plays well into the nineteenth century. His much altered *Romeo and Juliet* included an elaborate funeral procession for Juliet for which

William Boyce composed a choral dirge that was to be popular for many years. Even more successfully, Garrick developed an idea originating with Thomas Otway by causing Juliet to wake up in the tomb before Romeo dies, giving them the opportunity for a last conversation. The scene reads absurdly now – 'Bless me, how cold it is!' says Juliet – but was unquestionably effective when acted with conviction. In 1814 Hazlitt referred to 'the last scene at the tomb, which, however, is not from Shakespeare, though it tells admirably upon the stage'.[6] Much later, Bernard Shaw saw it at one of its late appearances and perhaps helped to hasten its demise by describing how 'Romeo, instead of dying forthwith when he took the poison, was interrupted by Juliet, who sat up and made him carry her down to the footlights, where she complained of being very cold, and had to be warmed by a love scene, in the middle of which Romeo, who had forgotten all about the poison, was taken ill and died.'[7] For all the derision that has been poured on Garrick's interpolation, the notion of pointing the irony of the situation by causing Juliet to show signs of life that can be discerned by the audience but not by Romeo has appealed to several modern stage directors and is perpetuated in Baz Luhrmann's 1996 film *William Shakespeare's Romeo + Juliet.*

No less popular was Garrick's *Catherine and Petruchio* (often given in a double bill with the abbreviated *Winter's Tale*) which supplanted the original until 1886, was occasionally acted after that, and continued to affect the image of *The Taming of the Shrew* as a primarily knockabout farce even after the adaptation was abandoned. It too was castigated by Shaw.[8]

Garrick was not the only adapter of Shakespeare's plays during this period. George Colman, for example, prepared a version of *King Lear* for the rival Covent Garden, also restoring some of Shakespeare's lines. The movement to return to Shakespeare's text was slowly gathering impetus. Ironically, one of the harshest attacks on Garrick as play-adapter came from the son of the adapter of *Richard III*, the play in which Garrick had made his name. Theophilus Cibber wrote bitterly around 1756 that Garrick's

68. *Opposite, top.* 'Give me the daggers' (2.3.51): a mezzotint based on Johan Zoffany's painting of David Garrick and Hannah Pritchard in *Macbeth.*

69. *Opposite, bottom.* Henry Fuseli's vision of the same scene, painted in 1812 from a sketch made in 1760.

houses are crowded, for what he designs [deigns?] to give must be receiv'd, it is *Hobson's* choice with the town. . . . *The Midsummer Night's Dream* has been minced and fricaseed into an undigested thing called *The Fairies; – The Winter's Tale* mammocked into a droll; *The Taming of the Shrew*, made a farce of; – and *The Tempest* castrated into an opera.[9]

As if to atone for his sins, Garrick was assiduous in paying public tribute to Shakespeare, and indeed deserves most of the credit both for establishing Stratford-upon-Avon as the centre of Shakespearian pilgrimage and for laying the foundations for the Romantic worship of Shakespeare. His interest in Stratford goes back at least to 1742 when he and Macklin, like Betterton before them, visited the town apparently in search of information about Shakespeare, and were entertained under the mulberry tree that Shakespeare was supposed to have planted in the garden of New Place.[10] The first recorded performance of a Shakespeare play in the town that was later to be the centre of the Royal Shakespeare Company's work stemmed from a desire to emulate the support given by the London theatrical managements to the erection of the Westminster Abbey memorial in 1741. According to the play-bill for a performance of *Othello* in the Town Hall in 1746 the strolling player John Ward (1704–73; later to become the grandfather of the great Sarah Siddons) had offered to devote the proceeds to restoring the monument in Holy Trinity which had 'through length of years and other accidents become much impaired and decayed'. A few years later the physical reminders of Shakespeare in the town suffered a severe blow when the Reverend Francis Gastrell (not a Stratford man), exasperated by interest shown in the mulberry tree, ordered it to be chopped down and cut up for firewood (luckily a Mr Thomas Sharpe had the commercial acumen to buy it and convert it into an endless series of souvenirs and relics). Worse still, in 1759 Gastrell had New Place pulled down. But the local authorities were waking up to the value of their Shakespearian heritage, and astutely saw Garrick, now a wealthy man, as the playwright's earthly surrogate.

They knew that Garrick loved to memorialize both Shakespeare and himself. As his wealth increased he had bought a fine villa beside the Thames, fashionably close to the royal residence of Hampton Court. In its grounds he

1746.

AS the generous proposals of the Proprietors of the two greatest Play-Houses in this Kingdom, were kindly accepted and encourag'd, in relation to each of them Acting a PLAY, for the Sole purpose of erecting a New Monument to the Memory of SHAKESPEARE, in *Westminster-Abbey:* And as the Curious Original Monument and Bust of that incomparable Poet, erected above the Tomb that enshrines his Dust, in the Church of *Stratford* upon *Avon Warwickshire,* Is through length of Years and other accidents become much impair'd and decay'd; An offer has been kindly made by the Judicious and much Esteem'd Mr. JOHN WARD, and his Company, To Act one of SHAKESPEARE'S PLAYS, *Viz.*

Othello, or the Moor of Venice.

in the Town-Hall   1746.

At *Stratford,* on *Tuesday* the *Ninth* of this instant *September:* The Receipts arising from which Representation are to be Solely Appropriated to the Repairing the Original Monument aforesaid.

The part of Othello, to be perform'd by Mr WARD,

See an Explanation of ye Beauties of this play in ye Guardian Vol.ye 1st. No. 37.

Jago,		Mr. Elrington, *a young man acts well.*
Caffio,		Mr. Redman, *a middle-ag'd man. too indifferent in Action.*
Brabantio,	by	Mr. Woodward, *an elderly man. something well, other wretchedly.*
Montano,		Mr. Butler, — *an old man. Comic part pretty well*
Roderigo,		Mr. Butcher, *a young man. low humour pretty well.*
Gratiano.		Mr. Bourne, *an elderly man. low humour very well.*

Doge of Venice --- by --- *Do*

Desdemona, } by { Mrs. Elrington, *a 2nd wife, but young a very agreeable actress*

Emilia, Mrs. Ward, *a middle-ag'd Woman a good Actress.*

Mr Elrington's voice is rather more agreeable than miss Wilson's, but miss Wilson has most judgment in musick.

With several Entertainments of SINGING, between the ACTS. by Mrs. Elrington. and Mrs. †Wilson.

†mr Wilson since married to Mr Butcher plays very well & genteelly on ye violin.

To begin punctually at 6 o'Clock.   Pit, 2 s. 6 d.   Gallery, 1 s.

It is therefore humbly wish'd, that such Persons as have a taste for the Inimitable Thoughts, the Sublime Expressions, the Natural and lively Descriptions and Characters of that Great Genius, and Consequently a Value for his Memory, will Encourage the propos'd method of perpetuating it, by attending the PLAY, at that juncture, for the laudable purpose of re-beautifying his Venerable Monument and Effigies.

N. B. The Money receiv'd on this Occasion, is to be Deposited in the Hands of the Church-Wardens.

70. The playbill for the first recorded performance of a Shakespeare play in Stratford, 1746.

built an octagonal temple, probably of his own design, with an alcove to
hold a statue of Shakespeare which he commissioned from the French-born
sculptor Louis François Roubiliac and for which, in a characteristic gesture
of self-identification, he himself probably posed. (He bequeathed the statue

71. David Garrick's temple to Shakespeare, restored in 1999,
showing a painting of the exterior.

to the British Museum; the Temple, restored and opened to the public in 1999, now holds an exhibition devoted to Garrick with copies of the statue and of Zoffany's fine conversation pieces showing Garrick and his wife entertaining guests there.) No doubt members of the Stratford Corporation had this in mind in 1768 when, deciding that they too would like a statue of Shakespeare to fill a niche above the entrance to their new Town Hall, but feeling disinclined to pay for one, they privately suggested to Garrick that he might care to present them with 'some statue, bust, or picture of Shakespeare'. They also appealed to his vanity by asking for a portrait of Garrick himself. More publicly they resolved unanimously that Garrick be made the first honorary freeman of the borough and directed that the document conferring this honour 'should be presented to him in a small neat chest constructed from a mulberry tree planted by Shakespeare himself'. The handsome casket, a fine example of the wood-carver's art which figures a representation of Benjamin Wilson's 1762 painting of Garrick as Lear, took four months to make; it is preserved in the British Museum. In response Garrick generously

72. The carved wooden casket that contained the scroll recording David Garrick's enrolment as the first freeman of Stratford-upon-Avon.

donated a statue, which still adorns the Town Hall, but suggested that it would be only fair for the Corporation to demonstrate gratitude by paying for the portrait of himself. They agreed and gave Thomas Gainsborough 60 guineas to rework his painting of 1766 showing Garrick leaning against a plinth surmounted by a bust of Shakespeare. It was duly placed in the Town Hall, but perished in a fire in 1946.

Garrick's association with Stratford and its town clerk soon precipitated a more elaborate ceremony of memorialization whose ripples spread far beyond both the Avon and Garrick's own time. Reporting the award of the freedom in May 1769, a newspaper announced that 'a jubilee to honour and to the memory of Shakespeare' would be held in September and that Garrick had kindly accepted the stewardship. He did not, we may suspect, take much persuading; certainly he threw himself heart and soul into preparing for the festivities. An octagonal building known as the Rotunda, holding a thousand persons, was erected on meadow land on the banks of the Avon, and Garrick worked tirelessly to energize artists, composers, builders, innkeepers, costumiers, medal makers and a host more of recruits to the occasion. Though he had to overcome many frustrations, hundreds of members of the nobility and gentry along with theatrical and other celebrities eventually crowded the town's limited accommodation for the three-day festival.

The jubilee began at dawn on Wednesday 6 September with the thunder of cannon, the chiming of bells, and the singing of mummers. At a formal ceremony Garrick, wearing a specially designed velvet suit and white gloves said to have belonged to Shakespeare himself, was installed as steward. Flowers were placed on the grave, and an oratorio, *Judith* – the name (by chance) of Shakespeare's daughter as well as the biblical personage – composed by Thomas Arne and dedicated to Garrick was sung in Holy Trinity. The church, indeed, with its monument and grave, still interested visitors to Stratford more than the house where he was born, but the first known representation of Shakespeare's Birthplace was published in the *Gentleman's Magazine* a couple of months before the jubilee. The visitors wore medals and ribbons designed by Garrick. There were songs written (by Garrick) in praise of Shakespeare – 'Sweet Willy-O' was a favourite, and 'Warwickshire Lads' – 'The lad of all lads was a Warwickshire Lad' – with a jolly tune by Dibdin which became the regimental quick march of the Royal Warwickshire

73. Shakespeare's Birthplace, 1769: the first known representation,
by Richard Greene.

regiment. A grand parade was led by Garrick. Buildings were decorated with large transparent paintings lit from the windows behind them. Garrick, with sensational success, spoke, to musical accompaniment, an ode he had written, already privately performed before the King and Queen; it includes the delightful song 'Thou soft-flowing Avon', with music by Arne, which can still be heard. At a fancy-dress ball the guests included James Boswell as an armed Corsican chief. There was horse racing – the Garrick Cup is still an annual Stratford fixture. And there was rain. There was indeed so much rain that a carefully prepared pageant of Shakespearian characters was cancelled and an amazing fireworks display had to be abandoned halfway through. Throughout all this, however, there was no word from the honorand. None of Shakespeare's plays – nor even an excerpt from one of them – was spoken throughout the entire festival. Unsurprisingly, the occasion has come to be known as the Garrick, not the Shakespeare, Jubilee. It showed a loss of £2,000, and although the original agreement was that responsibility should be shared between the town and Garrick, he generously agreed to defray it all himself, and eventually did so, helped by the colossal success of his witty and spectacular play *The Jubilee*, incorporating the cancelled pageant, which had an unprecedented run of ninety-one performances as an afterpiece at Drury Lane.[11]

Garrick died in 1779, provoking Johnson's famous tribute 'I am disappointed by that stroke of death which has eclipsed the gaiety of nations, and impoverished the public stock of harmless pleasure.' He was buried in Westminster Abbey at the foot of Shakespeare's statue in what was virtually a state funeral. His death was also grotesquely commemorated in George Carter's painting *The Apotheosis of Garrick*, exhibited at the Royal Academy in 1784 and now in the collections of the Royal Shakespeare Theatre, in which we see the actor, still looking very poorly, being wafted from his tomb by a pair of amply-winged angels to be welcomed to the slopes of Parnassus by Shakespeare in the company of the Muses of Comedy and Tragedy (Plate 9). Seventeen of Garrick's fellow-actors wave him a sad farewell, dressed, according to a contemporary key, 'in their favourite characters' – though why Joseph Vernon should have felt so warmly about Thurio, in *The Two Gentlemen of Verona* – one of the most colourless roles in the canon – is hard to comprehend (see p. 233).[12]

It was to be a while before a male actor of anything like comparable stature was to emerge, though Macklin, whose fame preceded Garrick's, long outlived him, attempting Shylock for the last time in 1789 when he was around ninety years old – his understudy had to take over after a short time. Two women, however, one supreme in comedy, the other in tragedy, were soon to make a major impact on the London scene. Sarah Siddons (1755–1831) had appeared with Garrick at Drury Lane at the age of twenty in roles that included Portia (in *The Merchant of Venice*) and Lady Anne (in *Richard III*), with little success. She went on to mature her art in the provinces, played over a hundred roles, including Hamlet, in Bath and Bristol, and returned to Drury Lane, now managed by Richard Brinsley Sheridan, in 1782 in a triumph comparable in its effect with Garrick's as Richard III over forty years before. Commanding in presence and voice, majestic in mien, intense and original in conception and execution of her roles, and conspicuously virtuous in private life, she brought an awesome new dignity to the profession. For some time she acted mainly in contemporary plays, but she had played Isabella in *Measure for Measure* and Constance in *King John* before making her London debut in the greatest of all her roles, Lady Macbeth, in 1785. This was a performance that made women faint and strong men tremble; indeed Mrs Siddons scared herself out of her wits while first studying it at night at the age of twenty: 'I went on with tolerable composure, in the silence of the night (a night I never can forget), till I came to the assassination scene, when the horrors of the scene rose to a degree that made it impossible for me to get farther. I snatched up my candle, and hurried out of the room in a paroxysm of terror' (Plate 14). Already when she was twenty-eight Sir Joshua Reynolds, one of the greatest among her many great admirers, had painted her as the Tragic Muse. Along with her brother John Philip Kemble, who joined her at Drury Lane, she was to dominate the London theatre scene for a quarter of a century.

In comedy, however, Siddons had to yield the palm to Dorothea – Dora – Jordan (1762–1816), a great beauty and enchanting stage presence who became the mistress of the Duke of Clarence, later King William IV, by whom she had ten children. She too learned her trade in the provinces before joining the Drury Lane company in 1785. Her principal Shakespearian roles were Viola and Rosalind (in which Siddons failed). Charles Lamb's recollection of how, as Viola, Mrs Jordan spoke 'the disguised story of her love for Orsino' suggests an ideal command of the poetry of the role:

> It was no set speech, that she had foreseen, so as to weave it into an harmonious period, line necessarily following line to make up the music . . . but, when she had declared her sister's history to be a 'blank', and that she 'never told her love', there was a pause, as if the story had ended – and then the image of the 'worm in the bud' came up as a new suggestion – and the heightened image of 'Patience' still followed after that, as by some growing (and not mechanical) process, thought springing up after thought, I would almost say, as they were watered by her tears.[13]

74. John Hoppner's
painting of
Dorothea Jordan
as Viola in
Twelfth Night.

She was painted as Viola by the fashionable and successful portrait painter John Hoppner (1758–1810) who, rivalling Reynolds with Siddons, had previously portrayed her (in 1786) as the Comic Muse.

★

Few Shakespearian activities in Garrick's lifetime do not, in one way or another, impinge upon him. His former school teacher Samuel Johnson, comparable in genius and accomplishment, was to become as eminent in Shakespearian scholarship as Garrick in acting. They travelled from Lichfield to London together in 1737 in search of their fortunes, sharing one horse between them if Garrick is to be believed. Johnson's ambitions at this point were as a tragic playwright, and Garrick, intended for the law, took up the wine trade before finding his true vocation. In 1745 Johnson, who was already displaying the skills that would enable him to compile his great *Dictionary*, published a short pamphlet called *Miscellaneous Observations on the Tragedy of Macbeth* consisting mainly of explanations of specific passages along with discussions of the way they had been handled by previous editors. He appends devastating criticisms of Hanmer's dilettantish treatment of the play in his edition which appeared as Johnson's pamphlet was in the press:

> There is no distinction made between the ancient reading, and the innovations of the editor; there is no reason given for any of the alterations which are made; the emendations of former critics are adopted without any acknowledgement, and few of the difficulties are removed which have hitherto embarrassed the readers of Shakespeare.

And Johnson appends a single folded leaf offering proposals for yet another new edition of Shakespeare, in ten relatively inexpensive volumes, 'with notes critical and explanatory'. Tonson, publisher of Pope and Theobald, soon squashed this idea, but it remained latent in Johnson's mind throughout his work on the *Dictionary*, for which he collected thousands of Shakespearian citations.

A few weeks after publishing his plan for the dictionary, in 1747, Johnson wrote the prologue for the opening performance at Drury Lane under Garrick's management – *The Merchant of Venice*, with Macklin as Shylock – and in the same year yet another complete edition appeared, this time edited by William Warburton, who had contributed notes to both Theobald's and Hanmer's editions and who arrogantly claimed to be presenting 'the genuine text . . . restored from the blunders of its first editors and the interpolations of the two last' (i.e. Hanmer and Theobald). Though Warburton was to become Bishop of Gloucester, his comments on his predecessors and colleagues, like those of many of his successors, are imbued with no spirit of Christian charity.

The demand for Shakespeare editions was great; explication and conjectural emendation of individual passages became a pastime for cultivated amateurs conducted frequently in the pages of the *Gentleman's Magazine,* and reprints of existing editions as well as new ones flowed from the presses. One of the most remarkable was, in its own day, the least successful, appearing without an authorized reprint – possibly because it is rather austerely presented, with no illustrations and only textual notes on the page. Its explanatory notes did not finally appear until two years after the editor died. He was Edward Capell (1713–81), a grumpy scholar whose official position as deputy inspector of plays gave him ample leisure to devote himself to the study of Shakespeare and his contemporaries. In the process he collected the largest and most important collection of early editions of Shakespeare's plays that had so far been assembled, and left them to Trinity College, Cambridge, to the great benefit of his successors. The depth of his dedication may be gauged by the fact that when his edition appeared, in 1767–8, he claimed, no doubt with justice, to have been working on it for twenty years, and that he is said to have transcribed the complete plays by hand ten times in the process. His avoidance of the practice regularly followed by editors of the complete works up to his time (and by most later editors), of sending to the press marked-up sheets of a previously edited text enabled him to avoid accumulated corruptions and the mindless repetition of inauthentic or unconsidered detail. And unlike earlier editors he realized the importance of working from the first reliable edition of each play.[14] As usual, Garrick comes into the picture: in 1759 he got Capell to help him to prepare a text of *Antony and Cleopatra,* 'fitted for the stage by abridging only', for the first performances of the original play since Shakespeare's time. Lavishly presented, and with Garrick as Antony, it nevertheless failed to please and had only six performances. The friends later fell out, perhaps because Garrick heard that Capell said he 'spoke many speeches in Shakespeare without understanding them'.

In the meantime Johnson, freed from his labours on the *Dictionary,* which appeared in 1755, returned to his Shakespearian project. A year or two earlier he had assisted a friend, Mrs Charlotte Lennox, by writing the Dedication (which appeared as if written by her) to the first attempt at a collected reprint, in three volumes, of Shakespeare's sources. Though the idea was good, it is hard to understand from Mrs Lennox's critical remarks why she bothered since, continuing to apply irrelevant neoclassical criteria, she frequently finds Shakespeare's works far inferior to those on which they are based: in *King Lear*, 'had Shakespeare followed the historian he would not have violated the rules of poetic justice'. Understandably the romances fare worst: *The Winter's Tale* 'is greatly inferior to the old paltry story that furnished him with the subject of it'. 'The whole conduct' of *Cymbeline* 'is absurd and ridiculous to the last degree'. Johnson was to write with similar contempt of the same play: 'To remark the folly of the fiction, the absurdity of the conduct, the confusion of the names and manners of different times, and the impossibility of the events in any system of life, were to waste criticism upon unresisting imbecility, upon faults too evident for detection, and too gross for aggravation.' So much for *Cymbeline*. Johnson inordinately admired Mrs Lennox, and it would be interesting to know to what extent he influenced her criticisms.

In 1756 Johnson both signed an agreement to prepare a new edition, in eight volumes, and published new *Proposals* for it. His commitment to complete the work within eighteen months may seem a little less over-optimistic if we remember that a great part of his aim was 'to explain what is obscure', and that he had already thought hard about Shakespearian meanings for his work on the *Dictionary*. Nevertheless it was to be another nine years before the edition finally appeared. Oddly to us, printing of the first volume had started within a year; similarly, Capell's volumes were in the press from 1760, seven years before publication, which gave him an excuse not to comment on Johnson's work. Textually Johnson's edition is of no great importance; its strengths lie in its Preface, which has become a classic of Shakespeare criticism, and in its explanatory and critical notes; and the strength in turn of these lies largely in the energy, trenchancy, and self-confidence of his prose style. Johnson's glosses and notes, unrivalled in terseness, still crop up in modern editions; and the Preface, though inevitably of its time in critical technique and attitude, particularly in its tendency to deliver sonorous generalities unillumined by example or illustrative quotation, reminds us at times that Johnson was a poet as well as one of our greatest writers of prose:

> Shakespeare's plays are not in the rigorous and critical sense either tragedies or comedies, but compositions of a distinct kind: exhibiting the real state of sublunary nature, which partakes of good and

evil, joy and sorrow, mingled with endless variety of proportion and innumerable modes of combination; and expressing the course of the world, in which the loss of one is the gain of another; in which, at the same time, the reveller is hastening to his wine, and the mourner burying his friend; in which the malignity of one is some-times defeated by the frolick of another; and many mischiefs and many benefits are done and hindered without design.

Here at last is an eloquent recognition that generic impurity may be truer to real life than a mechanical following of the rules.

The flow of literary editions was broken by the publisher John Bell who had the bright idea of publishing all twenty-four of the plays that were in the current theatrical repertoire at Covent Garden and Drury Lane 'regulated from the prompt-books, by permission of the managers', along with the remaining plays (minus *Pericles*) in standard texts marked with suggestions for cuts. The editor, Francis Gentleman, was a struggling actor and play-wright who in 1770 had published a series of criticisms of plays of the time, *The Dramatic Censor*. (Naturally he dedicated the first of the two volumes to Garrick, who was kind to him when he fell upon hard times.) Bell's pleasantly presented edition appeared from 1773 to 1775, the first volume adorned with plates of Shakespeare and Garrick, and is invaluable to theatre historians for its information about theatre practice in Garrick's late years and for its series of engravings for each play of a named actor (including Garrick as Macbeth – only) costumed for a specific role (even in plays that were not performed) and of a scene involving several characters.[15]

As the eighteenth century unfolds the editing of Shakespeare becomes an increasingly (and unrewardingly) tangled tale of reprints and newly revised editions, both of the complete works and of selected plays, the former incorporating by a process of accretion material from earlier ver-sions with increasing complexity and decreasing readability. In 1784 came the first single-volume of the works, edited by Samuel Ayscough and using tiny print, since the Fourth Folio. The tale is enlivened by occasional mischievous and malicious episodes such as George Steevens's attribution, in his edition of 1793, of his own obscene notes on bawdy passages to a couple of harmless clergymen who had offended him. The climax comes

75. Joseph Vernon (see p. 226), the singing Thurio in *The Two Gentlemen of Verona*, from Bell's theatre edition.

with the work of Edmond Malone (1741–1812), an Irish barrister who settled in London in 1777 as a man of letters after coming into a private income, and who formed friendships with many literary men including Johnson and, especially, Boswell, with whom he worked closely on his great *Life of Johnson*.

The best all-round scholar who had so far worked extensively on Shakespeare, Malone was exceptionally versatile and systematic in his investigations.

First, in 1778, came his much-needed, pioneering *Attempt to Ascertain the Order in which the Plays attributed to Shakespeare were Written*[16] in which he drew on his assiduous researches into publishing history and early printed books to produce a work which he revised several times and which in its final state has formed a generally sound foundation for all future studies of the topic. He was to make many important discoveries of documents relating to the Elizabethan stage, above all the papers of Philip Henslowe in Dulwich College (though deplorably he snipped bits out of them), and his 1790 edition of Shakespeare includes a long 'Account of the English Stage' based on much primary research. It's easy for us, to whom such information is commonplace, to underestimate the need for such work: Elizabeth Montagu had written in 1769, for instance, that 'Shakespeare's plays were to be acted in a paltry tavern, to an unlettered audience just emerging from barbarity.'[17] Malone was the first scholar to make a thorough search of the Stratford records for biographical information, correcting many of Rowe's errors, discovering the Quiney letter (p. 30), and persuading the vicar and town council to arrange for him to borrow the parish register and thousands of other documents, which he hung on to for an unconscionable length of time, returning them only when threatened with legal action. Regrettably he never completed his projected full biography. And he offended the burghers of Stratford by arranging for the bust in the church (which he believed, probably mistakenly, to have been done from a death mask) to be taken down and scrubbed free of its coloured paint under the misapprehension that this had been added when the monument was restored (p. 220). The colours were not restored until 1861.

Far less significant as a scholar but little less influential on the popular apprehension of Shakespeare was the notorious William Dodd (1729–77), writer, clergyman, immensely popular preacher who became chaplain to the King, but whose taste for high living led him to forge the signature of Lord Chesterfield on a bond for £4,200. In spite of support and petitions from, among others, Dr Johnson (no friend to Chesterfield), he was hanged for the crime. Among his voluminous publications, many of them religious in nature and including four volumes of sermons, was his two-volume *Beauties of Shakespeare* (1752), each extract supplied with a title and each volume with a thematic index, which went through at least thirty-nine versions by 1893,

1. The poet Sir John Suckling holding a copy of either the First or Second Folio open at *Hamlet*; painted by Sir Anthony Van Dyck (1599–1641). This is said to be the first English work of art in which a secular book appears.

2. *Above*. The front parlour of Shakespeare's Birthplace as newly displayed in 2000.

3. *Left*. A conjectural reconstruction of Shakespeare's study showing him at work; from the exhibition at the Shakespeare Centre.

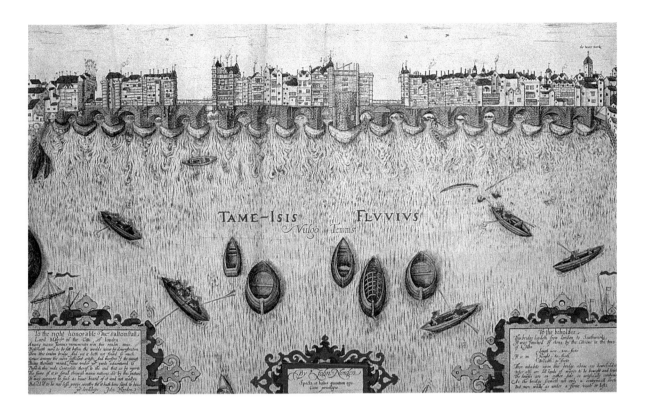

4. *Above*. John Norden's 1597 view of London Bridge. Norden records that the bridge is nearly 800 feet long, 60 feet high, and 30 feet broad.

'There inhabit upon this bridge above 100 householders where also are all kind of wares to be bought and sold. The houses are on either side so artificially [skilfully] combined as the bridge seemeth not only a continual street but men walk as under a high vault or loft.' Heads of executed criminals mounted on pikes are to be seen at the east end.

5. *Right*. Queen Elizabeth I: the Ditchley portrait, painted by Marcus Gheeraerts the Younger (1561/2–1636) in 1592, when the Queen was sixty years old, to commemorate a visit to Sir Henry Lee at Ditchley, in Oxfordshire. She carries a pair of gloves in one hand and a fan in the other.

6. *Left*. King James I, patron of Shakespeare's company from 1603: painting attributed to John de Critz the Elder (*c.*1552–1642).

7. *Below, left*. Henry Wriothesley, third Earl of Southampton, in the Tower of London: also attributed to John de Critz the Elder; Southampton allegedly had a cat named Trixie, but the animal may be emblematic of a desire for liberty.

8. *Below*. Robert Devereux, Earl of Essex: a miniature painting by Isaac Oliver (*c.*1565–1617).

9. *Right.* Shakespeare flirting with the Muse of Comedy while extending a propitiatory hand to the Muse of Tragedy, painted by Richard Westall in 1825.

10. *Below.* 'Give me a horse!' William Hogarth's painting of David Garrick awakening to remorse in the tent scene in Colley Cibber's adaptation of *Richard III.*

11. *Left*. Charles Macklin as Shylock in *The Merchant of Venice*, *c.*1768, painted by Johan Zoffany (1733–1810).

12. *Below*. 'Sir John, Sir John, do not yourself wrong' (*Henry IV, Part Two*, 3.2.251). William Hogarth's painting of Falstaff examining his ragged regiment.

13. *Above.* Susannah Cibber, Colley's daughter-in-law, as Cordelia with her maid Arante in Nahum Tate's adaptation of *King Lear*. This painting by Pieter Van Bleeck shows the disguised Edgar coming to her rescue as she is assailed by two of Edmund's ruffians.

14. *Right.* '*Enter Lady Macbeth, with a taper*' (*Macbeth*, 5.1.17). Henry Fuseli's painting of Sarah Siddons as Lady Macbeth, 1783.

15. *Above.* 'Waft him, angels, to the skies':
The Apotheosis of Garrick (1784): painting by
George Carter.

16. *Left.* 'Best draw my sword, and if mine
enemy / But fear the sword like me he'll
scarcely look on't' (*Cymbeline*, 3.6.25–6):
Charles Willson Peale's 1771 painting of Nancy
Hallam as Imogen, disguised (in irrationally
oriental costume) as the boy Fidele.

17. *Opposite, top.* A winged Puck looks on as a
tiny but perfectly formed Titania is serenaded
by an elfin band. This painting (*c.* 1850) by
Joseph Noël Paton (1821–1901) relates to
2.2. of *A Midsummer Night's Dream*, though
Puck is not present in the text at this point.

18. *Opposite, bottom.* 'Ill met by moonlight,
proud Titania' (*A Midsummer Night's Dream*,
2.1.60): the painting by Francis Danby
(1793–1861).

19. The golden fairies in Granville-Barker's 1914 production of *A Midsummer Night's Dream*.

20. *Left*. 'O for a horse with wings!' (*Cymbeline*, 3.2.48): Ellen Terry as Imogen, which she played with Henry Irving at the Lyceum Theatre, London in 1897. This anonymous miniature, done from a photograph, belonged to her great-nephew, John Gielgud.

21. *Opposite, top. Pity*: William Blake's colour print illustrating *Macbeth* (1.7.21–5).

22. *Opposite, bottom. Rosalind in the Forest*: a painting of *c*.1868 by John Everett Millais (1829–96).

23. '. . . in dreaming / The clouds methought would open and show riches / Ready to drop upon me' (*The Tempest*, 3.2.142–5): *Caliban's Dream*, by Odilon Redon (1840–1916).

24. *Above.* Mark Rylance (left) as Cleopatra and Danny Sapani as Charmian in an all-male production (1999) of *Antony and Cleopatra* at the reconstructed Globe with female roles played (inauthentically) by adult actors.

25. *Below.* 'Stay, stand apart. I know not which is which' (5.1.366): the moment of recognition in Tim Supple's Royal Shakespeare Company production of *The Comedy of Errors*, The Other Place, 1996.

26. *Above.* The set of postage stamps designed by David Gentleman for the Shakespeare quatercentenary, 1964.

27. *Below. Shakespeare with Queen Elizabeth I*, drawn by David Hockney in 1979 for a Folger Shakespeare Library exhibition, 'Shakespeare: the Globe and the World'.

28. *Right*. 'Now good digestion wait on appetite'
(3.4.37–8): a 'cel' of Macbeth for the Animated Tales
from Shakespeare series.

29. *Below*. 'Her beauty makes this vault / A feasting
presence full of light' (5.3.85–6). Juliet lies in state at the
end of Baz Lurhmann's film *William Shakespeare's
Romeo + Juliet*.

30. *Above.* Writer's block: Joseph Fiennes in the film *Shakespeare in Love*, directed by John Madden.

31. *Left.* 'Is this a dagger which I see before me?' (2.1.32): a page from *Macbeth: The Unabridged First Folio Text in Cartoon*, illustrated by Von, 1982.

provoked many imitations, and is said to be the form in which Goethe first encountered Shakespeare.

In his Preface Dodd declared it unnecessary to praise Shakespeare 'at a time when such universal and just applause is paid to him, and when every tongue is big with his boundless fame'. Though many equally hyperbolical eulogies abound, not all tongues wagged to the same tune. Charlotte Lennox's invidious comparisons were soon to be published, and Johnson's Preface of 1765 devotes several pages to listing Shakespeare's faults. Slowly, reasoned criticism paying close attention to the text was beginning to supersede this kind of judicial generalization, and frequently it centred on Shakespeare's powers of characterization.

A spirit of the age seems to have been operating: several critics were working along similar lines with no knowledge of each other's work. Thomas Whately (?–1772), a Member of Parliament from 1761, left unfinished at his death a remarkable and seminal comparison of the characters of Richard III and Macbeth – a rewarding topic – intended as part of a larger study and published by his brother in 1785. This is the first detailed study of any of Shakespeare's characters; Horace Walpole declared that it 'ought to be prefixed to every edition of Shakespeare as a preface, and will tend more to give a just idea of that matchless genius than all the notes and criticisms on his works'.[18] At around the same time William Richardson (1743–1814), a Professor of Humanity in the University of Glasgow, was at work on his *Philosophical Analysis and Illustration of Some of Shakespeare's Remarkable Characters*, published in 1774, aiming 'to make poetry subservient to philosophy, and to employ it in tracing the principles of human conduct'. Richardson followed this moralistic study of Macbeth, Hamlet, Jaques, and Imogen in 1784 with similar studies of Richard III, King Lear, and Timon of Athens, and in 1789 with an essay on the ever-popular Falstaff and Shakespeare's female characters. In 1775 Mrs Elizabeth Griffith, an actress and playwright, published (and dedicated to Garrick) *The Morality of Shakespeare's Drama Illustrated*, a substantial work heavily influenced by Johnson in which she claims that, however much Shakespeare may have sported with the unities of time, place, and action, 'he seldom sins against a fourth . . . namely, that of character'. And in 1777 (though written in 1774) appeared one of the most highly regarded of all early works of criticism, Maurice Morgann's *Essay on the Dramatic Character*

76. 'Give me some light. Away' (*Hamlet*, 3.2.257): Francis Hayman's painting
of the play scene from *Hamlet*.

of Falstaff, ostensibly a defence of the character against the charge of cowardice but actually, as Morgann writes, a far wider-ranging study extending to Falstaff's 'whole character; to the arts and genius of his poetic maker, Shakespeare; and through him sometimes, with ambitious aim, even to the principles of human nature itself'.

Musical adaptations of Shakespeare were still fairly rudimentary; they include a mock-opera by John Frederick Lampe, *Pyramus and Thisbe,* of 1745, which parodies Handel and other composers of *opera seria,* and J. C. Smith's *The Fairies,* put on by Garrick at Drury Lane in 1755. Music for theatre productions has not, except for that of Thomas Arne, made much impact on later ages, but the violin prodigy Thomas Linley Junior (1756–78), whose father was a successful composer and, for some fifteen years from 1776, director of music at Drury Lane; who became a close friend of Mozart; whose sister Elizabeth Ann, a great beauty and fine singer, married Thomas Sheridan; and who was accidentally drowned at the age of twenty-two when a boat capsized on the Duke of Ancaster's estate in Lincolnshire, composed two fine works based on Shakespeare which have been revived successfully in recent years and which justify Mozart's judgement that he was 'a true genius'. One is his *The Witches and Fairies: an Ode in Commemoration of Shakespeare,* performed at Drury Lane in 1776, the other a suite of music for *The Tempest* of 1777.

Though, as we have seen, the earliest illustrations of Shakespeare were done for editions, during the eighteenth century many artists were to follow Hogarth in finding Shakespeare's plays an ideal source of inspiration for portraits of actors and for independent works of art, sometimes directly of specific characters and scenes, at other times taking off from the plays more adventurously in pursuit of off-stage themes and images. Some topics frequently recur; Francis Hayman, for instance, who did the attractive illustrations for Hanmer's edition, followed Hogarth in painting both Falstaff and the Recruits and Garrick as Richard III; starting off as a scene painter he went on, in collaboration with Hogarth, to provide many of the panels with which the alcoves at Vauxhall Pleasure Gardens were adorned. The only Shakespearian one to survive is a fine version of the play scene from *Hamlet* which unusually focuses attention on the guilty Claudius's reaction to the play within the play.

For many years one of the Shakespearian themes most popular with artists was King Lear in the storm, the subject of a harrowing early oil painting (*c.*1760) by George Romney (1734–1802), a vivid drawing by the short-lived Scottish artist Alexander Runciman (1736–85) which provides an early depiction of the Fool at a time when he did not figure in stage productions, and an ambitious and impressive oil by Alexander's short-lived brother John (1744–68) which is of exceptional interest in that, rather than adopting a literal approach to the subject, it looks forward to the imagery criticism of the 1930s in its introduction of a storm at sea. Though these are not theatre paintings, in all of them the costumes resemble those used on stage at the time.

Theatre paintings continued to appear, some no less literalistic than Zoffany's of Garrick and Mrs Pritchard in *Macbeth*. A good example is the elegantly costumed scene from a Drury Lane *Twelfth Night* by Francis Wheatley (1747–1801) painted in 1772 which, though Elizabeth Younge as Viola is leaning sideways in a manner suggestive of sickness consequent upon a storm at sea, provides an interesting visual counterpart to a memorable piece of verbal description, Charles Lamb's account of James William Dodd as Sir Andrew:

> You could see the first dawn of an idea stealing slowly over his countenance, climbing up by little and little, with a painful process, till it cleared up at last to the fulness of a twilight conception – its highest meridian . . . A glimmer of understanding would appear in a corner of his eye, and for lack of fuel go out again.[19]

Garrick's Jubilee is often spoken of as a herald of the full-blown Romantic attitude to Shakespeare, and during the 1760s and '70s two of the most original and visionary artists associated with Romanticism in painting, Henry Fuseli (1741–1825) and William Blake (1757–1827), were coming to prominence. The Swiss Fuseli, an excellent linguist who studied Shakespeare in his youth, translating *Macbeth* into German, moved to England in 1764; the contrast between his and Zoffany's paintings of Garrick and Mrs Pritchard in *Macbeth*, painted within a year or so of each other, is a measure of the way things were going, even though Fuseli's idiosyncratic style was only beginning to emerge (pp. 218–19). Spending eight years in Rome (where he knew

77. John Runciman's painting (1767) of *King Lear in the Storm* conflates the heath
with an imagined sea.

Alexander Runciman who also spent time there) from 1770, Fuseli, a passionate admirer of Michelangelo, nevertheless dreamed of repainting the
ceiling of the Sistine Chapel with monumental characters from Shakespeare.
Fortunately this did not come to pass, but he was to draw and paint many
Shakespearian scenes, especially of supernatural and horrific subjects, some
of which were engraved by his younger friend Blake.

78. William Blake's drawing of Lear and Cordelia in prison.

Though Blake, like Fuseli, was attracted to plays of the supernatural – fairies as well as witches – his was a more lyrical, less awesome art than his friend's. His many Shakespeare drawings and engravings include the tender *Lear and Cordelia in Prison*, in which father and daughter are portrayed asleep in prison – a scene represented in Tate's adaptation but only imagined in the original play. More characteristic of Blake's visionary art, however, is the extraordinary colour engraving *Pity*, of around 1795 (Plate 21), which takes off from the dramatic situation to realize the images of Macbeth's lines,

> And pity, like a naked new-born babe,
> Striding the blast, or heaven's cherubin, horsed
> Upon the sightless couriers of the air,
> Shall blow the horrid deed in every eye
> That tears shall drown the wind. (*Macbeth*, 1.7.21–5)

The climax of the eighteenth-century interest in Shakespeare and the visual arts comes with the establishment in 1789 of the Boydell Shakespeare Gallery. Hatched at a dinner party attended by a number of distinguished painters in 1786, this was a bold and imaginative, as well as commercially inspired, venture.

John Boydell (1719–1804), who became an alderman of London in 1782 and Lord Mayor in 1790, was an engraver turned printseller and publisher of other men's engravings who made a fortune particularly by trading with the continent. Ostensibly the aim of his gallery was to found a British school of historical painting – regarded by Reynolds as the highest form of art – with Shakespeare as a prime source of subjects, but of course Boydell saw the commercial possibilities, planning to produce engravings of each painting which could both be sold separately, at home and abroad, and used to illustrate editions of the plays. To this end thirty-three of the best artists in the kingdom, headed by the super-eminent Sir Joshua Reynolds, were commissioned to produce between them one set of large paintings and one of small. The larger were to be reproduced as illustrations to a massive, elephant-folio edition in six volumes; issued serially from 1791, it appeared complete with one hundred plates in 1802 and is now an expensive collectors' item. The smaller set of paintings illustrated a reprint of Steevens's edition. In the event almost half of the paintings were done by four artists, William Hamilton (1751–1801), Robert Smirke (1752–1845), Richard Westall (1765–1836), and Francis Wheatley (1747–1801). Judging by the catalogue, which presents the enterprise partly as a contribution to the overseas tourist trade, and includes a substantial extract from each play illustrated, only thirty-four paintings were ready for the opening of the specially designed and built gallery, at 52 Pall Mall, London, in 1789. By 1802, 152 items are listed, the last of them seven paintings of the Ages of Man by Smirke. There were also some sculptures. The gallery was subsequently adorned by a splendid alto-relievo (also not ready for the opening) by the sculptor Thomas Banks (1735–1805), now to be seen in the Great Garden of New Place, Stratford-upon-Avon (see overleaf).

The gallery was not the money-making enterprise that had been hoped, partly because the bottom dropped out of the continental market as a result of the French Revolution – and Boydell had been generous with his commissioning fees. In 1804 he was obliged to ask Parliament's permission to dispose of his property by lottery, 22,000 tickets were sold; they saved him from bankruptcy, but he died before the lottery was drawn. The collection was dispersed; many of the paintings are now lost or badly damaged, known only by the engravings.

79. Thomas Banks's alto-relievo for the Boydell Gallery. According to the Gallery's catalogue, it 'represents Shakespeare seated on a rock, between Poetry and Painting. Poetry is on his right hand, addressing Shakespeare and presenting him with a wreath of bays, while she celebrates his praise on her lyre. Her head is ornamented with a double mask, to show she has bestowed the double power of Tragedy and Comedy upon her favourite son. Shakespeare is represented as listening to her with pleasure and attention. On his left is Painting, who is addressing a spectator with one hand extended towards Shakespeare's breast, pointing him out as the proper object of her pencil, while he leans his left hand on her shoulder, as if accepting her assistance.'

80. *Shakespeare Sacrificed*: James Gillray's satirical engraving.

The Boydell Gallery had its critics, one of whom, the caricaturist James Gillray (1757–1815), rapidly produced a harshly satirical etching, *Shakespeare Sacrificed – or – The Offering to Avarice*, showing Boydell, in his aldermanic robes, burning copies of the plays so that the smoke obscures a statue of Shakespeare and swirls upwards in the shape of various characters as portrayed in some of the best paintings in the Gallery. Gillray, who also did a number of Shakespeare-based caricatures satirizing royal and political figures of his day, was not without the commercial motives that he ascribes to Boydell; his print was very popular and sold in large numbers.

★

Garrick spent two long periods of time in France as a tourist, and was enthusiastically fêted on his second trip, in 1764, when he also visited Italy. Though he acted scenes from Shakespeare, sometimes in mime, to admiring private audiences, he gave no theatrical performances. France was taking an interest in Shakespeare, but still very much on its own terms. In 1746 Pierre-Antoine de la Place published (in London, surprisingly) French translations of selected scenes from the plays with a linking commentary. Adaptations by Jean-François Ducis of six plays, starting with *Hamlet*, were acted between 1769 and 1792 at the Comédie Française; Ducis, who knew no English but met Garrick in Paris, worked from translations and adapted heavily; his version of *King Lear* (1783), for instance, written (like de la Place's versions) in rhyming alexandrines, restructures the narrative even more comprehensively than Tate and bears relatively little resemblance to Shakespeare, whose name is not mentioned in the published text. But at least Ducis's versions were intended for the theatre; his *Hamlet*, which lacks many of Shakespeare's characters and in which Hamlet survives to rule Denmark, continued, with revisions, in the repertoire of the Comédie Française until 1852. A complete translation of the plays, literary rather than theatrical, by Pierre Le Tourneur (1736–88) – the first collected edition in a foreign language – appeared in twenty volumes from 1776 to 1782 with a Preface that looks forward to Romantic attitudes rather than backwards to the neoclassicism of Voltaire.[20]

Partly under the influence of Voltaire's adverse criticisms, Shakespeare was slow to make headway in Italy where, as in Germany, the first of his plays to be translated was *Julius Caesar*, in 1756,[21] by Domenico Valentini; and in 1782 the poet Lorenzo Pignotti published a poem, *Ombra di Pope*, in which, on Shakespeare's birthday, his ghost appears to the poet upon his own monument, and the figure of Fancy reveals a series of tableaux from the plays. The first Shakespeare-related play to be performed in the country appears to be an Italian version of Ducis's radical adaptation of *Hamlet*, in 1774.

Shakespeare seems to have exerted a readier appeal in the countries of northern than of southern Europe, perhaps because the northerners found it easier to shake off the shackles of neoclassicism than those born closer to Athens and Rome. In Germany, a landmark comparable to Le Tourneur's translation in France was the prose translation and adaptation by Christoph Martin Wieland of twenty-two of the plays published between 1762 and 1766, revised and completed by Johann Joachim Eschenburg in 1775. The spirit of Romanticism inspired Johann Herder, in a rhapsodic essay published in 1773, and his friend Johann Goethe (1749–1832) to an intoxicated enthusiasm for Shakespeare; in 1771 the latter made a speech, 'On Shakespeare's Day', given during a festivity in the family household modelled on the Garrick Jubilee, and he was to continue to write under Shakespeare's spell and to express his admiration for the rest of his long life. Lichtenberg's descriptions of Garrick's acting (see p. 215) in *Hamlet* and other plays were published in Hamburg in 1776, and the play was to exert a special attraction for the German sensibility from its rapturously received performance (in a heavily adapted version) by Konrad Ackermann's company in the city in the same year, which inaugurated a period of '*Hamlet* fever' throughout the country. The actor most responsible for Shakespeare's establishment on the German theatrical scene was a member of Ackermann's company, Friedrich Ludwig Schröder, who was to form the basis of the actor Serlo in Goethe's *Hamlet*-centred novel *Wilhelm Meister's Apprenticeship* (1795–6), with its famous if sentimental characterization of Hamlet as 'an oak tree planted in a costly jar, which should have borne only pleasant flowers in its bosom – the jar is shivered.' As director of the Hamburg theatre from 1776 to 1780 Schröder staged versions of eight of the plays; his own roles there and in Vienna included Hamlet, Shylock, Lear, Falstaff and Macbeth. His version of *King Lear*, which became standard for many years, was closer to Shakespeare than the Tate adaptation then regularly acted in England; it retains the Fool, and Lear is allowed to die, of a heart attack brought on by the false belief that Cordelia is dead; she recovers and ends the play grieving for him.[22] The English singer Michael Kelly later remembered that Schröder, known as 'the Garrick of Germany', was 'very great in *King Lear*: The scene where he asks after his fool was one of the most exquisite pieces of acting I ever beheld, and indeed, he was very great in most of Shakespeare's plays which had been translated into German.'[23]

In Russia, a radical, neoclassical adaptation of *Hamlet – Gamlet –* made probably from a French translation by the nobleman Alexander Sumarakov (1718–77) was acted in St Petersburg in 1750.[24] More surprisingly, in 1786 the Empress Catherine the Great (ruled 1762–96), a prolific writer in her spare time, embarked on versions of two Shakespeare plays in which she attempted to resist the influence of French neoclassicism by working from a German prose translation. Her version of *The Merry Wives of Windsor* under the title of *This is What it Means to Have a Buck-basket and Linen* (echoing Master Ford at 3.5.131–2), set in St Petersburg, satirizes her fashionable subjects' aping of western ways of life by turning Falstaff into a Frenchified Russian dandy, Polkadov, whose travels have given him a contempt for his countrymen. She also started, but did not complete, a moralistic version of *Timon of Athens*.[25] As in Germany and Italy, the first play in Russia to be translated from the original was *Julius Caesar*, in a version of 1787 by Nikolay Karamzin (1766–1826), who was familiar with English, French and German translations and criticism and who was ahead of his time in arguing that everything in Shakespeare's plays 'is brought together to compose a perfect whole which is in no need of improvement by our present-day *dramatic* authors'.[26] And even before this, King Stanislaus of Poland, visiting England in 1754, had had his faith in the importance of the three unities shaken by his experience of seeing a Shakespeare play. He too translated *Julius Caesar*, not into Polish but into French, the language spoken at his court. The first play to be performed in Czech was *Macbeth*, in 1786, acted by a band of patriots and proclaiming the end of tyranny. In 1790 all copies were ordered to be sold as waste paper; the same thing happened later to the first Czech versions of *Hamlet* and *Romeo and Juliet*, of which no copies survive.[27]

In America, Puritan opposition to the theatre inhibited interest throughout the seventeenth century. The age of Garrick has the distinction of being the first period during which Shakespeare began to make an impact on the American way of life; it also saw a revival of the practice of touring which had taken English actors to Europe in Shakespeare's time and later.[28] Though there are traces of a few earlier amateur and professional performances, and though the Cibber version of *Richard III* was given in New York and elsewhere in 1750, the first regular company to appear in America was one headed by Lewis Hallam that, after falling foul of the law restricting performances of plays to the patent theatres, braved the perils of the six-week sea voyage from London with their costumes, properties and scenery in 1752, rehearsing on the way their repertory of twenty-two plays, including half a dozen or so by Shakespeare. They played first in Williamsburg, Virginia, where they stayed for eight months, moving on from there to New York and, later, Jamaica. Hallam died there, but his son, also Lewis, went on to become one of America's leading actors for close on half a century or more, playing the first American Hamlet in 1759, and on another curious occasion playing Romeo to his mother's Juliet. Gradually the number of companies performing Shakespeare increased and the repertory extended. It is estimated that between 1750 and 1776 fourteen of the plays were professionally acted some 180 times. In 1770 another Hallam, Nancy, scored a special hit as Imogen in *Cymbeline*, and was charmingly painted in the role by Charles Willson Peale (Plate 16). In 1774 play-acting in America was officially, though not entirely successfully, forbidden by a law that was in force for at least eleven years; in some cities the ban was evaded by calling theatres 'schoolhouses' and billing plays as 'moral lectures' – *Richard III* became 'The Fate of Tyranny', *King Lear*, 'The Crime of Filial Ingratitude'. John Adams (1735–1826), first Vice-President and second President of the USA, is probably the first of many conservative politicians to see in Ulysses's 'degree' speech in *Troilus and Cressida* – 'Take but degree away, untune that string, / And hark what discord follows' (1.3.109–10) – support for his own views on social structures.[29] In 1786 he and Thomas Jefferson visited Shakespeare's Birthplace during a visit to England. For all Garrick's endeavours, Adams felt that the inhabitants undervalued Shakespeare; the Birthplace was still in private hands, and there were no regular theatrical performances in the town.

CHAPTER SIX

Regency and Romanticism: 1789–1843

'Shakespeare one gets acquainted with without knowing how. It is a part of an Englishman's constitution. His thoughts and beauties are so spread abroad that one touches them every where, one is intimate with him by instinct. No man of any brain can open at a good part of one of his plays, without falling into the flow of his meaning instantly.'

Henry Crawford in *Mansfield Park*, 1814,
by Jane Austen, Volume 3, Chapter 3

'Was there ever such stuff as great part of Shakespeare? only one must not say so! But what think you? – What? Is there not sad stuff? What? – What? I know it's not to be said! but it's true. Only it's Shakespeare, and nobody dare abuse him.'

King George III of England, reported by Fanny Burney, 1785

IF THE MID-EIGHTEENTH-CENTURY theatrical scene in England was dominated by one individual – David Garrick – at the turn of the century it was a family, the Kembles, who had a virtually proprietary hold on the staging of Shakespeare. The first to make an impact, as we have seen, was also the greatest: Sarah, who married William Siddons, a lesser actor who dwindled into her business manager. She continued to act until 1812 when, at what was announced as her last performance of Lady Macbeth, the play was brought to a close in tribute to her at the end of the sleepwalking scene (5.1). It is hard to over-estimate the reverence in which she was held. Regretting her brief but

81. George Henry Harlow's painting of the Kemble family and friends in the scene of Queen Katherine's trial (*Henry VIII*, 2.4).

ill-judged emergence from retirement in 1816, William Hazlitt was to write: 'She was not less than a goddess, or than a prophetess inspired by the gods. Power was seated on her brow, passion emanated from her breast as from a shrine. She was Tragedy personified . . . To have seen Mrs Siddons was an event in everyone's life.'[1] George Henry Harlow (1787–1819), commissioned to paint Mrs Siddons as Queen Katherine in *Henry VIII*, took it upon himself to add other members of the family (as well as himself) in a representation of Katherine's trial.

Sarah's slightly younger brother, John Philip Kemble (1757–1823), after gaining experience in the provinces, made a successful Drury Lane debut as

82. 'A goodly city is this Antium' (*Coriolanus*, 4.4.1): John Philip Kemble
as Coriolanus, painted by Thomas Lawrence.

83. The Theatre Royal, Drury Lane, in 1813. This is the auditorium in which Kemble,
and later Edmund Kean, had their greatest triumphs.

Hamlet in 1783. A well-educated man originally destined for the priest-
hood he was, like his sister, primarily a tragedian. Tall, handsome, noble
of feature and stately of mien, he had a statuesque quality especially suited to
heroic and classical roles, particularly Coriolanus, which he played in his own
bastardized version of an adaptation by Thomas Sheridan which borrowed
from a play on the same subject by James Thomson. Kemble was finely portrayed in the role by Sir Thomas Lawrence in 1798, and as Hamlet in 1801
– both wonderfully Romantic interpretations. Hazlitt had reservations about
Kemble's Coriolanus; he was to write unkindly that his 'supercilious airs and
nonchalance . . . remind one of the unaccountable abstracted air, the contracted
eyebrows and suspended chin of a man who is just going to sneeze'.[2] But
Hazlitt could also appreciate Kemble's merits, finding that his distinguishing
excellence was 'intensity' – a quality no less associated with his sister, and one
which, as we shall see, was highly valued by the Romantics in general – and

that 'in embodying a high idea of certain characters, which belong rather to sentiment than passion, to energy of will, than to loftiness or to originality of imagination, he was the most excellent actor of his time'.

Kemble was not as universally extolled as Sarah, coming under criticism for speech mannerisms and over-precise, declamatory diction, which was no doubt encouraged by the vast size of the patent theatres. When Drury Lane was rebuilt in 1794 its capacity was enlarged from 2,500 to 3,611 – well over twice the capacity of the Olivier auditorium today, where amplification is sometimes considered necessary. This also encouraged increasingly spectacular staging methods; Kemble's *Coriolanus*, in which his sister triumphed as a majestic and passionate Volumnia, introduced a ceremony after the hero's victory against the Corioles in which 'no fewer than 240 persons marched, in stately procession, across the stage'; they included 'sword-bearers, and standard-bearers, and cup-bearers, and senators, and silver eagle bearers, with the S.P.Q.R. upon them, and trumpeters, and drummers, and priests, and dancing-girls, &c., &c.'[3]

Like Garrick, Kemble was a complete man of the theatre. He was to all intents and purposes the manager of Drury Lane from 1788 to 1802, after which he ran Covent Garden with great success from 1803 till he retired in 1817. He revived no fewer than twenty-seven of Shakespeare's plays in twenty-nine years; he made great efforts to maintain high standards of production; like Garrick he amassed an important collection of texts; and he rethought the acting versions of the plays, publishing his own texts in versions that were long influential. One of his amiable eccentricities, no doubt useful in rehearsal, was to bestow names on minor, previously anonymous characters; so the outlaws in *The Two Gentlemen of Verona* become Ubaldo, Luigi, Carlos, Stephano, Giacomo, Rodolfo, Valerio, and so on.

Enthusiastic Shakespearian though he was, Kemble was no purist; while he sometimes restored passages of Shakespeare, at other times he put the clock back by reverting to adapted texts. Although Bell's edition of 1773–5 (which printed the plays as they were acted at the time) gives a shortened version of the original text of *The Tempest*, Kemble, in 1789, used much of the Restoration adaptation. He played Cibber's *Richard III*, Garrick's *Romeo and Juliet*, and in 1809 put back into *King Lear* much of Tate's verse that Garrick, half a century before, had banished in favour of Shakespeare.

The Kemble tradition was sustained by other members of the family. John Philip's portly younger brother Stephen (1758–1822) is remembered mainly for his ability to play Falstaff, which became his principal role, without padding, as he did at Covent Garden in 1806; he even played Hamlet when weighing eighteen stone. The still younger Charles (1775–1854), though not the best, was the most versatile actor of them all, equally successful in comedy and tragedy. In 1822 he succeeded John Philip as manager of Covent Garden and in the following year put on a revival of *King John*, playing the Bastard himself, which inaugurated a spectacular, historically oriented production style that came to dominate the English stage for close on a century. The costumes were designed by James Robinson Planché, a prolific playwright who

84. Stephen Kemble as Falstaff: a drawing of 1805 by Samuel Wilde.

85. Master Betty costumed as Hamlet standing before a bust of Shakespeare:
a painting by James Northcote (1746–1831).

was also a member of the College of Heralds and an expert on historical costume, who writes in his memoirs:

> When the curtain rose, and discovered King John dressed as his effigy appears in Worcester Cathedral, surrounded by his barons sheathed in mail, with cylindrical helmets and correct armorial shields, and his courtiers in the long tunics and mantles of the thirteenth century, there was a roar of approbation, accompanied by four distinct rounds of applause, so general and so hearty, that the actors were astonished.

After this, Planché claims, 'a complete reformation of dramatic costume became inevitable upon the English stage.'[4]

Charles Kemble's daughter Fanny (1809–93), a remarkable person by any standards, helped to save the fortunes of Covent Garden at a difficult time when, in 1829, she scored a great hit as Juliet with her father as Mercutio – his most famous role – and her mother as Lady Capulet. As Lewis Hallam had played Romeo to his mother's Juliet (p. 247), so Fanny was to play Juliet to her father's Romeo – he was fifty-seven – on a successful American tour in 1833–4, at the end of which she married a southern planter, Pierce Butler, who owned 700 slaves. This put an end to her theatrical career until she divorced him, largely because of her hatred of slavery, in 1848; later she made occasional appearances as actress and reader as well as publishing numerous volumes of her journals.[5] Her independence of mind made her a fitting dedicatee in 1832 of (Mrs) Anna Jameson's *Characteristics of Women, Moral, Poetical and Historical*, known in later reprints simply as *Shakespeare's Women*, one of a sequence of books written by women on this subject. Mrs Jameson, developing earlier interest in Shakespeare's characterization, writes well-informed essays on leading characters of the plays as women 'of intellect', 'of passion and imagination', 'of the affections', and as 'historical characters'. Later she was to become a distinguished historian of art.

A remarkable theatrical phenomenon of this period is Bettymania – the extraordinary success of the boy actor William Henry West Betty (1791–1874), known as Master Betty, or The Young Roscius (after the great Roman actor), who at the age of ten, after seeing Mrs Siddons as Elvira in

Sheridan's tragedy *Pizarro*, is said to have declared that he would expire if he did not become an actor.[6] After a number of rapturously received appearances in leading roles including Hamlet – which he is said to have memorized in three hours – in Ireland, Scotland, and the provinces, he was engaged at Covent Garden and Drury Lane late in 1803 for inflated fees; his success was sensational. The armed forces were called out to preserve order, and many persons were injured in the crush for admission. King George III personally presented him to the Queen and princesses, and William Pitt suspended Parliament so that members could see him as Hamlet. An anonymously published volume of *Memoirs*, along with a 'critique on his Principal Characters', was in a second edition by 1804.[7] In 1805, still only fourteen, he added Richard III and Macbeth to his Shakespearian repertoire. Gillray published a caricature showing Sheridan as Betty's principal puffer. Gradually the furore abated; he had little success as an adult actor, but was able to retire at the age of thirty-three with a large fortune.

Styles of acting swing from age to age like pendulums. As Garrick was to Quin, so Edmund Kean (*c.*1787–1833) was to Kemble. The day in January 1814 when Kean appeared at Drury Lane as Shylock sounded the death knell for the Kemble school of acting. Like Garrick, Kean was unimpressive in stature; he was often hoarse, especially in the vast recesses of Drury Lane and later in his short life when his voice was ravaged by heavy drinking. Scandal after scandal endangered his career. In 1825 the Drury Lane prompter, James Winston, whose journals provide eye-opening accounts of what went on behind the scenes, wrote that after going missing all night Kean was 'found in his room fast asleep wrapt up in a large white greatcoat. He then sent for some potence [presumably a cordial drink],[8] some ginger [regarded as an aphrodisiac], etc., and said, "Send me Lewis or the other woman. I must have a fuck, and then I shall do." He had it. They let him sleep till about six, when they awoke him, dressed him, and he acted but not very sober.' The role was Hamlet.[9]

In his brief prime Kean must have been – with the possible exception of Laurence Olivier – the most electrifying actor of the English stage, transcending his limitations by the imaginative intensity with which he identified himself with the characters he played. Coleridge famously remarked that to see Kean was 'like reading Shakespeare by flashes of lightning'. This may not

86. James Gillray's caricature of Richard Brinsley Sheridan puffing the merits of Master Betty. The large bubble shows the boy actor bestriding the conquered bodies of the actors Garrick, Kemble, and G. F. Cooke.

87. Edmund Kean
as Othello, drawn
and engraved by
F. W. Gear.

be an unequivocal compliment; Kean was an uneven – it might even be said flashy – performer. But even late in Kean's career, Leigh Hunt could write that he could not see him

without being moved, and moved too in fifty ways – by his sarcasm, his sweetness, his pathos, his exceeding grace, his gallant levity, his measureless dignity: for his little person absolutely becomes tall, and rises to the height of moral grandeur, in such characters as that of Othello. We have seen him with three or four persons round him, all taller than he, but himself so graceful, so tranquil, so superior, so nobly self-possessed, in the midst, that the mind of the spectator rose above them by his means, and so gave him a moral stature that confounded itself with the personal.[10]

Kean was at his greatest in strongly characterized figures – Shylock, Richard III, Lear, Othello, Iago, Macbeth – less impressive as Richard II and Romeo. He played Richard II in an odd version of 1815 by Richard Wroughton in which the Queen mourns over her husband's body in lines adapted from those of the dying Lear, with 'Pray you, undo my lace' instead of 'Pray you, undo my button', along with a snatch of *Titus Andronicus*. Kean must have been bitterly conscious of the irony that words not present in the version of *King Lear* that had been acted for the past 150 years were now being heard in a different play almost literally over his dead body. When he played Lear in 1823 he was at least allowed the death scene, though otherwise the text was mostly Tate's. As often in versions of the tragedies throughout the century, the curtain fell, to slow music, immediately after the hero's last words.

The eventual return to the stage of a wholly Shakespearian *Lear* – if not of the whole of Shakespeare's *Lear* – must be credited to William Charles Macready (1793–1873). One of the most reluctant actors in the history of the English stage, he despised his profession – especially as represented by the disreputable Kean – and made himself intensely disagreeable to many of its members. Careful and conscientious, he sought consistency and uniformity of characterization rather than the lightning flashes of Kean's sequence of crowd-pleasing moments known as 'points'; after playing Othello in 1836 he wrote in his amazingly voluminous and torturedly self-searching diaries that 'the audience seemed to wait for Kean's points, and this rather threw me off my balance'. Like Kemble, as manager of Covent Garden from 1837 to 1839, then of Drury Lane from 1841 to 1843, he sought attention to detail and discipline in his productions. He despised the adaptations still in use, writing in a characteristically lofty vein in 1838 of his astonishment 'at the base venality of the disgusting newspaper writers – the wretches – who dare to laud the fustian of Cibber, and tried to keep the many in ignorance by praising his trash called *Richard III*'. Nevertheless Cibber's adaptation continued to be played.

It was also in 1838 that Macready staged *Lear* in a version which, though shortened and rearranged, abandoned Tate and restored the character of the Fool (played by a woman). Similarly, his popular *Tempest* in the same year abandoned quite a bit of Shakespeare as well as the Dryden/Davenant changes. The trend towards spectacular staging continued: according to the paper *John Bull*, a 'mimic vessel was outrageously bumped and tossed about on waves that we can liken to nothing save tiny cocks of hay, painted green, and afflicted with a spasm'. And Ariel, also played by a girl, was 'whisked about by wires and a cogwheel, like the fairies in *Cinderella*'.

Perhaps the most revealing account not only of Macready as an actor but also of the relationship between performers and audiences at the time was written by Helena Faucit. At the age of twenty, in 1837, she played Hermione to his Leontes in *The Winter's Tale*. Of her descent in the final scene from the pedestal on which she had been standing motionless as the statue she writes:

> Oh, can I ever forget Mr Macready at this point! At first he stood speechless, as if turned to stone; his face with an awe-struck look upon it. Could this, the very counterpart of his queen, be a wondrous piece of mechanism? Could art so mock the life? He had seen her laid out as dead, the funeral obsequies performed over her, with her dear son beside her. Thus absorbed in wonder, he remained until Paulina said: 'Nay, present your hand.' Tremblingly he advanced, and touched gently the hand held out to him. Then, what a cry came with, 'O, she's warm!' It is impossible to describe Mr Macready here. He was Leontes' very self! His passionate joy at finding Hermione really alive seemed beyond control. Now he was prostrate at her feet, then enfolding her in his arms. I had a slight veil or covering over my head and neck, supposed to make the statue look older. This fell off in an instant. The hair, which came unbound, and fell on my shoulders, was reverently kissed and caressed. The whole change was so sudden, so overwhelming, that I suppose I cried out hysterically, for he whispered to me, 'Don't be frightened, my child! don't be frightened! Control yourself!' All this went on during a tumult of applause that sounded like a storm of hail . . . It was the finest burst of passionate speechless emotion I ever saw, or could have conceived.[11]

Macready was succeeded as manager of Covent Garden by Charles Mathews and his wife Elizabeth – Madame – Vestris, whose rule was notable for the production, in 1839, of *Love's Labour's Lost*, the last of Shakespeare's plays to

88. Elizabeth Vestris as the first female Oberon in her 1840 production of *A Midsummer Night's Dream* at Covent Garden.

be revived since his own time. Vestris played Rosaline in a text that was shorn of much of its comedy and wordplay. Then in 1840 they gave *A Midsummer Night's Dream*, which had always been subjected to adaptation, in a purely Shakespearian, if somewhat abbreviated, text prepared by Planché, who also designed what must have been a very pretty production. The thirteen songs were at least all set to words from the play. It was the year of Queen Victoria's marriage; she and Albert saw the production within a few days of their first anniversary. Vestris, a popular and talented singer, actress and theatre manager who often played male ('breeches') roles which enabled her to show off her famously shapely legs, and who had played Ariel to Macready's Prospero in 1824, took the role of Oberon; this first female casting of the role remained standard in both England and America until 1914.[12]

The comparison of Macready's *Tempest* to *Cinderella* reminds us that Shakespeare still belonged to the popular theatre. Even when Kemble, Kean, and Macready played the tragedies they were given as part of a mixed bill, characteristically followed by a comic afterpiece and interspersed with other entertainments, and other performances played fast and loose with Shakespeare's texts in the cause of entertainment. At Covent Garden between 1816 and 1828 the playwright Frederick Reynolds (1764–1841) mounted musical adaptations of several of the comedies which savaged the texts, interspersing them with pageants, spectacles and dances, and with songs, duets, glees, and choruses culled from many other sources, including Shakespeare's plays and poems, and charmingly set to music by Sir Henry Bishop (1786–1855). His song 'Lo, here the gentle lark', with words from *Venus and Adonis*, written for *The Comedy of Errors* (1819), is still a favourite with coloratura sopranos.[13] Even more skeletal versions of the plays include a 'Ballet of Music and Action', performed at the Royal Circus, or Surrey Theatre, in 1809 and *The History, Murders, Life and Death of Macbeth* which sounds from contemporary descriptions rather like a precursor of the silent film: 'Action was the thing, action heightened by music and expanded or interpreted by means of banners borne in by messengers, on which were written sentences like "By Sinel's death, Macbeth is Thane of Glamis", or "The wood of Birnam moves towards Dunsinane".'[14] The ordinary theatre-goer's familiarity with plays in the standard repertoire meant that playwrights could rely on them to pick up Shakespearian allusions in other works such as pantomimes and extravaganzas. Planché's 'fairy extravaganza' *The Fair One with the Golden Locks* (1843), for instance, includes a full-scale parody of Macbeth's 'dagger' soliloquy, beginning

> Is this a corkscrew that I see before me?
> The handle towards my hand – clutch thee I will!
> I have thee not – and yet I see thee still!
> Art thou a hardware article? or oh!
> Simply a fancy article, for show.
> A corkscrew of the mind – a false creation
> Of crooked ways, a strong insinuation![15]

This period also saw early manifestations of a curious sub-genre of Shakespearian imitation, burlesques, or parodies of complete plays. The pattern was set by John Poole's 1810 *Hamlet Travestie*, with 'Burlesque Annotations, after the manner of Dr Johnson and Geo. Steevens Esq., and the various Commentators'. Frequently reprinted and, in later years, performed, it was used for satire of Henry Irving as late as 1874 and has been revived in modern times. Poole parodies and paraphrases the play in rhymed couplets, including songs set to popular airs. Maurice Dowling's witless *Othello Travestie* (Liverpool, 1834) was so popular when given at the Strand in London that it helped to establish that theatre as a home of burlesque. The merry finale of his *Romeo and Juliet* (1837), based on Garrick's version, imitates that of Rossini's opera *La Cenerentola*, and Charles Selby's *Kinge Richard ye Third* (1845), successful in America as well as England, features a 'Gigantic Equestrian Pageant'; at the end Richard comes to life and begs the audience's favour in a finale set to 'Yankee Doodle'.

Although from the 1820s onwards pictorialism came to dominate Shakespearian production, a unique experiment in 1844 foreshadowed the much later reaction against it. Under the guidance of Planché, Benjamin Webster put on at the Haymarket Theatre a production of *The Taming of the Shrew* that attempted to reconstruct the conditions of its original performance (see overleaf). Considering that our only real pictorial evidence of the interior of an Elizabethan theatre, the Swan drawing (p. 63), was not discovered till 1888, his was a truly pioneering endeavour. Instead of Garrick's adaptation, then standard, the original text was given complete, running to three and a half hours. The Induction, revived for the first time since the Restoration, was played with full scenery, but *The Times* reported that for the rest of the play 'the whole dramatic apparatus' was 'only two screens and a pair of curtains'.

During the Romantic period some of the best writing about Shakespeare is inspired by the theatre. Encouraged by the rise of serious journalism and by the quality of individual performers, writers such as Charles Lamb, Leigh Hunt, William Hazlitt, and even John Keats[16] worked for newspapers and other periodicals, often saying as much about the plays as about the performances. Hazlitt, for example, wrote reviews and essays about the drama intermittently between 1813 and 1828. He was present, happily, at Kean's London debut as Shylock, and was to write memorably about the actor on many subsequent occasions. Hazlitt's reputation as a literary critic of Shakespeare rests mainly on his frequently reprinted book *Characters of Shakespear's*

89. An artist's impression of Ben Webster's production of *The Taming of the Shrew*, with the Lord and his servants to the left, Christopher Sly and his party to the right. They remained on stage throughout and were served drinks during the intervals.

Plays (1817). A year later he published *A View of the English Stage, or, A Series of Dramatic Criticisms,* collecting most of the reviews that he had written to that date. In fact, however, many paragraphs from those reviews had already appeared in the earlier book. This was possible because his reviews are rather in the nature of literary essays on the theatrical interpretation of certain roles than immediate reviews of a particular performance.[17]

Paradoxically Hazlitt, for all his appreciation of fine acting, often expresses a preference for reading Shakespeare over seeing the plays acted. This must be attributed partly to the frequently ramshackle standards of performance; Reynolds's *A Midsummer Night's Dream* of 1816, for example, incited him to an eloquent attack: 'All that is fine in the play, was lost in the representation.' In part too it is by way of a reaction against the heavily adapted texts still in use, which he deplores. But it also reflects a characteristically Romantic preference (which had been expressed in the previous year by Goethe in his essay *Shakespeare kein Ende* (Shakespeare Without End)) for the imaginary over the real, the solitary sublime to the gregariously shared experience. Charles Lamb's famous and eloquent essay 'On the Tragedies of Shakespeare, considered with reference to their fitness for stage representation' (1811) similarly complained that 'the Lear of Shakespeare cannot be acted . . . The contemptible machinery by which they mimic the storm which he goes out in, is not more inadequate to represent the horror of the real elements, than any actor can be to represent Lear.' Leigh Hunt, the earliest of our major theatre critics – he started in 1805 – was more tolerant of adaptation than Hazlitt but concurred with him in reacting against the neoclassical criticism of Dr Johnson, asserting that his remarks on *King John* are 'in the usual spirit of the Doctor's criticism, consisting of assertions very well founded, but careless of all proof ', and praising Hazlitt's *Characters of Shakespear's Plays* by saying that 'it must inevitably supersede the dogmatic and half-informed criticisms of Johnson'.[18]

The spirit of Romanticism evident in the finest acting of the period, with its emphasis on the individual psychology of characters represented, and in the response to this acting of theatre critics, is apparent too in more formal literary criticism and in other writings of the time.[19] Samuel Taylor Coleridge is one of the most highly respected of critics, but with the exception of a remarkable chapter, 'The Specific Symptoms of Poetic Power elucidated in a critical analysis of Shakespeare's *Venus and Adonis* and *Lucrece*' in his *Biographia Literaria* (1817), which represents the first substantial criticism of the poems, his views have to be reconstructed from scattered writings and lecture notes, with the result that it is scarcely unfair to turn back on him what he said of Kean: 'to read Coleridge on Shakespeare is like reading about Shakespeare by flashes of lightning'. Coleridge sought to define an organic unity within Shakespeare's works by tracing patterns of language in the search for a psychological subtext – he coined the very word 'psycho-analytical'. In this he resembled the German A. W. Schlegel (1767–1845), whose *Lectures on Dramatic Art and Literature* of 1811, translated into English in 1815, exerted strong influence on Coleridge and other English critics. Schlegel embarked upon a verse translation of Shakespeare's plays in 1791, completing sixteen texts by 1801 and adding one more (*Richard III*, thus completing the histories) in 1811; the enterprise was completed in 1833 under the supervision of Ludwig Tieck; though it has been largely superseded for theatrical use, it remains one of the classic texts of German literature in its own right. The Coleridgian search for organic unity is inclined to lead to the bardolatrous assumption that every detail in every work of Shakespeare is a figure in an intricately woven carpet, and that failure to see the point of every detail represents inadequacy on the part of the critic. Still, it led to greater understanding of Shakespeare's techniques of composition, and especially of his language and imagery. It was enormously influential, and largely beneficial, until well past the middle of the twentieth century.

Like Coleridge's, Keats's writings about Shakespeare are mostly to be found in his letters, though he has a fine sonnet 'On sitting down to read King Lear once again' which he wrote on 22 January 1818 on a blank page before the play in his copy of the first ever facsimile of the First Folio, a line by line, letter for letter reprint published in 1807. Keats also owned a seven-volume 1814 reprint of the plays which he gave to his friend Joseph Severn as he lay dying in Rome, and a volume of the *Poems* of 1817, and underlined and otherwise marked passages in all of them.[20] His critical remarks are mostly scattered through his letters in which his often wonderful prose is Shakespearian in its vivacity and glancing intelligence. He liked to imagine Shakespeare as a presiding spirit over his own genius, writing to the painter Benjamin Haydon 'When in the Isle of Wight I met with a Shakespeare' – an engraving – 'in the Passage of the House at which I lodged – it comes nearer to my idea of him than any I have seen – I was but there a Week yet the old Woman made me take it with me though I went off in a hurry – Do you not think this is ominous of good?'[21]

Comparisons with Shakespeare infuse Keats's deepest meditations about his own art; the 'poetical character', he writes, 'is not itself – it has no self – it is every thing and nothing – It has no character – it enjoys light and shade;

On sitting down to read King Lear once again.

O Golden-tongued Romance, with serene Lute!
    Fair plumed Syren, Queen of far-away!
    Leave melodizing on this wintry day
Shut up thine olden Pages and be mute.
Adieu! for once again, the fierce dispute,
    Betwixt Damnation and impassion'd clay
    Must I burn through, once more humbly assay
The bitter-sweet of this Shakspearean fruit.

Chief Poet! and ye Clouds of Albion,
    Begetters of our deep eternal theme!
When through the old oak forest I am gone,
    Let me not wander in a barren dream:
But when I am consumed in the fire,
Give me new Phoenix wings to fly at my desire.

Jan'. 22. 1818

90. The manuscript of Keats's sonnet 'On sitting down to read King Lear
once again'.

it lives in gusto, be it foul or fair, high or low, rich or poor, mean or elevated
– It has as much delight in conceiving an Iago as an Imogen.' And Keats's
struggle to define the quality that goes 'to form a Man of Achievement
especially in Literature and which Shakespeare possessed so enormously –
I mean *Negative Capability*, that is when man is capable of being in uncertainties, Mysteries, doubts, without any irritable reaching after fact and reason'
comes in a letter in which he says also that 'the excellence of every Art is its
intensity, capable of making all disagreeables evaporate, from their being in

close relationship with Beauty and Truth – Examine *King Lear* and you will find this exemplified throughout.'[22] Keats helps us to understand the quality of imagination that goes specifically to make a poetic dramatist, a writer who can submerge his own identity in that of the characters he depicts. And his remarks are typical of the Romantic attitude in their emphasis on intensity and on character rather than structure.

Keats was to visit Stratford, which was slowly becoming a centre of literary pilgrimage. The first visitors' book to Shakespeare's Birthplace, which was still in private ownership, shows that from 1812 to 1814 nearly 700 people visited the house each year.[23] In March 1818 Haydon wrote breathlessly to Keats 'I shall certainly go mad! In a field at Stratford upon Avon, in a field that belonged to Shakespeare; they have found a gold ring and seal, with the initial thus – *W. S. and a true lover's knot between*. If *this* is not Shakespeare who is it? – a true lover's knot.!! – ... As sure as you breathe, & that he was the first of beings the Seal belonged to him – O Lord! –'.[24] Keats replied with understandable though kindly scepticism.

But was this necessary? The ring, now in the possession of the Shakespeare

91. The gold seal ring bearing Shakespeare's initials found
in a field in Stratford in 1810.

Birthplace Trust, is on exhibition with a cautious inscription. The story of its discovery in 1810, eight years before Haydon wrote, is recounted by the Stratford solicitor Robert Bell Wheler in his *Guide to Stratford-upon-Avon* of 1814. The find was made by a labourer's wife named Martin in a field next to the churchyard; oddly – perhaps auspiciously – a man named William Shakespeare was working in the field at the time. The ring was nearly black with rust and although Wheler bought it (for the value of its weight in gold) on the day it was found, Mrs Martin had already had time to have it 'unnecessarily immersed in aquafortis to ascertain and prove the metal at a silver-smith's shop, which consequently restored its original colour' but regrettably destroyed what might have been useful evidence in the ring's encrustation. Wheler – a reputable local historian – tells that in spite of 'numerous researches into public and private documents' he found 'no Stratfordian of that period so likely to own such a ring as Shakespeare'. He also intriguingly noted that no seal is affixed to Shakespeare's will but that 'where the Scrivener had written "In witness whereof I have hereunto set my hand and Seal"' these words "and seal" were struck out,' as if Shakespeare had recently lost his seal ring. (In fact 'hand' is substituted for 'seal' in the will.) Early in the twentieth century the scholar E. K. Chambers, in his cautious way, proposed that the separation of the initials on the ring by a lovers' knot 'may indicate two persons rather than one'.[25] But this ignores the entire function of a seal ring, which is to emboss the initials of an individual on the wax with which a legal or other official document is sealed. The possibility that this ring is the only surviving personal relic of Shakespeare is stronger than has usually been supposed.

Later in 1818 Keats visited Stratford with his friend Benjamin Bailey, who records that they signed the visitors' book in the church and wrote their names on the wall of the Birthplace, where Keats also signed the visitors' book, giving as his 'place of abode' 'Everywhere'.[26] Another famous visitor, Sir Walter Scott, wrote in his journal for 8 April 1828, 'We visited the tomb of the mighty wizzard. It is in the bad taste of James Ist's reign but what a magic does the locality possess. There are stately monuments of forgotten families but when you have seen Shakespeare what care we for the rest?'[27] Scott was painted, probably by William Allen, standing bare-headed before the monument and looking down at the gravestone (see overleaf).

Celebration of Shakespeare was growing. The two-hundredth anniversary of his death was commemorated in a small way in 1816, and in 1820 Leigh Hunt wrote an essay, 'Shakespeare's Birthday', proposing that the occasion should be a regular 'subject for public rejoicing' and that within the family circle:

> If the enthusiasm is in high taste, the ladies should be crowned with violets, which (next to the roses of their lips) seem to have been [Shakespeare's] favourite flower. After tea should come singing and music, especially the songs which Arne set from his plays, and the ballad of 'Thou soft-flowing Avon'. If an engraving or bust of him could occupy the principal place in the room, it would look like the 'present deity' of the occasion; and we have known a very pleasant effect produced by everybody's bringing some quotation applicable to him from his works, and laying it before his image, to be read in the course of the evening.

Four years later the first Shakespeare Club was founded, in Stratford, to organize annual birthday celebrations, with a 'jubilee' every third year; it sponsored the building of the town's first permanent theatre, on Chapel Lane, opened in 1827. A festival in 1830 included performances by Charles Kean.

★

Though it is a back-handed compliment, Shakespeare's mounting fame encouraged the attentions of forgers. They had to contend with the deep scholarship of Edmond Malone (pp. 233–4). In 1790 he had revealed that the actor Charles Macklin, then in his nineties, had long previously – in 1748 – forged a pamphlet in which Ben Jonson was castigated for ingratitude to Shakespeare and to the playwright John Ford, and that Macklin's motive was the desire to gain publicity for a revival of one of Ford's plays in which the actor's wife was to appear.[28] In the process Malone, never one to use a nutcracker when a sledgehammer would do, wrote a new biographical sketch of Jonson and the first history of the Poet Laureateship.

92. *Opposite.* Sir Walter Scott paying homage at Shakespeare's grave; an oil painting attributed to William Allen (1782–1850).

A few years later Malone had more exciting material on which to exercise his skills. William Henry Ireland (1775–1835), a well-read and stage-struck congenital liar, was the son of a talented if credulous engraver and passionate collector of books, pictures, and curiosities, Samuel Ireland (d. 1800). The young man was especially fascinated by the story of Thomas Chatterton (1752–70), the 'marvellous boy' who had counterfeited many supposed medieval poetical and other documents. Though Malone exposed them as forgeries, he admired their literary merits. Around 1794, when Samuel was preparing a volume of *Picturesque Views of the Avon* which includes the first representation of Anne Hathaway's Cottage, the father and son made a pilgrimage to Stratford where the wheelwright John Jordan (p. 23) regaled them with anecdotes of dubious validity. They also heard a cock and bull story about the alleged destruction a couple of weeks before they arrived of basketfuls of Shakespeare manuscripts to make room for a bevy of young partridges.

This incident may have inspired William Henry to assuage his father's disappointment by filling the gap himself. He was employed in a lawyer's office where he had access to spare leaves of parchment and old paper, and to ancient seals. Before long he was proud to present his astonished and grateful father with a wonderful stream of papers including business documents about the Globe, letters to Shakespeare from Queen Elizabeth and the Earl of Southampton, a love letter (with a lock of hair) and verses written by Shakespeare to 'Anne Hatherrewaye', an appendix to Shakespeare's will making amends for the bequest to his widow of the second-best bed, a new manuscript of *King Lear* improved by the omission of bawdy passages and obscurities, manuscript extracts from *Hamlet*, and a ridiculous portrait of Shakespeare. He later offered his father two previously unknown Shakespeare plays, *Vortigern* and *Henry II*. They had all come, he explained, from a great chest in the house of a wealthy young man of his acquaintance who preferred to remain anonymous. From February 1795 Samuel invited selected literary and other luminaries to inspect the finds in his home. Among those who paid homage was James Boswell, who fell to his knees, kissed the relics, and declared that he could now die happy. He did, three months later. Though there were many sceptics, and satirical journalists had a field day, even authorities from the College of Heralds pronounced the papers authentic.

93. William Henry Ireland's attempt to convince his father that he had found a
new portrait of Shakespeare. Faced with scepticism, he tried to deflect it by forging
a letter in which Shakespeare described the picture as a 'whymsycalle conceyte'.

Malone was a disbeliever from the start, alerted by the fact that he was not
included among those invited to the private view, and struck by the resemblances between the spelling of the Shakespeare papers, full of unnecessarily
doubled letters and redundant final e's, to that of the Chatterton documents. It is astonishing, indeed, that anyone in the least familiar with papers
of Shakespeare's period and with his writings could have believed him at
any time of his life to have been capable of addressing to his beloved such
twaddle as:

> Is there inne heavenne aught more rare
> Thanne thou sweete Nymphe of Avon fayre
> Is there onne Earthe a Manne more trewe
> Thanne Willy Shakspeare is toe you.

On Christmas Eve 1795 Samuel Ireland published an impressive and expensive volume of facsimiles and annotated transcripts called *Miscellaneous Papers and Legal Instruments under the Hand and Seal of William Shakspeare: including the Tragedy of King Lear and a Small Fragment of Hamlet, from the Original MSS. in the Possession of Samuel Ireland, of Norfolk Street*. A few days later, in the 1 January issue of the *Gentleman's Magazine*, Malone made a preliminary strike, and only three months later, on 31 March, brought his sledgehammer to bear with the publication of a rapidly written and commercially successful volume of 400 pages, *An Inquiry into the Authenticity of Certain Miscellaneous Papers and Legal Instruments, Published Dec. 24, MDCCXCV. and Attributed to Shakspeare, Queen Elizabeth, and Henry, Earl of Southampton*.

Malone's passionate scholarship dealt the first death blow to the forgeries. The second came only three days later. The Irelands had persuaded John Philip Kemble to put on a performance of *Vortigern* at Drury Lane, with himself in the leading role. Sarah Siddons had diplomatically pleaded ill health. The first performance took place on 2 April, cautiously avoiding the inauspicious previous day. There were titters at the banal language during the early part of the play, and towards the end, when Kemble had to say 'And when this solemn mockery is o'er', the audience fell apart. The first performance was also the last. After some prevarication William Henry admitted the fraud, but his humiliated father, deceived and possibly self-deceived, continued to proclaim his son's innocence. He published the new plays in 1799 and continued, unsuccessfully, to try to have *Henry II* performed.[29]

The process of publishing Shakespeare's authentic plays during this period is one of both domestication and democratization. New reprints and editions poured from the presses, and publishers, who had previously catered largely for gentlemen's libraries, now also had middle-class, and even impoverished, households in mind. Whereas editors such as Pope had mainly relegated to the foot of the page passages that, for reasons of propriety and otherwise, they wished Shakespeare had not written, the first systematic expurgation of twenty of the plays was made by the chaste-minded Henrietta (1754–1830), sister of Thomas Bowdler (1754–1825), in the notorious 'Family Shakespeare, in which nothing is added to the original text, but those words and expressions are omitted which cannot with propriety be read aloud in a family'. Publication in 1807 of the four-volume edition was anonymous, perhaps, as Gary Taylor suggests, as a way of protecting Henrietta's reputation by not admitting to have 'understood things that no decent woman should understand'.[30] Henrietta's twin brother Thomas, a physician and philanthropist, completed the disembowelling and accepted responsibility for it in the ten-volume edition of 1818; he was concerned to remove what he regarded as frivolous biblical allusions as well as lewdness. Both editions, it's worth remarking, were published well before the Victorian era. Victorianism is a common pre-Victorian phenomenon, perhaps as a reaction against the excesses of the Regency.

Bowdler's Preface to the complete edition declares that 'Many words and expressions occur which are of so indecent a nature as to render it highly desirable that they should be erased . . . neither the vicious taste of the age, nor the most brilliant effusions of wit, can afford an excuse for profaneness or obscenity . . . To banish everything of this nature from his writings is the object of the present undertaking.' There are close parallels between the Bowdlers' enterprise and that of another brother and sisterly collaboration, which also first appeared in 1807, and which also offered initially an adaptation of twenty of Shakespeare's plays. This is Charles and Mary Lamb's *Tales from Shakespeare*, ascribed on its first publication to Charles, whose sister's name was not added to the title page until the seventh edition, of 1838, though Charles had made clear in letters to friends that Mary wrote fourteen of the tales and that he contributed only six – the tragedies, along with 'occasionally a tail piece or correction of grammar – and *all* of the spelling'.

Both enterprises were undertaken in a spirit both of education and of protectiveness for the young. The Lambs, explaining that the *Tales* are written mainly for 'young ladies . . . because boys are generally permitted the use of their fathers' libraries at a much earlier age than girls are', encourage brothers to explain the hard bits to their sisters, and even to read pleasing passages from the original plays to them, 'carefully selecting what is proper for a young sister's ear'. Similarly, Bowdler declares that his aim has been 'to

94. 'Round about the cauldron go' (4.1.4): the anonymous illustration for *Macbeth*, with hedgehog and toad, cat and bats, and perhaps a 'fillet of a fenny snake', in the first edition of Lamb's *Tales from Shakespeare*.

exclude . . . whatever is unfit to be read aloud by a gentleman to a company of ladies'. He can, he says, 'hardly imagine a more pleasing occupation for a winter's evening in the country, than for a father to read one of Shakespeare's plays to his family circle. My object is to enable him to do so without incurring the danger of falling unawares among words and expressions which are of such a nature as to raise a blush on the cheek of modesty, or render it necessary for the reader to pause, and examine the sequel, before he proceeds further in the entertainment of the evening.'

The Lambs idealize the plots and clean up the language; there are no bawds or brothels in their *Measure for Measure* or *Pericles*, and bawdy language is almost totally expunged. In *A Midsummer Night's Dream* the name 'Bottom' is avoided in favour of 'the clown', no doubt in an attempt to avert unwanted giggles. Charles and Mary were not completely successful in their enterprise; in *The Merchant of Venice*, both Mary Lamb and Henrietta Bowdler retain Graziano's bawdy closing couplet about 'keeping safe Nerissa's ring'; when brother Thomas came along, however, he noticed its double meaning in time to remove it from the collected edition. Some plays posed special challenges. Although in *Othello* Bowdler changes 'Your daughter and the Moor are now making the beast with two backs' to '. . . are now together', he allows the word 'whore' to remain, prefacing the play with a warning that in it he has 'depart[ed] in some degree from the principle on which this publication is undertaken'. And *Measure for Measure* defeated him altogether: 'Feeling my own inability to render this play sufficiently correct for family-reading, I have thought it advisable to print it . . . from the published copy, as performed at the Theatre Royal, Covent Garden' – that is, from John Philip Kemble's acting version.

Both Bowdler's edition and the Lambs' *Tales* were astonishingly successful. Though the *Family Shakespeare* is now relegated to library basements and mentioned only to be derided, it went through at least thirty-five reprints during the nineteenth century, including an American one in 1850; and the process of bowdlerization – the verb 'bowdlerize' was already in use by 1836 – continued in English school editions at least until the 1960s. Lamb's *Tales* took off to a slow start. One reviewer, who did not consider them 'proper studies for female children', pointed out that to tell girls that there are parts of Shakespeare that they should not read until they are older 'serves only as a *stimulus* to juvenile curiosity, which requires a *bridle* rather than a *Spur*.'[31] Still, eleven editions had appeared by the time Mary Lamb died, in 1847, and after that the stream became a flood, especially with the introduction of compulsory elementary education. In 1987 I discovered evidence of close on 200 editions in English up to that date, often supplemented by extracts from the plays, annotations, specimen examination questions and other teaching aids, along with translations into some forty languages as far flung as Burmese, Swahili, Macedonian, and the African dialects of Ga and Ewe.[32] It was through Lamb's *Tales* that Shakespeare first became available to readers in many countries, including China and Japan. Although much better prose versions of the plays, such as those of Leon Garfield,[33] are now available, the Lambs' is still frequently chosen by adults as a book suitable for them to give to children, less frequently I suspect by children as a book that they are anxious to read for themselves.

A pioneer in the cause of popular education was Charles Knight (1791–1873), who was associated with innumerable publishing enterprises designed to bring knowledge to the poor. The son of a Windsor printer and bookseller, he developed a keen interest in the processes of book production early in life. In his youth a customer of his father's – 'a clergyman who had received an appointment in India' – grateful for a good offer for his books, gave him a badly defective copy of the First Folio. Knight got access to a similar font of type along with (like Ireland before him, but with purer motives) leaves of old paper and, with the aid of the recently published facsimile, set himself 'the task of composing every page that was wholly wanting or was torn and sullied. When the book was handsomely bound I was in raptures at my handiwork.' But his father accepted a handsome offer for it from a tutor at nearby Eton College.[34] Knight's early interest in Shakespeare developed in later years when, after publishing in multiple parts a *Pictorial Bible* (from 1836) and a *Pictorial History of England* (from 1837) he turned his attention, in 1838, to *The Pictorial Shakespeare*, edited by himself and completed, in fifty-five parts, in 1841; it was frequently reprinted in both England and America in varying formats.

Knight was able to use the relatively new process of lithography for his illustrations. They are not of outstanding quality, but fine painters in various media continued to derive inspiration – and some of them to make a living –

from Shakespeare's works. The Boydell Gallery (pp. 241–3) represents a climax, and virtually an end, to the use of Shakespearian themes for grandiose historical paintings, though some of the contributors, including Fuseli and James Northcote, continued to draw on Shakespeare well into the nineteenth century. Richard Westall (1765–1836), a prolific book illustrator employed by Boydell and others, abandoned historical paintings when he found they did not sell. He created one of the most attractively Romantic images of Shakespeare, languorously and boyishly handsome in a Byronic pose (Westall had painted Byron), still young enough to sport a fine mop of curly hair, dallying with the Muse of Comedy who has descended in swirling clouds of diaphanous white tulle, while appearing to make a conciliatory gesture towards a disdainful and sombre Tragedy (Plate 9). In paintings by two of the most celebrated artists, J. M. W. Turner and John Martin, the ostensible subjects, Juliet and the Nurse for Turner and Macbeth, Banquo and the Witches for Martin, are dwarfed by their Romantically sublime surroundings. Oddly, Turner's Juliet lives in Venice, not Verona.

Artists of the Romantic era tended to prefer more intimate and imaginative themes, and a particular vogue, initiated by Fuseli and Blake (who saw fairies in his garden), grew up for supernatural and, especially, fairy paintings, drawing principally on *A Midsummer Night's Dream* along with *The Tempest*, the final scene of *The Merry Wives of Windsor*, and Mercutio's Queen Mab speech in *Romeo and Juliet*. Many of these paintings, from as early as Fuseli's *Titania and Bottom* (c.1790) onwards, are remarkable in their exploration of erotic and sinister aspects of the plays anticipating, and possibly influencing, interpretative trends that did not become explicit in criticism until the 1930s and in the theatre several decades later.

The great period of Shakespearian fairy painting in England can be dated fairly precisely from 1830 to 1850. These works tend to suggest the tininess of the fairy characters by portraying them against a minutely detailed natural background of flowers, mushrooms, and small animals. Many of them also rejoice in the freedom of a fantasy world to depict amorous exploits of nude, or teasingly semi-nude, male and female figures of idealized beauty, along with occasional suggestions of the grotesque. Francis Danby's hauntingly moonlit depiction of the quarrel between the sinuously graceful figures of Oberon and Titania – a favourite theme – is relatively decorous (Plate 18).

95. 'I do but beg a little changeling boy / To be my henchman' (*A Midsummer Night's Dream*, 2.1.120–21): a populous painting of 1849 by Joseph Noël Paton (1821–1901) of the quarrel between Oberon and Titania.

More explicitly sexual is Joseph Noël Paton's *The Quarrel between Oberon and Titania* (1849), in which Robin Goodfellow (Puck) is making a predatory leap upon a pleased-looking naked fairy, and various couplings are joyfully depicted. (Lewis Carroll is said to have counted 165 fairies in this painting.)[35] Richard Dadd and Edwin Landseer are among other artists inspired by *A Midsummer Night's Dream* to astonishingly intricate, sensuously beautiful paintings.

96. Priscilla Horton as a flying Ariel in W. C. Macready's
production of *The Tempest*, 1838, painted by
Daniel Maclise (1806–70).

At times, interplay can be discerned between the world of art and the
theatre. Androgynous characters such as Ariel, Oberon, and Robin Goodfellow were often acted by women in costumes that emphasized their physical
attributes. In 1838, for instance, Macready produced *The Tempest* at Covent
Garden with Priscilla Horton as Ariel, a role in which she was painted by
Daniel Maclise in a manner that draws as much on the traditions of painting

97. After Agincourt: Clarkson Stanfield's diorama for Macready's production of
Henry V (1839).

as on the stage. Maclise did many other Shakespearian paintings including at
least two of Macready as Macbeth.

This was a great period for English watercolourists, some of whom, such
as David Roberts (1796–1864) and David Cox (1783–1859), worked in the
theatres to supply scenery for the increasingly spectacular productions as well
as producing easel paintings. Clarkson Stanfield (1793–1867) created a great
diorama (a partly translucent painting which could change in appearance
with shifts in lighting) for Macready's *Henry V*.[36] During the early part of the
century the development of the process of steel engraving, which permitted
the reproduction of thousands of good copies from the same plate rather than

the few hundred that could be made from copper plates, made it possible to produce illustrated books in large quantities, and a demand grew up for drawings to adorn annual volumes for a polite, largely female readership with titles such as *The Keepsake* and *The Ladies' Polite Remembrancer*.[37] Among those who helped to supply the demand was John Massey Wright (1777–1866), a prolific and accomplished, if minor, artist who must have drawn thousands of Shakespearian characters and scenes, many of them in more than one version. It is hard to track them down as many of them are in private hands, but they often come up in sale rooms. I have a small collection, acquired for modest sums over the years, including a charming one of Falstaff being teased by children carrying torches and dressed as fairies, in the last scene of *The Merry Wives of Windsor*.

98. 'Pinch him, and burn him, and turn him about, / Till candles and starlight and moonshine be out' (5.5.100–1): John Massey Wright's watercolour of the last scene of *The Merry Wives of Windsor*.

It was during the 1820s that Shakespeare succeeded at last – if only temporarily – in conquering France. In his 1827 Preface to *Cromwell*, often regarded as the manifesto of the French Romantic movement, Victor Hugo (1802–85), repudiating neoclassicism as represented by Voltaire and declaring that 'the grotesque is one of the supreme beauties of the drama', hailed Shakespeare before the Académie Française itself as 'the deity of the theatre, in whom the three characteristic geniuses of our own stage, Corneille, Molière and Beaumarchais, seem united, three persons in one'.[38] And in the same year a group of English actors, including the up-and-coming young Harriet Smithson, who had given many performances with Edmund Kean at Drury Lane, travelled to Paris to play (in English), with occasional guest stars, at the Odéon Theatre.[39] Their first Shakespeare play, on 11 September, was *Hamlet* with Charles Kemble as the Prince and Smithson as Ophelia. The growing interest in Romanticism, and therefore in Shakespeare, made this a fashionable event, attended by many of Paris's leading intellectuals and artists. Though the play suffered the usual cuts – ending for instance with 'The rest is silence' – it was far closer to what Shakespeare wrote than Ducis's familiar version. The style of acting surprised the audience by its relative naturalism, and the occasion was a triumph for Shakespeare, for Kemble, and above all for Harriet Smithson, overwhelmingly tragic as Ophelia. Like Garrick and Kean before her, she became a star overnight. Three days later *Romeo and Juliet*, also with Kemble and Smithson, enjoyed a similar success. They were the toast of the town.

Perhaps the farthest-reaching consequence of these performances was the effect they had, both personally and – of more consequence to posterity – professionally, on the twenty-three-year-old composer Hector Berlioz (1803–69). Never notable for emotional stability, he was knocked out by both Shakespeare and Smithson. 'The impression made on my heart and mind by her extraordinary talent, nay her dramatic genius, was equalled only by the havoc wrought in me by the poet she so nobly interpreted . . . Shakespeare, coming upon me unawares, struck me like a thunderbolt.'[40] This was the more surprising in that Berlioz knew no word of English. He haunted the theatre obsessively throughout the winter, eager for glimpses of Harriet, dreaming of marriage to the woman he had not yet met, and he continued to suffer love after her return to England. For a while he seemed to have recovered and became engaged to a pianist, Marie (but known as Camille) Moke; but she jilted him for Camille Pleyel, a wealthy piano manufacturer. In 1832 Harriet, whose career was languishing, chanced to attend a concert of Berlioz's music in Paris at which she could not fail to recognize herself as the idealized being celebrated in his *Symphonie Fantastique* and its sequel *Lélio*. At last they met, and after many vicissitudes including a Romeo-like suicide attempt by Berlioz in which he took an overdose of opium in Harriet's presence and vomited for two hours, they married in October 1833. She died in 1854. Ten years later, in a bizarre episode that could only have happened to Berlioz, her body had to be exhumed for reburial. After the rotting coffin had been wrenched open, the gravedigger, watched by the composer, 'picked up the head, already parted from the body – the ungarlanded, withered, hairless head of "poor Ophelia" – and placed it in a new coffin ready for it at the edge of the grave' before the remains were reburied next to those of Berlioz's second wife.[41]

No composer – not even Verdi – has been inspired by Shakespeare to write more great music than Berlioz. Shakespeare permeates his work. Much of the sprawling, six-part *Lélio* (1831, revised 1855) is made up of a spoken narration celebrating Berlioz's passion for Shakespeare; it concludes with a magical but rarely played fantasy (1830) for chorus and orchestra based on *The Tempest*, in which airy spirits sing a blessing on Miranda as she leaves the island. Even Berlioz's grand opera *The Trojans* (1856–8), though primarily based on the *Aeneid*, sets part of the last act of *The Merchant of Venice* as a love duet. The lack of a sense of proportion which made him his own worst enemy in his private life is reflected both in the eccentric form of his Shakespearian works and in the demands they make on their performers, factors which have given them less circulation than the music in them deserves. The sombrely magnificent funeral march for the last scene of *Hamlet* (1844) calls uneconomically for a large orchestra along with a wordless chorus which sings nothing but 'Ah!' from time to time. Most readily pleasing is the late *opéra-comique Beatrice and Benedick* (1860–2) which projects the lovers in music of sparkling wit and vivacity foreshadowed in the overture but, jettisoning the Dogberry plot, substitutes a rather inept subplot of musical satire. Characteristically, the longest and most beautiful number in the work is a ravishing nocturne sung by two minor women characters, Hero and Ursula. Greatest of all is the 'dramatic symphony' *Romeo and Juliet*, rarely heard complete in the concert hall – it takes a full evening – but happily restored to circulation through recordings. Based partly on Garrick's adaptation it presents the story by sung narration rather than by dialogue; only two characters – Mercutio and the Friar – are represented by solo singers. Otherwise the chorus stand in for Montagues and Capulets, and the love scene, though closely following details of the play, is purely orchestral, anticipative of Wagner in the eroticism of its long-breathed melodies but exquisitely delicate too in its pictorialism. The overwhelmingly affirmative Finale, led by the Friar, lays great emphasis on the reconciliation of the houses.

Berlioz understandably regarded the music composed by his friend Felix Mendelssohn (1809–47) for *A Midsummer Night's Dream* as 'ravishing', and posterity has concurred.[42] The overture, a work of the greatest delicacy and humour in its evocation of the fairy world and of the mechanicals, astonishing from a seventeen year old, came first, in 1826, the remaining pieces in 1843 for a production by Ludwig Tieck in Berlin, but in style they hang together perfectly. Although Tieck undertook scholarly research into the theatres of Shakespeare's time, designing a reconstruction of the Fortune Theatre in 1836,[43] his production – given repeatedly over the next fifty years – drew on the conventions of Romantic theatre and ballet. Mendelssohn's music, with for instance the famous wedding march lasting some seven minutes, is tied to these conventions but became immensely popular and was used internationally for virtually all productions of the play until Granville-Barker's of 1914. Still frequently performed in concert and recorded, sometimes with extracts from the play, it has itself formed the basis of ballets from Marius Petipa (1876) to, among others, Georges Balanchine (1962) and Frederick Ashton (1964).

The principal French artist of the Romantic era to be influenced by Shakespeare was Eugène Delacroix (1798–1863), who saw Kean play some of his finest roles, including Shylock, Richard III, and Othello, during a visit to London in 1825. He was present too at the performance of *Hamlet* in Paris that had so great an effect on Berlioz, and returned to the play repeatedly in his work for the rest of his life, even though he is not known to have seen it again. His 1844 series of lithographs based on the play were rejected by

99. A balletic episode in Ludwig Tieck's production of *A Midsummer Night's Dream* in Potsdam, 1843, in which Mendelssohn's incidental music was heard complete for the first time.

publishers, so he had them printed in an edition of eighty copies at his own expense. His Hamlet is indeed a young and tender prince, almost feminine in his beauty – Delacroix modelled him on a woman friend – but is capable too of violent bursts of emotion.[44] Delacroix also based many paintings

100. 'Her clothes spread wide, / And mermaid-like a while they bore her up'
(*Hamlet*, 4.7.147–8): *The Death of Ophelia*, a lithograph by Eugène Delacroix.

on tragedies by Shakespeare and, in 1847, helped to design costumes for Alexandre Dumas's adaptation of *Hamlet* (which he heartily disliked).

Shakespeare was associated with the spirit of Romanticism in many European countries other than France and Germany. In Russia his influence profoundly affected the blank verse tragedy *Boris Godunov*, by Alexander Pushkin (1799–1837), who declared even Byron 'petty' by comparison with him, and wrote a verse tale, *Angelo*, based on *Measure for Measure*. The first great Russian critic, Vissarion Belinsky (1811–48), a Shakespeare enthusiast, wrote a long essay (1838) on *Hamlet* which includes a scene-by-scene description of a performance at the Maly Theatre in Moscow by the actor Pavel Mochalov.[45] The Polish Adam Mickiewicz (1798–1855), friend of Pushkin, exiled to Russia, found Shakespeare's history plays especially appropriate to the political situation following the Decembrist Revolution of 1825. His fellow countryman Juliusz Słowacki (1809–49), who saw Kean as Richard III in London in 1831, translated excerpts from *Macbeth* and *King Lear*, incorporating part of the latter into his verse play *Kordian* (1834).

Though there was a good deal of interest in Shakespeare among Italian intellectuals, exemplified by the championship of the dramatist and novelist Alessandro Manzoni, neoclassical attitudes descending from Voltaire tended to prevail and performances with even remote claims to authenticity were few and far between. Nevertheless Shakespeare filtered through in, for example, Antonio Salieri's sub-Mozartian opera *Falstaff* (1795) (composed, however, in Vienna), and Gioacchino Rossini's *Otello* (1816) based on Ducis's French adaptation and revised in 1819 to permit a happy ending. Rossini's score, with fearsomely demanding roles for three tenors, is especially successful in its portrayal of Desdemona; it is still performed, as occasionally is Salieri's *Falstaff*, but both works have been overshadowed by the great Verdi operas on the same subjects.[46]

In America the appetite for Shakespeare on the stage was supplied partly by visitors from England. G. F. Cooke (1756–1812), an exciting actor who had challenged Kemble in some of his best roles in London but whose career, like Kean's, was blighted by habitual drunkenness and whoremongering, had a sensational but temporary success in visits to American cities, including New York, in 1810–11; on a return engagement during the following season, in broken health, he caused little stir and died in New York in September 1812. Edmund Kean, who had similar problems, overcame prejudicial advance publicity to triumph when he brought his greatest roles to New York, Philadelphia, Boston, and Baltimore in 1820 but an ill-advised return visit to Boston late in the season flopped; Kean had to return home in disgrace after cancelling a performance because he feared he would have a poor house. During a return visit in 1825 he enjoyed success in New York but a foolish attempt to recapture his popularity in Boston resulted in insults and riots which damaged the theatre and caused him to flee the city. A subsequent visit to Canada offered consolation in the form of an honorary chieftainship in the Huron tribe of Indians who not only gave him the name of Alanienouidet but also the costume to go with it, which he delighted to wear in the streets of London.

A British-born actor whose emigration was ultimately to have far more

101. 'There's not a shirt and a half in all my company; and the half shirt is two napkins tacked together and thrown over the shoulders like a herald's coat without sleeves' (*Henry IV, Part One* 4.2.42–5): an engraving made from a daguerreotype of James Henry Hackett as Falstaff.

serious consequences for the nation than theatre riots was Junius Brutus Booth, the first actor to play Lear after the death in 1820 of George III, whose supposed madness had caused a ban on performances of the play. In the following year, as James Winston put it, 'shortly after Booth got leave of absence from Drury Lane . . . he set off for America with [a] shop-keeper's daughter in the night-time'.[47] He went on to perform Shakespearian roles all over the States. An excellent actor at his best, he suffered bouts of madness: 'In the swordfight at the end of *Richard III* (Cibber's) he would sometimes refuse to be downed by Richmond and would drive his amazed opponent off the stage, out the stage door, and into the street.'[48]

The theatrical traffic between England and America was two-way. James Henry Hackett (1800–71), one of the earliest native American actors to achieve eminence, was famous mainly for his Falstaff, which he played for forty years in London as well as America. In preparing an imitation of Kean's

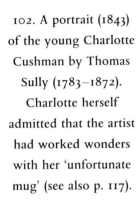

102. A portrait (1843) of the young Charlotte Cushman by Thomas Sully (1783–1872). Charlotte herself admitted that the artist had worked wonders with her 'unfortunate mug' (see also p. 117).

Richard III he wrote minutely detailed notes on that performance, with the result that what Kean did and how he spoke the role can be more closely reconstructed than any earlier performance.[49] Probably the greatest male American actor of this period, however, was Edwin Forrest (1806–72), handsome, heroic in build – Fanny Kemble called him 'a mountain of a man' – and, when he wanted, in voice, he excelled as Othello, Lear, and, later in life, Coriolanus, a role in which he was sculpted at larger even than his own life size.[50] The first great American actress was the extraordinary Charlotte Cushman (1816–76) whose career got off to a false start when, at the age of nineteen, she was miscast as the Countess in Mozart's opera *The Marriage of Figaro* to the Susanna of Clara Fisher who, even more of an infant phenomenon than Master Betty, had played Richard III at Drury Lane at the age of six. Cushman realized her true métier when she turned to the drama, scoring a success as Lady Macbeth with Macready in America when she was twenty-seven. A highly intelligent woman with a remarkable contralto voice and virtuoso talents as a performer, she pursued an illustrious career on both sides of the Atlantic, specializing in masculine roles. In a new permutation on the family relationships between performers of Romeo and Juliet she played Romeo opposite her sister, Susan, and had the independence of mind to abandon Garrick's adaptation; her other roles were to include Orsino, Hamlet and Cardinal Wolsey.[51]

As the century wore on Romanticism gave way in England to Victorianism, the libertarian attitudes of the Regency theatre to the more middle-class respectability of a rapidly growing population increasingly liable to value education at least as highly as entertainment. Traditional adaptations of the plays were losing their grip. And in 1843 the Act for Regulating the Theatres abolished the monopoly of Covent Garden and Drury Lane, which were seen to be too big for serious performances of Shakespeare, legalizing the performance of 'legitimate' drama in smaller houses. Cheap labour reduced the cost of books and in the theatre made possible ever-increasingly spectacular production methods with elaborate scenery and, even in theatres of reduced size, hundreds of extras. Both at home and abroad, improvements in systems of communication were facilitating cultural exchange – steamships helped actors to tour overseas and, along with the beginnings of the railway age, increased the flow of visitors to and from England and within England itself. Attitudes to Shakespeare were changing, but his works continued to evolve with, and to influence, the times.

CHAPTER SEVEN

Victorian Shakespeare: 1843–1904

'I loved thee, spirit, and love, nor can
The soul of Shakespeare love thee more.'

Alfred, Lord Tennyson, *In Memoriam* (1850), Lyric 61

WITH THE RISE OF the middle classes and the growth in popular education during the nineteenth century the gap between legitimate and popular theatre in England widened. Audiences seeking social and educational advancement encouraged the development of productions that were more earnest, more decorous, more pictorially instructive, and more professedly educational. Perhaps inevitably they were also less exciting. And many theatre-goers preferred actors who could hold their place in respectable society. The great star of the Regency period had been Edmund Kean, base-born, drunken, hell-raising, whoremongering genius; the leading actor of the 1850s was his son Charles (1811–68), educated at Eton, unimpeachably married to a fine actress, proud of his status as a Fellow of the Society of Antiquaries, director of theatricals at Windsor Castle (see overleaf) for Queen Victoria (he hoped, in vain, for a knighthood): conscientious, determined, uninspired. On the other hand theatres still attracted a wide spectrum of spectators. The subversive counter-movement of burlesque, travesty, and make-shift performances in fit-up theatres grew in force: the Victorians were capable of laughing at themselves.

Macready, in his speech of retirement as manager of Drury Lane, had advocated abolition of the patent houses; he pointed out that they were too big for serious performances of Shakespeare and that the growth in London's

103. *'The Merchant of Venice' at Windsor Castle*, 1848, from Benjamin Webster's
The Dramatic Entertainments at Windsor Castle (1849).

population called for theatres in outlying areas. Smaller theatres permitted
productions that did not need to coarsen their effects. In 1847 Covent Garden
became an opera house, as its replacement after the disastrous fire of 1856 still
is. Drury Lane came to be used for spectacular shows with only occasional
productions of Shakespeare. After visiting London in the 1850s the German

novelist Theodor Fontane (1819–98), recording his impressions of many Shakespeare productions, was able to list fifteen theatres where 'Shakespeare's plays either are actually performed or at least can be'.[1] During the second part of the century Shakespeare production was dominated by actor-managers running their own theatres and companies for most of their careers. The most important were Samuel Phelps (1804–78), Charles Kean, Charles Calvert (1828–79; he worked mainly in Manchester),[2] and Henry Irving (1838–1905). Developing the methods of Kemble and Macready, they worked in a tradition that put great emphasis on pictorialism, often to the detriment of text.

Phelps's management from 1842 to 1862 of Sadler's Wells theatre, in the London suburb of Islington, was a direct result and rapid vindication of the 1843 act. In the smaller house in an unfashionable area he was able to mount genuine ensemble productions for audiences that were eager to take an interest in Shakespeare's plays as works of art rather than as vehicles for virtuoso actors. Phelps integrated his own performances in leading roles with those of his company. As Henry Morley (1822–94), a theatre critic who was also, significantly, first Professor of English at University College, London put it, 'Although only in one or two cases we may have observed at Sadler's Wells originality of genius in the actor, we have nevertheless perceived something like the entire sense of one of Shakespeare's plays.'[3] It was at last possible to think of productions as interpretations of the complete play rather than as showcases for particular roles.

Phelps's earnestness of approach is shown by both the range of his repertoire and his rethinking of texts. During eighteen years of management he put on every play in the canon except for the three parts of *Henry VI*, *Richard II* (much less popular at this time than *King John*), *Titus Andronicus*, and *Troilus and Cressida*, still not acted since before the Restoration. In 1845 he displaced Cibber's *Richard III* with a version of Shakespeare's (though he reverted to Cibber in 1861) and played a more genuinely Shakespearian *King Lear* with a man as the Fool, as well as an exceptionally full text of *The Winter's Tale*. His *Macbeth* of 1847 dispensed with the traditional balletic and operatic interpolations in the witches' scenes, in 1849 he put on the rarely played *Antony and Cleopatra*, and in 1851 had an unexpected success with *Timon of Athens*. Admittedly with *Pericles* he resorted to rewriting, collapsing the two brothel scenes – no more to his taste than to Bowdler's – into one and purging the text in a manner that enabled the critic of *The Times* to write, 'although the plot of the drama is not compromised by a false delicacy, there remained not a syllable at which true delicacy could have conceived offence'. The staging of the last act called for a travelling panorama of the journey from Mytilene to Ephesus. But Phelps is best remembered for his 1853 *A Midsummer Night's Dream*, with himself as a poetically imaginative Bottom. This production, through its textual and imaginative integrity, triumphantly vindicated the play against Hazlitt's criticism that 'poetry and the stage do not agree together'. Morley wrote that 'as in dreams, one scene is made to glide insensibly into another . . . over all the fairy portion of the play there is a haze thrown by a curtain of green gauze placed between the actors and the audience . . . Very good taste has been shown in the establishment of a harmony between the scenery and the poem.'[4]

Working to a tight budget, Phelps resorted to considerable ingenuity in achieving spectacular effects; in *Henry V*, for the march past that took place before Agincourt, he had Madame Tussaud model eighty wax heads; wicker frames with one of these heads mounted on each side were carried by forty extras whose own heads appeared in the middle; they paraded behind a shoulder-high wall, creating the illusion of an army marching three abreast. 'As they tramped past, banners streaming, drums beating, trumpets braying, the stage seemed crowded with soldiers, and the illusion was so perfect that the audience never once discovered the artifice.'[5]

The middle of the nineteenth century was not a great time for Shakespearian acting. Charles Kean, who began to emerge from behind the shadow of his father's reputation around 1838, was at his best in gentlemanly melodrama; his wife, Ellen Tree, was the better actor. His place in Shakespearian stage history rests mainly on his management of the Princess's Theatre from 1850 to 1859. Kean's approach epitomizes the auto-didacticism and search for self-improvement associated with Victorianism. Admirable in itself, it was not conducive to exciting theatre. His passion for archaeology and historical research overwhelmed his productions with irrelevant detail. Of his first important Shakespeare production, *King John* in 1852, his hagiographic biographer J. W. Cole claimed that its 'total purification of Shakespeare, with every accompaniment that refined knowledge, diligent research, and chrono-

104. The extensive programme for Charles Kean's 1858 production of *The Merchant of Venice*, in which it was his 'object to combine with the poet's art a faithful representation of the picturesque city; to render it again palpable to the traveller who has actually gazed upon the seat of its departed glory; and at the same time, to exhibit it to the student, who has never visited' the city.

logical accuracy could supply, was suited to the taste and temper of the age, which had become eminently pictorial and exacting beyond all former precedent'.[6] A less charitable judgement would be that under Kean's management the plays were turned from dramas into museum pieces, offering a didacticism that appealed to theatre-goers seeking self-improvement.

Kean's antiquarianism impinged as heavily on the comedies as on the histories. Readers of his voluminous three-panelled programmes packed with information were assured that Bottom and his crew used 'furniture and Tools

... copied from discoveries at Herculaneum', and that in *The Winter's Tale* Autolycus's costumes derived from the *Hamilton Vases* (vol. 1, pl. 43) and from 'a Vase, engraved in Gerhard's *Auserlesene Vasenbilder*, taf. 166'. But Kean's passion for authenticity did not extend to the text – Cibber's *Richard III* and the Dryden/Davenant singing witches, but not Shakespeare's Porter, were good enough for him, and *Macbeth* finished with a tableau immediately following the hero's death. Victorian actor-managers liked to have the last word. Kean's Shakespeare productions are, I believe, the first to be photographically recorded, though only in portraits of individuals or small groups;

105. In Charles Kean's production of *The Winter's Tale* the go-cart pulled by Ellen Terry, playing the boy Mamillius, was copied from a terracotta model in the British Museum. On the first night she pulled it 'with such vigour that I tripped over the handles and came down on my back!'

the image of him as Richard II is clearly modelled on the painting of Richard in Westminster Abbey.[7]

As well as historical accuracy, Kean also offered spectacle, in *The Tempest* (1857) 'requiring the aid of above one hundred and forty operatives nightly'. Kean was a skilful stage manager, able to deploy large numbers of extras to stunning effect, and he hired fine artists to design and paint elaborate scenery, including panoramic vistas that unfolded before the audience's eyes to give an illusion of movement from one location to another. In *Richard II* he interpolated 'the triumph of the entry of Bolingbroke with Richard into London,

106. The Westminster Abbey portrait of Richard II.

107. Charles Kean as Richard II: an early theatrical photograph.

108. The triumphal entry into London of Bolingbroke with the humiliated
King Richard from Charles Kean's production of *Richard II*, 1857.

which is a fine piece of stage-effect'.[8] According to Cole it employed between
500 and 600 performers, 'all moving in trained regularity or organized disorder' which, Cole naïvely claims, 'gave a reality to the play it was never
supposed to possess'. Magical visual effects adorned a heavily abbreviated
Midsummer Night's Dream, which encompassed a shadow dance of fairies.
(Morley, who thought that poetry was sacrificed to painting, complained that
it would have been truer to the nature of fairies if they had appeared to have
no shadows.) Puck, who rose out of the ground on a mushroom, was played
by Ellen Terry, aged nine, whom Fontane found 'altogether intolerable: a
precocious child brought up in the true English manner, old before her
years'. Queen Victoria, however, thought she played the part 'delightfully'.[9]

To make his rapid exits Puck 'appeared to stand on a board that propelled him off-stage with one bound; the second time a device made it seem as though he flew through the air just like an arrow. Both were effective.'[10]

Incorrigible to the end, Kean boasted in his farewell speech as manager that he had never 'permitted historical truth to be sacrificed to theatrical effect'. But not everyone took him as seriously as he might have wished. Of *The Winter's Tale* the magazine *Punch* claimed 'authority to state that the Bear at present running in Oxford Street is an archaeological copy from the original bear of Noah's Ark', and during the play's long run a charming and entertaining burlesque of both play and production, William Brough's *Perdita, or The Royal Milkmaid*, drew crowded audiences to the Lyceum.[11] Brough handles his original freely, sometimes parodying passages from other plays; a line from *Othello* is easily adapted to refer to the nagging Paulina: 'Silence that dreadful bell[e].' The discussion between Leontes and Camillo about the possible murder of Polixenes is based on *Macbeth*; Leontes concludes with

> Oh never shall sun that fine day see.
> We made him welcome: he's himself made free.
> I bid him come to court; but on my life,
> I little thought he'd come to court my wife!

There is a pleasant skit on the love-at-first-sight convention in the meeting of Florizel and Perdita:

> FLORIZEL: What's that? My stars!
> PERDITA: Oh my!
> FLORIZEL: Oh lor!
> PERDITA: Oh dear!
> FLORIZEL: Smitten completely! Yes I'm done for surely.
> PERDITA: Oh! something's struck me here, I feel quite poorly.
> FLORIZEL: Fair maid!
> PERDITA: Fair sir!
> FLORIZEL: I – that is, how d'ye do?
> PERDITA: Considerably worse for seeing you.

Duncombe's Edition.

ROMEO AND JULIET:

" AS THE LAW DIRECTS."

AN OPERATICAL BURLESQUE BURLETTA,

IN

One Act.

BY M. M. G. DOWLING, Esq.
Author of Othello—" According to Act of Parliament."

THE ONLY EDITION CORRECTLY MARKED, BY PERMISSION,
FROM THE PROMPTER'S BOOK:
To which is added,
A DESCRIPTION OF THE COSTUME—CAST OF THE CHARACTERS,
THE WHOLE OF THE STAGE BUSINESS,
SITUATIONS—ENTRANCES—EXITS—PROPERTIES AND
DIRECTIONS,
AS PERFORMED AT THE
NEW STRAND THEATRE.

EMBELLISHED WITH A FINE ENGRAVING,
By Mr. Findlay, from a Drawing taken expressly in the Theatre.

LONDON:
PRINTED AND PUBLISHED BY J. DUNCOMBE & CO.
10, MIDDLE ROW, HOLBORN

1837.

Romeo & Juliet Travestie.

TYBALT   Thou wretched boy
Where's the young girl from home you did decoy ?
And you, I know not what you'd both be at.
You must go home —.
ROMEO   This shall determine that .
(*They fight. Comic business &c*)

Act 1. Scene 9.

109. The frontispiece and title page to Maurice Dowling's burlesque of *Romeo and Juliet.*

Not all was comedy; the playlet includes patriotic topical references and a grand ballet danced before a 'brilliantly illuminated scene' which achieved an independent life of its own. Granville-Barker was even to suggest that when, in the last scene, Antigonus enters 'followed by the bear respectably dressed', Brough perhaps had 'a better sense of the fitness of things than Shakespeare'.[12]

Florizel and Perdita is only one example of the increasingly successful series of burlesques and travesties that flourished in Victorian theatres. At their best they reached a high level of sophistication and produced at least one star actor, Frederick Robson (?1822–64), who scored his greatest success as Shylock in Francis Talfourd's *Shylock: or The Merchant of Venice Preserved*

(1849). The *Times* reviewer wrote that 'The only regret in observing his execution of Mr Talfourd's Shylock is that he had not made trial of Shakespeare's in preference', and the *Illustrated London News* found that 'many of his bursts are truly tragic, and might have done credit to Edmund Kean in his best days'. These pieces abound in that staple of Victorian humour, the pun, particularly rampant in *The Rise and Fall of Richard III; or, A New Front to an Old Dicky* (1868) by F. C. Burnand, who edited *Punch* from 1880 to 1906. In it the Duchess of York travesties Macbeth's 'Hang out our banners on the outward walls!' with 'Hang up my bonnet in the outer hall!', and Catesby and Tyrrell fall over a coal scuttle to provoke the comment 'Oh! they're more shinned against than shinning.'

Burlesques reach their apogee in W. S. Gilbert's *Rosencrantz and Guildenstern* which originally appeared in the magazine *Fun* in 1874 in reaction to the great success of Henry Irving's Lyceum performances. First performed in 1891, with 'a little harmless mimicry of Mr Irving', this is less a parody of the play than a comic commentary on its interpreters. Ophelia remarks on the variety of different actors' appearances in the central role:

> Sometimes he's tall – sometimes he's very short –
> Now with black hair – now with a flaxen wig –
> Sometimes an English accent – then a French –
> Then English with a strong provincial 'burr'.
> Once an American, and once a Jew –
> But Danish never, take him how you will!
> And, strange to say, whate'er his tongue may be,
> Whether he's dark or flaxen – English – French –
> Though we're in Denmark, A.D. ten-six-two –
> He always dresses as King James the First!

Ophelia also shows wide familiarity with critical commentary:

> Some men hold
> That he's the sanest, far, of all sane men –
> Some that he's really sane, but shamming mad –
> Some that he's really mad, but shamming sane –

Some that he will be mad, some that he *was* –
Some that he couldn't be. But on the whole
(As far as I can make out what they mean)
The favourite theory's somewhat like this:
Hamlet is idiotically sane
With lucid intervals of lunacy.

At a much lower level of theatrical endeavour are the popular and provincial theatre performances unforgettably described by Dickens. In his essay 'Private Theatres' (*Sketches by Boz*, 1836) he writes vividly if uncharitably of 'minor theatres' run by 'an ex-scene-painter, a low coffee-house keeper, a disappointed eighth-rate actor, a retired smuggler, or uncertificated bankrupt' where ambitious amateurs may pay for the privilege of performing – Richard III costs two guineas, Buckingham fifteen shillings, the Lord Mayor of London a mere two shillings and sixpence. And Dickens's accounts in *Nicholas Nickleby* of the Crummles family's theatrical exertions and in *Great Expectations* of Mr Wopsle's Hamlet suggest how deeply some, at least, of Shakespeare's plays had permeated the popular consciousness:

> Whenever that undecided Prince had to ask a question or state a doubt, the public helped him out with it. As for example; on the question whether 'twas nobler in the mind to suffer, some roared yes, and some no, and some inclining to both opinions said 'toss up for it;' and quite a Debating Society arose. When he asked what should such fellows as he do crawling between earth and heaven, he was encouraged with loud cries of 'Hear, hear!' . . . On his taking the recorders – very like a little black flute that had just been played in the orchestra and handed out at the door – he was called upon unanimously for Rule Britannia. When he recommended the player not to saw the air thus, the sulky man said, 'And don't *you* do it, neither; you're a deal worse than *him*!' And I grieve to add that peals of laughter greeted Mr Wopsle on every one of these occasions.

It is perhaps a measure of the increasingly artificial nature of Shakespeare production that continental actors performed in England sometimes in their

George Cruikshank

110. Illustration by George Cruikshank (1792–1878) to Dickens's essay 'Private Theatres': 'That snuff-shop-looking figure, in front of the glass, is Banquo, and the young lady with the liberal display of legs, who is kindly painting his face with a hare's foot, is dressed for Fleance. The large woman, who is consulting the stage directions in Cumberland's edition of *Macbeth*, is the Lady Macbeth of the night; she is always selected to play the part, because she is tall and stout, and LOOKS a little like Mrs. Siddons – at a considerable distance. That stupid-looking milksop, with light hair and bow legs – a kind of man whom you can warrant townmade – is fresh caught; he plays Malcolm to-night, just to accustom himself to an audience. He will get on better by degrees; he will play Othello in a month, and in a month more, will very probably be apprehended on a charge of embezzlement. The black-eyed female with whom he is talking so earnestly, is dressed for the "gentlewoman." It is HER first appearance, too – in that character. The boy of fourteen who is having his eyebrows smeared with soap and whitening, is Duncan, King of Scotland; and the two dirty men with the corked countenances, in very old green tunics, and dirty drab boots, are the "army".'

own languages. Charles Fechter, educated in France, was bilingual; he played Iago, Othello and Hamlet with success and in English (though with the pronounced accent noted by Gilbert's Ophelia) at the Princess's in 1861 and at the Lyceum in 1864. Tommaso Salvini (1829–1915) played Othello in his native Italian at Drury Lane in 1875 in a heavily mutilated text; at other times he played in Italian while his fellows spoke English. He brought to the role a passion that Anglo-Saxon actors have rarely matched: 'he seizes [Desdemona] by the hair of the head, and, dragging her on to the bed, strangles her with a ferocity that seems to take a delight in its office . . . Nearing the end, he rises, and at the supreme moment cuts his throat with a short scimitar, hacking and hewing with savage energy, and imitating the noise that escaping blood and air may together make when the windpipe is severed.'[13]

111. A photograph of
Adelaide Ristori
as Lady Macbeth.

112. *Julius Caesar*: the forum scene in the Duke of Saxe-Meiningen's production.

English actresses tended to decline the honour of playing Desdemona with him. Ernesto Rossi (1827–96) played Hamlet, Lear, Macbeth, and Romeo with an Italian company in Italian at Drury Lane in 1876 but a few years later failed as an Italian Lear with an otherwise English-speaking cast in New York and London. The Italian Adelaide Ristori (1822–1906) travelled as far as Australia with her acclaimed Lady Macbeth (sometimes in brief excerpts and in a bizarre version 'trimmed so as to bring the heroine into every possible prominence'),[14] first in Italian and later in English. And in 1881 the Duke of Saxe-Meiningen brought to London his German-speaking company which had an unrivalled reputation for ensemble playing, for historical reconstruction, and for the handling of crowd scenes; in *Julius Caesar*, their most famous production, the forum scene offered 'the most startling effect ever seen –

those forests of hands and arms, those staccato shouts, that brilliancy of emphasis, the whirl and rout and maddened frenzy of an excited mob'.[15]

After the end of Charles Kean's management – following which he and his wife toured to America, Canada, and Australia – the centre of gravity of British Shakespeare production shifted for a while to Manchester where Charles Calvert, a disciple of Phelps, embarked as actor-manager of the Prince's Theatre in 1864 on a series of serious-minded productions. But English acting was not to rise to greatness again until the advent of Henry Irving, who in 1895 became the first English actor to be knighted. After playing Hamlet for the first time in 1874 he took over the management of the Lyceum four years later; it rapidly became the most important London theatre of its time, housing major Shakespeare productions, native and foreign, even when Irving was on tour with his company in England and America. He was not handsome and had a tendency to drag one leg. His idiosyncrasies invited, and received, caricature, and Poole's *Hamlet Travestie* was revived as a parody of his performance; Henry James wrote of the 'strange tissue of arbitrary pronunciations which floats in the thankless medium of Mr Irving's harsh, monotonous voice'.[16] These were the early days of sound recording. Irving's voice may still – just – be heard rasping through the pop and crackle of the old cylinders in a few extracts, but it takes a trained and trusting ear to gain from them any sense of the impact that it undoubtedly made on his contemporaries.[17]

Along with his natural disadvantages Irving also had marvellously expressive features, a sardonic sense of humour, admirably suited to Richard III and even to Hamlet, dignity, pathos, and – most important of all – a mesmeric control over his audiences. He was an interior actor who, by gesture, facial expression, and intonation could suggest a character's state of mind. And he had a perfectionist's attention to detail along with an instinctive sense of what would work in the theatre. His acting style was not primarily heroic or lyrical; he did not attempt Richard II and failed as Romeo, Othello, Coriolanus, even Lear; his Macbeth (Ellen Terry, in her wonderful memoirs, said he looked in the last act 'like a great famished wolf')[18] split opinion. But he had the proper touch of high comedy for Benedick – along with an unrivalled Beatrice in Ellen Terry – an irresistible, picturesque pathos as Shylock (a role that he played over a thousand times); he could convey the shifting complexity of

113. A drawing of Henry
Irving as Shylock by his
admirer and biographer
Percy Fitzgerald
(1834–1935).

Hamlet's inner life and the callous intellectuality of Richard III and Iago. No less important, he was a theatre professional to his fingertips, employing highly skilled set designers, painters (including Sir Lawrence Alma-Tadema), costume designers and composers (such as Sir Arthur Sullivan) to enhance his productions. Text however tended to be sacrificed to pictorialism. Of his *Cymbeline* Bernard Shaw – who wrote letters virtually coaching Terry in the role of Imogen (Plate 20) – complained that 'every part is spoiled except the governor's' (Irving wisely played Iachimo). He cut almost half of *Lear*, not much less of *Hamlet*, nearly 800 lines of *Much Ado* and more than 500 even from relatively short plays including *The Merchant of Venice* (which occasionally also lost its last act so as to give Irving, as Shylock, the final curtain).[19] But

114. The painting by John Singer Sargent (1856–1925) of Ellen Terry wearing her beetle-wing dress as Lady Macbeth, which she played at the Lyceum Theatre in 1895.

Irving's silences could be more eloquent than other actors' speeches. For much of his career he had the inestimable advantage of the collaboration of the loyal and enchanting Ellen Terry (1847–1928), at her best in high comedy and in pathetic roles; recordings made late in life, when she toured as lecturer and reader, enable us to sample her Portia and Ophelia. Lady Macbeth was not her greatest part, but John Singer Sargent painted a splendid portrait of her holding the crown over her head and dressed in her stunning robe embroidered with green beetles' wings.

Bernard Shaw contrasted Irving's handling of Shakespeare's text with that of the younger Johnston Forbes-Robertson (1853–1937) in a review which is a classic of English prose. Praising Forbes-Robertson's 'true classical Hamlet' of 1897 for its textual integrity as well as for the acting, Shaw wrote that

> Instead of cutting every line that can possibly be spared, he retains every gem, in his own part or anyone else's, that he can make time for in a spiritedly brisk performance lasting three hours and a half with very short intervals. He does not utter half a line; then stop to act; then go on with another half line; and then stop to act again, with the clock running away with Shakespear's chances all the time. He plays as Shakespear should be played, on the line and to the line, with the utterance and acting simultaneous, inseparable and in fact identical.

There was, however, an unrevealed subtext to Shaw's review: he had himself served as Forbes-Robertson's textual adviser.

Scholarship in this period suffered from the last (so far – and so far as we know) of the great Shakespeare forgers. Unlike William Henry Ireland, John Payne Collier (1789–1883) was a serious and learned scholar who made real discoveries – he was the first to bring to light Manningham's diary and the Forman papers – but was all too inclined to augment them with documents of his own fabrication designed to support his conjectures. The skill with which he did so means that any documents that passed through his hands, such as the Henslowe papers, must be subject to the suspicion that they contain undetected additions or alterations. His most ambitious venture came in 1852 when he announced that he had bought a copy of the Second (1632) Folio said to have belonged to one Thomas Perkins and containing thousands of changes to the dialogue and stage directions, including the addition of nine whole lines, all written in an early hand which Collier claimed could include authentic corrections derived from manuscripts and performance. He incorporated many of them into editions of 1853 and 1858. Some scholars expressed scepticism without, initially, implying intention to deceive. Collier sued for libel, but scientific tests carried out in 1859 revealed the annotations to be fraudulent, showing that they had been written first in pencil then traced over with modern ink. Gradually Collier's reputation crumbled, but he continued to protest his innocence and to carry out scholarly work; at the age of eighty-nine he issued yet another edition of Shakespeare, of only fifty-eight copies, which anticipated late twentieth-century scholarship by including, and advocating Shakespeare's authorship of, the apocryphal play *Edward III.* Collier's forgeries, like Ireland's, now fetch high prices from collectors.[20]

Even reputable scholars were liable to adopt a cavalier attitude to the materials with which they worked. Like Collier and many of his contemporaries, James Orchard Halliwell, later Halliwell-Phillipps (1820–89), was incredibly industrious over a wide area of scholarship. He, along with Charles Knight, Collier, and Alexander Dyce founded the Shakespeare Society in 1840 and (like Collier) wrote extensively for it. Halliwell published a series of biographical studies culminating in the *Outlines of the Life of Shakespeare,* which grew through successive editions from 192 pages in 1881, to 848 in 1887, the last edition to appear in his lifetime. This is still valuable for its thorough investigation of primary sources which yielded genuine new information about Shakespeare and the Stratford of his time. From 1853 to 1865 he published a handsome and extensively annotated folio edition of the works in only 150 copies. But Halliwell's integrity, too, was suspect. As a young man he was accused of stealing manuscripts from Trinity College, Cambridge; he claimed that he bought them from a London bookseller. An indefatigable collector of rare books and manuscripts, even in his years of relative poverty before the death in 1867 of his rich father-in-law, the antiquary Sir Thomas Phillipps (who had discovered Shakespeare's marriage bond), he treated them in an extraordinarily prodigal fashion. 128 volumes of neatly bound scrapbooks containing material for notes on the works now housed in the Shakespeare Centre library include many hundreds of pages ripped from early printed books and manuscripts, often unidentified.[21] Yet Halliwell-Phillipps worked with unselfish dedication to enhance Stratford's attractions as a place of pilgrimage, in initiating in 1863 the purchase for the town of property associated with New Place, and in acting as joint secretary of the tercentenary celebrations, until a quarrel with the corporation caused him to sever relations and revoke bequests in 1884.[22]

More blameless scholars than Collier and Halliwell-Phillipps were the husband-and-wife team of Charles (1787–1877) and Mary (1809–98) Cowden Clarke. Charles, friend and teacher in his youth of Keats, delivered and published several series of lectures which did a lot to arouse popular interest in Shakespeare, but Mary's was the more significant achievement. Together they produced an edition (1864–8) of the complete works, originally published in weekly instalments, a 'work of peculiar pride and gratification', Mary wrote in 1896, 'inasmuch as it made me the first (and as yet only) woman editor of our great poet'.[23] Mary herself undertook the arduous task – it took her sixteen years – of compiling by hand the first *Complete Concordance to Shakespeare*[24] and in 1851–2 published in three volumes the often-reprinted work by which she is best but not always fairly remembered. The subtitle of *The Girlhood of Shakespeare's Heroines* – 'in a Series of Fifteen Tales' – is often ignored: though its style is dated, this is not a naïve specimen of character criticism but a work of imaginative fiction – a series of long short stories – as intellectually respectable an enterprise as for instance Robert Nye's novel *Falstaff* (1976) or John Updike's *Gertrude and Claudius* (2000). Clarke ingeniously builds anticipations of the play into the tales, and each ends with the first words of Shakespeare's text spoken by the character. So in 'The Thane's Daughter' a ball with which young Gruach and a pageboy are playing on the battlements of Glamis Castle lands out of their reach in a martlet's nest. The tender-hearted boy scruples to harm the nest in the attempt to reach it, but the future Lady Macbeth fixes the point of an arrow 'into the caked mud and earth which fastened the nest to the jutting point, loosened it, raised it, and in another moment, the martlets' home with its unfledged tenants spun whirling into the air, and was scattered to pieces, striking against the buttresses and rough-hewn walls'. The tale ends as she receives Macbeth's letter telling of Duncan's approach: 'Glamis thou art, and Cawdor, and shalt be / What thou art promised.' Later in the century Oscar Wilde was to fictionalize Shakespeare's relationship with the young man of the Sonnets in his 'Portrait of Mr W. H.' of 1889, which Wilde revised in a version that remained unpublished until 1921, long after his death. The premise of the story, that W. H. is a boy actor named Willie Hughes, whose name is punned upon in Sonnet 20 – 'all hues in his controlling' – comes close to the speculations of less avowedly fictional writing.

Collier's, Halliwell's, and the Clarkes' editions are now largely ignored, but other editorial projects of the later nineteenth century are of more abiding importance. The meticulously prepared if austere Cambridge Shakespeare (1863–6, revised in 1891), edited jointly by W. G. Clark and W. Aldis Wright, is still useful to textual scholars for its recording of variant readings over the centuries; moreover it formed the basis of the plain-text Globe edition of 1864 which was to remain standard for a century and more. More ambitious still is the American New Variorum (i.e. *cum notis variorum*, with the notes of various commentators)[25] founded in 1871 by H. H. Furness (1833–1912) with his own edition of *Romeo and Juliet*, continued by his son, H. H. Furness Jr. (1865–1930), and still only about two thirds of the way towards completion, now under the direction of the Modern Language Association of America. And in 1891 appeared the first volume of the Arden edition, now in its third series.

The strangest aberration of Victorian scholarship is the growth of attempts to show that Shakespeare's works were written by someone else.[26] The Rev. James Wilmot had suggested in 1847 that Francis Bacon was their author, but did not publish his conclusions. The idea next appears in a book with the apparently unrelated title of *The Romance of Yachting* (1848) by an eccentric New York lawyer, Colonel Joseph C. Hart. Influenced by a denigratory life of Shakespeare in Dionysus Lardner's *Cabinet Cyclopaedia*, which found that the plays 'absolutely teem with the grossest impurities, – more gross by far than can be found in any contemporary dramatist', Hart fantasized that Shakespeare 'purchased or obtained surreptitiously' other men's plays which he then 'spiced with obscenity, blackguardism and impurities'. Hart did not identify the original author or authors. The first extended attempt to suggest that Bacon was a possible author came in an article by (no relation) Delia Bacon (1811–59), also an American, of 1856. Convinced that the plays could not have been written by one whom she conceived of as an 'ignorant, low-bred, vulgar country fellow, who had never inhaled in all his life one breath of that social atmosphere that fills his plays',[27] she thought it more likely that they were written by a committee including Bacon, Raleigh, and Spenser. In 1853 she raised funds for a visit to England where she spent three years writing a book on the subject. Moving to Stratford in 1856, a sick woman, she spent a night in Holy Trinity Church with a lantern and tools intending personally to open Shakespeare's grave where she hoped to find documents that would confirm her theory, but gave up the idea as dawn approached. Publication of her book, *The Philosophy of the Plays of Shakespeare Unfolded*, was subsidized in 1857 without her knowledge by the novelist Nathaniel Hawthorne, then American

115. 'William Shakespeare, his method of work', from *Poets' Corner* (1904) by Max Beerbohm (1872–1956). Francis Bacon surreptitiously hands Shakespeare the manuscript of *Hamlet*.

116. The poster for the sale of Shakespeare's Birthplace.

consul in Liverpool; it was not well received. Later that year she came to believe that she was no longer Delia Bacon but 'the Holy Ghost and surrounded by devils'.[28] A nephew managed to get her back to America, where she died in an asylum the following year. Others took up her obsession, and an English Bacon Society was formed in 1885, followed by an American one in 1892.

In Stratford, purchase of the site of New Place in 1863 was one in a series of events destined to make the most of the town's Shakespearian heritage. When the Birthplace had come up for sale in 1846 one of those interested in buying it was Phineas T. Barnum, of Barnum and Bailey's Circus, who wanted to put it on a wagon for exhibition all over America. In the event the house was bought for the nation in 1847 with money raised by local and

117. An early photograph, *c.*1850, of Shakespeare's Birthplace before restoration,
with elegant onlookers.

London committees. It was in a dilapidated state, as may be seen from a
photograph taken before restoration. In the following year Dickens took the
role of Justice Shallow in a series of amateur performances of *The Merry Wives
of Windsor* – Mary Cowden Clarke played Mistress Quickly – with the aim of
establishing the dramatist Sheridan Knowles, who had fallen on hard times,
as curator; but this did not come to pass. In Birmingham during the 1860s
the local Shakespeare club founded a Shakespeare library, now subsumed into
the civic collection, which has grown into a resource of international importance with special strengths in editions and in stage history. The Shakespeare
Birthplace Trust was formed in 1866 with the aim of preserving the Birthplace and associated houses as a national memorial and of establishing a
library and museum. Both Collier and Halliwell-Phillipps were among the

first Life Trustees. The Trust was incorporated by Act of Parliament in 1891 and acquired Anne Hathaway's Cottage in the following year.

Stratford took centre stage in 1864 for the celebrations of Shakespeare's three-hundredth birthday. A local committee was headed by Robert Hunter who held office for six months, after which, he wrote, 'I resigned, and subsequently rapidly recovered my health and spirits.'[29] There were many problems. Someone tactlessly asked the French Fechter to play Hamlet; Phelps took offence: *Hamlet* was not performed. Advertising was bad; on the first day of the two-week festival, though the weather was fine, there was 'a degree of ominous quietude throughout the streets which on such an occasion was most remarkable'. The two weeks that followed saw a similar mixing of good and bad fortune. Fireworks were splendid but 'the brilliancy of the finale' – an illuminated portrait of Shakespeare – 'was sadly marred by the density of the smoke'. A balloon was to have made an ascent but, astonishingly, there was not enough gas to inflate it. But the birthday banquet, attended by 750 guests, was a great success. Toasts, interspersed with songs, went on for hours. William Creswick, described as '*tragedian*, London', responded on behalf of The Drama with singular if orotund eloquence:

> To the unreflecting mind it doubtless seems strange and curious that the great Ruler [God, not Queen Victoria] should inspire the greatest genius, humanly speaking, the world has known – not to advise men from the senate, not to judge men from the bench, not to dictate to them from the closet, not to admonish them from the pulpit, but to touch, soften, mould, and instruct them from the stage – (*cheers*) – to pierce their hearts with glowing eloquence, to fire them with ambition, to warm them into love, to move them with the soft presence of beauty and goodness, to place before them the true nobleness of virtue; to establish the strong, to sustain the weak, to fright the guilty, and uphold the free; to thrill their hearts with new delights, and to gently chide them to repentant tears. (*Great cheering*)[30]

The proceedings also included several concerts of Shakespearian music, Handel's *Messiah*, a fancy-dress ball, an elaborate pageant of Shakespearian characters, eloquent and uplifting sermons, and (moderately) successful performances of several plays including *The Comedy of Errors* with real twin brothers, Charles and Henry Webb, as the Dromios. The secretary was able to draw final melancholic satisfaction from the fact that 'no widow or orphan associates his or her bereavement with this joyful occasion'.

Out of the festival emerged an idea that has had momentous consequences. Performances took place in a temporary structure; the small and unsatisfactory theatre built in the gardens of New Place in 1827 was pulled down in 1872 by Halliwell-Phillipps to permit the extension of the Great Garden of New Place. Two years later the brewer Charles Edward Flower offered a site and a generous donation to found a national memorial made up of a new theatre to permit annual celebrations of the birthday with performances of plays, along with a picture gallery and library. Flower was something of a pioneer in fostering relations between the theatre and the study. In 1880,

118. The Webb twins as the twin Dromios, 1864.

119. Frank Benson
the sportsman:
a portrait of 1910
by Hugh Goldwin
Rivière (1869–1956).

assisted by the actor William Creswick, he embarked on the Memorial Theatre edition aiming to present the plays as acted in Stratford; the edition, which eventually included even those plays, such as *Measure for Measure* and *Troilus and Cressida*, which were not acted, was completed in 1891.

The Shakespeare Memorial Theatre opened on Shakespeare's birthday in 1879 with a performance of *Much Ado About Nothing* in which Helena Faucit, now in her sixty-second year, came out of retirement to play Beatrice. Faucit, who married Sir Theodore Martin, Queen Victoria's private secretary and biographer of Prince Albert, published *On Some of Shakespeare's Female Characters* in 1885 (revised 1891); her vivid account of playing Hermione to Macready's Leontes is quoted on p. 260.

Between 1886 and 1919 Frank Benson directed twenty-eight spring and around six summer festivals at Stratford, each only one or two weeks long, producing all Shakespeare's plays except *Troilus and Cressida* and *Titus Andronicus*. A first-rate athlete who won the three-mile race for Oxford against Cambridge, he became a protégé of Ellen Terry and acted with Irving before establishing his own repertory company – or companies, because at one time he was responsible for three simultaneously – with which he toured the provinces and overseas with productions of Shakespeare and other classics. Versatile, immensely energetic, enormously popular in Stratford, he was perhaps too easily mocked for his athletic prowess; his company was especially valuable as a training ground for the young, who were most welcome if they displayed sporting skills. Max Beerbohm indeed felt that these spilled over into their acting, writing of Benson's *Henry V*:

> Every member of the cast seemed in tip-top condition – thoroughly 'fit'. Subordinates and principals all worked well together. The fielding was excellent, and so was the batting. Speech after speech was sent spinning across the boundary, and one was constantly inclined to shout 'Well *played*, sir! Well played *indeed!*' As a branch of university cricket, the whole performance was, indeed, beyond praise. But, as a form of acting, it was not impressive.'[31]

But Benson had more respect for Shakespeare's text than most of his contemporaries; in 1899 he gave the first 'complete' *Hamlet*, known as the 'eternity' version, at Stratford and in the following year at the Lyceum, where, Bayreuth-style, it lasted from 3.30 to 11.00 p.m. with a one-and-a half-hour break for dinner. And C. E. Montague, in a classic review, wrote with great admiration of one of Benson's least athletic roles, Richard II, a performance 'brilliant in its equal grasp of the two sides of the character, the one which everybody sees well enough, and the one which nearly everybody seems to shun seeing, and in the value which it rendered to the almost continuous flow of genuine and magnificent poetry from Richard.'[32] Benson was knighted by George V, using a property sword, on the stage of Drury Lane after a performance of *Julius Caesar* in 1916.

Charles Edward Flower's incorporation of a picture gallery, opened with a loan exhibition in 1881, into the Memorial Theatre was an imaginative acknowledgement of the close relationship, fostered by Victorian styles of production, between the theatre and the visual arts. At the age of sixteen Ellen Terry married the much older painter George Frederic Watts (1817–1904); the union rapidly collapsed, but not before Watts had painted her as Ophelia (c.1864), a role in which she was to score one of her greatest successes when she first acted with Irving. When the Pre-Raphaelite Brotherhood drew up their list of 'Immortals' in 1848, Shakespeare and Jesus Christ alone were awarded three stars. The leading members of the Brotherhood, Holman Hunt, Dante Gabriel Rossetti, and John Everett Millais, all painted scenes from Shakespeare. Hunt's *Claudio and Isabella* is haunting in its representation of the dejected young man, and Millais's minutely detailed *Ophelia* has become one of the best-known of all Shakespeare paintings; no less attractive is his *Rosalind in the Forest* (Plate 22).

Improved methods of transport which, as we have seen, facilitated relatively easy interchange of actors between England, America, and Europe virtually made possible the career of the first great black interpreter of Shakespeare, Ira Aldridge (?1807–67), known as the African Roscius. Legends accrued about his early life, such as that he came from Senegal or was the son of a slave, but in fact he seems to have been born in New York to a straw-seller who was also a lay preacher.[33] Realizing that there was no future for him as a black actor in America, he emigrated to England when he was around seventeen, and soon made a reputation in London and the provinces. Othello was naturally among his roles, but from 1830 he played white as well as black men, including Macbeth, Shylock and Richard III, using white make-up. Edmund Kean encouraged him, and in April 1832, one month after the performance at Covent Garden of *Othello* in which the sick, forty-five-year-old Kean collapsed into his son's arms, saying 'I am dying – speak to them for me', Aldridge made his London debut in the role at the same theatre. Notices were mixed and not without racial prejudice: the *Athenaeum* protested that Ellen Tree, his Desdemona, should not be subjected to 'the indignity of being pawed about' by a 'black servant', but the performance was repeated two nights later. Around 1847, anxious to find another black role, Aldridge acted Aaron in a version (known only by report) so grotesquely altered as to turn the villainous Moor into the play's virtuous hero. In 1852

120. Ira Aldridge as
Aaron in an adaptation
of *Titus Andronicus*
given at the Britannia
Theatre, Hoxton,
in 1852.

he embarked on the first of numerous continental tours during which he played with great success in Western and Eastern Europe, receiving many state honours and gifts. From time to time he returned to England, playing Othello at the Lyceum in 1858 when the *Athenaeum* wrote much more favourably, if patronizingly, of 'the sable artist', but, although he longed to return to America, he never had the confidence to do so. He was especially admired in Russia, making his debut as Lear in St Petersburg in 1858, but also travelling extensively in remote provinces, playing sometimes in English with Russian-speaking fellow actors. Tolstoy presented him with a portrait inscribed (in English) with admiration for 'his intellectual and cultivated mind – also his pure and elevated soul!' Aldridge became a British citizen in 1863 but died in Poland four years later. He was indisputably great both as actor and as an ambassador for his race.

The best remembered white American actor of the century is Edwin Booth (1833–93), son of Junius Brutus (p. 290). Of moderate height, elegant, handsome, with deep-set eyes, black curls, and a melodious voice, he hated playing lovers but could not escape Romeo. He built, and for some years managed, a splendid theatre in New York – Booth's, no longer standing – intending to emulate Charles Kean at the Princess's, and in 1864 put on a *Hamlet* in supposedly tenth-century costume which ran for a record one hundred performances. Three weeks after the run ended his brother, John Wilkes Booth, shot dead Abraham Lincoln in a box at a theatre in Washington. Edwin withdrew from the stage for a while, and though he was acting again within a year, his career understandably suffered. One of his more remarkable achievements was a visually splendid *Julius Caesar* (1871) which ran for eighty-five performances in which Booth started as Brutus but then played Cassius followed by Mark Antony for a week each. A malicious newspaper writer exclaimed 'How he could have maintained his composure during that awful scene in which, in mockery, he played the part which John Wilkes Booth played with such fearful earnestness, no one but Edwin Booth and his God can tell.' He was later to alternate Iago and Othello at the Lyceum with Irving; the general view was that both were excellent as Iago, neither as Othello. In Berlin and Vienna he triumphed in his Shakespearian roles with a German-speaking company. One of the earliest (1890) – and most crackly – of all theatrical recordings, of two of Othello's speeches to the Senate, gives a sense of the beauty and intelligence of Booth's delivery and his respect for the iambic metre. There is little sign of an American accent, and, like Irving, he usually – but not invariably – pronounces 'my' as 'mi' – 'rude am I in mi speech' – 'mi boyish days'.

At this time Germany was taking Shakespeare very seriously indeed, and there was a strong interplay with Britain. The Duke of Saxe-Meiningen's Shakespeare productions (pp. 307–8) had been influenced by Charles Kean's, whose work he saw on a visit to England in 1857. Among the speakers at the 1864 tercentenary lunch in Stratford was G. W. Leitner, Professor of Arabic at King's College, London, who formally presented an illuminated address from the German Hochstift in Frankfurt, the birthplace of Goethe, whose house, like Shakespeare's, had been 'rescued' from 'falling into the hands of the stranger'. Speaking on behalf of the German nation he declared 'We have

121. A photograph dated 25 November 1864 of John Wilkes Booth as Mark Antony, Edwin Booth as Brutus, and Junius Brutus Booth, Jr as Cassius in *Julius Caesar*.

read Shakespeare, we have criticised Shakespeare, we have perused everything bearing on him and his times, till, when we thoroughly understood him, we fell down and worshipped.' In the same year the German Shakespeare Gesellschaft was established in Weimar to disseminate knowledge of Shakespeare. Its annual publication, the *Shakespeare Jahrbuch*, still appearing, has had a longer consecutive run than any other Shakespeare periodical and the society, originally made up of around thirty enthusiasts, now has well over 2,000 members. Weimar in 1864 was also the scene for the first ever production anywhere, by Franz Dingelstedt (1814–81), of Shakespeare's two history cycles, performed together over eight days and repeated in Vienna in 1873–4.

In France the first flush of enthusiasm following the visit of the English actors in 1827 was not consolidated by extension of the repertoire or by wholesale abandonment of the old adaptations. The original, 1868 version of Ambroise Thomas's opera *Hamlet* is based on an adaptation by Alexandre Dumas *père* and Paul Meurice in which Hamlet survives and is proclaimed king at the end. (In a version prepared for Covent Garden Hamlet commits suicide.) The tercentenary year had seen the publication in English and German as well as in French of Victor Hugo's substantial book *William Shakespeare*, dedicated 'To England' and described as 'The Glorification of her Poet', which he offered as a foreword to his son, François-Victor's, eighteen-volume translation (1859–66). It is impossible to understand how anyone can ever have taken seriously this rhapsodic and self-indulgent series of sustained digressions from its ostensible topic. Towards the end of the century, however, things began to look up. Sarah Bernhardt, the charismatic and immensely talented idol of the French theatre, had played Cordelia in 1868, Desdemona ten years later, Lady Macbeth in 1884, and Ophelia in 1886, all in standard adaptations. When, in 1899, she came to play Hamlet, however – only one in a long line of women to do so both before and after – she commissioned a new translation of the full text which broke with tradition by being composed not in alexandrines but almost entirely in prose; 'So profoundly', she said, with justice, 'am I imbued with the religion of Shakespeare that I cut out much less of Hamlet than you do on the English stage.'[34] Nevertheless the staging was very much of its time: it divided the play into fifteen tableaux arranged in five acts with currently popular music including a Strauss waltz and the ballet music from Gounod's *Faust* played during the intervals.

One point of the translation had almost fatal consequences. In the original, Gertrude says of Hamlet 'He's fat and scant of breath.' The translators preferred the emendation 'hot' to 'fat': '*Il a chaud; il est hors d'haleine.*' Bernhardt (who, though aged fifty-four, sought – aided by a brilliant vocal technique – to play the Prince as a twenty-year-old) understandably concurred. But at

the premiere a newspaper critic, Georges Vanor, asserted that Hamlet was
fat and that Bernhardt was consequently completely unsuited to the role,
whereas the poet and critic Catulle Mendès – 'a corpulent man' – vehemently
defended her right to play it. The argument developed into a quarrel, Mendès
challenged Vanor, a duel ensued, and Mendès was seriously wounded.

Bernhardt's performance, seen in France, Switzerland, Austria, Hungary,
South America, London, and (on a single occasion) Stratford, was admired
by many but ridiculed by others, most memorably by Max Beerbohm, who
deplored her undertaking: 'Her friends ought to have restrained her. The
native critics ought not to have encouraged her. The custom-house officials

122. Sarah Bernhardt as Hamlet, 1899.

at Charing Cross ought to have confiscated her sable doublet and hose. I, lover of her incomparable art, am more distressed than amused when I think of her aberration at the Adelphi.' And his review ends with the words, 'the only compliment one can conscientiously pay her is that her Hamlet was, from first to last, *très grande dame*'.[35]

Textual restoration was taken a step further in 1904 when André Antoine gave *King Lear* in Paris in a translation by Pierre Loti which represented the first French production of the unadapted text and has been described as the first ever Paris production of a complete Shakespeare play.[36] It is natural for us to feel that departure from Shakespeare's text represents derogation, while restoration is a step forward. At the same time it has to be admitted that some adaptations of the plays, including manifest simplifications and vulgarizations such as Cibber's *Richard III*, Tate's *Lear*, and Garrick's *Romeo and Juliet*, have had immense theatrical success in their own right. Even now very few theatre-goers would insist that every word of every play should be spoken unchanged in stage performance, and some of the most exciting performances of our time, such as Peter Brook's *Lear* or his Bouffes du Nord *Hamlet* (2000), or the Barton/Hall *Wars of the Roses*, have drastically shortened and otherwise altered the plays on which they were based. We are aware too that derivative works in different media may be masterpieces of their kind. Some of these owe relatively little to their originals. Tchaikovsky's purely orchestral fantasy overture *Romeo and Juliet* of 1869 (usually heard in its revision of 1880), for example, owes something to the play's structure in its musical layout; though it begins with a theme for Friar Laurence, it soon moves into a brilliant evocation of the play's opening street quarrel in which we can hear swords and rapiers clashing, then develops into a struggle between the full-blown romanticism of the great love theme surging in the strings against the orchestral depiction of continuing family strife, and concludes with funeral drumbeats, the grief of the families, and the admonitions of the Friar. But all of this could derive from a straightforward retelling of the basic narrative – as does Bellini's opera *I Capuleti ed i Montecchi*, of 1830, whose libretto owes nothing to Shakespeare. Still, it may be that Tchaikovsky's musical inventiveness would have been less rich had he not experienced the linguistic detail of Shakespeare's play, even in translation. (He did in fact sketch a duet based on the love theme with words ineptly paraphrased from the lovers' dawn parting.)[37]

Occasionally, however, transformation of a play into a different medium stays relatively close to the original while achieving total artistic independence as a masterpiece in its own right. There are no better examples than Giuseppe Verdi's two late Shakespeare operas, *Otello* and *Falstaff*. His earlier *Macbeth* (1847, revised 1865), though uneven in quality, includes masterly passages, especially the hypnotic sleepwalking scene. Verdi's choice of *Othello* for a subject in 1887, when he was seventy-four years old, shows his affinity with the Italian actors who had found the leading role so rewarding. Long though the play is, it is often regarded as the most concise of Shakespeare's tragedies, and as the one that focuses most intensely on its central characters. Verdi, guided by his librettist, Arrigo Boito, outdoes it in both respects, narrowing the focus still further upon Iago, Othello, and Desdemona. The opera blazes with passionate energy from the opening discords portraying a storm at sea experienced by the citizens of Cyprus, a passage which culminates in the entry of Othello from shipboard with a ringing cry of '*Esultate!*' – 'Rejoice!' – which tests a tenor's mettle – and his high notes – like no other entry in opera. Omitting the first act, Boito reshapes Shakespeare's play with great skill to permit the composition within a continuous score of such set pieces as Iago's *Credo*, a declaration of evil as sinister in its musical setting as in its words; the duet in which Othello and Desdemona celebrate their love, as erotic in its way as that in Wagner's *Tristan und Isolde*; the thrilling climax to the second act as, trumpets blaring, Iago exults over Othello's capitulation to his deception; and the moments of poignant repose in the last act represented by Desdemona's 'Willow' song and – Boito's addition to Shakespeare – her *Ave Maria*. The words *un bacio* – a kiss – and the musical phrase to which they are set at the end of the love duet become unbearably poignant on their repetition at the very end as Verdi's Othello, like Shakespeare's, dies upon a kiss and, as in theatre versions of the time, the curtain comes slowly down with the dead lovers centre stage.

As a play, *The Merry Wives of Windsor* has theatrical merits that are often underrated, but it would be a rash bardolater (a word coined, incidentally, by Shaw) who did not admit that if Verdi matches Shakespeare's greatness in *Otello*, he surpasses it in his last opera, *Falstaff*, based mainly on *The Merry Wives* and dating from 1893 when he was eighty years old. The German Otto Nicolai (1810–49) had composed a fine opera based on the comedy in 1849, but in England at least it is, sadly if understandably, neglected in favour of Verdi's supreme comic masterpiece. Again Verdi had Boito as a skilful librettist, this time treating the text with more freedom in, for instance, his importing, from the *Henry IV* plays, of Falstaff's soliloquy on honour and other passages including his reminiscences of himself as a page to John of Gaunt in the brief '*Quand 'ero paggio*' – 'When I was a pageboy'. This can still be heard on a recording by the original singer of the role, the French baritone Victor Maurel, who had also first sung Iago. Boito's changes go some way towards answering the objections of those who find the Falstaff of the comedy a sad letdown from the character found in the history plays. And Verdi's score is as rich as it is concise. His love music for Fenton and Nanetta (Anne Page), coming and going, oblivious to the world around them, a harp rippling sympathetically as the tenor and soprano voices breathe out their happiness in long, sustained phrases, is more poetical than any words Shake-speare gives them to speak. Ford's jealousy has an emotional weight which counterpoises the mirth of the wives, their laughter echoed by the orchestra in music whose comedy uniquely matches that of words and situation, and the fairy music of the last scene is a match for Mendelssohn. Indeed as an opera *Falstaff* achieves the perfection of *A Midsummer Night's Dream* as a play.

Towards the end of the nineteenth century there are signs of a dip in Shakespeare's reputation. The social realism associated with Ibsen, the cool rationality of thinkers such as Bernard Shaw, the popularity of the novel, all worked against him. Shaw's writings on Shakespeare, whose works he knew intimately, reveal a constant ambivalence of response, a tension between his intellectual rejection of many of their conventions and values along with a reluctant acknowledgement that they transcend the limitations of their age. 'With the single exception of Homer', he wrote in a review of Irving's *Cymbeline* in 1896,

> there is no eminent writer, not even Sir Walter Scott, whom I can despise so entirely as I despise Shakespear [the idiosyncratic spelling seems a form of insult in itself] when I measure my mind against his. The intensity of my impatience with him occasionally reaches such a pitch, that it would positively be a relief to me to dig him up and throw stones at him, knowing as I do how incapable he and his

worshippers are of understanding any less obvious form of indignity. To read *Cymbeline* and to think of Goethe, of Wagner, of Ibsen, is, for me, to imperil the habit of studied moderation of statement which years of public responsibility as a journalist have made almost second nature to me.

Yet, he continues, as if annoyed with himself for having to admit it,

I am bound to add that I pity the man who cannot enjoy Shakespear. He has outlasted thousand of able thinkers, and will outlast a thousand more. His gift of telling a story (provided someone else told it to him first); his enormous power over language, as conspicuous in his senseless and silly abuse of it as in his miracles of expression; his humour; his sense of idiosyncratic character; and his prodigious fund of that vital energy which is, it seems, the true differentiating property behind the faculties, good, bad, or indifferent, of the man of genius, enable him to entertain us so effectively that the imaginary scenes and people he has created become more real to us than our actual life – at least, until our knowledge and grip of actual life begins to deepen and glow beyond the common.[38]

In Russia, though writers such as Turgenev (1818–83), Dostoevsky (1821–81), and Chekhov (1860–1904) were steeped in and greatly admired Shakespeare, especially *Hamlet*, Leo Tolstoy wrote a virulent attack in a long essay, 'On Shakespeare and the Drama', published in Moscow and, in translation, by the left-wing Free Age Press in England and America in 1906. The pamphlet also contains an essay on 'Shakespeare and the Working Classes' by Ernest Crosby, an American social reformer and friend of Tolstoy, accusing Shakespeare of manifesting an 'utter lack of sympathy' with those classes, along with extracts from letters written by Shaw to Tolstoy's translator which essentially repeat what Shaw had said in his review of *Cymbeline*. Tolstoy declares that he had repeatedly read the plays in Russian, German, and English, with 'repulsion, weariness and bewilderment'. His severest criticism is directed at *King Lear*, which he summarizes at length and derisively; like Mrs Lennox in the eighteenth century (p. 230–1), he finds that the whole of the old play of *King Leir* is 'incomparably and in every respect superior to Shakespear's adaptation.'

Tolstoy was not alone. In 1883 Henry James (echoing Lamb) had found it 'impossible to imagine a drama that accommodates itself less to the stage,'[39] and at the time of Irving's production of a much altered text in 1892 newspaper writers declared that 'Shakespeare is, as a poet and playwright, at his worst in *King Lear*' which 'would not be tolerated if produced without the name of Shakespeare'.[40] And Max Beerbohm wrote, less specifically, that 'throughout the fabric' of Shakespeare's work 'you will find much that is tawdry, irrational, otiose – much that is, however shy you may be of admitting that it is, tedious'.[41] Or 'sad stuff', as King George III had said. (p. 240)

Such criticism did not, however, stem the tide of Shakespearian production and publication. Staging methods associated with spectacular theatre were growing stale, but the seeds had already been sown of a reaction that was to revolutionize Shakespeare production. In 1881 the eccentric William Poel, who hated the production methods of his time, directed and played the main role in a single performance of the first, short quarto (1603) of *Hamlet* at St George's Hall, London. There was no scenery or interval (though a curtain rose and fell briefly from time to time), and the performance lasted only two hours. The discovery in 1888 of the de Witt drawing of the Swan (p. 63) fuelled Poel's enthusiasm; in 1893 he attempted a portable reconstruction of the stage of the Fortune playhouse of 1600 which he set up, however incongruously, in the modern Royalty Theatre for a performance of *Measure for Measure* with himself as Angelo. In 1895 he established the Elizabethan Stage Society. Gradually, helped by Shaw's championship, the movement made headway, and Poel was to direct many plays, mostly rare, until the early 1930s.

For all his antiquarianism, Poel was not a textual purist. He did terrible things to *Richard II*, *Measure for Measure*, and *Coriolanus*. Believing that actors should be chosen largely for the timbres of their voices he was liable to cast roles irrespective of gender. Women played, for instance, Thersites in *Troilus and Cressida* and Valentine in *The Two Gentlemen of Verona*. Of the latter, Poel's biographer, Robert Speaight, tells of a rehearsal in which 'Poel's voice was raised in querulous criticism of the lady who was to play the role: "I am disappointed", he said, "very disappointed indeed. Of all Shakespeare's heroes

123. William Poel's production of the first quarto text of *Hamlet*, which obeys
the instruction unique to that text, Ophelia 'playing on a lute, and her hair down,
singing' (4.5.20).

Valentine is one of the most romantic, one of the most virile. I have chosen
you out of all London for this part, but so far you have shown me no virility
whatsoever." '[42] But Poel showed how much could be gained by speaking
Shakespeare swiftly, by avoiding the long pauses and textual rearrangements
necessitated by naturalistic scenery, by intelligent use of an apron stage and
an upper level, and by concentrating attention on the acting rather than the
settings. He also had a talent for spotting and training newcomers. His *Troilus
and Cressida* of 1912, though given in a mangled text, was the first fully staged
English performance of the play since Shakespeare's time; the milliner Edith
Evans, soon to be recognized as the greatest English actress since Ellen Terry,
virtually created the role of Cressida, her first major stage appearance. Even
more important for the future of Shakespeare production was Poel's casting,
in 1899, of the 22-year-old Harley Granville-Barker as Richard II, as we shall
see in the next chapter.

Poel's approach to staging was paralleled elsewhere. A so-called 'Shake-speare Stage' built by Jozca Savits in 1889 in the Munich Hoftheater helped Poel to develop his own ideas, and in 1895 a mock-Elizabethan stage set up at Harvard University was the first of many such endeavours in America.[43]

*

A new impetus to what it becomes increasingly just to call the Shakespeare industry[44] came from the growing use of the plays to replace the Greek and Roman classics as instruments of secondary and tertiary education. During the 1890s well over a hundred editions of the complete works, or of substantial selections, some of them illustrated with newly commissioned engravings, photographs of actors, and so on, were published in England and America; they include scholarly editions, facsimiles, abbreviated texts for children and for schools, miniature sets, acting editions (notably the Henry Irving Shake-speare (1888–90, etc.), which, rather like Bell's eighteenth-century volumes but in a more heavily pedantic manner, indicates passages recommended for cutting), a shilling Shakespeare, and even a sixpenny Shakespeare. School texts of this period such as A. W. Verity's Pitt Press edition (started in 1890) and the Warwick Shakespeare (from 1893) were to continue in use until the middle of the twentieth century and beyond. Their notes, excellent in their way, reflect the strongly philological emphasis in teaching, as if the plays had been written in a dead language for purely literary study. And the Lambs' *Tales* were unalluringly reprinted in many versions as an educational tool, with a high emphasis on character and moral values along with specimen examination questions such as 'Name three men whose characters you admire and give your reasons' (1899), and 'Can you justify Desdemona's choice of husband?' (1904).

On the tertiary level Shakespeare was increasingly studied and taught in universities both in England and overseas. The German Alexander Schmidt's *Shakespeare Lexicon* (1871) is still a standard work of scholarly reference, and academic studies deriving from doctoral dissertations along with critical studies and essays were published in Germany, America, and elsewhere. The trickle that had sprung by the end of the nineteenth century was to grow into a great flood in subsequent decades. 1904 saw the publication of A. C. Bradley's *Shakespearean Tragedy*, based on lectures given in the University of

Oxford and devoted principally to what have become known (unfairly to the others) as the 'great' tragedies – *Hamlet, Othello, King Lear,* and *Macbeth.* This was the most substantial and sustained work of criticism that had so far been devoted to Shakespeare, and one of the most influential. Though its reputation has fluctuated with changes in critical attitude it has never lost respect and is still a standard work.

Further afield, performances of Shakespeare had been given in India both in English and in translation from early in the century. Slowly Shakespeare began to impinge upon the East, if only through the medium of the Lambs' ubiquitous *Tales*; the first Japanese theatre adaptation was of *The Merchant of Venice* in kabuki form in 1885, and the *Tales* were translated around the same time; a company run by the British-born but American-based George Crichton Miln gave the first complete productions of Shakespeare plays at the Gaiety Theatre in Yokohama in 1891.[45] A translation of ten of the Lambs' *Tales* constituted the first published appearance of Shakespeare in China in 1903.

At the very end of the century a new medium appeared which was to have a colossal impact on the worldwide dissemination of Shakespeare. The very first surviving film of Shakespeare – silent, of course, and only one minute in length – shows Herbert Beerbohm Tree – half-brother of Max Beerbohm – taking an unconscionable time a-dying as King John, and appears to be one of several extracts made as a trailer for his spectacular production – which remedied Shakespeare's omission of a scene showing the signing of Magna Carta – at Her Majesty's Theatre. Before long, too, Sarah Bernhardt would film the duel from *Hamlet* for the Paris Exhibition of 1900 along with recorded sound effects of the clashing of swords which have not survived. We are entering the age of revolutionary new media.

CHAPTER EIGHT

From Victoria to Elizabeth: 1903–1952

I read Shakespeare *directly* I have finished writing, when my mind
is agape & red & hot. Then it is astonishing. I never yet knew
how amazing his stretch & speed & word coining power is, until
I felt it utterly outpace and outrace my own, seeming to start
equal and then I see him draw ahead & do things I could not in
my wildest tumult and utmost press of mind imagine . . . Why
then should anyone else attempt to write. This is not 'writing' at
all. Indeed, I should say that Shre surpasses literature altogether,
if I knew what I meant.

Virginia Woolf, diary entry for 13 April 1930

Brush up your Shakespeare, start quoting him now.
Brush up your Shakespeare, and the women you will wow.
Just declaim a few lines from *Othella*
And they'll think you're a helluva fella.
Brush up your Shakespeare, and they'll all kow-tow.

Sam and Bella Spewack, from *Kiss Me Kate* (1948);
music by Cole Porter

IT IS FITTING THAT Sir Herbert Beerbohm Tree (1852–1917), the last major
exponent of spectacular stage Shakespeare, should have been the first actor
to be filmed in a Shakespeare role, because the spectacular presentation of
Shakespeare was to continue on film while it gradually lost its grip on the
stage. Tree's heyday as a Shakespeare actor and director came during his

management of Her (later His) Majesty's Theatre, from 1897 to 1915. Though he was not as great an actor as Irving he assumed, and later inherited, Irving's mantle as a producer. Like Irving, he employed distinguished artists and composers along with masses of extras in the creation of splendid spectacles which were enormously popular with the theatre-going public. His 1900 production of *A Midsummer Night's Dream*, with Mendelssohn's full score, in which Julia Neilson, as a singing Oberon, wore 'an electric coronal and breastplate' and the stage was carpeted with 'thyme and wild-flowers, brakes and thickets full of blossom'[1] has become notorious for the live rabbits which disported themselves in the sylvan setting. According to the critic of *The Athenaeum*, 'In presenting the poetic aspects of *A Midsummer Night's Dream*, Mr Tree has not only gone beyond precedent and record, he has reached what may, until science brings about new possibilities, be regarded as the limits of the conceivable.'[2] Those new possibilities lay just around the corner; it has been observed that the production 'belongs to the same genre as Walt Disney'.[3] And Max Reinhardt, whose production of the same play in Berlin in 1905, with real trees in the forest, was to be the first of his twelve or so versions, would stretch the limits of the conceivable in his Hollywood film of 1935 (see overleaf), in which Titania and her followers materialize from a moonbeam and Oberon shelters his attendants under a vast black cape of night.

Even Tree was not impervious to the mounting winds of change. In art, literature, theatre, and ballet the spirit of modernism was in the air. A festival which Tree put on at His Majesty's in 1905 broad-mindedly included productions by not only Frank Benson but even the visually austere William Poel. At the same time as Tree was sustaining the old tradition of visually spectacular, textually cavalier presentation at His Majesty's, movements were afoot which would lead to less naturalistic, more symbolic production styles and acting methods conducive to the use of far purer texts. Ellen Terry's son Edward Gordon Craig (1892–1966), who acted with – and idolized – Irving – is a key figure, though he worked little in England. In 1903 he designed a *Much Ado About Nothing* in London in which his mother played Beatrice, a role in which she had triumphed in very differently designed sets with Irving. Craig was unhappy with the production, which was under-prepared and inadequately rehearsed, but his designs were revolutionary in their suggestive simplicity: the church scene, using 'nothing but candles and a corridor of

124. 'Night and silence. Who is here? / Weeds of Athens he doth wear' (2.2.76–7):
Puck (Mickey Rooney) comes upon the sleeping Lysander (Dick Powell)
in Reinhardt's film of *A Midsummer Night's Dream*.

draperies' lit by coloured shafts of light,[4] was 'incomparably finer than any other attempt that has been made to suggest a cathedral on the stage', wrote Max Beerbohm.[5] This was Craig's only English Shakespeare production; he went on writing idealistically about theatre for many years, offering designs for imaginary productions, and in 1908 agreed to design and co-direct a *Hamlet* for Stanislavsky's Moscow Arts Theatre; it was three years before the production materialized, and Craig disowned it, but his designs, using movable screens to both symbolical and practical ends, were revolutionary in their effect. Unfortunately the screens crashed to the ground at the dress rehearsal and had to be hastily patched together again.[6] But the production remained in the company's repertoire for many years and its Hamlet, V. I. Kachalov, was still playing the role in 1940, when he was sixty-five.[7]

More practically efficacious, and even more significant for its effect on the English theatre, was the work of Harley Granville-Barker (1877–1946), who was to take Poel's ideas, purged of their eccentricity, into the mainstream not only of the professional theatre but of criticism and scholarship. Barker's most important productions, given at the Savoy Theatre from 1912 to 1914, were of *The Winter's Tale*, *Twelfth Night*, and *A Midsummer Night's Dream* (which was also given in New York, in 1915). Responsive to new artistic trends, in 1912 Barker invited Duncan Grant to design costumes for a production of *Macbeth* which went into rehearsal but, because of the financial strain of *The Winter's Tale*, was replaced by *Twelfth Night*, considered likely to do better at the box office. Plans for *Macbeth* were revived in 1913 and Grant continued to work on his designs, but the production never materialized.[8] In 1914, too, Jacques Copeau invited Grant to design costumes for a minimally set, long-lived *Twelfth Night* at the Vieux-Colombier in Paris which Barker was to review enthusiastically and at length, though he felt that Grant's costumes, though they were 'enchanting, gay and reposeful' in colour, 'shamefully betrayed' Copeau by their inappropriateness to the play.[9]

Though Barker was a disciple of Poel, he was far from antiquarian in his approach to scenic design, and far more of a purist about texts. He gave the plays almost complete in a theatre in which an attempt had been made to break down the distancing effect of the proscenium arch. While not dispensing with scenery he formalized it, not permitting it to hinder the forward movement of the play. Costumes and lighting were imaginative, even bizarre

– his gold-plated fairies were not universally admired (Plate 19). Like Poel, Barker built out an apron stage and encouraged rapid delivery of the lines without unnecessary pauses and interpolated business. Unlike Poel he engaged fully professional casts whom he rehearsed rigorously. The plays were brushed clean, stripped of conventional accretions – folk tunes arranged by Cecil Sharp, the pioneer collector, replaced Mendelssohn's music in the *Dream* – thought out afresh from beginning to end.

After abandoning the practical theatre Granville-Barker (he hyphenated his name after his second marriage, in 1918) turned to writing. His *Prefaces to Shakespeare*, mostly published between 1923 and 1947, are among the few critical writings that belong to the history of Shakespeare production as much as to that of criticism. They consider the plays from the point of view of one whose main concern is to present them in the theatre. They were largely influential in demonstrating the stage-worthiness of certain plays, such as *Love's Labour's Lost* and even *King Lear*, and in furthering the understanding of Shakespeare's stagecraft in terms of the theatres for which he wrote. Like Poel, Granville-Barker saw the need to understand Shakespeare as a man of his time; but he was also aware of the need to translate such understanding into terms that were attractive to the modern theatre-goer.

Though Granville-Barker's three productions are now regarded as land-marks in the development of Shakespearian staging, moving away from scenic excess towards a style that permitted a far fuller exploration of the text than had previously been possible, they met with hostility and incomprehension in some quarters. The ultra-conservative American G. C. D. Odell, for instance, whose two-volume work *Shakespeare from Betterton to Irving*, published in 1920, remains the most comprehensive survey of Shakespeare production to the beginning of the twentieth century, writes rapturously of Tree but derisively of 'theorists, amateurs and visionaries' such as Craig, Poel, and Granville-Barker, expressing the hope that the 'silly and vulgar way of presenting Shakespeare' represented by Granville-Barker's *A Midsummer Night's Dream* had 'died with all other vain, frivolous, un-simple things burnt up by the great war-conflagration'.[10] More sympathetic critics felt they had experienced a revelation; John Masefield praised Granville-Barker's *Twelfth Night* as 'much the most beautiful thing I have ever seen done on the stage', and John Palmer considered *The Winter's Tale* 'probably the first performance in England of a play by Shakespeare that the author would himself have recognized for his own since Burbage – or at any rate Davenant – retired from active management'.[11]

Devotees of the spectacular could derive pleasure of a kind, divorced though it was from the spoken word, in the products of the burgeoning film industry. The very concept of silent films based on plays by the greatest of poetic dramatists may seem as crazy as operas without music. But the early cinema in England, America, and on the Continent frequently drew scenarios from Shakespeare's plays. Partly this was in the hope of asserting claims to cultural respectability. Competing with live theatre, cinema sought to capitalize on the reputations of established classical performers while offering them the opportunity to reach wider audiences and hopes of immortality in a medium less transient than that of theatre. Such hopes were illusory. Many of the early films have vanished, or survive only in damaged or incomplete copies too frail for public showing. Beerbohm Tree's qualities as an actor are more readily apparent in the sound recordings of his sonorous vocal delivery, crackles notwithstanding, and still more in the review of his production of *King John* written by his half-brother Max Beerbohm,[12] than in the filmed excerpt from that production, valuable though this is as a document. For all that, it is fascinating to be able to see, for instance, Johnston Forbes-Robertson in a 59-minute 1913 version of *Hamlet* in which the sixty-year-old actor mouths the lines as if he were in the theatre, or the 23-minute compression of F. R. Benson's Cibber-influenced *Richard III* filmed on stage in the Shakespeare Memorial Theatre, revelatory as a record of staging in the early years of the century.

Plays with a supernatural element appealed to early film makers as a way of showing off the capabilities of the medium. Even in Benson's theatre-based *Richard III* the ghosts use filmic devices, and an American *Midsummer Night's Dream* employs trick photography to show fairies appearing and disappearing before our very eyes; Bottom becomes an ass on screen instead of having to go off stage for his transformation, but the actor visibly pulls a string to manipulate the jaw of the ass's head even though no audible words issue from it. Absence of spoken language assisted internationality and stars used film to spread their reputation outside their native country. Italian films of *The Merchant of Venice* and *King Lear* starring the eminent tragedian Ernesto

125. Asta Nielsen in silent soliloquy as Hamlet.

Novelli helped him gain recognition in English-speaking countries and elsewhere. Both films used stencil colouring, pretty but erratic, painted directly
on to the film, and both were made on location: Lear goes mad in bright sun-
shine. It is often difficult to tell whether the melodramatically exaggerated
gestures accurately reflect the acting style of the period or result from the effort
to convey emotion without words, but Novelli mimes powerfully as Lear and
plays an interestingly merry Shylock against fascinating glimpses of Venice in
1910. His voluminous wife Olga looks more like a Brunnhilde than a Portia.[13]
   While the trend in stage production was towards a new textual integrity,
the demands of the film medium favoured even more radical abbreviation

and adaptation than had been common in the theatre, sometimes with interesting effect as in the silent Danish expressionist version of *Hamlet* (1921), lasting over two hours and imaginatively directed by Svend Gade. In this film Hamlet is not only played by a woman, Asta Nielsen, who during the war had been a pin-up girl of both Allied and German troops, but actually *is* a woman. The idea comes from an earnestly argued study, *The Mystery of Hamlet. An Attempt to Solve an old Problem* (1881) by an American, Edward P. Vining. In the film, following Vining's hypothesis, the Queen, having given birth to a daughter, conceals the baby's true sex 'for reasons of state'. At the University of Wittenberg Hamlet falls in love with Horatio (Vining had supposed that the closeness of affection between them was explicable only if one of them was a woman), who, however, falls in love with Ophelia; Horatio discovers Hamlet's true sex only as he gropes to find the death wound in 'his' chest, after which a title card proclaims 'Death reveals the tragic secret. Now I understand what bound me to that matchless form.' This film has attracted much attention from critics interested in media studies, feminism, and sexuality.[14]

The new theatrical seriousness evinced in the work of Granville-Barker and other followers of Poel finds its counterpart in the development of major resources for the scholarly study of Shakespeare. Henry Clay Folger's passion for Shakespeare was sparked by a lecture given by Ralph Waldo Emerson as early as 1879. As Folger's business interests prospered and he became an oil millionaire, he and his wife Emily, who was to write a thesis on 'The True Text of Shakespeare', started to amass a collection of books, promptbooks, playbills, manuscripts, paintings, and other objects relevant to Shakespeare which grew so vast that it had to be stored in packing cases until a suitable home could be found for it. One rarity succeeded another and Folger's acquisitiveness even resulted in the discovery of at least one uniquely valuable item. In 1904 press reports of his expenditure of a large sum on a Bible with alleged signatures of Shakespeare caught the eye of a post office clerk in Sweden; remembering a shabby old edition of a Shakespeare play that had belonged to his father he took it to a university librarian for evaluation, and before long Folger had paid £2,000 for the only surviving copy of the first edition of *Titus Andronicus*, important especially because it revealed that all edited texts to that date had included inauthentic lines.[15]

At one time the Folgers even considered housing their library in Stratford-upon-Avon, but they eventually settled upon Washington, DC. Folger died in 1930, but his wife lived on to see the completion of the splendid building where the couple's ashes now rest beneath a reproduction of the memorial bust of Shakespeare. The Folger Shakespeare Library, which its donor described as 'a gift to the American people', opened on Shakespeare's birthday in 1932. Its holdings have been kept up to date and it is now an invaluable and hospitable resource for scholars from all over the world (Plate 27). Perhaps its chief glory is its collection of around eighty of the surviving 250 or so copies, in various states of completeness, of the First Folio.

In the meantime discoveries remained to be made in British libraries. The American Charles William Wallace, with his wife Hulda, became a fanatical and self-sacrificing searcher of uncatalogued and unread documents in the Public Record Office in London, hoping originally to find information relating to Elizabethan child actors. They unearthed valuable finds to do with the Globe and its finances and above all, in 1909, the twenty-six depositions and other documents of the Belott-Mountjoy case (pp. 75–7), which added substantially to knowledge of Shakespeare's life in London as well as providing an additional signature. Back home, a newspaper announced 'Professor Wallace's Remarkable Analysis of 3,000,000 Documents Which Prove the Immortal Bard Never to Have Been a Roistering, Reckless Profligate'. Wallace returned to America in 1916 and though his hope of establishing a Shakespeare Foundation with a million members came to nothing, he struck gold in another way, buying land which became one of the most valuable of American oil fields.[16] Investigations of the Elizabethan theatre included the building of reconstructions at several American universities, including Harvard, which managed to persuade Forbes-Robertson, accustomed to very different surroundings, to play Hamlet on its replica Globe stage in 1904; he enjoyed it so much that he returned in 1916 for performances that celebrated both the tercentenary of Shakespeare's death and his own retirement from the professional stage.[17] And in England the grandiose 'Shakespeare's England' exhibition at Earl's Court during the summer of 1912 saw the building of the first full-scale English reconstruction of the Globe; half-hour excerpts from the plays were presented before audiences which included extras in period costume.[18]

126. The reading room of the Folger Shakespeare Library, Washington, DC, designed to resemble an Elizabethan Great Hall.

127. 'Had Shakespeare asked me . . .' : Max Beerbohm's drawing of Frank Harris
offering himself to Shakespeare, who shudders at the thought.

Far less scholarly in biographical endeavour than the Wallaces was the loud-mouthed womanizer, editor, and miscellaneous writer Frank Harris (1856–1931), who became obsessed with Shakespeare early in life. 'Frank Harris is upstairs', wrote Wilde in a letter of 1899, 'thinking about Shakespeare at the top of his voice'. Had Harris known Shakespeare he would have done anything for him. 'Homosexuality?' he declared during a Café Royal lunch, 'No, I know nothing of the joys of homosexuality. My friend Oscar can no doubt tell you all about that. But I must say that if *Shakespeare* asked me, I would have to submit.' (This incident inspired one of Max Beerbohm's racier cartoons.) A result of Harris's thinking aloud was a series of articles published in the *Saturday Review* (which he edited) and later developed into a book, *The Man Shakespeare and his Tragic Life-Story* (1909). Harris believed that the plays encoded Shakespeare's autobiography, along with the lives of his relatives and friends, at different stages of his career. Now ignored, his book created a sensation in the popular press; the novelist Arnold Bennett (not without encouragement from Harris) declared it a masterpiece which 'has destroyed nearly all previous Shakespearean criticism' and would be 'the parent of nearly all Shakespearean criticism of the future'. He was wrong. Harris also wrote a fatuous play, *Shakespeare and his Love* (1904), which Beerbohm Tree wisely declined to produce, and a sequel to the biography, *The Women of Shakespeare* (1911), which similarly identified heroines of the plays with real-life personages.

More acceptable fictions about Shakespeare were those that identified themselves as such. Clemence Dane's once-popular romantic drama *Will Shakespeare: An Invention in Four Acts*, written partly in verse, now seems badly dated, but Maurice Baring's playlet *The Rehearsal*, written, like Gilbert's *Rosencrantz and Guildenstern*, to be read remains eminently suitable for amateur performance. Republished from the *Morning Post* in his *Diminutive Dramas* (1910), it offers an entertaining if unhistorical reconstruction of an early rehearsal of *Macbeth* which anticipates modern theories about the collaborative nature of playwriting:

[*Enter Mr Burbage, who plays Macbeth*]

MR BURBAGE: That scene doesn't go. Now don't you think Macbeth had better walk in his sleep instead of Lady Macbeth?

THE STAGE MANAGER: That's an idea.

THE PRODUCER: I think the whole scene might be cut. It's quite unnecessary.

LADY MACBETH: Then I shan't come on in the whole of the fifth act. If that scene's cut I shan't play at all.

THE STAGE MANAGER: We're thinking of transferring the scene to Macbeth. – It wouldn't need much altering. Would you mind rewriting that scene, Mr Shakespeare? It wouldn't want much alteration. You'd have to change that line about Arabia. Instead of this 'little hand' you might say 'All the perfumes of Arabia will not sweeten this horny hand.' I'm not sure it isn't more effective.

THE AUTHOR: I'm afraid it might get a laugh.

MR BURBAGE: Not if I play it.

THE AUTHOR: I think it's more likely that Lady Macbeth would walk in her sleep, but –

MR BURBAGE: That doesn't signify, I can make a great hit in that scene.

LADY MACBETH: If you take that scene from me, I shan't play Juliet tonight.

THE STAGE MANAGER [*aside to the Producer*]: We can't possibly get another Juliet.

THE PRODUCER: On the whole, I think we must leave the scene as it is.

Baring is also the author of an imaginary letter from Goneril to Regan which anticipates Peter Brook's 1962 production in ironically finding justification for the sisters' treatment of their father:

I went to Papa and told him frankly that the situation was intolerable; that he must send away some of his people, and choose for the remainder men fitting to his age. The words were scarcely out of my mouth than he called me the most terrible names, ordered his horses to be saddled, and said that he would shake the dust from his feet and not stay a moment longer in this house.

Her final postscript is 'It is wretched weather. The poor little ponies on the heath will have to be brought in.'[19]

The tercentenary of Shakespeare's death, in 1916, came at a bad time for England, in the middle of the First World War. Plans to commemorate the anniversary had been in hand for over a decade, and were associated with the long-abortive attempt to found a National Theatre; Bernard Shaw's playlet *The Dark Lady of the Sonnets*, of 1910, in which Granville-Barker played Shakespeare when it was acted at the Haymarket, is a blatant but entertaining piece of propaganda for that cause. Though celebrations were muted, they included the publication by Oxford University Press of a massive and handsome *Book of Homage to Shakespeare 1916*, edited by Israel Gollancz, who wrote that 'the dream of the world's brotherhood to be demonstrated by its common and united commemoration of Shakespeare, with many another fond illusion', had been 'rudely shattered' by the war. Still, he assembled an international team of 106 'Homagers', as he calls them, mostly from the worlds of literature and the academy, to pay tribute in verse and prose written in a wide range of languages, living and dead, including Romanian, Icelandic, Polish, Finnish, Japanese, Chinese, Persian, Armenian, Urdu, Burmese, Welsh, Greek, Latin, Hebrew, Sanskrit, and English – not all of them with translations. The volume is headed by a poem, 'To Shakespeare after 300 Years', by Thomas Hardy, which doesn't seem to have come easily to him – 'Bright baffling Soul, least capturable of themes, / Thou, who display'dst a life of commonplace . . .' and magnanimously includes an essay on 'The German Contribution to Shakespeare Criticism' by C. H. Herford, editor of Ben Jonson.

Germany celebrated Shakespeare, too. In 1916, the dramatist Ludwig Fulda, claiming that Shakespeare was 'more frequently performed in Germany during a single year than during a whole decade in his native country', declared that Shakespeare had been born in England by mistake: 'Our Shakespeare! . . . Thus we may call him by right of spiritual conquest. And should we succeed in vanquishing England in the field, we should, I think, insert a clause into the peace treaty stipulating the formal surrender of William Shakespeare to Germany.'[20] Could Fulda have had his tongue in his cheek?

In 1914 London had acquired a new centre for the performance of Shakespeare which was to operate for the next half-century. The Old Vic (more formally the Royal Victoria Theatre), situated (like the original Globe) on the unfashionable, south side of the Thames, had been briefly run as the

'Royal Victoria Coffee Music Hall' by William Poel during the 1880s. During the early years of the next century scenes from Shakespeare were performed during intervals, and in April 1912 the indomitable Lilian Baylis (1874–1937) took over the management with the aim of presenting both opera and classical drama at moderate prices. In October 1914 *Romeo and Juliet* became the first of eight Shakespeare plays to be performed during the opening season, and by 1923 the Old Vic company had chalked up a record by presenting every play in the canon except *Cymbeline.* The full-text *Hamlet* became an annual rite. Audiences, paying less than in the West End – thanks partly to private subsidy along with Baylis's capacity to cajole her artists into working for practically nothing – had an earnestness akin to those that saw Phelps's productions at Sadler's Wells. Economy of production style was a financial necessity as much as an ideological tenet, but several of Baylis's producers had worked with Poel, whose ideas, mediated by Granville-Barker, were infiltrating the London stage.

Baylis had an extraordinary capacity to attract talented young actors, partly no doubt because she gave them the chance to play so wide a range of great roles. During the war Sybil Thorndike (1882–1976) took parts as varied as Lady Macbeth and Rosalind, Imogen and Queen Margaret, and – because so many men were at the front – Prince Hal, Ferdinand, Lancelot Gobbo, and Lear's Fool. In the 1925–6 season Edith Evans played Portia in both *Julius Caesar* and *The Merchant of Venice*, Rosalind, Cleopatra, Beatrice, and Juliet's Nurse. John Gielgud, at the start of a career that was to last to the end of the century, led the company as Richard II and Hamlet, two of his greatest roles, in 1929, followed in the next year by Prospero and Lear, with Ralph Richardson as Caliban and Kent. In 1932 Peggy Ashcroft was the leading lady, as Imogen, Rosalind, Portia (in *The Merchant of Venice*), Perdita, Juliet, and Miranda; the following season saw Charles Laughton as Henry VIII (capitalizing on his success as Henry in Alexander Korda's film *The Private Life of Henry VIII*), Angelo, Prospero, and Macbeth; in 1934 Maurice Evans, soon to emigrate to America where he was to become Broadway's leading classical actor and to achieve popular success during the Second World War as the GI Hamlet, played a string of leading roles, and from 1936 to 1938 Laurence Olivier starred as Hamlet, Henry V, Macbeth, Iago, and Coriolanus. Some of the finest twentieth-century actors were cutting their teeth on the great roles,

128. John Gielgud as Hamlet at the New Theatre, London,
directed by himself, 1934.

129. John Barrymore as Hamlet on Robert Edmund Jones's set for New York and
London, 1922–25.

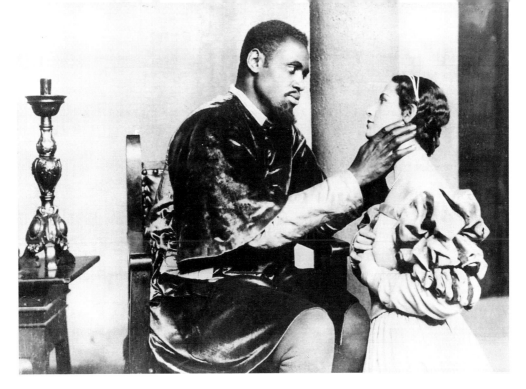

130. 'How do you, Desdemona?' (3.4.35): Paul Robeson as Othello and Peggy Ashcroft as Desdemona at the Savoy Theatre, London, 1930.

most of which they were to play again later, sometimes in more sophisticated productions, but not always with greater personal success.

During these years too new perspectives were opening up elsewhere. In America the first two decades of the century represent a low point in Shakespeare production, but there was a sudden change for the better in 1920 with the emergence in John Barrymore (1882–1942) of a first-class actor in a production of *Richard III* directed by Arthur Hopkins in which the great designer Robert Edmund Jones (1887–1954), who had worked with Granville-Barker, established his reputation. Heavily influenced by Gordon Craig, but more practical and more interested in actors, Jones was a brilliantly imaginative and innovative designer of skilfully lit expressionist settings that permitted fluidity of action while suggesting locality and, above all, mood. The British critic James Agate was to describe his set for *Hamlet* as 'the most beautiful thing I have ever seen on any stage. The vast arch at the back served as the battlements, and was hung with curtains for the indoor scenes, played on two platforms intersected by a flight of steps.'[21] The Ghost 'was represented by a shaft of wavering greenish light projected onto a cyclorama beyond the arch'.[22] Barrymore himself, handsome, magnetic in presence, brought a new immediacy to the verse-speaking both as Richard III and in his *Hamlet* which ran for 101 performances (one more, not without calculation, than Edwin Booth's previous record) in New York in 1922 and was repeated in London three years later.[23] His later career was blighted by drink, but he played Mercutio in the Hollywood film of *Romeo and Juliet* in 1936. Paul Robeson (1898–1976), son of a slave and the first great American black performer to emerge since Ira Aldridge (p. 322–3), had, like Aldridge, a career chequered by racial prejudice and political problems. A magnificent figure of a man with a deep bass voice of exceptional beauty and power, he was primarily a singing actor, but he played Othello in three different productions. The first was in 1930 at the Savoy Theatre, London, adjoining the hotel to which he had been refused admission because of his colour; Peggy Ashcroft was Desdemona and Sybil Thorndike Emilia (p. 353). The second, and most successful, was in New York in 1943; it had 296 performances before going on an extended tour. Finally, at Stratford in 1959, when he was a little over sixty, Robeson appeared in an over-naturalistic production in which his performance, though sonorously spoken, seemed stately and unimpassioned, especially in contrast with the conversational, 'method' style of Sam Wanamaker as Iago.

The first major modern-dress Shakespeare performance, of *Hamlet*, was directed by Max Reinhardt in Berlin in 1920, and in 1923 the Birmingham Repertory Theatre, under the management of Sir Barry Jackson, followed suit with *Cymbeline* and, later, *Hamlet* (in plus fours) and a *Macbeth* set in the First World War. Perhaps the most influential modern-dress production of this era was Michael MacOwan's *Troilus and Cressida* at the Westminster Theatre in 1938. In spite of pioneering productions by Poel and by the Marlowe Society of Cambridge in 1922, the play had not yet established itself in the repertory; at Stratford in 1936 it had been dismissed as a museum piece. Now the immediacy of modern dress and music helped to reveal its relevance to a world about to plunge once again into war. In the profundity of its concerns with irrationalities of war and sex it became a play in which the twentieth century would uniquely see its own reflection.

An important event at Stratford was the appointment in 1919 – the year Benson withdrew as festival director – of William Bridges-Adams (a follower of Granville-Barker, and known because of his textual principles as Unabridges-Adams) as artistic director with a year-round contract for a

131. 'My niece is horrible in love with a thing you have, sweet Queen' (3.1.94–5): Paul Rogers as Pandarus, Wendy Hiller as Helen, and Ronald Allen as Paris in Tyrone Guthrie's Edwardian-style production of *Troilus and Cressida* at the Old Vic, 1955.

permanent Shakespeare company, freeing the theatre from its dependency on touring companies. He was a fine director of true integrity, but his work was hampered by a backward policy from the governing body. Disaster struck Stratford in 1926, when the Memorial Theatre burnt down. It was an outdated building: Shaw is said to have sent a telegram of congratulation to his fellow governors (and contributed handsomely to the rebuilding fund). Performances continued in the local cinema until the opening on Shakespeare's birthday in 1932 – the day that also saw the inauguration of the Folger Shakespeare Library – of a replacement designed by Elisabeth Scott, the only woman candidate in the competition to choose an architect. Shaw, patronizingly, said that 'although the architect is a woman, hers was the only plan which showed any theatre sense'. The building (which has undergone both internal and external changes), looking at night when approached from the bridge like a river steamer, makes fine use of its location, but was designed in a manner that took too little note of developing performance styles; in spite of Poel's and Granville-Barker's attempts to bring performers closer to audiences by escaping from the tyranny of the proscenium arch, the very basis of this theatre, whose design resembles cinema architecture of the time, is just such an arch. Baliol Holloway is reported to have said that performing on its stage was like acting to Calais from Dover Cliff.

Though most productions in Stratford during the 1930s were conservative in nature, experiments occurred there, too. Increasingly the director was replacing the actor as the motive force behind productions – indeed, the term 'director' was superseding 'producer' as the name for the artistic controller. In Theodore Komisarjevsky's six productions from 1932 to 1939, *The Merchant of Venice* and *The Comedy of Errors* were fantasticated into the style of *commedia dell'arte* and *Macbeth* was played on a metallic set with potent allusions to modern warfare and expressionist devices such as 'amplifiers drumming out incantations which Macbeth's conscience speaks, and shadows projected for bodies'. (In 1936, too, Orson Welles produced his all-black 'Voodoo' *Macbeth*, set in Haiti, in New York.) Like Granville-Barker, Komisarjevsky was destroying his audience's preconceptions, but he seems often to have substituted theatrical virtuosity and vivid but generalized mood painting for Granville-Barker's patient exploration of text. The exception was *King Lear*, played on a severely simple set of stairs and platforms backed by a cyclorama which, when subtly lit, acted as a vast 'reflector of mood'; for once the director subjugated himself to the play and to Randle Ayrton's powerful performance in the title role. The young Peter Brook (b. 1925), who had already worked with Barry Jackson in Birmingham, directed a production of the then rarely played *Love's Labour's Lost* which, with its Watteau-esque settings, was revelatory in its demonstration of the humanity lying behind a text that had been considered sterilely artificial, along with an iconoclastic *Romeo and Juliet*, at Stratford in 1946 and a great *Measure for Measure* (1951) with Gielgud as Angelo.

John Gielgud and Laurence Olivier were the two greatest male Shakespeare actors to emerge from the Old Vic of the 1930s. Each excelled in roles that the other did not attempt. In Shakespeare, Gielgud was the supreme lyric actor; he could be intensely passionate, but the passion was vocal rather than bodily; he was ideal as Prospero and Richard II. His Hamlet, given many times in various productions between 1929 and 1944, and recorded for radio but not on film, was a classic, especially in its 1940 incarnation directed by

132. 'Attend the lords of France and Burgundy, Gloucester' (1.1.34): Randle Ayrton as the king in Komisarjevsky's production of *King Lear*, Shakespeare Memorial Theatre, 1936.

George Rylands, in the beauty, intelligence and energy of its speech, and in its emotional range. Gielgud conveyed superbly the inward agony of Cassius (in the Joseph Mankiewicz film of 1953 as well as on stage) and Angelo, and was a marvellously tortured Leontes in Peter Brook's *Winter's Tale* of 1951. Granville-Barker came out of retirement to direct him as Lear in 1940 in a production that showed it was possible to stage the tragedy effectively in a full text and in Elizabethan costume; Gielgud played the role again at Stratford in 1950 and 1955, and on a sound recording in 1994, to celebrate his ninetieth birthday, sixty-five years after he first played it at the Old Vic.

Olivier was a far more physical actor. His voice was less naturally beautiful, but he made of it a wonderfully pliant, vibrant and heroic instrument, capable of plangent pathos as well as sardonic irony, bitter invective, rousing ferocity, and anguished agony. He was a virtuoso in the line of Garrick, Kean, and Irving, excelling in unexpected transitions, athletic excitement, and startling physical transmutations. His protean quality is shown in the range of his roles. In 1935 at the Old Vic, along with Gielgud, he played successively Mercutio and Romeo in a production adorned with the Juliet of Peggy Ashcroft and the Nurse of Edith Evans. In 1944, with the Old Vic company at the New Theatre, he first gave his brilliantly ironic Richard III. In the next season, along with Richardson as one of the greatest of Falstaffs, he played a strongly characterized, virile Hotspur in *Henry IV, Part One* and transformed himself into the aged Justice Shallow in *Part Two*. His Titus Andronicus in Brook's revelatory Stratford production of 1955 was astounding in its tragic intensity; in the same season he was a memorable Macbeth and a grotesquely comic Malvolio. In 1959, also at Stratford, the emergent Peter Hall directed him as Coriolanus in a performance that encompassed all the character's heroism, hauteur, and bewildered self-examination; to these Olivier added a wry irony, discovering unexpected comedy in the tension between the hero's sense of himself and the demands that others made on him. The culminating death leap, after which Olivier dangled like, in Kenneth Tynan's words, 'the slaughtered Mussolini', set the seal on a performance of searing intensity. I was present at the first night, and nearly jumped out of my seat with the thrill of this ending. Afterwards I walked the streets of Stratford alone, unwilling to break the spell by anything so mundane as conversation. No less powerful was Olivier's Othello for the National Theatre Company in 1964, for which he found bass notes in his naturally light voice.

Olivier was not only a great actor but also one of the finest directors of Shakespeare on film. When he started, competition, such as it was, came from Hollywood, which had bridged the gap between silent films and talkies with a slapstick version of *The Taming of the Shrew* starring Mary Pickford and Douglas Fairbanks in 1929, originally intended to be silent but finally made in both forms. Only the great popularity of the stars made it a commercial proposition, and even then a studio worker is said to have apologized 'Sure, we're making *The Taming of the Shrew*, but we're turning it into a cah-medy.'[24] As Kate declares her intention to obey her husband she winks broadly at Bianca, showing that she has the upper hand after all. The best of the pre-war films is Max Reinhardt's expensive, kitsch, but cinematically brilliant *A Midsummer*

133. *Opposite*. 'Kill, kill, kill, kill, kill him!' (5.6.130): Coriolanus (Laurence Olivier) dangles in the air before being despatched by Aufidius (Anthony Nicholls).

Night's Dream (1935), which adventurously cast James Cagney, famous in gangster roles, as Bottom and the young Mickey Rooney as Puck. It was followed in 1936 by a respectful but slow-moving *Romeo and Juliet* starring Leslie Howard and Norma Shearer, then aged forty-three and thirty-six respectively. After that Hollywood avoided Shakespeare for nearly twenty years.

Olivier played Orlando in a British film of *As You Like It*, also of 1936, with Elisabeth Bergner as Rosalind, and the growth of the native film industry during the war made possible his filming of *Henry V* (1944), which, dedicated to the 'Commandos and airborne troops of Great Britain, the spirit of whose ancestors it has been humbly attempted to recapture in some ensuing scenes', was in part an instrument of propaganda. It is far more; indeed, the leading historian of Shakespeare on film writes that it 'not only launched, indeed invented the modern Shakespeare film, but also showed that the Shakespeare movie could survive in the Palace theatre as well as in the rarified art houses'.[25] Olivier's instant mastery of the film medium, and of the problems of translating theatre into cinema – achieved partly by opening with, and returning to, a performance in the Globe – is astonishing. Substantial shortening of the text – as in virtually every Shakespeare film – works towards a glamorization of the warrior-hero akin to that of the play's Chorus, and no actor could have sustained this image better than Olivier. Few things on film are more thrilling than the great, pounding cavalry charge of Agincourt with the culminating whistle of arrows released for slaughter, few recorded speeches more stirring, despite changes in style of vocal delivery, than Olivier's 'Once more unto the breach', and both are wonderfully supported by William Walton's magnificent musical score.

Olivier let himself down by prefacing his film of *Hamlet* (1948) with the hero's lines 'So, oft it chances in particular men / That, for some vicious mole of nature in them . . . Shall in the general censure take corruption / From that particular fault', followed by the statement that this is 'the tragedy of a man who could not make up his mind'. This over-simplifies both play and film. The black-and-white photography (making a virtue out of the need for economy) is haunting, and in spite of studio-bound sets and over-genteel speaking of some roles, the film bears comparison with any of its successors. *Richard III* is more closely based on the stage production, though fully translated into filmic terms, whereas *Othello*, though vocally thrilling, is visually disappointing; based closely on the stage production it was filmed hastily in a studio, and the scale of Olivier's magnificent performance is not adjusted to the demands of the screen.

The early decades of the century witness the influence of psychoanalytical theory on the interpretation of Shakespeare. Sigmund Freud's Oedipal interpretation of Hamlet, proposing subconscious sexual desire for his mother, was developed by his disciple and biographer Ernest Jones in a series of studies culminating in *Hamlet and Oedipus* (1949) which influenced performance as well as criticism. Arthur Hopkins's production of *Hamlet*, with John Barrymore, featured Freudian interpretations of the so-called 'closet' scene and of Ophelia's sexuality;[26] Dover Wilson refers to the closet as a bedroom in his Cambridge edition and to the scene as the 'Bedroom Scene' in his lively book *What Happens in Hamlet* (1935), and a bed appeared on stage, apparently for the first but by no means for the last time in a New York production starring Gielgud in the following year, when also Tyrone Guthrie, always adventurous, directed Olivier in an Oedipal reading at the Old Vic, which carried over into his film.[27]

Freudian investigations of homosexuality also affected interpretation of Shakespeare. Homosexual interpretations of the Sonnets were nothing new: they go back at least as far as the eighteenth century, and were often repudiated with irrational passion; Coleridge, for example, inaccurately told his son Hartley that in all Shakespeare's works there is 'not even an allusion to that very worst of all possible vices' and defended Shakespeare's 'pure love' for his fair friend.[28] He ignores, to give only one example, Thersites's description, in *Troilus and Cressida*, of Patroclus as Achilles's 'masculine whore' (5.1.17). But although the later part of the nineteenth century saw major developments in studies of sexuality and in the categorization of homosexuality, I know of no attempts to identify homosexuality in the plays, or to portray it in performance, until the twentieth century. It may be significant that *Richard II*, whose hero is susceptible to this interpretation, was little played during the nineteenth century and that Benson's performance, which he gave over a period of thirty years from 1896, was described as effeminate, perhaps a way of suggesting homosexuality without actually mentioning it. But gradually explorations of psychological subtext identified homosexuality in relationships such as those of Antonio and Bassanio in *The Merchant of Venice*, Antonio and

Sebastian in *Twelfth Night*, and Coriolanus and Aufidius. When Olivier was to play Iago under the direction of Tyrone Guthrie in 1938 they went together to consult Ernest Jones, who told them that 'to his mind the clue to the play was not Iago's hatred for Othello, but his deep affection for him. His jealousy was not because he envied Othello's position, not because he was in love with Desdemona, but because he himself possessed a subconscious affection for the Moor, the homosexual foundation of which he did not understand.'[29] Olivier's attempt to translate this interpretation into theatrical terms had only limited success. He described how, in rehearsal with his Othello, Ralph Richardson, 'I flung my arms round Ralph's neck and kissed him. Whereat Ralph, more in sorrow than in anger, sort of patted me and said, "Dear fellow, dear boy", much more pitying me for having lost control of myself, than despising me for being a very bad actor.'[30] The idea that the jealousy of Leontes, in *The Winter's Tale*, similarly derives from an 'early fixation of his affections upon his friend' Polixenes, whom he believes to be committing adultery with Hermione, was put forward by J. I. M. Stewart in his book *Character and Motive in Shakespeare* (1949), but as the characters are scarcely seen together the idea would be difficult to realize on stage.

After the First World War a number of works of scholarship appeared which have laid the foundations for the great upsurge of academic study of Shakespeare that has proliferated ever since. Sir Edmund Chambers produced exhaustive studies in the four volumes of *The Elizabethan Stage* (1923) and the two of *William Shakespeare: A Study of Facts and Problems* (1930). The *New (Oxford) English Dictionary*, which began to appear in 1888 and reached completion in 1928, provided material for more exhaustive studies of Shakespeare's complex language than had previously been possible, feeding the notes of, for example, the American G. L. Kittredge's highly regarded editions of individual plays collected posthumously as *Sixteen Plays of Shakespeare* (1946). In Britain the New (Cambridge) Shakespeare, edited by John Dover Wilson with various collaborators, pursued a stately and sometimes eccentric progress from 1921 until 1966 when the aged, nearly blind but still sprightly Wilson completed the series with the Sonnets. Early volumes are remarkable for literary stage directions in the manner of Shaw or James Barrie: in *A Midsummer Night's Dream*, for example, 'Another part of the wood. A grassy plot before a great oak-tree; behind the tree a bank overhung with creepers, and at one side a thorn-bush. The air is heavy with the scent of blossom.' Even Beerbohm Tree would have found it hard to compete with that. Legend has it that Wilson's wife would lock him into his study to encourage him to get on with his work, whereupon he would escape out of the window to play golf. But he achieved much.

It may be no coincidence that publication of the final instalments of the *Dictionary* was followed by the development of a school of criticism much concerned with close verbal analysis associated in England especially with Cambridge, and in America with Yale. Caroline Spurgeon's *Shakespeare's Imagery and What it Tells Us* appeared in 1935, and Wolfgang Clemen's *The Development of Shakespeare's Imagery*, in its original German version, in 1936 (Clemen studied in Cambridge). L. C. Knights's provocatively titled *How Many Children had Lady Macbeth?* (1933), parodying the title of some of the less happy appendices in A. C. Bradley's *Shakespearean Tragedy*, proposed that 'a Shakespeare play is a dramatic poem' rather than a series of character portrayals; in its emphasis on poetry rather than drama Knight's essay now seems to belong to its time no less than Bradley's does to its. And G. Wilson Knight pursued a series of complex, highly romantic studies in Shakespearian interpretation working from the assumption of a Coleridgean 'organic unity' and of the play as an 'extended metaphor'. These studies were readerly, not theatrical, in their orientation.

The Oxford *Dictionary*, begun in the Victorian era, was prurient in its approach to sexual language. Eric Partridge attempted to fill the gap in his *Shakespeare's Bawdy* of 1947, but that work was first issued in a limited edition of 1,000 copies selling at the high price of two guineas (at a time when that sum would have bought forty-two Penguin paperbacks). Certain features of its publication aligned it with erotic literature (or, in the vulgate, dirty books) such as might be perused with impunity by the wealthy and learned but should be placed and priced out of the reach of anyone else. Partridge follows the time-honoured custom of resorting to the sanitizing influence of Latin for expressions which plain English would have rendered offensive. So for instance he suggests that, in the Constable's words in *Henry V*, that his mistress 'was not bridled' (3.7.50), 'There may even be a pun on "to put the bridle-bit in her mouth": *"penem in vaginam inmittere"*' – to insert the penis into the vagina. On occasion Partridge seems even to have coined latinisms for sexual activity: his word 'penilingism', presumably meaning 'tonguing of the penis', is not recorded in either the original *Dictionary* or its broader-minded Supplements. Increasing frankness about Shakespeare's sexual language has resulted in a reinstatement of frequently bowdlerized passages in performance.

★

The perennial fascination for creative artists of the figure of Falstaff is witnessed by a spate of musical works, the first and greatest of which is Sir Edward Elgar's 'symphonic study' *Falstaff* (1913). This was fed not only by the *Henry IV* plays but also by the critical writings of the Victorian Edward Dowden, whose book *Shakspere: A Critical Study of his Mind and Art* (1875) was popular for over a century, and the early essay by Maurice Morgann (pp. 235–7) which Elgar quoted to characterize the aspects of Falstaff that he wished to capture in sound: 'in a green old age, mellow, frank, gay, easy, corpulent, loose, unprincipled, and luxurious'. Elgar's music is indeed wonderfully mellow, above all in the two episodes for small orchestra, one a 'Dream Interlude' in which Falstaff, asleep, looks back to his youth as page to the Duke of Norfolk with a nostalgia of which Elgar was a master, the other, 'Shallow's Orchard', a bucolic interlude with music for pipe (oboe) and tabor. The work reaches a great, characteristically Elgarian climax with the entry of Hal for his coronation and his repudiation of his old friend, and ends elegiacally with the fat knight's death.

Two other British composers wrote stage works centred on Falstaff which, though they have not retained a place in the operatic repertoire, may be enjoyed in recordings. Early in his career, Ralph Vaughan Williams (1872–1958) composed incidental music for Benson's Stratford productions; his opera based on *The Merry Wives of Windsor*, *Sir John in Love* (1929), which incorporates lyrics from other plays by Shakespeare and his contemporaries such as Jonson's 'Have you seen but a white lily grow?', makes use of folk songs including 'Greensleeves', heard in an early version of the composer's ever-popular Fantasia. *Sir John in Love* is at once a jolly and richly lyrical piece with brilliant writing for soloists, chorus and orchestra. It is a mystery why this highly enjoyable and quintessentially English work – the second-best,[31] and perhaps the most easily enjoyable, English Shakespeare opera – is not more often performed. When it failed on the stage Vaughan Williams

134. The Prologue to Prokofiev's ballet *Romeo and Juliet*, with Galina Ulanova as Juliet and Yury Zhdanov as Romeo at the Bolshoi Theatre, Moscow, 1956.

reclaimed parts of it in a cantata, 'In Windsor Forest'. But his greatest Shake-speare-inspired works are the haunting 'Serenade to Music' of 1938 and the three part songs of 1951, which include a magical setting of 'Full Fathom Five'. The Serenade, composed for the golden jubilee of the conductor Sir Henry Wood, is surely one of the greatest pieces of occasional music ever written; sixteen solo voices – at the first performance the finest in England – intertwine over a rich bed of orchestral sound in a setting of lines from the last scene of *The Merchant of Venice* – 'How sweet the moonlight sleeps upon this bank . . .'.[32] The other Falstaff-inspired opera is Gustav Holst's one-acter *At the Boar's Head*, based largely on the tavern scenes in both parts of *Henry IV* and drawing extensively on folk songs; particularly effective are the settings of two sonnets sung by the Prince disguised as a barman.

In Russia the play of Shakespeare's with the most romantic image provided the scenario for a work in the medium most associated with romanticism, the ballet. Developing the nineteenth-century tradition, most closely associated with Tchaikovsky, of creating full-length narrative works, Sergei Prokofiev both devised and composed his *Romeo and Juliet* in 1935–6. Initially turned down by the Bolshoi Ballet, it was first danced in Brno, Czechoslovakia, finally reaching Moscow only in 1946. Since then it has become probably the most frequently danced of all Shakespeare ballets, and independent selections of the music have found a place in the concert hall. Prokofiev, of course, uses none of Shakespeare's words, and not many crop up in Cole Porter's delightful musical *Kiss Me Kate*, freely adapted from *The Taming of the Shrew* and first performed on Broadway in 1948. Leonard Bernstein's musical *West Side Story* (1957), brilliantly innovative in its use of jazz rhythms, derives from *Romeo and Juliet* only its framework of the story of young lovers caught between the strife of feuding gangs on the New York waterfront.

With the rise of fascism Shakespeare's plays suffered new transmutations in the service of propaganda and political comment. Some productions in Germany implicitly criticized the Nazi regime. *Coriolanus*, with its struggles between plebeian and aristocratic factions, has always been peculiarly susceptible to political interpretation; in Germany, where it had been considered critical of militarism, the author of a radio translation in 1932 was exiled by the Nazis, after which the play was adopted 'as a schoolbook to demonstrate to Hitler Youth the unsoundness of democracy and to idealize Martius as an heroic *führer* trying to lead his people to a healthier society, "as Adolf Hitler in our days wishes to lead our beloved German father-land".'[33] On the other hand, in Russia and Poland productions of 1934 and 1935 had criticized the hero as 'a would-be superman who has detached himself from the people and betrayed them'.[34] And fascist partisans in Paris saw a 1933 production as a stimulus for demonstrations against the left-wing government; feelings ran so high that police shut the theatre down after rioting during a performance.[35] In a 1937 *Richard III* in Berlin Werner Krauss as Richard resembled Joseph Goebbels, 'his bodyguards wore black SS-type uniforms, the costumes of the murderers of the princes suggested the outfits of other Nazi ruffians, and the Scrivener spoke his revealing lines' (3.6), in which he reports that the document announcing Hastings's execution had been commissioned when Hastings still 'lived, / Untainted, unexamined, free, at liberty' – 'directly to the audience'. Though 'the production caused great offence in official quarters . . . the allusions, though perfectly comprehensible to those who wanted to see, were ambivalent enough to prevent the director from having to suffer serious consequences'.[36] In the same year in New York Orson Welles, playing Brutus, directed a modern-dress *Julius Caesar* pointedly set in Mussolini's

Italy. And in a notoriously anti-Semitic interpretation of *The Merchant of Venice* in Berlin in 1943 Krauss, this time playing sympathetically to Nazi policy, portrayed Shylock so as to suggest 'the pathological image of the typical eastern Jew in all his outer and inner uncleanness'.[37]

The dangers of wartime London led to an increase in the number of Shakespeare productions touring the provinces in the hope – often successful – of improving national morale. The indomitable veterans Dame Sybil Thorndike – an actress who combined keen intellect with an extraordinarily warm and generous personality – and her Poel-trained husband Sir Lewis Casson took a portable *Macbeth* on a ten-week tour of thirty-eight Welsh mining towns, she playing a witch as well as Lady Macbeth. In 1937 Donald Wolfit (1902–68), who had acted at the Old Vic and Stratford (where he played Hamlet), had established his own company with which he played (invariably) leading roles, mostly in Shakespeare, for fourteen seasons, touring extensively in the provinces and overseas while occasionally also playing in London. During the war he and his company braved the bombs in London to give hour-long lunch-time performances of selected scenes. There was more than a touch of Dickens's magniloquent Vincent Crummles, in *Nicholas Nickleby*, about Wolfit. In the manner of the old actor-managers he often surrounded himself with inferior colleagues, his speaking could be orotund to the point of fruitiness, and when he was on stage he was rarely not at its centre. His acceptance of applause when, clutching the edge of the curtain with an obeisance that threatened to pull it to the ground, he would declare, with Hamlet, 'Beggar that I am, I am even poor in thanks' was a performance in itself. But at his best, as when he accepted the challenge of playing Iago to the Othello of the great German-born, Czech-trained Frederick Valk, and especially as Lear, unquestionably his greatest role, he could be both powerful and deeply moving. Of *Othello* Kenneth Tynan wrote, with conscious hyperbole, 'I have lived for three hours on the red brink of a volcano, and the crust of lava crumbles still beneath my feet.' Ronald Harwood's affectionately satirical play *The Dresser* (1980, also filmed) is closely based on his experiences of acting with Wolfit in *Lear*, and Harwood also wrote an eloquent composite account of a wartime London performance of the play in his biography of Wolfit.[38]

In England the war against fascism was seen, like Henry V's war against France, as a fight between the heroic and happy few against the evil many.

Dover Wilson was to declare that Henry's words before Agincourt – 'We few, we happy few, we band of brothers' (*Henry V*, 4.3.60) – and Winston Churchill's after the Battle of Britain – 'never in the field of human conflict was so much owed by so many to so few' – came 'from the same national mint'.[39] Both Olivier's morale-boosting film of *Henry V* and E. M. W. Tillyard's influential book *Shakespeare's History Plays*, arguing that the two tetralogies from *Richard II* to *Henry V* constitute a national epic, appeared in 1944. They set the tone for an image of Shakespeare as a pillar of orthodoxy whose works could be invoked as exemplars of true-blue Britishness and upholders of the status quo. Undoubtedly Shakespeare had served as a source of spiritual consolation and as a stimulus to patriotic fervour, though Olivier's film sacrifices almost half of the play's text, including passages that might detract from the image of Henry as the 'mirror of all Christian kings', and Tillyard's thesis has been attacked as an over-simplification. With the end of the war Shakespeare's political function was to change gradually from that of a bolsterer of national morale to an instrument of cultural propaganda. But internationally his function was far more than political. In some countries the plays would increasingly become means of figuring forth, and covertly commenting upon, their own political problems. But they remained also deeply human projections of basic human situations, as well as stimuli to other sorts of artistic creation, challenges and opportunities to performers, and sources of instruction and, in the broadest sense of the word, entertainment, to millions. And it was around the middle of the century that the Shakespeare industry really took off, especially in academic circles.

CHAPTER NINE

Shakespeare Worldwide

This man, whose vision ranged
Life's whole from bliss to woe,
Perceived how love, warped or estranged,
Will bring the highest low.
Today his birthday fell.
But he is born once more
Each time we come beneath his spell
And to his genius soar.

C. Day-Lewis, 'Hymn for Shakespeare's Birthday'

THE STORY OF SHAKESPEARE to be told in this chapter is one of political and cultural initiatives, of the growth of international interest, and of the development of major performing companies, not least the Royal Shakespeare Company. It encompasses new developments in, especially, biographical and textual scholarship, along with revolutionary approaches to criticism. In theatre buildings, archaeological discoveries accompanied reconstruction. Film, video, and television leapt forward as media that disseminate Shakespeare performances with greater speed and economy, and over greater distances, than ever before. The interaction between Shakespeare and artists, especially writers, has operated with increasing subtlety, and he has been paid the backhanded compliment of massive attention from anti-Stratfordians (pp. 314–16) and eccentrics.

Shakespeare's emergence as a truly global writer, aided by the increasing use of English as an international language and by the worldwide desire for universally acceptable cultural icons, was in part the result of a deliberate campaign. As Britain tried to pull itself together at the end of the Second World War in 1945, stressing cultural rather than militaristic values, an impetus to international appreciation and, indeed, appropriation of Shakespeare came from a sense that enjoyment and discussion of his works formed a meeting ground which transcended national boundaries. Shakespeare was considered in some quarters to be above politics and therefore as a potent healing force in the international arena. A seminal event was the organizing in 1947 of a small international conference on Shakespeare in Stratford-upon-Avon by the British Council, whose function was, in part, to serve as a force for the propagation of British culture. This led to the founding there in 1951 of the Shakespeare Institute as a centre for postgraduate study of Shakespeare and his contemporaries, and of a biennial international conference.

Internationalism was a keynote too of the celebrations in 1964 of the four-hundredth anniversary of Shakespeare's birth, but naturally they centred on Stratford where they bore a strong resemblance to the Garrick Jubilee – again there were a ball, a banquet, a firework display, a race meeting, a special church service, and an impressive musical programme including specially commissioned compositions. And this time many of Shakespeare's words were heard – supplemented, admittedly, by pastiche from John Barton in the three-play sequence of history plays, *The Wars of the Roses*, along with the plays of the second tetralogy, which he adapted and directed with Peter Hall.[1] Though not pure Shakespeare this was epic political theatre performed by the Royal Shakespeare Company at the height of its powers. A large pavilion on the south bank of the Avon housed a splendid, imaginative, and extravagant exhibition of Shakespeare's life and times. Enlivened with music and scents, it included sculptures, models, and tableaux commissioned from distinguished artists, a long gallery full of original portraits, early printed books and jewellery, and a reduced model of the Globe with a *son et lumière* display. Revived in the following year, it nevertheless lost a lot of money for its sponsors. A commemorative set of postage stamps featured for the first time a head – Shakespeare's, of course – beside that of the sovereign (Plate 26).

As part of London's contribution, Olivier gave his historic Othello at the National Theatre and Frederick Ashton choreographed *The Dream* for the

Royal Ballet, with music predictably by Mendelssohn; on television, the Beatles performed a skit based on *Pyramus and Thisbe* from *A Midsummer Night's Dream*. Further afield, a group of Stratford actors gave a reading in the Vatican before the Pope and had to correct his misapprehension that the Theatre's prized copy of the First Folio taken for him to inspect was a gift. Celebrations in Turkey included six productions in Istanbul and two in Ankara; an audience of 15,000, mainly peasants and local inhabitants, saw the State Theatre's performance of *Julius Caesar* in a Roman amphitheatre. The University of Munich founded the Shakespeare Bibliothek, a research centre funded initially by the Volkswagen Foundation and headed by the doyen of German Shakespeare scholars, Wolfgang Clemen, who, although he opposed the Nazis, had been conscripted into the German army. This re-affirmation of Germany's commitment to Shakespeare was significant in the European process of reunification.

The post-war period saw major developments in the theatrical presentation of Shakespeare both at home and overseas. In London the Old Vic, damaged in the war, reopened in 1950; in 1953, under Michael Benthall, it embarked on a plan to present all the plays of the First Folio in five years. This culminated in 1953 – Coronation year – in a *Henry VIII* which brought back two of the theatre's greatest pre-war luminaries, John Gielgud and Edith Evans, as Cardinal Wolsey and Queen Katherine. In Canada 1953 saw the first productions of the Stratford, Ontario Shakespeare Festival with plays directed by Tyrone Guthrie on an open stage incorporating Elizabethan features and designed by Tanya Moiseiwitsch which has influenced the design of many later theatres (see overleaf). It was originally covered by a tent; the permanent building opened in 1957 and has seen successful Shakespeare productions starring both Canadian and British actors. In 1954 Joseph Papp founded the New York Shakespeare in the Park company giving free performances of Shakespeare plays in Central Park. Stratford-upon-Avon celebrated its one-hundredth season (the calculation was a bit dodgy) in 1959 with an all-star programme including Olivier and Edith Evans, magnificent respectively as Coriolanus and Volumnia, Charles Laughton as Bottom and Lear, Paul Robeson as Othello, and Evans as a wonderfully poetic and tender Countess in Guthrie's scintillating production of *All's Well That Ends Well*, which he had already directed in Ontario. With actors like that the end-of-term party was a remarkable affair:

135. The Ontario Festival Stage, designed by Tyrone Guthrie and Tanya Moiseiwitsch; the theatre holds 1820 people, but no seat is more than 65 feet from the stage.

Olivier performed sketches from Osborne's *The Entertainer*, Edith Evans sang Ben Jonson's 'Drink to me only' as a duet with the young Albert Finney, and Robeson contributed spirituals as only he could. The climax came with a brief, virtually wordless sketch in which the young actors responsible for holding Olivier by the ankles as he dangled in his death leap as Coriolanus gazed empty-handed into the void beneath them exclaiming 'Sir? SIR!'

The director of *Coriolanus* was Peter Hall, who became overall director of the theatre the following year, inaugurating many important changes including the founding of a London base which turned the company from a local to a national and, eventually, international organization. He engaged as co-director John Barton, with a special brief for developing the company's verse-speaking. Exceptionally in their time, both were university trained and had as their guru the Cambridge don George Rylands (p. 357) whose theory and practice of verse-speaking influenced generations of actors. A new intellectualism was in the air, expressing itself in radical approaches and attracting many fine actors of a similar background. With their colleagues, Hall and Barton were to direct many great productions, not least the *Troilus and Cressida* of 1960, set simply but boldly against a bloodshot backcloth with the action taking place in an octagonal pit of white sand ('Ban the horse!' the actors scrawled in it at the height of the anti-nuclear campaign). Fine individual performances justified Hall's company ethos, but the production's greatest triumph lay in its realization of the play's deepest poetic structures. Moments such as Cressida's sifting of sand through her fingers, the black-clad Myrmidons' brutal slaughter of the half-naked Hector, and the final appearance of a decrepit Pandarus shattering the boundary between players and audience with a frightening immediacy all acquired symbolic resonance; 'director's theatre' was triumphantly justified.

136. Dorothy Tutin as Cressida in the sandpit of the Peter Hall / John Barton Royal Shakespeare Company production of *Troilus and Cressida*, 1960.

137. 'Come, wait upon him, lead him to my bower' (3.1.189): the triumphant conclusion to the first part of Peter Brook's production of *A Midsummer Night's Dream*, the Royal Shakespeare Theatre, 1970; Sara Kestelman as Titania, David Waller as Bottom.

Among the company's many later triumphs was Peter Brook's *A Midsummer Night's Dream* of 1970, as revolutionary in its way as Granville-Barker's; the play was set (as Granville-Barker had said it should be) in a white box; costumes were timeless – loose satin garments in bright colours. The production was self-consciously iconoclastic: Oberon and Theseus, like Titania and Hippolyta, were played by the same actor, setting a trend that has often been followed. Adult males played the fairies. Oberon and Puck swung on trapezes, and Titania descended sitting on a great scarlet feather; there was

138. Hugh Quarshie and Gerard Murphy in *The Two Noble Kinsmen*, directed by Barry Kyle in Japanese style; the opening production at the Swan Theatre, Stratford-upon-Avon, 1986.

rampant sexuality in her encounter with Bottom who processed to the union between Beauty and the Beast mounted on the shoulders of another actor whose forearm protruded phallically between his legs. Confetti showered down, actors skimmed paper plates, a snatch of Mendelssohn's 'Wedding March' played, and the house lights rose for the interval in a glow of euphoria. Though it seemed so fresh and original, the text was played complete and was given with rapid clarity. The production did little to realize the grace, charm and humour of Shakespeare's play, but its self-confident assertion of its own values made it a great happening in its own right. It toured the world and has become a legend.

Gradually the Royal Shakespeare Company's work expanded, in 1974 with the conversion of a rehearsal shed into a small studio theatre, the Other Place, in 1982 with the acquisition of a new London base in the Barbican, and in 1986 with the rebuilding of the shell of the 1876 theatre as an open-stage, medium-sized auditorium, The Swan, which opened with the first professional Stratford performance of *The Two Noble Kinsmen*.[2] Immensely increasing its number of productions of classic and modern plays as well as Shakespeare and his contemporaries, the company has come to be recognized as perhaps the finest in the world. Not least among its strengths is its openness to a wide range of production styles, from the relatively conservative to the out-and-out experimental. It has fostered the careers of too many eminent directors and actors even to list here, but Judi Dench must be mentioned as the natural successor to her fellow Dames Ellen Terry, Edith Evans, and Peggy Ashcroft in a wonderfully versatile series of performances including Isabella, Viola, Beatrice, Lady Macbeth and later, for the National Theatre, a passionately volatile Cleopatra.

139. 'She never told her love, / But let concealment, like a worm i'th'bud, / Feed on her damask cheek' (2.4.110–12): Judi Dench as Viola/Cesario and Charles Thomas as Orsino, in John Barton's Royal Shakespeare Company production of *Twelfth Night*, Stratford-upon-Avon, 1969.

140. This photograph of Trevor Nunn's Royal Shakespeare Company production of *Macbeth* at The Other Place, 1976, shows members of the audience encircling the witches' circle of the stage. The white-clad and prostrate Duncan (Griffith Jones) is attended by Macbeth (Ian McKellen). The witches huddle together at the left, and other members of the cast sit on crates watching the action.

The establishment after many years of frustration of a National Theatre company in 1963, with its own buildings from 1976, was a landmark in the history of the British theatre; understandably Shakespeare has figured less prominently in its repertoire than in that of the Royal Shakespeare Company, but some of its productions, such as the opening *Othello* with Olivier, Hall's 1984 *Coriolanus* with Ian McKellen, Richard Eyre's 1997 *King Lear* with Ian Holm, and Trevor Nunn's *Troilus and Cressida* and *The Merchant of Venice* (1999) have passed into theatrical legend. Though the National successfully ventured an all-male *As You Like It* as early as 1967, and a *Richard II* with Fiona Shaw as Richard in 1995, the most consistently experimental productions have come from touring companies such as the English Shakespeare Company,[3] especially successful in their modern-dress sequence of history

141. 'You have simply misused our sex in your love prate' (*As You Like It*, 4.1.191–2):
Celia (Simon Coates) berates Rosalind (Adrian Lester) in Declan Donellan's
Cheek by Jowl production, 1995.

plays, *The Wars of the Roses* (1986, filmed 1989), and Cheek by Jowl,[4] which offered a no-less successful all-male *As You Like It* (1991, 1994); strikingly, so far from being homoerotic in effect, this struck me as emphasizing the elements of play, of the action as a game in which the audience were required to use their imaginations so that all was indeed as they liked it.

Overseas, innovation has been even more prominent. In Germany in 1975 Peter Zadek directed an iconoclastic and brutal *King Lear* set in a circus tent in which Lear sexually assaulted Cordelia during the reunion scene and carried her on stage stark naked in death. The Japanese Yukio Ninagawa mingled Japanese with Western theatrical techniques both in native-based productions and, bravely but less successfully, in his English-language *King Lear* for the Royal Shakespeare Company, with Nigel Hawthorne as the King and the Japanese Hiroyuki Sanada as the Fool. Ariane Mnouchkine has employed the techniques of Far Eastern theatre in her French-language Shakespeare productions. In the Italian Giorgio Strehler's long-running *Tempest* (1978 onwards) inspired by Jan Kott (see pp. 381–2), Prospero's magic was equated with the magic of theatre; it became one of the most highly praised productions of its time.

142. 'Approach, my Ariel, come!' (1.2.189): Giorgio Strehler's production of *The Tempest*, first given at the Piccolo Theatre, Milan in 1978.

One manifestation of the conscious internationality which distinguished post-war Shakespearian activities has been the establishment of new Shakespeare periodicals and associations in many different countries. In 1979 India became the first country to establish a journal, the twice-yearly *Hamlet Studies*, devoted to a single play, and in 1997 Pakistan celebrated the fiftieth anniversary of its independence with the inaugural conference of its Shakespeare Association on the theme 'Shakespeare around the Globe'.

Partly for reasons of funding, America tended to take the lead in Shakespearian scholarship and criticism, though the products often appeared from British university presses. The immense resources of the Folger Shakespeare Library made possible Charlton Hinman's monumental study of the First Folio, for which, using a collating machine of his own devising, he made a minute comparison of the typography of some thirty of the library's eighty or so copies, subsequently publishing an authoritative study, *The Printing and Proof-Reading of the First Folio of Shakespeare*,[5] along with what is now the standard facsimile, *The Norton Facsimile: The First Folio of Shakespeare*,[6] an 'ideal copy' made up of the clearest and best pages from thirty different specimens of the original.

In biographical studies the British historian A. L. Rowse was ambitious of discovery. He wrote in a lively, idiosyncratic, opinionated fashion of Shakespeare's life and times, and with vitriol in his pen about literary scholars, 'third-raters' to a man; but his much trumpeted claim that he had identified the 'dark lady' of the Sonnets (p. 85–9) was undermined when I pointed out to him during a radio broadcast that he had misread Simon Forman's statement that his candidate, Emilia Lanier, was 'brave' – that is, showy or flamboyant – 'in youth' as 'brown in youth', his only evidence that she was dark. Much more substantial biographical work was done by S. – Sam – Schoenbaum, who was fond of telling how his first date with his future wife, Marilyn, was to see Robeson as Othello in the 1943 New York production.

Rather as, earlier in the century, E. K. Chambers had found it necessary to write a two-volume study of the medieval stage, followed by a four-volume one of the Elizabethan stage, before progressing to the two volumes of his *William Shakespeare: A Study of Facts and Problems*, so Sam, intending to write a biography of Shakespeare, started by clearing the ground with his monumental, and continuously entertaining, study of others' efforts to do so in his

Shakespeare's Lives (1970, revised 1991). In the Preface he relates that the book had been conceived during the 1964 international conference:

> I wandered down to the Avon, speckled white with swans, and entered (for the first time) the splendid Collegiate Church of the Holy Trinity. It was late afternoon; the tourists had departed. Although outside the late summer sun still shone brilliantly, I could barely make out the monument and bust in the shadows of the north chancel.

Thinking of 'the pilgrims, many thousand strong, who had looked up as I now did and pondered the inconceivable mystery of creation', it occurred to him 'that some interest might attach to a little book narrating the quest for knowledge of Shakespeare the man'. In the event the 'little book' was well over 800 pages long, and established its author as one of the heroes of Shakespeare scholarship. He followed it with his no less authoritative *William Shakespeare: A Documentary Life* (1975), a magisterial photographic reprint of all the central documents accompanied by a learned and sprightly narrative which, in its revised, compact form of 1985, shorn of most of the facsimiles, has come to be regarded as the standard life. This in itself was followed by a supplementary study, *William Shakespeare: Records and Images* (1981), aiming to reproduce and comment on many other relevant facsimiles. Sadly, Sam never wrote the planned biography in which he would have contextualized the information in the *Documentary Life*. Maybe he had been unwise to tell so much of the story in that book. Anyhow in his late years he was plagued by serious illness which would have made yet another major work beyond even his capacities. He died in 1996. One morning during the following Shakespeare conference his widow, like Sam before her, made her way down to the Avon where she scattered his ashes into the river that flows past Holy Trinity church.

Radical attitudes towards Shakespeare's text in the theatre, and also in scholarship, have been accompanied by a revolution in criticism. The Polish writer and man of the theatre Jan Kott reached a wide public with his politically inspired *Shakespeare Our Contemporary*, published in English in 1964, the year of the quatercentenary celebrations. Painting with a broad brush to

143. 'Hark in thine ear' (4.6.148): Paul Scofield as Lear and Alan Webb as Gloucester in Peter Brook's 1962 Royal Shakespeare Company production of *King Lear*.

expressionistic effect, often flying high above the text – notoriously his chapter '*King Lear* and *Endgame*', drawing parallels with the work of Samuel Beckett, makes no mention of Cordelia – creating fantasies around plays rather than exploring their intricacies as in his essay on *A Midsummer Night's Dream*, 'the most erotic of Shakespeare's plays', Kott nevertheless provided a stimulating challenge to received opinion. His book anticipated and influenced revolutionary productions by, especially, Peter Brook, whose bleak but powerful 1962 *King Lear* (filmed in 1970) for the Royal Shakespeare Company, with Paul Scofield as an authoritatively authoritarian king, found sympathy for Goneril in the riotous behaviour of Lear's knights and, like Kott, echoed Beckett especially in the desolation of the Dover Cliff encounter between blind Gloucester (played by Alan Webb) and mad Lear. In Brechtian style, this disturbing production provoked thought rather than emotional identification, but was no less moving for that. No one present on the first night is likely to forget the slow, stumbling exit of the newly blinded Gloucester as the house lights went slowly up for the interval.

During the later part of the century, in criticism as in theatre, an alternative, iconoclastic, subversive Shakespeare has emerged, much abetted by an explosion in academic activity and by the development of a variety of theoretical approaches, each with its own terminology which too often has seemed more concerned to obscure than to convey meaning, or at least to communicate only with a select band of like-minded devotees. But fresh thought has succeeded in cracking some of the intellectual encrustation that had been stifling the potential underlying Shakespeare's texts; those who see him as a supporter of feminism, of political dissension, of anti-racism and sexual liberation, an opponent of the royalist regime of his own time who can also be harnessed in support of radicalism today, have freshened and extended the range of meaning that can be extrapolated from the plays – or, to apply an aphorism of Terence Hawkes, have increased the ways in which we can mean by Shakespeare.[7]

The massive increase at all levels in academic activity on Shakespeare resulted in a proliferation of editions of many different kinds. The American tradition in both multi-volume editions, such as the paperback Signet and Pelican (later gathered together in collected form) and in complete ones such as the Bevington and the ambitious Riverside favours presentation of the plays with relatively light annotation as works to be studied in the classroom. In Britain editions of the complete works still come as books for reading, presented with little editorial matter, though multi-volume editions are, in the tradition established in the late nineteenth century by the Arden series, more likely to assume readers avid for assistance with the complexities of the text. In planning the New Penguin edition during the early 1960s a group of scholars (myself among them) spent hours discussing whether to place notes at the foot of the page – as tends to be favoured by students – or at the back of the book, in line with Dr Johnson's view that, while 'Notes are often necessary . . . they are necessary evils', and that 'The mind is refrigerated by interruption'.[8] The Johnsonian view, which is in accord with the Penguin philosophy of catering for 'the common reader' (in Johnson's phrase), prevailed. This enabled the edition to provide clean-page texts that are actor-friendly along with annotation which, because it does not have to be crammed on to the foot of the page, can be discursive in style. We avoided notes such as (to quote one from a rival edition) '*the Pleiades*. Cf. 1H4, 1. ii. 16.

See Amos, v. 8 and Job, xxxviii. 31, marginal note in A.V. to Pleiades: "Cimah or the seven stars". Cf. note to III. iv. 152.' (That is a quotation from – well, let's say another edition.)

We abandoned the practice of abbreviating speech headings, which produces barbarities such as (in *Othello*) 'Rod.' (for Roderigo), 'Cas.' (for Cassio), 'Bra.' (for Brabanzio), 'Des.' (for Desdemona), and '1 Off.' (for First Officer). And, acknowledging that act and scene references have little to do with theatrical practices in Shakespeare's time, we made them far less prominent than in many previous editions.

The Oxford edition of *The Complete Works*, published in 1986, has been described by John Carey in the *Sunday Times* as 'the most interesting since the First Folio'. It is also controversial. My involvement with it is so close that it would be artificial not to write about it from a personal point of view. It was in the late 1970s that I was invited to assume the general editorship of a new edition for Oxford University Press. Their edition then in print dated from 1891, well before the discoveries of major bibliographical scholars of the early twentieth century such as R. B. McKerrow, who had in fact been commissioned to prepare a new Oxford edition in old spelling. A number of plays edited by him advanced as far as the proof stage but were not published when he died in 1940. His assistant, Alice Walker, was appointed in his place but oddly succeeded only in editing two plays for the New (Cambridge) Shakespeare, apparently because she had lost faith in old spelling. Realizing that it was unrealistic to expect scholars to produce a major new edition while holding full-time university posts, the Press took the bold step of establishing a Shakespeare department, with me at its head, charged with the responsibility of preparing an entirely new edition of the complete works. The plan as it evolved went through various changes. At first it was simply to prepare a new plain-text edition in spelling modernized according to freshly considered principles. After consultation with American colleagues we decided to print explanatory notes on the page. The Arden series was in the doldrums, so it seemed viable also to commission from scholars outside the Press a parallel multi-volume series to rival that. Cambridge University Press latched on to the same idea, appointing Philip Brockbank as general editor of a new series for them; at one point he even telephoned me to propose that we might join forces on an intervarsity edition. And before long, stimulated no doubt by the competition, the Arden editors pulled up their socks, almost completing what is now known as Arden2 before embarking on Arden3 in 1995. As time passed I was joined by Gary Taylor, first as my assistant – I wanted, I told him, someone to disagree with – eventually as joint general editor, along with other scholars drafted in to help to complete a task which grew increasingly demanding and complex as we decided to add a complete text printed in the spelling of Shakespeare's time along with a volume explaining our textual thinking. The full story is too long to be told here. Suffice it to say that after many vicissitudes plain-text editions of *The Complete Works* in both modern and original spelling appeared in 1986, to be followed a year later by the substantial *Textual Companion*, for which much of the work was undertaken by Gary Taylor.

Before the edition appeared, information that I was working on it was apt to be received in Oxford with a curl of the upper lip and a rising of the left eyebrow along with the words, 'Will it be any different from all the others?' Condescension turned in some quarters to consternation when it turned out to be very different indeed. I felt strongly that there was no point in a timid conservatism that shied away from the application of hypotheses which, though they might be ultimately unprovable, had the weight of rational thought behind them. And, knowing that the almost invariable practice in previous editions (Capell's – p. 230 – was an honourable exception) had been to mark up an earlier version, leaving many of the conventions of presentation including spelling, punctuation, and even stage directions to stand, I was determined that we would work from the original printings to produce a text genuinely designed for the modern reader, rethinking conventions from the ground upwards, and that we would act on the best recent thinking about textual issues even if it challenged orthodoxy. In the Oxford Shakespeare Iago is Ensign not Ancient Iago, the Forest of Arden is the Forest of Ardenne (a favourite of mine which persuades scarcely anyone), *Macbeth* and *Timon of Athens* are ascribed to Shakespeare and Middleton, the play previously known as *Henry VIII* is *All is True*, and, horror of horrors, Falstaff in *Henry IV, Part One* is Oldcastle. Well, if we hadn't done it there would still be no possibility of reading the play as it was first acted. This is a destabilizing edition which emphasizes the plurality of Shakespeare's texts, the fact that there is nothing definitive about works written for the practical theatre. Most radically, we adopt the hypothesis, mooted by a few earlier scholars but never consistently acted upon, that some of Shakespeare's plays survive in both revised and unrevised forms, that the traditional conflated texts represent neither one thing nor another, and that the only proper procedure is to edit each version in its own right. In this policy we were putting into practice ideas that were still being thrashed out at the time we were working, and to which indeed we ourselves – especially Gary Taylor – contributed. Also, since Shakespeare was so much a man of the practical theatre, it seemed proper to give priority to the revised versions representing the plays as acted, rather than before they were put into performance: in practice, this usually means preferring Folio to quarto alternatives. The result is an edition in which, conspicuously, there are two separate texts of *King Lear*, one edited from the 1608 quarto, the other from the 1623 Folio, and in which *Hamlet* is printed without passages (including the final soliloquy, 'How all occasions do inform against me') found only in the quarto – though the omitted lines are given as 'Additional Passages'.[9] The publishers were brave in supporting us in our radicalism, and we ourselves were conscious of working during a period in which the ideas that we adopted were still being thrashed out.

One of the problems of planning a complete edition is what to include. It was only just becoming customary to regard the collaborative *The Two Noble Kinsmen* as part of the canon. While we were working Eric Sams revived claims which we, along with most other scholars, did not accept, for an anonymous manuscript play, *Edmund Ironside*. Support grew for Shakespeare's authorship of parts, at least, of the anonymously published *Edward III* (1596); although I doubt Shakespeare's sole authorship, we should probably have included it if we had been working a few years later. We rethought the minor poems, rejecting parts of *The Passionate Pilgrim* traditionally included even though they are definitely not by Shakespeare, and adding a few short items which could be. We got into terrible trouble over an ingeniously rhyming lyric, 'Shall I die?', which Gary Taylor re-discovered – it had never really been lost – in the Bodleian Library in a seventeenth-century manuscript where it is firmly ascribed to William Shakespeare. (It is not true, as is often stated, that Taylor himself made the ascription, though he did defend it.) This became an international media event of astonishing proportions and a number of scholars applied themselves with great assiduity to the task of disembarrassing Shakespeare of responsibility for the poem. I still think he may have written it.

Also during this period the possibility was mooted that Shakespeare wrote the 578-line poem 'A Funeral Elegy: in memory of the late virtuous Master William Peter of Whipton near Exeter', published in 1612 as 'By W. S.'. Peter had been stabbed to death near Exeter in a dispute over a horse after a hard day's drinking. The case was put more positively in 1996 and three American editors hastened to add the poem (generally admitted to be dead boring whoever wrote it) to their complete editions. I was among the British scholars who were more sceptical, and support is now growing for the idea that the author was Shakespeare's late contemporary John Ford (even though he has the wrong initials).[10] Development of computer-assisted authorship studies has raised false hopes. Computers can help in the analysis of authorial tics such as the use of abbreviations and colloquial forms (''em' for 'them', for instance), characteristic oaths (''Slid'), asseverations ('Pish' and 'Tush'), and function words such as 'but', 'by', and 'for'; they can count more quickly than human beings and can synthesize information in a variety of ways, but they are no more intelligent or learned than the minds that control them. In order to demonstrate that a particular author wrote something it would ideally be necessary to eliminate every other author of the period, as well as all the writings that are lost.

Disputes about who wrote separate items pale in ferocity beside questions about whether William Shakespeare wrote anything at all. In *Shakespeare's Lives* Schoenbaum devoted one hundred ironical pages, headed 'Deviations', to attempts to prove that the works were written by over fifty candidates ranging from Francis Bacon through Queen Elizabeth I to Daniel Defoe. In recent years the most vociferous and long-winded claims have been made on behalf of Christopher Marlowe and Edward de Vere, seventeenth Earl of Oxford. Marlowe is particularly implausible. His death in 1593 is one of the best-documented events of English literary history. The suggestion that this flamboyant character could have lived on for some twenty-five years not only concealing his own authorship from everyone in the busy world of the theatre but also leaving no traces of his continued existence while obligingly allowing an actor called William Shakespeare to take credit for an unexampled string of masterpieces is patently ludicrous. The Earl of Oxford died in 1604, which requires him to have left around a dozen plays ready to be filtered through to the King's Men as opportunity arose. He too was modest enough to allow the man from Stratford the credit for his entire body of work for the public theatre, as well as his poems, while also concealing his authorship from all his contemporaries.

These and similar theories are heavily publicized. Over the past fifteen years or so I have frequently been called upon in public debating places ranging from a day-long mock-trial in the Middle Temple, where I was cross-examined by an eminent QC (Shakespeare won the day), to a debate in the Theatre Royal, Bath where the respective claims of Bacon, Marlowe, and Oxford were aired – one began to get the feeling that it didn't really matter who wrote the works so long as it wasn't Shakespeare. Fanaticism prevails. The anti-Stratfordians are impervious to reason. All their cases rely upon conspiracy theory – the belief that all those who knew the truth conspired together to conceal it from their contemporaries while obligingly leaving tiny, cryptic clues to be discovered hundreds of years later – which means that by their very nature they can neither be proved nor disproved.

Who knows what motivates the theorists? Is it snobbery, a belief that a man of relatively humble origin is less likely to have written the plays than an aristocrat? Those who take this line tend to understate the value of a Stratford education, and to overvalue the talents of the aristocracy. Is it the desire for ten minutes of fame? – the media readily latch on to supposed news about Shakespeare, especially when real news is in short supply. Or is it mere eccentricity, bordering even on mental instability of the kind that impelled poor Delia Bacon to spend her fearful night in Holy Trinity Church (pp. 314–16), a perverse desire to challenge orthodoxy in the face of reason?

This is all theory. More exciting for anyone interested in Shakespeare the dramatist was the material discovery in 1989 of remains of the Elizabethan Rose Theatre, where we know *Titus Andronicus* and at least one part of *Henry VI* were acted (p. 52). This was soon followed by identification of the site, and of a small part of the remains, of the Globe. The circumstances were dramatic: discovery of the Rose occurred unexpectedly as the result of building development; there was a danger that the remains would be reburied, even bulldozed into oblivion, within days of their being found. Scholars and actors flocked to the site, joining the archaeologists in protest; a stay of execution was granted. To look down on the newly revealed space where Shakespeare had done much of his early theatre-going held the same kind of excitement

– sentimental, perhaps, but real for all that – as seeing the amphitheatres of Ancient Greece, or hearing Mozart played on his own piano. Another bridge had been made with the past. And information newly gleaned was invaluable for scholars. But investigation of the Globe site has been hampered by bureaucracy, and the remains of the Rose, now in the basement of a huge office block, are covered by a protective shell while attempts are made to find funding for their full display. Work continues, and visitors to the site can watch an informative video as they meditate on what lies below.

New knowledge of the Globe would have been particularly welcome at a time when the building of a reconstruction of the theatre close to its original site was entering its final stages. Sam Wanamaker's project, financed by dona-tions from all over the world, mostly from enthusiasts who hoped to be able to see productions of the plays as they had first been given, had been long in the making; Wanamaker did not live to see its fulfilment. Though not exactly the great Globe itself – some compromises and best guesses had to be made – it comes as close to the original as the efforts of scholars could achieve, and is a splendid piece of craftsmanship. Since its inception the artistic director has been the actor Mark Rylance; a few productions have laid claims to authen-ticity of presentation, and some, such as the *Antony and Cleopatra* (1999) in which Rylance himself played Cleopatra, or the *Cymbeline* performed by six actors in 2001, have been overtly experimental. The approach has been on a largely populist level, but a few productions, such as the *King Lear* of 2001 with Julian Glover as an authoritative king, have come some way towards showing us how plays might have worked in a similar space in Shakespeare's time.

Intellectual approaches to Shakespeare may make little direct impact on the majority of those who enjoy his plays in the theatre or on film, but may nevertheless filter through into the more popular media without those who enjoy them being aware of it. As we have seen, Freudian ideas affected main-stream interpretations of plays including *Hamlet* and *Othello* during the earlier part of the century. In the cinema, more avant-garde approaches tend to be associated with low-budget films which do not reach the large audiences of the commercial public circuits. *The Tempest* is the starting point for films by both Derek Jarman (1980) and Peter Greenaway (1991) that have made their mark while appealing primarily to minority audiences, Jarman's by virtue of its deployment of a gay sensibility. Its high point comes with an overtly camp

144. 'Stormy weather', Elisabeth Welch in Derek Jarman's film of *The Tempest*.

rendering of the song 'Stormy Weather' sung by the blues singer Elisabeth Welch, while a bunch of sailor boys dance. Greenaway's *Prospero's Books*, though packed with nudity and visually stunning, is a far more cerebral affair; full of esoteric literary, artistic, scientific, architectural and mythological significances, it has been described as 'a *Finnegans Wake* of visual art'.[11] The greatest of stage Prosperos, John Gielgud, by now well into his eighties, gamely appears naked in the opening sequence while also speaking not just Prospero's lines but most of the rest of the text. The experimentalism of films such as these pales beside Jean-Luc Godard's post-modern *King Lear* (1987) in which an editor, William Shakespeare, Jr, the Fifth, played by Peter Sellars, seeks for the lost text of his ancestor and Godard, as Professor Pluggy, Lear's Fool, speaks out of the corner of his mouth as a way of suggesting the limitations of language as a medium for conveying ideas.[12]

If avant-garde films reach only small audiences – and may be understood by only a small proportion of them – more mainstream films have come to assume enormous importance in spreading interest in, and enjoyment of, Shakespeare to the general public both in English-speaking countries and in the rest of the world. The long-popular *Shakespeare Wallah* (1965), which adapts the actor Geoffrey Kendal's diary of his travels in India as a Shakespeare actor in 1947, includes well-performed scenes from a number of plays; the film as a whole finds in the slow demise of the travelling company an elegiac metaphor for the end of the British Raj.[13] Even relatively highbrow films, such as Orson Welles's *Macbeth* (1949), *Othello* (1951), and *Chimes at Midnight* (1966; another celebration of Falstaff) reach far larger audiences than most stage productions, and foreign translations and adaptations have done much to increase Shakespeare's internationalism. It is a curious experience to listen to the Russian soundtracks of Grigori Kozintsev's fine *King Lear* and *Hamlet* while reading selections from the original text projected as subtitles. Akiro Kurosawa's films based on *Macbeth*, as *Throne of Blood* (1957) and *King Lear*, as *Ran* ('Chaos', 1985) are brilliantly creative adaptations rather than translations into another medium.

Far more popular in appeal have been the Shakespeare films of Franco Zeffirelli, whose *Romeo and Juliet* (1968) – like many Victorian theatre productions – is ravishingly beautiful to look at though less successful as a realization of the text. Hollywood films require a high level of funding, and have been known to pander to the popular market. Zeffirelli's *The Taming of the Shrew* (1966), exploiting the popular appeal of Elizabeth Taylor and Richard Burton, shamelessly takes the play back via its Fairbanks/Pickford predecessor to the farcical traditions of Garrick's adaptation. Other films, such as Joseph Mankiewicz's *Julius Caesar*, with James Mason, Marlon Brando, and John Gielgud, have been more successful in maintaining artistic integrity while deploying famous stars. In *Antony and Cleopatra* (1972), Charlton Heston was reduced to recycling episodes from *Ben Hur* in the battle scenes,[14] and Olivier failed in his efforts to persuade the studios that his *Macbeth* would be commercially viable; the same is true – so far – of Kenneth Branagh.

During most of the 1970s and 1980s no major feature film of Shakespeare appeared. The period between 1978 and 1985, however, saw the filming by the BBC of the entire canon for television. Some of the products of this bold enterprise were over-conventional, with mainly representational settings and traditional costumes, but many distinguished actors took part, and some of the lesser-known plays, such as *All's Well That Ends Well*, directed by Jonathan Miller with settings reminiscent of Vermeer, *Henry VIII*, filmed at the historic Leeds Castle, and Jane Howell's brilliant production of the early histories performed as a consecutive series on an adventure playground, succeeded best. The continued availability of the series on video has been of great educational value.

An interesting attempt to extend the lower age-range of audiences for Shakespeare is the Animated Tales, a series of half-hour reductions of twelve Shakespeare plays shown on television in over fifty countries from 1992. This international undertaking was organized from Wales with funding from Japan and America. The children's writer Leon Garfield skilfully filleted the texts making only minimal changes for the sake of narrative continuity. For anyone who knows the texts it is of course frustrating to hear a fine actor such as Brian Cox speaking only a line or two of Macbeth's soliloquies, but the films' purpose is introductory. Russian artists working in Moscow created the animation using three different techniques. Some of the films, such as the brilliantly imaginative *A Midsummer Night's Dream*, employ the traditional 'cel', i.e. celluloid, method, which requires around 30,000 individual paintings, all minutely different from the others, for each half-hour film (Plate 28). Others use flexible puppets some ten inches high, sometimes with more than one for the more important characters – and even two subtly different ones for the twins in *Twelfth Night* – to enable a variety of expressions. They are moulded by degrees and repeatedly photographed to give the illusion of movement. It is a laborious technique, permitting the filming of only about nine seconds' worth of action within a whole day, but produces excellent results, funny in *Twelfth Night*, where the puppet plays Malvolio with timing that a professional actor might well envy, mysteriously beautiful in *The Tempest*. Rarest of the techniques, and one that produces exquisite effects, is that in which images painted in oil on glass are slowly altered, detail by detail, until they exist no more; this makes for a hauntingly supernatural *Hamlet*. The best of these films are, like all good adaptations, independent works of art, transmuting their raw material into something rich and strange in its own right.

The drought of feature films was broken in 1989 when Branagh, young, handsome, immensely talented, often referred to as the new Olivier (though his distinctive qualities as an actor are very different), followed his great success as Henry V on stage at Stratford with a film version directed by himself.

145. *Opposite.* Kenneth Branagh with the bodies of the slaughtered boys
in his film of *Henry V*, 1989.

Eschewing the jingoism of Olivier's film, he emphasized the suffering of war, most memorably in the long tracking shot in which a devastated Henry carries the body of the boy killed by the French through the carnage of the muddy battlefield. Branagh followed up the success of this film with a cheerful and pretty *Much Ado About Nothing* (1993), by playing Iago in Oliver Parker's film of *Othello* (1995), and most remarkably by his own, full-text *Hamlet* (1996). Almost all Shakespeare films before this had been even more drastic in their shortening of texts than the standard Victorian theatre versions; indeed, it had become axiomatic that abbreviation was a necessary part of the transition from a primarily verbal to a pictorial medium. Branagh disproved this in his four-hour *Hamlet*, which, though lacking nothing in visual excitement, offered a complete text of this longest of plays. Shakespeare's ultimate moment of glory came when his script was nominated for an Academy Award.[15] The film has outstanding performances from a mixture of Hollywood 'names' along with seasoned British Shakespeare actors, many of whom had already worked with Branagh. Derek Jacobi as Claudius and Julie Christie as Gertrude are outstanding, and performers of cameo roles include Charlton Heston, Jack Lemmon, Gérard Depardieu, and Richard Attenborough. Wordless interpolated episodes feature John Gielgud as Priam and Judi Dench as Hecuba, the comedian Ken Dodd as Yorick, and a nude sex scene between Hamlet and Ophelia, played by Kate Winslet, who is harrowing in madness. There is an abbreviated version, but most cinemagoers seem to prefer the full one; I very much welcomed the opportunity to see and hear the play complete.

One reason for the proliferation of Shakespeare films – and one that has affected their techniques – has been the growth of a profitable market for video versions. It has helped to extend the range of plays filmed and to encourage adventurous treatments. Richard Eyre's and Richard Loncraine's *Richard III*, adapted from Eyre's National Theatre production, offered a version thrillingly updated into the 1930s with Ian McKellen as a rivetingly Hitlerish Richard. Baz Luhrmann's *William Shakespeare's Romeo + Juliet*, which had the commercial advantage of casting the teenage heart-throb Leonardo DiCaprio as Romeo, brilliantly juxtaposed Shakespeare's text against a modern American setting to wittily imaginative effect (Plate 29). It was instructive to compare this with Michael Almereyda's *Hamlet*, starring Ethan

Hawke, which fails to do more than superimpose the text on a New York setting, making no creative use of the conjunction.

A Midsummer Night's Dream continued to assert its popularity in versions directed by Adrian Noble (1996) and Michael Hoffman (1999) and even in one performed entirely by children,[16] and the repertoire of Shakespeare on film was surprisingly and pleasingly extended by Julie Taymor's exciting and visually imaginative *Titus Andronicus* and Branagh's *Love's Labour's Lost* (much cut and enjoyable mostly for its 1930s song and dance episodes), the first feature films to be made of both plays. The most commercially successful of all Shakespeare-related films of the 1990s was *Shakespeare in Love*, nominated for thirteen Academy Awards and winner of seven, with a script written by Tom Stoppard and Marc Norman that owes something to the comic novel *No Bed for Bacon* (1941) by Caryl Brahms and S. J. Simon. This is even sometimes spoken of as a Shakespeare film, whereas in fact of course it is a witty and sexy romantic comedy which makes extensive use of passages from Shakespeare plays, especially *Romeo and Juliet*. For all its convincing reconstruction of the Rose Theatre and the picturesqueness of its presentation of the Elizabethan court and theatre, viewers looking for documentary realism would receive as false an impression of Shakespeare and his theatrical environment as anyone going to *King Lear* for accurate information about England in the eighth century BC (Plate 30).

Shakespeare in Love is only one of many fictional treatments of Shakespeare's life, which extend even to works purporting to be biographical. Garry O'Connor's lively *William Shakespeare: A Life* (1991, revised 1999) hovers between fact and fiction, seeming often to have information about both the outer and inner lives of Shakespeare and his family that can only have been psychically acquired. Somehow O'Connor can 'authoritatively affirm' (in spite of the Manningham anecdote, p. 83) that Shakespeare gave up womanizing 'in the middle, or towards the end, of the 1590s', that he smoked a pipe as he wrote *Hamlet*, and that at his death his 'body was disembowelled and carefully embalmed for display: led by the High Bailiff, Julius Shaw, one of the witnesses to his will, perhaps 500 or more people came through the door of New Place to register their grief and pay their respects'.[17] Well, perhaps they did. But there again, perhaps they didn't.

Edward Bond, who reworked *King Lear* in his sombre *Lear* (1971), offered a Marxist-inspired biographical study in his play *Bingo* (1973) entertaining in its portrayal of encounters between Shakespeare and Jonson but pessimistic in its view of Shakespeare's involvement in the Welcombe enclosures (pp. 34–41) and misanthropic in its interpretation of Shakespeare's supposedly suicidal last days. Anthony Burgess took advantage of the quatercentenary to publish a highly readable novel, *Nothing Like the Sun* (1964), much preoccupied with Shakespeare's sex life, and followed it with a straight (well, straight for a novelist) biography in 1970. Robert Nye, who shares some of Burgess's verbal exuberance, won prizes for his fictional life of a fictional character in *Falstaff* (1976) and followed it with novels devoted to *Mrs Shakespeare: The Complete Works* (1993) – Anne Hathaway's bawdy diary – and to her husband (*The Late Mr Shakespeare*, 1998). The last occasioned a letter to me from a lady so shocked by its imagined scenes of Shakespeare's sexual initiation that she asked if I could have it banned from bookshops with which I might be associated.

Other fictional offshoots make subtler use of their origins. Tom Stoppard's now classic play *Rosencrantz and Guildenstern Are Dead* places two of *Hamlet*'s minor characters at the centre of its action, and his two short, linked plays, *Dogg's Hamlet* and *Cahoot's Macbeth* also use Shakespeare as a basis for theatrically philosophical speculation. John Updike's *Gertrude and Claudius* resembles Mary Cowden Clarke's *Girlhood of Shakespeare's Heroines* (p. 313) in imagining events before the beginning of the play. Marina Warner's *Indigo* (1992) reverberates subtly with resonances from *The Tempest*, and it would be possible to read Jane Smiley's novel *A Thousand Acres* (1991) without realizing that it is based on *King Lear*.

Shakespeare has also provided grist to the mill of innumerable popular entertainers. An entertainment giving a whistle-stop tour of all his plays within a single performance (and usually quoting rather than parodying them – the comedy comes from what lies in between the quotations) has been offered by the R(educed) S(hakespeare) C(ompany), and has had a far longer uninterrupted London run than any of Shakespeare's individual plays ever. The script is published in an edition which, like John Poole's *Hamlet Travestie* of 1810 (p. 263), offers mock-scholarly annotations. Plays have even been presented – sometimes with complete, unaltered texts – in comic strip form (Plate 31). The use of Shakespearian situations and quotations in popular culture – radio programmes, television comedies, pop songs, films, comic papers, even pornography – has spawned an independent subdivision of academic scholarship and criticism, though rather for the light it throws upon various branches of modern society than as a way of illuminating Shakespeare.[18]

Any performance of a Shakespeare play – perhaps of any play – and any work derived from it, is an adaptation, a palimpsest in which the original text – unstable in itself – is overlaid with images derived to varying degrees, and with more or less exercise of the creative imagination, from that text. The most successful performances and derivative works are those that engage most actively and imaginatively – which may also mean most freely – with the original. Most operatic versions have strayed far from the text; an exception is Benjamin Britten's *A Midsummer Night's Dream* (1960) – 'the most successful Shakespeare opera since Verdi'[19] – for which Britten and the tenor Peter Pears devised a libretto which, though it omits about half of the lines, makes virtually no changes in what it keeps. Britten's choice of play was characteristic: he was greatly preoccupied with night and sleep. Playing down the roles of the lovers, the opera starts in the forest, magically evoking the fairy world with slithering phrases on the strings; Oberon is sung to ethereally beautiful if somewhat sinister effect by a counter-tenor, the first operatic role written for this high male voice since the eighteenth century, Titania by a high soprano, and the fairies by boy sopranos. The emotional climax of the opera comes with the awakening of the lovers and their quartet in which Shakespeare abets Britten by allowing them to express their wondering sense of having only partially emerged from the world of dreams, the words 'Mine own, and not mine own' sung to dropping and overlapping musical phrases in a moment where time stands still. Bottom too has his moment of musical communion with the dream kingdom. Britten does musical justice to the comedy of the play within the play in uproarious operatic parody, giving Thisbe a Donizettian mad scene, and the work ends exquisitely with a rocking lullaby for all the lovers sung by the cast's unusually wide range of high voices. Britten also found Shakespeare's Sonnet 43 – 'When most I wink, then do mine eyes best see . . .' – useful as the final song of his *Nocturne*, a setting for tenor and orchestra of poems about sleep. Musical settings of the sonnets are comparatively rare, but the German composer Hans Werner Henze's second piano concerto of 1967 is a complex response to

Sonnet 129 ('Th'expense of spirit in a waste of shame . . .'). Seven sonnets were set as songs by the Polish pianist and composer André Tchaikovsky who, on his premature death in 1982, bequeathed his skull to the Royal Shakespeare Company for use in *Hamlet*. Wrapped in a brown-paper parcel it arrived on the general manager's desk one morning along with the rest of the post.

★

By its very nature this book can have only a provisional ending. As the twenty-first century progresses there is every sign that Shakespeare's international presence continues to increase and to develop. Activity in some of the areas on which I have focused has increased, in others it has waned, and of course new ones have been added. A highly selective sampling will give at least an overall impression of the way things are going.

Interest in Shakespeare's historical and physical environment – vulgarly but not entirely inaccurately known as 'the heritage industry' – flourishes. Naturally, much of this is centred on Stratford. Research into archives along with tree-ring analysis of timbers resulted in the discovery in 2000 that the farm in nearby Wilmcote which John Jordan (p. 23) in the eighteenth century decided was Mary Arden's House had been built too late for the identification to be correct. On the other hand, what had formerly been known as Glebe Farm, a couple of hundred yards away, was positively identified as the house that had belonged to Shakespeare's mother's family. Happily the Shakespeare Birthplace Trust already owned both. Labels were rapidly changed – the former Mary Arden's House is now called Palmer's after its early owner. A rethought presentation of the renovated Birthplace aimed at bringing its interior closer than before to the way it would have looked in Shakespeare's time, and a glover's workshop was added; swathed in ribbon of the colours devised for the Garrick Jubilee – it makes a nice tie – the house was re-opened by Judi Dench and her husband Michael Williams as part of the birthday celebrations for 2000.

Tourists who find Stratford UK difficult to access may more easily visit Stratford Ontario with swans imported from its namesake, or the theme-park village in Japan which includes replicas of Shakespeare's Birthplace, Anne Hathaway's Cottage, and the house formerly known as Mary Arden's, or the full-size replica of Anne Hathaway's Cottage, packed with sixteenth-century antiques, in Victoria, British Columbia. Wherever they go they will have no trouble in picking up Shakespeare-related souvenirs ranging from the 'tasteful' through the tacky to the obscene – models of the Birthplace and Anne Hathaway's Cottage, tea towels, bottle-stoppers, pencils, erasers, fridge magnets, thimbles, candles, chocolate bars, key rings, even (at the Vermont festival) Shakespeare condoms, all adorned with choice images and quotations. 'Look, Mummy, William Shakespeare,' I heard a little boy say as I walked along Henley Street. 'O yes,' she replied, 'his head's on a tea bag.' A more expensive relic was the copy of the First Folio sold in New York in October 2001 for £4,166,216.

Among areas in which Shakespeare's influence has dwindled is music. I have the impression that fewer composers are turning to him for inspiration, but new incidental music and settings of the songs continue to appear, and both performances and recordings of associated musical works flourish. Similarly, fewer visual artists of any great distinction seem to look to his works for inspiration, but in Stratford-upon-Avon a series of impressive sculptures on Shakespearian themes by the American Greg Wyatt are being erected in New Place gardens (see overleaf) along with others by younger artists in the tree garden adjoining Anne Hathaway's Cottage.

Archaeological and other forms of research may bring us closer to Shakespeare's physical world, and works of art inspired by him may bear witness to the transmutative power of his genius. Criticism and scholarship, in all their diversity, seek to increase understanding of the works themselves, in relation both to the times in which they were conceived and to their impact on later ages, including our own. Activity here is frenetic, seeing the publication of an amazing number of monographs, reference works both scholarly and popular, and critical books and articles. Shakespearian websites abound. New volumes in all the ongoing editions continue to appear. Interest in Shakespeare's life is growing, especially as a result of the supposed Lancashire connection (pp. 21–5). Full-length biographies that vie for attention include Park Honan's scholarly and accessibly written study for Oxford University Press, thorough though not ground-breaking, and Katherine Duncan-Jones's provocative *Ungentle Shakespeare: Scenes from his Life* (2001) which portrays Shakespeare as mercenary, selfish, ungiving, quarrelsome, sexually promiscuous and exploitative, gluttonous, and drunken in his last months – rather as

146. *King Lear*: a sculpture by Greg Wyatt installed in the Great Garden
of New Place, Stratford-upon-Avon, 2001.

147. The 'Sanders' portrait, re-discovered in Canada in 2001.

Edward Bond does in *Bingo* (pp. 395–6) A fat book by Harold Bloom, *Shakespeare and the Invention of the Human* (1998), has sold in tens of thousands in the teeth of much critical disapproval; Sir Frank Kermode's slimmer, more scholarly and critically acute *Shakespeare's Language* (2000) has been well received. Claims for an alleged Shakespeare portrait of 1603 now in Canada which were investigated and rejected early in the twentieth century have been revived. It may well be a genuine portrait of the period, but reasons to identify the sitter as Shakespeare are slim; a now almost illegible label giving the date of his death as well as of his birth was clearly added years after the portrait was painted.

Dottinesses are no less in evidence than before. A Sicilian teacher claimed that Shakespeare was born in Messina as Michelangelo Florio *Crollalanza*

(= shake-spear). South African scientists proposed that Shakespeare smoked cannabis on the basis of a misinterpretation of a phrase ('keep invention in a noted weed') in Sonnet 76 along with the discovery that pipes found in Stratford (but not of Shakespeare's time, let alone ever in his possession) showed traces of the drug. A German scholar claimed to have found evidence that Elizabeth Vernon, who married the Earl of Southampton, was the dark lady of the Sonnets, and that Shakespeare had an illegitimate daughter by her; since the daughter, Penelope, went on to marry the second Baron Spencer, this would mean that the Princes William and Harry are directly descended from Shakespeare.

Performances of the plays in every sort of style, from the pseudo-authentic to the wildly experimental, and in many languages, flourish. The Royal Shakespeare Company celebrated the millennium with exciting performances of the histories from *Richard II* to *Henry V* in three different auditoria in Stratford and London, and took the earlier plays in the series to Michigan, USA.[20] The plays were given in their historical order under the title *This England*, with no attempt to impose uniformity of style. At the Globe Vanessa Redgrave played Prospero and it was possible within a year or two to see an Indian version of *King Lear*, a South African one of *Macbeth*, and an adaptation into the Japanese comic form known as kyogen of *The Comedy of Errors* undertaken by the distinguished scholar Yasunari Takahashi, former President of the Shakespeare Society of Japan. Japan itself, it appears, presented more performances of Shakespeare, in one form or another, than any other non-English-speaking country. In Lapland, a six-metre-high replica of the Globe hewn out of blocks of ice will offer performances of Shakespeare to winter audiences. And in 2001 the Norwegian town of Bergen witnessed a production of *Macbeth* given on a table top in which Macbeth was represented by a tomato, Duncan by a can of tomato purée, and other leading characters by a can of lager and a thermos flask. As a friend of mine quipped, paraphrasing Macbeth, 'Tomato and tomato and tomato.'[21]

★

A narrow focus on Shakespeare and on all who display an interest in him and his works obviously ignores those who do not. They are many. There is no moral obligation even on English men and women to like Shakespeare, no shame in not doing so. Many of those who visit Stratford do so for other reasons. Millions of people all over the world have never heard of him. But it is difficult for anyone in the English-speaking world, and for many people outside it, to avoid him altogether. The English language is permeated with expressions derived from and relating to his works. Writers and artists of all kinds and of every generation have come under his influence. His plays, both in English and in translation, are central to the international theatrical repertoire. Films, television series, reports in the media carry his name to all corners of the earth. He is a source of aesthetic pleasure and intellectual stimulus to millions. There is no holding him back. He is in the water supply, and is likely to remain there until the pipes run dry.

Notes

One: Shakespeare and Stratford

1. This was first suggested by Thomas de Quincey in his life of Shakespeare in the seventh edition of *Encyclopædia Britannica* (21 vols., Adam Black, Edinburgh, 1830–1842).

2. According to the monument in Holy Trinity Church, Shakespeare was fifty-three when he died on 23 April 1616; this can only be taken to mean that he had started his fifty-third year, i.e. was born on or before 23 April 1564.

3. Edgar I. Fripp, *Master Richard Quyny* (Oxford University Press, Oxford, 1924), p. 115.

4. *Mount Tabor, or Private Exercises of a Penitent Sinner* (London, 1639), pp. 110ff.

5. *The Elizabethan Home, discovered in Two Dialogues, by Claudius Hollyband and Peter Erondell*, ed. M. St Clare Byrne (Methuen, London 1925, rev. 1949), pp. 11–12.

6. Admittedly there was an English translation.

7. Greene's diary (also quoted on pp. 40–1) is printed in facsimile and transcribed by C. M. Ingleby in a rare volume, *Shakespeare and the Welcombe Enclosures* (R. Birbeck, Birmingham, 1885). The verses are transcribed on p. 5.

8. *The Diary of John Manningham of the Middle Temple, 1602–3*, ed. Robert Parker Sorlien (University Press of New England, Hanover, New Hampshire, 1976), p. 202.

9. Quoted in S. Schoenbaum, *William Shakespeare: A Compact Documentary Life* (Clarendon Press, Oxford, 1977), p. 87.

10. Andrew Gurr, 'Shakespeare's First Poem: Sonnet 145', *Essays in Criticism 21* (1971), pp. 221–6.

11. Anthony Burgess, *Shakespeare* (Jonathan Cape, 1970, repr. 1972), pp. 56–60 etc.

12. S. Schoenbaum, *William Shakespeare: Records and Images* (Scolar Press, London, 1981), pp. 160–61.

13. The theory was revived and discussed at length in E. A. J. Honigmann, *Shakespeare: the 'lost years'* (Manchester University Press, Manchester, 1985).

14. Mark Eccles, *Shakespeare in Warwickshire* (University of Wisconsin Press, Madison, Wisconsin, 1961), p. 74. Strong additional evidence against the identification is given by Robert Bearman in ' "Was William Shakespeare William Shakeshaft?" revisited', *Shakespeare Quarterly* 53, Spring 2002, pp. 83–94.

15. *Minutes and Accounts of the Corporation of Stratford-upon-Avon*, vol. 2, ed. Edgar I. Fripp (Dugdale Society, London, 1924), p. 54.

16. *Minutes and Accounts of the Corporation of Stratford-Upon-Avon*, vol. 4, p. 149.

17. Robert Bearman, 'Stratford's Fires of 1594 and 1595 Revisited', *Midland History* 25 (2000), 18–90.

18. On 24 January Sturley had written to Quiney 'I am left in the greatest need of £30 that possibly may be.' Fripp, *Mastor Richard Quyny*, p. 128. But Quiney's expenses were great (p. 160).

19. Fripp, *Master Richard Quyny*, p. 160.

20. Fripp, *Master Richard Quyny*, pp. 185–6.

21. Fripp, *Master Richard Quyny*, p. 121.

22. Our direct knowledge of the appearance of New Place depends on a drawing of the frontage, containing the gate house and servants' quarters, by George Vertue made in 1737 but based on reports of what it looked like before restoration. Frank Simpson, 'New Place: The Only Representation of Shakespeare's House from an Unpublished Manuscript', *Shakespeare Survey* 5 (1952), 55–7.

23. Robert Bearman, *Shakespeare in the Stratford Records* (Alan Sutton, Stroud, 1994), p. 42.

24. Schoenbaum, *William Shakespeare: Records and Images*, pp. 57–64.

25. This episode forms the basis of Peter Whelan's play *The Herbal Bed*, successfully acted by the Royal Shakespeare Company in 1996 at The Other Place, only a few hundred yards from Hall's Croft.

26. For Greene's diary, see Chapter 1, note 7.

27. Park Honan, *Shakespeare: A Life* (Oxford University Press, Oxford, 1997), pp. 406–7, imaginatively reconstructs Shakespeare's last illness.

28. By Sir Francis Fane, in a manuscript of *c.* 1655–6.

Two: Shakespeare in London

1. Chettle does not mention Shakespeare by name, but the identification is generally accepted.

2. I discuss the relationship between the plays more fully in my Oxford Shakespeare

edition (2000) of *King Lear*. Another play owned by the Queen's Men, *Felix and Philiomena*, performed at court on 3 January 1585 but now lost, appears from the characters' names to be based on *Diana* by the Portuguese Jorge de Montemajor (*c.*1521–61), which provides the main source of *The Two Gentlemen of Verona*, and must have had some relationship with that play.

3. The excellent study by Scott McMillin and Sally-Beth Maclean, *The Queen's Men and their Plays* (Cambridge University Press, Cambridge, 1998) includes a list of all their recorded performances.

4. *Material London, ca. 1600*, ed. Lena Cowen Orlin (University of Pennsylvania Press, Philadelphia, 2000), pp. 22 and 57. The total population of England and Wales is estimated at around 4 million.

5. The first three books were published in 1590, the remainder in 1596.

6. The only other example is the poem 'Let the Bird of Loudest Lay', also known as 'The Phoenix and Turtle', published in 1601. The Sonnets are a special case since there is nothing to show that Shakespeare had anything to do with their publication.

7. Barnfield's poem, 'A Remembrance of Some English Poets', appeared in his *Poems in Divers Humours* (London, 1598); Weever's lines, headed '*Ad Gulielmum* Shakespeare', in his *Epigrams in the Oldest Cut and Newest Fashion* (London, 1599).

8. Printed in John Davies of Hereford's collection *The Scourge of Folly* (*c.*1610) with the title 'To our English Terence Mr. Will. Shakespeare'.

9. *Shaw on Shakespeare*, ed. Edwin Wilson (Dutton, New York, 1961; Cassell, London, 1962), p. 85.

10. Park Honan, *Shakespeare: A Life* (Oxford University Press, Oxford, 1997), p. 312.

11. A mine of information about actors is *Playhouse Wills 1558–1642*, ed. E. A. J. Honigmann and Susan Brock (Manchester University Press, Manchester, 1993).

12. Edward Guilpin, *Skialethia* (London, 1598): 'But see yonder, / One like the unfrequented Theatre / Walks in dark silence, and vast solitude.'

13. James Burbage died in February 1597.

14. The complicated legal documents relating to this episode are analysed by e.g. E. K. Chambers, *The Elizabethan Stage* (4 vols., Oxford University Press, Oxford, 1923), vol. 2 and Herbert Berry, *Shakespeare's Playhouses* (AMS Press, New York, 1987), chapter 1.

15. Anthony Arlidge, *Shakespeare and the Prince of Love* (Giles de la Mare, London, 2000).

16. In *Love's Labour's Lost* and the second editions of both *Richard II* and *Richard III*.

17. *The Three Parnassus Plays, 1598–1601*, ed. J. B. Leishman (Ivor Nicholson and Watson, London 1949).

18. In *The Spanish Tragedy* (*c.*1587), by Thomas Kyd.

19. It is recorded in the 1674 edition of William Camden's *Remains*.

20. E. K. Chambers, *The Elizabethan Stage*, vol. 2, p. 308.

21. G. P. V. Akrigg, *Shakespeare and the Earl of Southampton* (Hamish Hamilton, London, 1968), p. 96.

22. Extracts from the documents concerning the Essex plot are reprinted by E.K. Chambers in *William Shakespeare: A Study of Facts and Problems* (2 vols., Clarendon Press, Oxford, 1930), vol. 2, pp. 323–7.

23. *The Diary of John Manningham of the Middle Temple, 1602–3,* ed. Robert Parker Sorlien (University Press of New England, Hanover, Hampshire, 1976), pp. 208–9.

24. Ben Jonson, *The Alchemist and Other Plays*, ed. Gordon Campbell, World's Classics (Oxford University Press, Oxford, 1995), 4.2.83–5.

25. In the original document these words are followed by the deleted words 'giving each other's hand to the hand'.

26. It's sometimes suggested that the knowledge of French that he displays in *Henry V* is a result of his stay with them, and Mountjoy is the title of the Herald in that play, but the name is in Holinshed, and there is no certain evidence that Shakespeare knew the Mountjoys by 1599, when he wrote the play.

27. S. Schoenbaum, *William Shakespeare: A Compact Documentary Life* (Clarendon Press, Oxford, 1977), pp. 222–3.

28. Schoenbaum, *William Shakespeare: A Compact Documentary Life*, p. 275.

29. Wilkins's chequered career is described in 'The Life of George Wilkins', by Roger Prior, *Shakespeare Survey* 25 (1972), 137–52.

30. A. L. Rowse's book *Simon Forman: Sex and Society in Shakespeare's Age* (Weidenfeld and Nicolson, London, 1974), characteristically slapdash and opinionated, is nevertheless an interesting pioneer study. More scholarly, though inclined to concentrate on Forman's medical interests, is Barbara Howard Traister's *The Notorious Astrological Physician of London: Works and Days of Simon Forman* (University of Chicago Press, Chicago and London, 2001). An excellent selective study is S. P. Cerasano's 'Philip Henslowe, Simon Forman and the Theatrical Community of the 1590s', *Shakespeare Quarterly* 44 (1993), 145–58.

31. Philip Stubbes, *The Anatomy of Abuses*, first published in 1583. The word 'sodomite' could be used of any kind of sexual offender.

32. A. L. Rowse, *Shakespeare the Man* (Macmillan, Basingstoke, 1973).

33. The tale is discussed by Jonathan Bate in his *The Genius of Shakespeare* (Picador, London, 1997), pp. 24–5.

34. *Shakespeare's Bawdy* (Routledge, London, 1947, repr. 1990), p. 25.

35. A reading of the Glossary suggests that he means heterosexual anal intercourse, though 'artifice' seems a funny word for it.

36. The exceptions are 99, which has an additional opening line; 126, which has twelve lines rhyming in couplets; and 145, in octosyllabics.

37. William Wordsworth, 'Scorn not the Sonnet'; Robert Browning, 'House'.

38. Other plays that Forman discusses include one about Richard II, but judging by his description it is not Shakespeare's play. He does not explicitly state that he saw *Cymbeline* at the Globe.

39. The astrologer William Lilly (1602–81) had this story from Forman's widow.

40. Stanley Wells, Gary Taylor, et al., *William Shakespeare: A Textual Companion* (Oxford University Press, Oxford, 1987), pp. 163–4.

Three: Shakespeare the Writer

1. *The Letters of John Keats*, ed. Maurice Buxton Forman, 4th edn (Oxford University Press, Oxford, 1952), p. 306.

2. Cited in E. K. Chambers, *William Shakespeare: A Study of Facts and Problems* (2 vols., Oxford University Press, Oxford, 1930), vol. 2, p. 210.

3. Here and in the following extracts from *Love's Labour's Lost*, spelling and punctuation are modernized.

4. The principal exception is Thomas Morley's setting of 'It was a lover and his lass' (*As You Like It*, 5.3); Morley also arranged a setting of 'O mistress mine' (*Twelfth Night*, 2.3) for mixed consort. Settings of songs from *The Winter's Tale*, *Cymbeline*, and *The Tempest* have been attributed to the court lutenist and composer Robert Johnson (*c.*1583–1633). Traditional tunes would have been used for e.g. Ophelia's mad songs and Desdemona's 'Willow' song.

5. The point is made by K. Duncan-Jones, *Ungentle Shakespeare*, Arden Shakespeare (Thomson Publishing, London, 2001), p. 112.

6. It was included in the 1997 reprint of the Riverside edition of the *Complete Works*, and has been contracted for the Arden edition. From time to time claims are made for Shakespeare's authorship of other works; see e.g. Chapter 9, p. 386–7.

7. The Oxford edition offers a fully reconstructed text of this play, with an exact transcript of the 1609 version in its original-spelling edition.

8. Scene 11 in the Oxford edition.

9. In his 'Ode to Himself'.

10. From his *Specimens of English Dramatic Poets Contemporary with Shakespeare* (Longman, Hurst, Rees, and Orme, London, 1808); quoted in *The Romantics on Shakespeare*, ed. Jonathan Bate (Penguin Books, Harmondsworth, 1992), p. 556.

11. T. W. Baldwin, *Shakespeare's 'Love's Labour's Won'* (Southern University Press, Carbondale, Illinois, 1957).

12. This discovery is discussed in more detail on p. 343.

13. G. E. Bentley, *The Profession of Dramatist in Shakespeare's Time* (Princeton University Press, Princeton, 1971), pp. 111–16.

14. In music, Mozart, Beethoven and Verdi come to mind – and Verdi owes much to Shakespeare.

15. *Shaw on Shakespeare*, ed. Edwin Wilson (Dutton, New York, 1961; Cassell, London, 1962), p. 50.

16. Geoffrey Bullough (ed.), *Narrative and Dramatic Sources of Shakespeare* (8 vols., Routledge, London, 1957–75).

17. *2 Henry IV*, 1.2.9–10.

18. *The Wheel of Fire* (Oxford University Press, Oxford, 1930), p. 15.

19. Or possibly to a lost play already based on it.

20. In a letter to Hall Caine, quoted in Caine's *Recollections of Rossetti* (Elliot Stock, London, 1882).

21. I treat this theme at greater length in 'Shakespeare Without Sources', *Shakespearian Comedy*, Stratford-upon-Avon Library 14 (Edward Arnold, London, 1972), pp. 58–74.

22. Preface, in *Johnson on Shakespeare*, ed. Arthur Sherbo (2 vols., Yale University Press, New Haven and London, 1968), vol. 1, p. 69.

23. Eric Griffiths, 'Prospero is Shakespeare making positively his last disappearance', *TLS*, 1 September 2000, p. 3.

24. J. W. Binns, *Intellectual Culture in Elizabethan and Jacobean England* (Francis Cairns, Leeds, 1990), offers a thorough study of the Latin writings of the period.

25. Keith Thomas, 'The Meaning of Literacy in Early Modern England', *The Written Word; Literacy in Transition*, ed. Gerd Baumann (Oxford University Press, Oxford, 1986), pp. 97–131.

26. 'Latin was . . . a more developed language than English, with a greater flexibility of syntax and an ability to formulate concepts that Elizabethan English lacked' (Binns, *Intellectual Culture*, p. 297).

27. Marvin Spevack, who compiled the *Harvard Concordance* on the basis of the Riverside edition, states 'there are 20,138 lemmata' (i.e. headwords in a dictionary) in Shakespeare; see his 'Shakespeare's Language', *William Shakespeare: His World, His Work, His Influence*, ed. J. F. Andrews (3 vols., Charles Scribner's Sons, New York, 1985), pp. 343–61 (352). Alvin Kernan, however, using a different but undisclosed criterion, states 'As counted in the *Harvard Concordance* the Shakespearean oeuvre, a total of 884,647 words (680,755 in verse, 203,892 in prose), uses 29,066 different words' (*Shakespeare, the King's Playwright* (Yale University Press, New Haven and London, 1995), p. 194).

28. The *Oxford English Dictionary* lists the first recorded use of words and forms; because its compilers paid special attention to Shakespeare it may well over-estimate his originality, but the figures are impressive all the same.

29. Bryan A. Garner, 'Shakespeare's Latinate Neologisms', *Shakespeare Studies* 15 (1982), 149–70.

30. The most reliable guide to Shakespeare's use of the Bible is Naseeb Shaheen, *Biblical References in Shakespeare's Plays* (University of Delaware Press, Newark, 1999). Shakespeare's use of proverbs and similar expressions is detailed in R. W. Dent's *Shakespeare's Proverbial Language: an Index* (University of California Press, Berkeley, California, 1981).

31. A useful guide is Lee A. Sonnino, *A Handbook to Sixteenth Century Rhetoric* (Routledge and Kegan Paul, London, 1968).

32. *Piers Penniless his Supplication to the Devil* (1592), in *Thomas Nashe: Selected Works*, ed. Stanley Wells, Stratford-upon-Avon Library 1 (Edward Arnold, London, 1964), pp. 64–5.

33. Frank Kermode, *Shakespeare's Language* (Penguin Books, London, 2000), p. 8.

34. Preface, *Johnson on Shakespeare*, ed. Sherbo, vol 1, p. 74.

35. *More Theatres: 1898–1903* (London, 1969), p. 582, parodying the gravediggers in *Hamlet*, 5.1.

36. *Romeo and Juliet*, 2.1.44.

37. 4.1.393.

38. *Henry IV, Part One*, 2.5.486.

39. 5.2.282; 4.15.51.

40. 11.55.

41. 5.3.109.

42. 5.1.186–7.

43. 5.2.205.

44. 5.1.49–51.

45. 5.2.288.

46. 5.3.183.

47. *An Oxford Anthology of Shakespeare*, ed. Stanley Wells (Clarendon Press, Oxford, 1987).

48. *Biographia Literaria*, Chapter 13.

49. 'John Ford', in *Selected Essays* (Faber and Faber, London, 1932), pp. 193–204 (p. 193).

50. *Letters*, ed. Forman, p. 227.

Four: The Growth of the Legend: 1623–1744

1. Robert Gell to Sir Martin Stuteville, quoted in E. K. Chambers, *William Shakespeare: A Study of Facts and Problems* (2 vols., Clarendon Press, Oxford, 1930), vol. 2. p. 348.

2. Hallett Smith, '"No Cloudy Stuffe to Puzzell Intellect": A Testimonial Misapplied to Shakespeare', *Shakespeare Quarterly* 1 (1950), 18–21: 'All the key words in Benson's tribute to Shakespeare appear in May's poem . . . five years earlier' (p. 20).

3. By Anthony Wood; quoted in Mary Edmond, *Rare Sir William Davenant* (Manchester University Press, Manchester, 1987), p. 14; this excellent biography supersedes all earlier work on Davenant's life.

4. Edmond, *Rare Sir William Davenant.* No baptismal entry for William Davenant is known, and Edmond has found no William other than Shakespeare after whom the child is likely to have been named.

5. The painting is discussed by e.g. S. Schoenbaum, *William Shakespeare: Records and Images* (Scolar Press, London, 1981), pp. 175–80; Mary Edmond ascribes it to one John Taylor, 'The Chandos Portrait: a suggested painter', *Burlington Magazine* CXXIV (1982), 146–9.

6. *The Shakespere Allusion Book*, ed. E. K. Chambers (2 vols., Oxford University Press, Oxford, 1932), vol. 1, p. 373, reprints versions of the story by Rowe, Dryden, Tate, and Charles Gildon. I follow Gildon.

7. Malcolm Rogers, 'The Meaning of Van Dyck's Portrait of Sir John Suckling', *Burlington Magazine* CXX (1978), 741–5.

8. Brian Vickers, *Shakespeare: The Critical Heritage* (6 vols., Routledge and Kegan Paul, London, 1974–81), vol. 1, pp. 421–2.

9. From the Preface ('The Grounds of Criticism in Tragedy') to Dryden's *Troilus and Cressida, or Truth Found Too Late* (1679).

10. *The Diary of John Evelyn*, ed. E. S. de Beer (Oxford University Press, Oxford, 1959), p. 431.

11. They are *Othello, The Merry Wives of Windsor, Henry IV, Part One, Hamlet, Twelfth Night,*

Romeo and Juliet, A Midsummer Night's Dream, Henry VIII, Macbeth, Henry V, The Taming of the Shrew, and *The Tempest*.

12. Cited from Louis Marder, *His Exits and his Entrances* (John Murray, London, 1963), p. 61.

13. Quoted in Edmond, *Rare Sir William Davenant*, p. 191.

14. According to Elizabeth Howe, *The First English Actresses* (Cambridge University Press, Cambridge, 1992), p. 56, the Prologue was spoken by Jane Long who played Hippolito.

15. It is reviewed by John Russell Brown, *Shakespeare Survey* 13 (1960), 137–45.

16. G. C. D. Odell, *Shakespeare from Betterton to Irving* (2 vols., Scribner, New York, 1920), vol. 1, p. 50.

17. His only settings of Shakespeare (apart from a song beginning 'If music be the food of love' but then departing from Shakespeare's words) are the songs 'Come unto these yellow sands' and 'Full Fathom Five' for the libretto of Shadwell's operatic *Tempest*.

18. This is available on a video, *Shakespeare Silents*, issued by the British Film Institute 1999.

19. Colley Cibber, *An Apology for the Life of Mr Colley Cibber* (London, 1740), ed. Robert W. Lowe (2 vols., John C. Nimmo, London, 1889), vol. 1, pp. 100–102; repr. Stanley Wells, ed., *Shakespeare in the Theatre: An Anthology of Criticism* (Oxford University Press, Oxford, 1997), p. 18.

20. From *The Laureat* (1740), cited in A. C. Sprague, *Shakespearian Players and Performances* (Adam and Charles Black, London, 1954), p. 13.

21. The quotation is from William Cooke's *Memoirs of Charles Macklin* (London, 1804), quoted in *A Biographical Dictionary of Actors*, ed. Philip H. Highfill et al. (16 vols., Southern Illinois University Press, Carbondale and Edwardsville, 1973–93), vol. 10, p. 8. Hereafter referred to as *Actors' Dictionary*.

22. Peter Holland's Introduction to the 1999 facsimile reprint of Rowe (Pickering and Chatto, London, 1999), pp. vi–xxx, is a valuable study to which I am indebted. Like many of its successors Rowe's edition soon appeared in a smaller, cheaper format.

23. Pope's edition is discussed by John Butt in *Pope's Taste in Shakespeare* (Oxford University Press, London, for the Shakespeare Association, 1936), and by Gary Taylor in *Reinventing Shakespeare* (Weidenfeld and Nicolson, London, 1989), pp. 81–7.

24. It is discussed by Gary Taylor in his Oxford Shakespeare edition of *Henry V* (Oxford University Press, Oxford, 1982).

25. Frequently quoted, e.g. by S. Schoenbaum, *William Shakespeare: A Compact Documentary Life* (Clarendon Press, Oxford, 1977), pp. 257–8.

26. *Reinventing Shakespeare*, p. 93.

27. Vickers, *Shakespeare: The Critical Heritage*, vol. 1, p. 43.

28. Vickers, *Shakespeare: The Critical Heritage*, vol. 2, p. 33.

29. Gary Taylor, in his excellent essay '*Hamlet* in Africa', *Travel Knowledge: European 'Discoveries' in the Early Modern Period*, ed. Ivo Kamps and Jyotsna G. Singh (Palgrave, Basingstoke, 2001), pp. 223–48 (234).

30. There is an account of the play in an appendix to G. R. Hibbard's Oxford Shakespeare edition of *Hamlet* (Oxford University Press, Oxford, 1987).

31. There are useful discussions of the work of the English comedians, as touring companies were known, in Jerzy Limon, *Gentlemen of a Company* (Cambridge University Press, Cambridge, 1985); Simon Williams's *Shakespeare on the German Stage*, Vol. 1: *1586–1914* (Cambridge University Press, Cambridge, 1990); and Zdenek Stříbrný, *Shakespeare and Eastern Europe* (Oxford University Press, Oxford, 2000).

32. Quotations are from Thomas R. Lounsbury's highly censorious (of Voltaire) study *Shakespeare and Voltaire* (David Nutt, London, 1902), pp. 63 and 143–4.

Five: The Age of Garrick: Shakespeare Celebrated: 1741–1789

1. *The Champion*, quoted in Jenny Uglow, *Hogarth* (Faber and Faber, London, 1997), p. 398.

2. The quotation is from Cibber's adaptation.

3. Joseph R. Roach, *The Player's Passion: Studies in the Art of Acting* (University of Delaware Press, Newark, Delaware, 1985), p. 58: 'Hamlet, Prince of Denmark, flipped his wig.'

4. *Shakespeare in the Theatre: An Anthology of Criticism*, ed. Stanley Wells (Clarendon Press, Oxford, 1997), pp. 24–8.

5. The *Morning Post*, 22 May 1776; reprinted in Wells (ed.), *Shakespeare in the Theatre*, pp. 28–9.

6. Reprinted (as 'Miss O'Neill's Juliet') in e.g. *Hazlitt on Theatre* (Dramabooks, Hill and Wang, New York, n.d.), reprint of Hazlitt, *Dramatic Essays*, ed. William Archer and Robert W. Lowe (Walter Scott, London, 1895), p. 19.

7. *Shaw on Shakespeare*, ed. Edwin Wilson (Dutton, New York, 1961; Cassell, London, 1962), p. 246.

8. *Shaw on Shakespeare*, pp. 178–82.

9. Quoted in G. C. D. Odell, *Shakespeare from Betterton to Irving* (2 vols., Scribner, New York, 1920), vol. 1, p. 365.

10. E. K. Chambers, *William Shakespeare: A Study of Facts and Problems* (2 vols., Oxford University Press, Oxford), vol. 2, p. 274.

11. The best factual account of the jubilee is Johanne M. Stochholm's *Garrick's Folly: The Stratford Jubilee of 1769* (Methuen, London, 1964).

12. Vernon was a singer, and composed a song for the play; the role is not fattened in Bell's theatre edition, but Vernon is the actor chosen for illustration (p. 233) so must have made a hit in the role.

13. *Charles Lamb on Shakespeare*, ed. Joan Coldwell (Colin Smythe, London 1978), p. 51.

14. Capell's work is surveyed by Alice Walker, 'Edward Capell and his Edition of Shakespeare', *Studies in Shakespeare*, ed. Peter Alexander (Oxford University Press, London, 1964).

15. The edition is a bibliographer's nightmare since many of the plays seem to have been printed separately, not necessarily with both plates, and then bound together.

16. It appeared in volume one of the second edition of Steevens's revision of Johnson's edition.

17. Quoted in Brian Vickers (ed.), *Critical Heritage*, vol. 5, p. 328.

18. Quoted in Vickers, *Critical Heritage*, vol. 6, p. 407.

19. *Lamb on Shakespeare*, p. 56.

20. Christopher Smith, 'Shakespeare on French Stages in the Nineteenth Century', *Shakespeare and the Victorian Stage*, ed. R. Foulkes (Cambridge University Press, Cambridge, 1986), pp. 223–9.

21. Lacy Collinson-Morley, *Shakespeare in Italy* (Shakespeare Head Press, Stratford-upon-Avon, 1916), p. 39. Pignotti's poem is described on pp. 59–61.

22. Simon Williams, *Shakespeare on the German Stage*, Vol. 1: *1586–1914* (Cambridge University Press, Cambridge, 1990) is an invaluable source of information to which I am greatly indebted.

23. Michael Kelly, *Reminiscences* (1826; repr. Oxford University Press, Oxford, 1975), p. 106.

24. There is an account of this version in Z. Stříbrný, *Shakespeare and Eastern Europe* (Oxford University Press, Oxford, 2000), pp. 27–9.

25. Stříbrný, *Shakespeare and Eastern Europe*, pp. 29–32.

26. Quoted in Stříbrný, *Shakespeare and Eastern Europe*, p. 34.

27. Stříbrný, *Shakespeare and Eastern Europe*, pp. 60–61.

28. The authoritative source of information is Charles Shattuck's *Shakespeare on the American Stage: From the Hallams to Edwin Booth* (Folger Shakespeare Library, Washington, DC, 1972).

29. Esther Cloudman Dunn, *Shakespeare in America* (Macmillan, New York, 1939), p. 91.

Six: Regency and Romanticism: 1789–1843

1. William Hazlitt, *The Examiner*, 16 June 1816, *Hazlitt on Theatre* (Dramabooks, Hill and Wang, New York, n.d.), p. 94.

2. *Hazlitt on Theatre*, p. 117.

3. Julian Charles Young, from his *Memoirs of Charles Mayne Young* (1840), pp. 40–41; repr. in Wells, ed., *Shakespeare in the Theatre: An Anthology of Criticism* (Oxford University Press, Oxford, 1997), pp. 37–8.

4. James Robinson Planché, *Recollections and Reflections* (2 vols., Tinsley Bros., London, 1872), pp. 56–7.

5. Selections are reprinted in *Fanny Kemble's Journals*, ed. Catherine Clinton (Harvard University Press, Cambridge, Mass., 2000). Her attitudes to slavery are examined in Catherine Clinton, *Fanny Kemble's Civil Wars* (Simon and Schuster, New York, 2001).

6. Giles Playfair pours scorn on the authenticity of this anecdote: *The Prodigy* (Secker and Warburg, 1967), pp. 18–19.

7. By J. Merritt, according to a pencilled note in the Shakespeare Centre copy.

8. No appropriate sense is recorded in the *Oxford English Dictionary*.

9. James Winston, *Drury Lane Journals*, ed. Alfred L. Nelson and Gilbert B. Cross (Society for Theatre Research, London, 1974), p. 107.

10. *Dramatic Essays by Leigh Hunt*, ed. William Archer and Robert W. Lowe (Walter Scott, Ltd., London, 1894), p. 225.

11. Reprinted in Wells, *Shakespeare in the Theatre*, pp. 67–72.

12. Gary Jay Williams, *Moonlight at the Globe* (University of Iowa Press, Iowa City, 1997), p. 93.

13. Selections have been recorded under the title *Shakespeare at Covent Garden* by the Musicians of the Globe, directed by Philip Pickett (Philips, 1999).

14. A. C. Sprague, 'Shakespeare and Melodrama', *Essays and Studies 1965*, 1–12 (p. 2).

15. Stanley Wells, 'Shakespeare in Planché's Extravaganzas', *Shakespeare Survey* 16, 103–17 (p. 106).

16. See Wells, *Shakespeare in the Theatre*, pp. 50–5.

17. Hazlitt was nothing if not economical with his prose. In 1814 he published a brief notice of Kean as Othello; two months later, after seeing the performance again, he wrote a long essay on the role published in two parts in the *Examiner*; he reprinted this in 1817 in a volume of essays by himself and Leigh Hunt called *The Round Table*, in the

same year he worked much of it into his essay on the play in *Characters of Shakespeare's Plays*, and then he reprinted it all again in *A View of the English Stage*.

18. Stanley Wells, 'Shakespeare in Leigh Hunt's Dramatic Criticism', *Essays and Studies 1980* (1980), 11–38.

19. Jonathan Bate's anthology, *The Romantics on Shakespeare* (Penguin, Harmondsworth, 1992), provides many of the main texts along with an excellent Introduction. To it I owe the information about the word 'psycho-analytical'.

20. His markings are reproduced and studied in Caroline Spurgeon's *Keats's Shakespeare* (Oxford University Press, Oxford, 1928).

21. *Letters of John Keats*, ed. J. Buxton Forman (Oxford University Press, Oxford, 1952), p. 29.

22. *Letters of John Keats*, pp. 71, 70.

23. Roger Pringle, 'The Rise of Stratford as Shakespeare's Town', *The History of an English Borough: Stratford-upon-Avon 1196–1996*, ed. Robert Bearman (Sutton Publishing, Stratford-upon-Avon, 1997), pp. 160–74, p. 169.

24. In *Letters of John Keats*, p. 114.

25. E. K. Chambers, *William Shakespeare* (2 vols., Oxford University Press, Oxford 1930), vol. 2, p. 240.

26. Privately communicated by Roger Pringle, Director of the Shakespeare Birthplace Trust.

27. *The Journal of Sir Walter Scott*, ed. W. E. K. Anderson (Oxford University Press, Oxford, 1972; repr. Edinburgh, 1998, p. 509).

28. Peter Martin, *Edmond Malone* (Cambridge University Press, Cambridge, 1995), pp. 188–9.

29. Accounts of the Ireland affair are given by Bernard Grebanier in *The Great Shakespeare Forgery* (Heinemann, London, 1966) and Jeffrey Kahan in *Reforging Shakespeare: the Story of a Theatrical Scandal* (Lehigh University Press, Bethlehem, 1998). Kahan notes performances of *Vortigern* in London in 1997. Schoenbaum tells the story with inimitable verve in *Shakespeare's Lives* and also in *Records and Images*, and there is a briefer account in Martin's biography of Malone.

30. Taylor, *Reinventing Shakespeare* (Weidenfeld and Nicholson, New York), pp. 207–8.

31. *The Anti-Jacobin Review* (26 March 1807), p. 298.

32. Stanley Wells, 'Tales from Shakespeare', British Academy Annual Shakespeare Lecture 1987, reprinted in *British Academy Annual Shakespeare Lectures 1980–89*, ed. E. A. J. Honigmann (Oxford University Press, Oxford, 1993), pp. 184–212.

33. *Shakespeare Stories* (Gollancz, London, 1985), with a second volume in 1994.

34. Charles Knight, *Passages of a Working Life* (1864–5; repr. Irish University Press, Shannon, 1971), p. 80.

35. Quoted in Christopher Wood, *Fairies in Victorian Art* (Antique Collectors' Club, Woodbridge, 2000), p. 47.

36. Illustrated in Sybil Rosenfeld, *A Short History of Scene Design in Great Britain* (Blackwell, Oxford, 1973), p. 109.

37. Martin Hardie, *Water-Colour Painting in Britain* (3 vols., Batsford, London, 1966–8), vol. 3, pp. 22–3.

38. *Romantics on Shakespeare,* ed. J. Bate (Penguin Books, Harmondsworth, 1992), pp. 226–7.

39. Peter Raby's *Fair Ophelia: Harriet Smithson Berlioz* (Cambridge University Press, Cambridge, 1982) provides an excellent account of her life.

40. *The Memoirs of Hector Berlioz*, tr. and ed. David Cairns (Victor Gollancz, London, 1969, repr. 1974), p. 109.

41. *The Memoirs of Hector Berlioz*, p. 611.

42. *The Memoirs of Hector Berlioz*, p. 357, n.

43. Reproduced in Simon Williams, *Shakespeare on the German Stage* (Cambridge University Press, Cambridge, 1990), p. 177.

44. Michael Marqusee, Introduction to *William Shakespeare: Hamlet: with sixteen lithographs by Eugène Delacroix* (Paddington Press, London, 1976).

45. Z. Stříbrný, *Shakespeare and Eastern Europe* (Oxford University Press, Oxford, 1975), pp. 44–5.

46. Bellini's opera *I Capuleti ed i Montecchi*, often said to be based on *Romeo and Juliet*, in fact has no direct connection with it; similarly Weber's *Oberon* is often mistakenly said to be based on *A Midsummer Night's Dream*.

47. Winston, *Drury Lane Journals*, p. 26

48. Charles Shattuck, *Shakespeare on the American Stage: From the Hallams to Edwin Booth* (Folger Shakespeare Library, Washington, DC, 1972), p. 46.

49. *Oxberry's 1822 Edition of King Richard III, with the Descriptive Notes Recording Kean's Performance by James H. Hackett*, ed. Alan Downer (Society for Theatre Research, London, 1966).

50. Shattuck, *Shakespeare on the American Stage*, p. 66.

51. Joseph Leach, *Bright Particular Star: The Life and Times of Charlotte Cushman* (Yale University Press, New Haven and London, 1970) offers a highly readable account of her life. A more scholarly study emphasizing Cushman's sexuality is Lisa Merrill's *When Romeo*

was a Woman: Charlotte Cushman and her Circle of Female Spectators (University of Michigan Press, Ann Arbor, 1999).

Seven: Victorian Shakespeare: 1843–1904

1. Theodor Fontane, *Shakespeare in the London Theatre, 1855–58*, tr. Russell Jackson (The Society for Theatre Research, London, 1999), p. 7.
2. Richard Foulkes, *The Calverts* (The Society for Theatre Research, London, 1992).
3. Morley's *Journal of a London Playgoer* (1866; repr. Routledge, London, 1891) forms only a tiny part of a prodigious output which includes a ten-volume history of English literature up to the time of Shakespeare.
4. Morley, *Journal of a London Playgoer*, p. 57; this review is reprinted in Wells, *Shakespeare on the Stage: An Anthology of Criticism* (Oxford University Press, Oxford, 1997), pp. 87–92.
5. John Coleman, *Memoirs of Samuel Phelps* (Remington and Co., London 1886), p. 217.
6. J. W. Cole, *The Life and Times of Charles Kean, F. S. A.* (2 vols, Richard Bentley, London, 1859), p. 26.
7. Reproduced in Richard W. Schoch, *Shakespeare's Victorian Stage* (Cambridge University Press, Cambridge, 1998), p. 91.
8. *Journal of a London Playgoer,* p. 142.
9. *Queen Victoria goes to the Theatre*, ed. George Rowell (Paul Elek, London, 1978), p. 71.
10. Fontane, *Shakespeare in the London Theatre 1855–58*, pp. 46–7.
11. See Stanley Wells, ed., *Shakespeare Burlesques* (5 vols., Diploma Press, London, 1977), vol. 3, Introduction and pp. 151–203.
12. In his essay 'Exit Planché, Enter Gilbert', *The Eighteen Sixties* (Cambridge University Press, Cambridge, 1932), p. 134.
13. Review by Joseph Knight, repr. Wells, *Shakespeare in the Theatre*, pp. 112–17.
14. Bartolomeo Galletti, *High Art in a Foreign Tongue*, tr. and ed. Tony Mitchell (Australasian Drama Studies Association, Brisbane, 1995).
15. Quoted by G.C.D. Odell, *Shakespeare from Betterton to Irving* (2 vols., Scribner, New York 1920), vol 2, p. 424.
16. Henry James, *The Scenic Art*, ed. Allen Wade (Rupert Hart-Davis, London, 1949), p. 105.
17. These and other classic recordings are reissued from time to time, e.g. *Great Historical Shakespeare Recordings*, 2 CDs, Naxos AudioBooks, 2000.
18. *The Story of My Life* (Hutchinson, London, 1908), p. 303

19. Irving's productions are studied in Alan Hughes, *Henry Irving, Shakespearean* (Cambridge University Press, Cambridge, 1981).

20. Collier is the subject of chapters 10 and 11 of Part IV of Schoenbaum's *Shakespeare's Lives* (Oxford University Press, Oxford, 1970, revised 1991).

21. A similar collection totalling fifty-six volumes is in the Folger Library, Washington. Schoenbaum points out that some of the pages may derive from copies that were already badly defective, but also gives evidence that this was not always so.

22. A colleague of Halliwell-Phillipps on the committee of the New Shakespeare Society was Richard Simpson (1820–76) who in 1871 proposed that part of the *Sir Thomas More* manuscript (pp. 104–8) was by Shakespeare. Simpson, a convert to Catholicism who tried to prove that Shakespeare was a Catholic, was also a composer who achieved the remarkable feat of setting every one of Shakespeare's sonnets to music, some of them several times. Most of his settings remain in manuscript, though a few were posthumously published.

23. *My Long Life* (Fisher Unwin, London, 1896), p. 138. There's a sense in which Henrietta Bowdler had anticipated her as a woman editor.

24. It had been partially anticipated by Samuel Ayscough's *Index to the Remarkable Passages and Words Made Use of by Shakespeare* (1790) and was superseded first by John Bartlett's *New and Complete Concordance* (1894), still in print, and by Marvin Spevack's electronically compiled *Harvard Concordance*.

25. The first full variorum is James Boswell's 21-volume edition of 1821 based on Malone.

26. The classic account of the subject is by S. Schoenbaum in *Shakespeare's Lives*.

27. From a letter, quoted in 'Delia Bacon in Stratford, 1856–58', by Bryan Homer, *Warwickshire History* x, 3 (1997), 93–112 (p. 95).

28. Homer, 'Delia Bacon in Stratford', p. 107.

29. Robert E. Hunter, *Shakespeare and Stratford: A Memorial of the Tercentenary Celebration of 1864* (Whitaker and Co., London, 1864), p. 100.

30. Hunter, *Shakespeare and Stratford*, p. 187.

31. Max Beerbohm, *Around Theatres* (1924; repr. Rupert Hart-Davis, London, 1953), p. 143.

32. Originally printed in the *Manchester Guardian*, 4 December, 1899; repr. in Wells, *Shakespeare on the Stage*, pp. 165–70, 170.

33. The standard biography is by Herbert Marshall and Mildred Stock, *Ira Aldridge – The Negro Tragedian* (1958; revised edn, Southern University Press, Carbondale, Ill., 1968).

34. Cited by Gerda Taranow in her exhaustive study, *The Bernhardt Hamlet: Culture and Context* (Peter Lang, New York, 1996), to which I am indebted.

35. Max Beerbohm, *Around Theatres*, pp. 34–7.

36. Robert Speaight, *Shakespeare on the Stage* (Collins, London, 1973), p. 183.

37. Roger Fiske, 'Shakespeare in the Concert Hall', *Shakespeare in Music*, ed. P. Hartnoll (Macmillan, London, 1964), pp. 177–241 (204–8). The duet was completed and orchestrated by Sergei Taneiev and is occasionally to be heard.

38. *Shaw on Shakespeare*, ed. Edwin Wilson (Dutton, New York, 1961; Cassell, London, 1962), 50–51.

39. James, *The Scenic Art*, pp. 178–80.

40. The *Idler* and the *Illustrated London News*, cited by Alan Hughes, *Henry Irving, Shakespearean*, p. 118.

41. Max Beerbohm, *More Theatres: 1898–1903* (Rupert Hart-Davis, London, 1969), p. 343.

42. Robert Speaight, *William Poel and the Elizabethan Revival* (Heinemann, London, 1954), p. 121.

43. Marion O'Connor, 'Reconstructive Shakespeare', in *The Cambridge Companion to Shakespeare on Stage*, ed. Sarah Stanton and Stanley Wells (Cambridge University Press, Cambridge, 2002).

44. The phrase, however, was first put into circulation by Ivor Brown and George Fearon in their book *Amazing Monument: A Short History of the Shakespeare Industry* (Heinemann, London, 1939).

45. Kaori Kobayashi, 'Touring in Asia: the Miln Company's Shakespearean Productions in Japan', in Edward J. Esche, ed., *Shakespeare and His Contemporaries in Performance* (Aldershot, Ashgate, 2000), pp. 53–72.

Eight: From Victoria to Elizabeth: 1903–1952

1. *The Times*, 11 January 1900, quoted in G. C. D. Odell, *Shakespeare from Betterton to Irving* (2 vols., Scribner, New York, 1920), vol. 2, p. 454.

2. Quoted in Odell, *Shakespeare from Betterton to Irving*, vol. 2, p. 454.

3. Ralph Berry, 'The Aesthetics of Beerbohm Tree's Shakespeare Festivals', *Nineteenth-Century Theatre Research* 9 (1981) p. 44, quoted in Dennis Kennedy, *Looking at Shakespeare* (Cambridge University Press, Cambridge, 1993), p. 68.

4. Kennedy, *Looking at Shakespeare*, p. 46

5. *The Saturday Review*, 30 May 1903; repr. Stanley Wells, ed., *Shakespeare in the Theatre: An Anthology of Criticism* (Oxford University Press, Oxford, 1997), pp. 171–4.

6. Kennedy, *Looking at Shakespeare*, pp. 44–57.

7. Z. Stříbrný, *Shakespeare and Eastern Europe* (Oxford University Press, Oxford, 2000), p. 56.

8. Frances Spalding, *Duncan Grant* (Pimlico, London, 1997), pp. 133, 145.

9. *Shakespeare in the Theatre: An Anthology of Criticism*, pp. 187–94; 189–90.

10. Odell, *Shakespeare from Betterton to Irving*, vol. 2, p. 468.

11. Wells, *Shakespeare in the Theatre*, p. 183.

12. Wells, *Shakespeare in the Theatre*, pp. 160–3.

13. All the films mentioned above except that of Forbes-Robertson's Hamlet are available on the British Film Institute's video *Shakespeare Silents* (1999).

14. The best critical and historical survey of Shakespeare on film is Kenneth S. Rothwell's *A History of Shakespeare on Screen: A Century of Film and Television* (Cambridge University Press, Cambridge, 1999).

15. J. Q. Adams, Introduction to *Shakespeare's 'Titus Andronicus': The First Quarto 1594* (Charles Scribner's Sons, New York and London, 1936), pp. 12–13.

16. S. Schoenbaum, *Shakespeare's Lives* (Oxford University Press, Oxford, 1970, revised 1991), pp. 464–72.

17. C. J. Shattuck, *Shakespeare on the American Stage*, vol. 2 (Folger Shakespeare Library, Washington, DC, 1987), pp. 204–5.

18. Reconstructions are surveyed in Marion O'Connor, 'Reconstructive Shakespeare', *The Cambridge Companion to Shakespeare on Stage*, ed. Stanton and Wells, Cambridge 2002, pp. 76–97.

19. Maurice Baring (1884–1945), from *Dead Letters* (1910), reprinted in Frank Muir (ed.), *The Oxford Book of Humorous Prose* (Oxford University Press, Oxford, 1990), pp. 513–6.

20. Quoted in Wilhelm Hortmann, *Shakespeare on the German Stage: The Twentieth Century* (Cambridge University Press, Cambridge, 1998), p. 4.

21. James Agate, *Brief Chronicles* (Jonathan Cape, London, 1943) p. 249.

22. Michael A. Morrison, 'Shakespeare in North America', *The Cambridge Companion to Shakespeare on the Stage*, p. 24–7.

23. An analysis of the production by the American critic Stark Young is reprinted in Wells, *Shakespeare on the Stage*, pp. 195–201.

24. Kenneth S. Rothwell, *A History of Shakespeare on Screen* (Cambridge University Press, Cambridge, 1999), p. 29.

25. Rothwell, *A History of Shakespeare on Screen*, p. 52

26. Michael A. Morrison, *John Barrymore, Shakespearean Actor* (Cambridge University Press, Cambridge, 1997), pp. 129–323.

27. A. C. Sprague and J. C. Trewin, *Shakespeare's Plays Today* (Sidgwick and Jackson, London, 1970), p. 19.

28. Hyder Rollins, ed., *The Sonnets*, New Variorum edition of Shakespeare (2 vols., J. B. Lippincott, Philadelphia, 1944), vol. 2, pp. 232ff.

29. Marvin Rosenberg, *The Masks of Othello* (University of California Press, Berkeley, Calif., 1961), p. 158.

30. Julie Hankey, ed., *Othello* (Plays in Performance, Bristol Classical Press, Bristol, 1897), p. 133

31. The best is Britten's *A Midsummer Night's Dream* (p. 397).

32. Happily the original performers recorded the work.

33. *Coriolanus*, The Oxford Shakespeare, ed. R. B. Parker (Oxford University Press, Oxford, 1994), pp. 123–4, citing M. Brunkhorst, *Shakespeare's Coriolanus in Deutscher Bearbeitung* (Berlin and New York, 1973), p. 157.

34. *Coriolanus*, ed. Parker, p. 127.

35. *Coriolanus*, ed. Parker, p. 123.

36. Wilhelm Hortmann, 'Shakespeare on the Political Stage in the Twentieth Century', in *The Cambridge Companion to Shakespeare on the Stage*, ed. Stanton and Wells, pp. 212–29

37. Wilhelm Hortmann, *Shakespeare on the German Stage: The Twentieth Century*, p. 136.

38. Tynan's review of *Othello* is reprinted in Wells, *Shakespeare in the Theatre*, pp. 239–243; the same volume includes Harwood's account of Wolfit's Lear (pp. 224–30).

39. J. Dover Wilson, ed., *Henry V*, New Shakespeare (Cambridge University Prress, 1947), p. xxxi.

Nine: Shakespeare Worldwide

1. Barton's contribution amounted to some 1,400 lines: *The Wars of the Roses*, adapted by John Barton in collaboration with Peter Hall (BBC Publications, London, 1970).

2. The play had been acted in an open-air production by Reading University Drama Society in 1959.

3. Directed by Michael Bogdanov and Michael Pennington, active mainly between 1985 and 1994.

4. Founded in 1981 by Declan Donnellan and Nick Ormerod.

5. 2 vols. (Clarendon Press, Oxford, 1963).

6. Norton and Co., New York, 1968, 2nd edn 1996.

7. Terence Hawkes, *Meaning by Shakespeare* (Routledge, London and New York, 1992), p. 3.

8. *Johnson on Shakespeare*, ed. Arthur Sherbo (2 vols., Yale University Press, New Haven and London, 1968), vol. 1, p. 111.

9. The text of the Oxford edition was adopted, with certain modifications, for the Norton Shakespeare of 1997. Had we had space enough and time, I should like to have given double texts of *Hamlet*, *Othello*, and *Troilus and Cressida* as well as *Lear*. We should also have included the full text of *Sir Thomas More* (pp. 104–8) had we not been conscious of the need for economy.

10. In June 2002, as this book was in proof, Drs Donald Foster and R. Abrams, chief proponents of Shakespeare's authorship of 'A Funeral Elegy', conceded that it is more likely to have been written by Ford.

11. Rothwell, *A History of Shakespeare on Screen*, p. 209.

12. Rothwell, *A History of Shakespeare on Screen*, pp. 211–15.

13. Rothwell, *A History of Shakespeare on Screen*, pp. 168–9

14. Rothwell, *A History of Shakespeare on Screen*, p. 163.

15. Rothwell, *A History of Shakespeare on Screen*, p. 254.

16. *The Children's Midsummer Night's Dream*, directed by Christine Edzard, 2001.

17. Garry O'Connor, *William Shakespeare: A Life* (Hodder and Stoughton, London, 1991), pp. 141, 181, 302.

18. An example is Richard Burt, *Unspeakable Shaxxxspeares: Kiddie Culture, Queer Theory, and Loser Criticism* (St Martin's Press, New York, 1998).

19. Winton Dean, in *Shakespeare in Music*, ed. Phyllis Hartnoll (1964), p. 118.

20. Only the early histories were performed in America.

21. This remark was perpetrated by Dr Russell Jackson.

Index